Reflexivity
&
VOICE

Reflexivity & VOICE

Rosanna Hertz, Editor

SAGE Publications
International Educational and Professional Publisher
Thousand Oaks London New Delhi

For information:

SAGE Publications, Inc.
2455 Teller Road
Thousand Oaks, California 91320
E-mail: order@sagepub.com

SAGE Publications Ltd.
6 Bonhill Street
London EC2A 4PU
United Kingdom

SAGE Publications India Pvt. Ltd.
M-32 Market
Greater Kailash I
New Delhi 110 048 India

Printed in the United States of America

Library of Congress Cataloging-in-Publication Data

Main entry under title:

Reflexivity & voice / editor, Rosanna Hertz.
    p. cm.
  Includes bibliographical references.
  ISBN 0-7619-0383-6 (acid-free paper).—ISBN 0-7619-0384-4 (pbk.:
  acid-free paper)
    1. Sociology—Research—Methodology. 2. Social sciences—
  Research—Methodology. 3. Sociology—Field work. 4. Social
  sciences—Field work. 5. Women's studies—Research. I. Hertz,
  Rosanna.
  HM48.R435 1997
  301'07'23—dc21   97-4619

97 98 99 00 01 02 03 10 9 8 7 6 5 4 3 2 1

Acquiring Editor:	Peter Labella
Editorial Assistant:	Corinne Pierce
Production Editor:	Michèle Lingre
Production Assistant:	Denise Santoyo
Copy Editor:	Joyce Kuhn
Typesetter/Designer:	Danielle Dillahunt
Cover Designer:	Ravi Balasuriya
Print Buyer:	Anna Chin

Contents

PART II: VOICE

Cover: Watercolor by Areyah Rothman, Kibbutz En Hamifratz, Israel.
The original colors have been altered for use as the cover of this edition.

Introduction: Reflexivity and Voice

Rosanna Hertz, Editor

For the past three years, I've been involved in a study group with women from the greater Boston area. Part of what we have been concerned with is how to create a new kind of ethnography—that is, a qualitative study where the author's voice and those of her respondents are situated more completely for the reader. New conventions in how we present ourselves and our respondents have also challenged us to rethink ethical issues surrounding social research. This collection will hopefully challenge the reader to reconsider research projects in light of the ideas and criticisms raised by the contributing authors.

As we puzzle through the problematics and the new conventions of ethnographic writing, two issues are at the forefront: reflexivity and voice. They are the subject of this edited book, which has as its basis a special issue I put together for the journal *Qualitative Sociology.* This book is a significant expansion of that special issue, and it is intended to address the concerns of contemporary writers of ethnographies.

REFLEXIVITY

Reflexivity implies a shift in our understanding of data and its collection—something that is accomplished through detachment, internal dialogue, and constant (and intensive) scrutiny of "what I know" and "how I know it." To be reflexive is to have an ongoing conversation about experience while simultaneously living in the moment. By extension, the reflexive ethnographer does not simply report "facts" or "truths" but actively constructs interpretations of his or her experiences in the field and then questions how those interpretations came about (Clifford and Marcus 1986; Rabinow 1986; Van Maanen 1988). The outcome of reflexive social science is reflexive knowledge: statements that provide insight on the workings of the social world *and* insight on how that knowledge came into existence (Myerhoff and Ruby 1982). By bringing subject and object back into the same space (indeed, even the same sentence), authors give their audiences the opportunity to evaluate them as "situated actors" (i.e., active participants in the process of meaning creation).

The best definition of reflexivity I have found is Helen Callaway's (1992):

> Often condemned as apolitical, reflexivity, on the contrary can be seen as opening the way to a more radical consciousness of self in facing the political dimensions of fieldwork and constructing knowledge. Other factors intersecting with gender—such as nationality, race, ethnicity, class, and age—also affect the anthropologist's field interactions and textual strategies. Reflexivity becomes a continuing mode of self-analysis and political awareness. (p. 33)

Reflexivity, then, is ubiquitous. It permeates every aspect of the research process, challenging us to be more fully conscious of the ideology, culture, and politics of those we study and those we select as our audience.

Since researchers are acknowledged as active participants in the research process, it is essential to understand the researcher's location of self (e.g., within power hierarchies and within a constellation of gender, race, class, and citizenship—see especially DeVault 1990, 1995; Edwards 1990; Riessman 1987; Williams and Heikes 1993). Through personal accounting, researchers must become more aware of how their own positions and interests are imposed at all stages of the research process—from the questions they ask to those they ignore, from who they study to who they ignore, from problem formation to analysis, representation, and writing—in order to produce less distorted accounts of the social world (Harding 1986, 1987).

Recent articles on reflexivity have highlighted the clash of identities between researchers and their informants and how they reconcile personal differences and similarities with these respondents. Some scholars are interested in telling their audiences about how they became sympathetic to those whose views they do not share (Ginsberg 1989; Klatch 1988; Stacey 1990). Others write of their inability to find common ground with their respondents (see Wasserfall in this collection) or how barriers between their own beliefs and those they studied could not be crossed (see El-Or in this collection).

CONTRIBUTORS ON REFLEXIVITY

Shulamit Reinharz (Chapter 1) provides a framework for analyzing how "the self is the key fieldwork tool" (Van Maanen, Manning, and Miller 1989). She explores both the self we bring to the field and the self we create in the field. By analyzing her field notes from a kibbutz study, she is able to identify 20 "selves" that she configures into three major categories: "research-based selves," "brought selves," and "situationally created selves." Her chapter focuses on the "research-based selves" to explain poignantly the importance of the self to fieldwork.

Reinharz argues that reflexive feminist ethnography combines material on the way the researcher gained knowledge of the field with a discussion of how the researcher's attributes became meaningful in the course of the fieldwork. As we write up our research reports we need to display the full process of the interaction between self and respondents in order to understand not simply "what I know" but also "how I know it." But she reminds us that we need to strike a balance between the extremes of unreflective ethnographic accounts and narcissism.

Patricia Adler and Peter Adler (Chapter 2) transform their everyday roles as parents into unique vantage points from which to learn about youth culture. They combine an examination of the ethical concerns of studying one's own backyard, specifically one's own children, with a discussion of how the self can sustain the dual roles of parent and researcher. Yet this duality favors the parental role that will take priority when aspects of youth culture become problematic. Highly regarded by these preadolescents as "cool parents," they were already members within the social worlds of the teens.

Raymond Michalowski (Chapter 3) pushes the discussion of reflexivity into the realm of political awareness by arguing that more focus should be placed on the macropolitical forces that shape ethnographic narratives. He is particularly interested in how geopolitical conflicts—the tensions between the United States and Cuba—"inscribe" themselves on the influence as well as the choice of the researcher's interactions with informants in Cuba and audiences for one's work in the United States. These political tensions produce particular kinds of uncertainties that he labels "disciplinary anxiety" and "discursive anxiety."

Generations of scholars have debated whether we should study familiar territory or unfamiliar turf. In her feminist revisiting of the "insider/outsider" debate, Nancy Naples (Chapter 4) reconceptualizes the dichotomy as "ever-shifting and permeable social locations that are differentially experienced and expressed by community members." Locating this debate within both the classical presentations and later feminist scholarship, she argues that the insider/outsider distinction is contested terrain over epistemological assumptions, methodological strategies, and political claims making. Using fieldwork in two rural towns, she illustrates how race-ethnicity, gender, and class relations are intertwined to form the "outsider" and how outsiders change as the community's population shifts.

Hale Bolak (Chapter 5) examines the equally shifting boundaries between self and other as she reflects upon her experiences as an indigenous researcher in Turkey. Through personal accounting she details how different demographic characteristics and parts of her biography became salient at different points in her research and how they affected her ability to gain access. She illustrates how she contextualized her experiences and the various reactions to her by differing categories of respondents. Gender becomes intertwined with other biographical variables and it is from this unique positionality that she comes to rethink her understanding of her country of origin. Finally, she raises questions about future research that needs to bridge the roles of researcher/researched as well as insider/outsider.

To blur the distinction between researcher and respondent, Carolyn Ellis, Christine Kiesinger, and Lisa Tillmann-Healy (Chapter 6) explore how the time-consuming and emotionally demanding process of "interactive interviewing" creates a self-reflective exchange between participants. Through a series of narrative exchanges the authors (and respondents of this chapter) explore both the development of their interactive interviewing project and multiple accounts of their experiences with body image, food, and eating disorders. This research project incorporates not simply the self of a single researcher but a group of researchers who are exploring and measuring their own reactions against the experiences and feelings of the other members. In this way, each member's narrative reflects the prior narratives as relationships between members are developed and modified. The multiple-voice approach they use in writing up this project should aid researchers looking for clues as to the many silences and unanswered questions that other researchers studying the same topic through more traditional methodologies may overlook. The comfort level for personal disclosure varies enormously and raises further ethical questions about the therapeutic dimension of in-depth interviewing that many researchers experience as they conduct qualitative interviews.

Serious examinations of the self should make researchers aware of being both subject and object, thus empowering them to a deeper understanding of themselves and their respondents. But this does not necessarily mean that awareness of the self makes one more sympathetic toward one's respondents. Two chapters raise important challenges to reflexivity: If a mandate of feminist research includes a working partnership with one's respondents, under what conditions may feminist research and reflexivity be incompatible? Can the practice of reflexivity bridge the differences between the researcher and her respondents?

Following a detailed discussion of the relationship between feminism and reflexivity, Rahel Wasserfall (Chapter 7) writes that the practice of reflexivity may not always lessen the tensions that exist in doing feminist fieldwork, particularly in situations where the divide is deeply engrained in the life histories of both the researcher and her respondents. Finally, she raises questions about whether or not it is possible to conduct feminist reflexive research if no common ground can be identified. Yet as we become more intimate with our respondents we become trusted actors in their lives. Tamar El-Or (Chapter 8) questions the extent of intimacy between herself and a female respondent in a riveting ethnographic account of everyday life among Hassidic women. Despite the desire of each woman to share with the other for the sake of research, there is a mutual recognition of the delicate line they establish. Both women experience the limits of intimacy when their separate world views became insurmountable barriers.

Finally, these chapters on reflexivity also challenge another long-standing myth about ethnographic research. Respondents learn who we are in the field as we participate in their lives or as we actively interact with them in shaping their telling of stories about their lives. Douglas (1985) refers to this exchange as a "creative search for mutual understanding" (p. 25; see also Hertz 1995; Holstein and Gubrium 1995). Respondents react to us as individuals, with ideas of their own, not simply in a role of researcher. In plain talk, they "size us up" in order to situate us. The interaction between their locating us and our own subject positionality produces a unique account that can only be more fully evaluated by the audience when social scientists acknowledge this relationship and depict it more fully as part of how we know what we know about the social world.

VOICE

Voice is a struggle to figure out how to present the author's self while simultaneously writing the respondents' accounts and representing their selves. Voice has multiple dimensions: First, there is the voice of the author. Second, there is the presentation of the voices of one's respondents within the text. A third dimension appears when the self is the subject of the inquiry.

Reflexivity encompasses voice, but voice focuses more upon the process of representation and writing than upon the processes of problem formation and data gathering. However, in the final product, voice typically is informed by the selection of an empirical problem, methodology, and theoretical tradition. Voice is how authors express themselves within an ethnography. The voice of the author may be absent as in the third-person "realist tales" (Van Maanen 1988), or the author's voice may be the subject of inquiry as in "experimental representations" (Richardson 1994). In between there are many different ways in which the author's voice appears in ethnography—from using a school's code language to demonstrate the author's theoretical alliances (Walton, cited in Becker 1986:38-39) to the author as a visible narrator and coparticipant in the text (see, e.g., Harper 1982).

The respondents' voice is almost always filtered through the author's account. Authors decide whose stories (and quotes) to display and whose to ignore. The decision to privilege some accounts over others is made while developing theories out of the data collected. As they shift between data and theory, scholars make decisions about the voices and placement of respondents within the text. The voice of respondents may be altered in other ways as well. In some settings, their voice is meant to be silent when a collective ideology and collective voice supersede individualism (see Wichroski in this collection). Finally, as both respondent and author, losing voice leads to interactional problems rendering the self invisible (see Robillard in this collection).

Writing about writing in this postmodern period, Richardson (1994) put it this way:

> Although we are freer to present our texts in a variety of forms to diverse audiences, we have different constraints arising from self-consciousness about claims to authorship, truth, validity, and reliability. Self-reflexivity unmasks complex political/ideological agendas hidden in our writing. Truth claims are less easily validated now; desires to speak "for" others are suspect. The greater freedom to experiment with textual form, however, does not guarantee a better product. (p. 523)

These "experimental representations" allow the author to push the boundaries of prescribed ways of conducting social science (see also Ellis and Bochner 1996). Drawing upon self-knowledge as a central source of data, personal experience—a "forbidden pool of data" as Michelle Fine (1984, cited in Reinharz 1992:263) aptly termed it—is increasingly becoming another acceptable scholarly basis of understanding social life and human behavior (for examples of the centrality of the self, see particularly Ellis 1995; Kondo 1990; Paget 1993; Williams 1991; Zola 1982). In this way, the self becomes both the subject of the study and the narrator. Multiple voices also mark new frontiers (Butler and Rosenblum 1991; Krieger 1983; also Ellis, Kiesinger, and Tillmann-Healy in this collection), as do studies that juxtapose self-discovery with the research participant's narrative (Behar 1993).

As "situated actors" we bring to each interview our own histories (Manning, 1967). To make sense of what we observe or what people tell us, we may draw on the richness of our own experience, particularly if what we are studying we also have experienced. Parts of an interview may echo our own thoughts or prompt us to recall parts of our own lives. But in the writing rarely does the author let the audience know how the author's life may parallel the respondents'. By presenting the author's voice in the account, the audience can situate the author in order to assess the author's perspective with regard to a topic or why particular actors' voices may be featured over others'. Without detracting from the case studies that Rubin (1996) presents, she skillfully interjects her voice into the life histories of her subjects. Rubin is not only a narrator of each case but also by placing her own voice, at selected points, alongside the subjects she locates for the reader how an individual's history might be evaluated as representative of a more common experience or feeling (at least the author's experience or feeling). A writer who is skillful can integrate both general and particular experiences. The placement of an author's voice, in this way, validates the respondent's experience.

Finally, the intent of the author may not always be shared by the audience. Audiences also bring themselves to the product. An acquaintance of mine who is a photographer told me about an experiment she conducted: She asked her female friends to recommend men that she did not know who would be willing to have their pictures taken with her. Using a self-timer, these strangers posed with her. She told me that when she asked other people to view the pictures and tell her what they saw, the viewers automatically assumed that she and the stranger were intimately involved. Elements in any seeing may touch off association for people. We selectively resonate and associate to produce a perspective. This is not unlike the musician for whom a music score is a reference point she brings to life through her own interpretation, even if her version is unintended by the original composer.

Framing the material to disarm an audience with preconceptions is not easy. Audiences read ethnographic accounts as "tests" of their own positionality while calling into question the "objectivity" of the author if she strays from her audiences' preformed judgments. In this regard, audiences are engaged in misdirection—focusing their attention on their author's positionality as problematic instead of on the respondents' accounts. In order to untangle the voice of the author from the voices of one's subjects the author must shift audiences' focus away from herself toward the subjects. The subjects must be given voice independent of the author's in order to focus the "seeing" in another direction.

CONTRIBUTORS ON VOICE

Social scientists learn to present their findings through disciplinary guidelines, which, in fact, also establish the presentation of the author's voice. Kathy Charmaz and Richard Mitchell (Chapter 9) debunk the myth of voiceless writing, even though most disciplines prefer camouflaged voices. Voice, they argue, is not a technical feature of writing but an interactive and emergent part of the empirical experience and the theoretical frame of a study. Using their own empirical work, they analyze two excerpts as examples of how each of their own voices emerge from and reflect different genres. The crispness they bring to this chapter demonstrates another dimension—how the relationships they establish with their respondents facilitate a voice shaped by their involvement and excitement about their individual studies.

Personal writing, Marjorie DeVault (Chapter 10) suggests, challenges an implicit assumption of social science: namely, that as part of the replicable process of conducting social research, individuals are interchangeable. The consequences of the personal voice in writing will require new ways to think about ethical issues of confidentiality as well as new ways to evaluate the product. Further, DeVault makes an important point about the politics of personal writing: She argues that personal writing must be grounded in a larger conversation, or the writers run the risk that their accounts will be marginalized within the social sciences. As she states poignantly "In each particular case, then, it seems important to consider what a personal element does in an analysis and how it contributes to a larger project."

Using a previously published autobiographical essay, Eric Mykhalovskiy (Chapter 11) explores a charged issue: that scholars who write narratives about the self are self-indulgent. Writing about our lives also "produces our subjectivities." To write about one's self, he argues, is to write about social experiences. Finally, Mykhalovskiy also captures the layering of different voices in order to break out of a particular kind of academic discourse that stifles other possible ways of doing sociology. By violating how sociology has been previously written through placing himself at the center and engaging multiple voices, Mykhalovskiy challenges sociologists to think about the following: Who should be the subjects of our work? How do we represent the self and position our own voices? What does experimental writing tell us about mainstream ethnography?

Albert Robillard's (Chapter 12) experience with his own illness challenges assumptions about using the self as the focus for our research. If a goal of social science is to understand how the everyday world unfolds, Robillard's own insights into the interactional problems he encounters as a product of loss of his own voice has led to understanding how the everyday world is constructed. Loss of his voice becomes a disruption demonstrating how caregivers react and how the displacement of the self by monitor screens renders Robillard an invisible patient. He painstakingly analyzes those who are willing to learn to communicate through alternative methods and those who resist. He treats the failure of his body as a way to examine structures of communication.

Mary Anne Wichroski (Chapter 13) adds an interesting twist on how she comes to understand her respondents' voices. This piece poses a novel question: What happens when the respondents are not supposed to have a voice? In particular, she discusses a culture in which individual voice is suppressed and participants speak collectively. She refers to the cloistering of nuns as an "inversion of the life on the outside." Silence is essential, and the individual is subsumed within the group. These differences make the study of a religious order problematic. She learns to communicate through nonverbal cues and to understand as a scholar how to speak about aspects of this community that lacks a spoken language.

The reception of ethnographic work is rarely discussed, despite the fact that authors typically have audiences in mind when they begin to write their tales from the field. The relationship between audiences and voice of both the author and her subjects has been overlooked. An exception to this is the research by Faye Ginsburg (Chapter 14). Aware that her audiences were familiar with right-to-lifers and had already formed opinions prior to reading her ethnographic account, she developed strategies for enabling audiences to set aside preconceptions. She wanted to develop accounts of her subjects that would not permit audiences to dismiss her work as simply misplaced advocacy by a sympathetic researcher. To ensure that audiences would not conflate her voice with that of her subjects, she used life histories to engage audiences in a relationship with her subjects' accounts. She states "life stories allowed me to present to readers long sections of narratives in which subjects interpreted their own actions, deflecting attention away from me as an ethnographer and forcing a vicarious encounter between the reader and the subjects." By distinguishing between herself and the voices of her subjects, she disarms her audiences, forcing them to confront their own preconceptions in order to understand her "counterintuitive encounter" as she came to know the world view of her subjects.

Through a provocative depiction of different readings of poetry, how the audience understands voice is highlighted by Geeta Patel (Chapter 15). Not only must the content be separated from the author's voice but also the author's voice and signature need to be uncoupled from the gender of the person who performs and composes poetry. Voice appears in several ways: for example, through the author's intention, which may depend on the context (e.g., women allowed to write as women), or through audiences' assumptions, which may help promote the passing of one gender for the other. Further, Patel demonstrates how the signature of the composer genders the meaning of the poem for the audience.

CONCLUDING REMARKS

In concluding this introduction, I want to draw special attention to the ethical questions that arise in the new self-reflexive ethnography. As several of the authors in this collection admit, revealing oneself is not easy. For example, how much of ourselves do we want to commit to print? How do we set the boundary between providing the audience with sufficient information about the self without being accused of self-indulgence? Do we risk appearing foolish to our colleagues (and a lay audience) when we admit to naïveté, ignorance, and/or uncertainty, that is, when we let slip the cloak of authority that traditionally has set us apart from the people we study?

The ethics of how we mask our respondents also becomes problematic. In earlier periods it was sufficient to mask the individual by making the individual representative of a category. The more we display about the individual and the more we allow our respondents to speak for themselves (whether through life histories or through being collaborators in our writing) the greater risk we run of not being able to provide guarantees of anonymity. Further, although the scholar/ researcher remains obligated to understand the respondent's viewpoint, following the thinking of the early Chicago School, these founders seemed to assume fairly comfortably that there is some general perspective from which others' perspectives can be gathered and evaluated.

Finally, it is important to admit that we study things that trouble or intrigue us, beginning from our own subjective standpoints. But what makes writing about our lives social science and not a novel? How do we find the parallels in our experiences to make sociological sense of our own routines, or chaos for that matter? Do we need permission from family and friends to write their lives into the telling of our own? What one person considers private, another may not: Must we ask everyone who is included in our account to read it and approve it before it is printed?

I end with these questions because at the core of our enterprise are concerns about confidentiality, validity, replication, and generalization. There is a large literature on each of these topics, but new questions arise as we shift into a more complete telling of the process through which we acquire knowledge.

REFERENCES

Becker, H. S. 1986. *Writing for Social Scientists.* Chicago: University of Chicago Press.

Behar, R. 1993. *Translated Woman: Crossing the Border with Esperanza's Story.* Boston: Beacon.

Butler, S. and B. Rosenblum. 1991. *Cancer in Two Voices.* San Francisco: Spinsters Book Company.

Callaway, H. 1992. "Ethnography and Experience: Gender Implications in Fieldwork and Texts." Pp. 29-49 in *Anthropology and Autobiography,* edited by J. Okely and H. Callaway. New York: Routledge, Chapman & Hall.

Clifford, J. and G. E. Marcus, eds. 1986. *Writing Culture: The Poetics and Politics of Ethnography.* Berkeley: University of California Press.

DeVault, M. 1990. "Talking and Listening from Women's Standpoint: Feminist Strategies for Interviewing and Analysis." *Social Problems* 37:96-116.

———. 1995. "Ethnicity and Expertise: Racial-Ethnic Knowledge in Sociological Research." *Gender & Society* 9:612-31.

Douglas, J. 1985. *Creative Interviewing.* Beverly Hills, CA: Sage.

Edwards, R. 1990. "Connecting Method and Epistemology: A White Woman Interviewing Black Women." *Women's Studies International Forum* 13:477-90.

Ellis, C. and A. P. Bochner, eds. 1996. *Composing Ethnography: Alternative Forms of Qualitative Writing.* Walnut Creek, CA: AltaMira Press.

Ellis, C. 1995. *Final Negotiations: A Story of Love, Loss, and Chronic Illness.* Philadelphia: Temple University Press.

Fine, M. and M. Fine. 1984. "Women's Voices in the Research Relationship: Feminist Alternatives to Objectivity." Paper presented at the annual meeting of the American Psychological Association, Toronto, Canada, August.

Ginsburg, F. 1989. *Contested Lives.* Berkeley and Los Angeles: University of California Press.

Harding, S. 1986. *The Science Question in Feminism.* Ithaca: Cornell University Press.

———. 1987. *Feminism and Methodology.* Bloomington: Indiana University Press.

Harper, D. 1982. *Good Company.* Chicago: University of Chicago Press.

Hertz, R. 1995. "Separate but Simultaneous Interviewing of Husbands and Wives: Making Sense of Their Stories." *Qualitative Inquiry* 1(4): 429-451.

Holstein, J. and J. Gubrium. 1995. *The Active Interview.* Thousand Oaks, CA: Sage.

Klatch, R. 1988. "The Methodological Problems of Studying a Politically Resistant Community." *Studies in Qualitative Methodology* 1:73-88.

Kondo, D. 1990. *Crafting Selves.* Chicago: University of Chicago Press.

Kreiger, S. 1983. *The Mirror Dance: Identity in a Women's Community.* Philadelphia: Temple University Press.

Manning, P. K. (1967). Problems and interpreting interview data. *Sociology and Social Research* 51:301-316.

Myerhoff, B. and J. Ruby. 1982. "Introduction." Pp. 1-35 in *A Crack in the Mirror: Reflexive Perspectives in Anthropology,* edited by J. Ruby. Philadelphia: University of Pennsylvania Press.

Paget, T. with M. DeVault. 1993. *A Complex Sorrow: Reflections on Cancer and an Abbreviated Life.* Philadelphia: Temple University Press.

Rabinow, P. 1986. "Representations Are Social Facts: Modernity and Post-Modernity in Ethnography." Pp. 234-61 in *Writing Culture: The Poetics and Politics of Ethnography,* edited by J. Clifford and G. E. Marcus. Berkeley: University of California Press.

Reinharz, S. 1992. *Feminist Methods in Social Research.* New York: Oxford University Press.

Richardson, L. 1994. "Writing: A Method of Inquiry." Pp. 516-29 in *Handbook of Qualitative Research,* edited by N. Denzin and Y. Lincoln. Thousand Oaks, CA: Sage.

Riessman, C. K. 1987. "When Gender Is Not Enough: Women Interviewing Women." *Gender & Society* 1:172-207.

Rubin, L. 1996. *The Transcendent Child: Tales of Triumph over the Past.* New York: Basic Books.

Stacey, J. 1990. *Brave New Families.* New York: Basic Books.

Van Maanen, J. 1988. *Tales of the Field: On Writing Ethnography.* Chicago: University of Chicago Press.

Van Maanen, J., P. Manning, and M. Miller. 1989. "Editors' Introduction." Pp. 5-6 in *Psychoanalytic Aspects of Fieldwork,* by Jennifer C. Hunt. Qualitative Research Methods Series No. 18. Newbury Park, CA: Sage.

Williams, P. 1991. *The Alchemy of Race and Rights.* Cambridge, MA: Harvard University Press.

Williams, C. and E. Heikes. 1993. "The Importance of Researcher's Gender in the In-Depth Interview: Evidence from Two Case Studies of Male Nurses. *Gender & Society* 7:280-91.

Zola, I. 1982. *Missing Pieces: A Chronicle of Living with a Disability.* Philadelphia: Temple University Press.

PART
I

Reflexivity

1 | Who Am I?

The Need for a Variety of Selves in the Field

Shulamit Reinharz

This chapter deals with the self of the researcher while conducting field-work. Presumably, this is an essential topic because, as the editors of an important research methods book series boldly proclaimed, "the self is the key fieldwork tool."[1] Why, then, does so little of the methodological literature on fieldwork actually focus on the self? Why does the vast majority of fieldwork literature concern the research *role* in the field rather than the researcher's *self*? The familiar topics—the ethics of covert research, the deficits of active participation, the mechanics of recording data, the preferred stance toward member beliefs, appropriate responses to illegal or immoral behavior, taking sides in the field—are all role related. But what about the self, "the key fieldwork tool"?

This chapter offers a framework to explain how the self actually does serve as "the key fieldwork tool." I propose that we both *bring* the self to the field and *create* the self in the field. The self we create *in the field* is a product of the norms of the social setting and the ways in which the "research subjects" interact with the selves the researcher brings *to the field*.

In sum, "being a researcher" is only one aspect of the researcher's self in the field. Although the researcher may consider "being a researcher" one's most salient self, community members may not agree. Methodological literature currently overlooks the variety of attributes that researchers bring to the field;

similarly, it minimizes the wide range of selves created in the field. Because these "brought" and "created" selves are those that are relevant to the people being studied, they shape or obstruct the relationships that the researcher can form and hence the knowledge that can be obtained. Thus, these selves affect the researcher's ability to conduct research.

More dramatically, I would say that unless the researcher (and subsequent reader) knows what the researcher's attributes mean to the people being studied, the researcher (and reader) cannot understand the phenomenon being studied. In anthropologist Pat Caplan's words,

> There are . . . a number of factors which determine the kinds of data we collect, and our interpretation of them. One of the most important of these is our positionality—who are we for them? Who are they for us? Such questions have to be considered . . . in terms of such factors as our gender, age and life experience, as well as our race and nationality.[2]

It is through understanding the relevance and creation of different characteristics of the researcher in the setting that the self becomes the key fieldwork tool. Like Pat Caplan,

> I have become aware that being an ethnographer means studying the self as well as the other. In this way, the self becomes "othered", an object of study, while at the same time, the other, because of familiarity, and a different approach to fieldwork, becomes part of the self.[3]

Similarly, in *Living the Ethnographic Life,* Dan Rose emphasizes that anthropologists (and sociologists) should learn how they are perceived. He suggests we focus on the "unnamed space" where "our" study of "them" meets and clashes with "their" study of "us." If we adopt this framework, then fieldwork reports will combine a full discussion of what the researcher *became* in the field with *how the field revealed itself to the researcher.* Field research will then strike a balance between self and other in its reporting and will also report the process of change.

FIELD NOTES, THEORY, AND RETROSPECTIVE ACCOUNTS

My discussion of the variety of selves in the field draws on a study I undertook in 1979-1980 of elderly kibbutz members' quality of life. After leaving the field,

I analyzed my field notes in various ways, including a chronological review of references to myself. This process transformed me into a data-based object of study. I found that I referred to myself in different ways throughout the year because different aspects of myself became salient over time and across contexts.

Besides the study of my field notes, my argument reflects feminist and poststructuralist theory, in particular its sensitivity to hidden voices and identities.[4] This theory helped me see that to understand "the key fieldwork tool," I also had to understand who I was *not* in the field. Thus, my field notes do not mention that I was *not* an Arab, Sephardi Jew, or lesbian. Only later did I understand the salience of these nonidentities, any of which would have stood in the way of establishing trust and relationships with most kibbutz members. Only in retrospect do I recognize the privileged position of being a heterosexual Ashkenzi Jew.

My analysis also reflects my reading of other experiential accounts of fieldwork. After doing fieldwork in North Catalonia, for example, Oonagh O'Brien commented that "housing is of vital importance in fieldwork" as are "choices about which part of the village to stay in," both of which I did recognize during my fieldwork. But her question about "whether to stay with a family or not" was a significant question I had neglected.[5]

A VARIETY OF SELVES IN THE FIELD

Analysis of my field notes reveals approximately 20 different selves that I have categorized in three major groups:

- *Research-based selves:* being sponsored (removing myself from the sponsor), being a researcher, being a good listener, being a person who has given feedback, being a person who is leaving
- *Brought selves:* being a mother, having relatives, being a woman, being a wife, being an American, being a Jew, being an academic, being 33 years old, being a dance enthusiast, being a daughter
- *Situationally created selves:* being a resident ("temporary member," not true member), being a worker, being a friend, being a psychologist/social worker, being chronically exhausted, sick, and sometimes injured

Although these selves are clear in my field notes, the categories into which I have clustered them are arbitrary. For example, I list "being a worker" as a situationally created self because in the field I learned that understanding this community required sharing people's experience of working. The work assignments I received were linked to my being a woman. My acceptance of physical assignments stems from my upbringing. Similarly, I am not typically conscious of "being an American," but this background feature of my identity was highlighted in the kibbutz in countless ways. In the field, the salience of my various selves varied among subsettings. Here, though, there is room to discuss only a few of these selves.

RESEARCH-BASED SELVES

Being Sponsored, Being a Researcher

Entry into the field begins with the desire and opportunity to study a particular setting. In my case, I wanted to do a field study in Israel, preferably in a kibbutz and dealing with gerontology because I suspected that kibbutzim had innovative approaches to aging. I hoped to study kibbutz elderly by living among them for an extended period of time and participating fully in their lives.[6] I planned to combine empirical information (e.g., how many hours do they work?) with an examination of their definitions of the situation (e.g., how do they feel about growing old on a kibbutz?).[7]

A friend of mine showed a kibbutz member friend of his who was visiting in the United States a book I had recently published and told him of my interest in doing fieldwork. This kibbutz member then contacted me and invited me to carry out the study on his kibbutz contingent on its approval. We next began to negotiate the conditions for my stay, and thus, like many other researchers, I relied on a sponsor to gain access to the study site.[8]

Eventually, this man brought a proposal to the weekly town meeting of his kibbutz, which I will call Kibbutz Emek ("valley"). By bringing this request to the town meeting he obtained the status of "my sponsor" in the eyes of the community, and I was a person "sponsored" by him. The following are segments of official minutes from the meeting:

> January 20, 1979: *Research team on old age in Emek: Proposal of [my sponsor].*[9] We are talking about 3 researchers with their families: a neurologist, a social worker and a sociologist. . . . The intent is that the researchers together with a parallel staff[10] would study the elderly only of Emek and would focus on the problems of Emek. 'I am interested in the future of Emek.'
>
> Conditions for selection of staff: a) Every one would know some Hebrew;[11] b) They would live in the kibbutz for a certain period; c) They would study the people of Emek only.

The researchers want to test community life not in terms of questionnaires but, rather, using the method of community anthropology. At the end of the year, a final report will be delivered with practical suggestions for the kibbutz. The researchers will be permitted to use the research for their own purposes, without the disclosure of names. Members who are affected by this topic are requested to take part. We must provide one room[12] for a year or two and a second room[13] for a half year. . . .

Discussion:

M. R.*:[14] There is a lot of demand for rooms of this type. A building with 5 rooms [in one area of the kibbutz] is about to be torn down. We don't have sufficient space to house our soldiers who are released from the army.[15] And in the [certain neighborhood in the kibbutz], there are no available rooms. If this proposal is accepted, it will compete with the establishment of a neighborhood[16] for young people.[17]

M. M.:* There are problems—a) housing; b) the cost of caring for the child; and c) will this research be specific to Emek? I personally am not enthusiastic about this research.

T. S.: The topic was brought to the executive committee more than a year ago. The financial aspect is not really a factor. It is likely that this project will help solve problems of the elderly. There is a technical problem of housing, but we should resolve it for the larger good of the research.

I.:* Advises acceptance of the proposal and points out that the kibbutz founders are the first generation of older people on the kibbutz. There is alienation between these people and the younger generation. Every effort to solve this problem is desirable.

D.: Accepts the idea but asks who the anonymous people are who will do the research. It is clear that someone will be affected by the housing shortage. With regard to the research, expresses concern from the last experience that the researchers will end up not working in the kibbutz and that in actuality we will have to support the researchers and that will cost us money.

T. Y.:* It seems to me that old people are not a problem; the real problem is the next generation.

M.: I was elected to the committee that helps new members become integrated into kibbutz life and I was warned that we have no rooms; the research will cause additional difficulties.

Outcome of the vote: 26 in favor, 6 opposed. The research proposal was endorsed.

Only 32 of the 200+ members voted, reflecting either small attendance or few votes; 20% were opposed. These minutes show that although the project received formal approval there was little enthusiasm or interest, including among the elderly themselves. Thus, the first perception that kibbutz members had of me before I even arrived was as a person who would consume valuable housing to do a project of questionable value. My sponsor wrote to me in the United States simply that "the project was approved."

As I was to find out, the "town meeting" vote represented only the first figurative gate that had to be unlocked before I would be accepted as a researcher in this kibbutz. In every setting, there is a difference between formal acceptance and social integration. I was soon to learn that I would have to perform much additional "entry work," and my study would hinge on my performance. I would have to (a) free myself from my sponsor and get new allies to ward off opponents; (b) integrate my daughter into her children's house; (c) find suitable workplaces for myself; (d) gain permission to attend "town meetings"; (e) get invitations to committee meetings; (f) demonstrate adherence to kibbutz policies; (g) be visible to community members; (h) earn the trust and cooperation of each individual separately; and (i) develop friendships.[18] Each gate had to be unlocked with its own "key"; each way of entering the community formed my selves. The reward of getting through each invisible "gate" was the sense of having proved myself to the kibbutz members and the ability to go on.

Seven months following approval of the project, my 2½-year-old daughter and I moved to Kibbutz Emek with the status of "temporary member" for 6 months, renewable for another 6 months if the kibbutz and I agreed. Shortly after arriving, I tried to learn more about the town meeting discussion:

> 18:4: I asked one of the "mazkirim" (elected kibbutz leaders) to tell me who had been in *favor* of and who had *opposed* the project.[19] But he said that at the meeting *"no one* spoke against it," *even though my sponsor . . . had introduced the proposal!*

I thus learned (as I had suspected) that being affiliated with my particular sponsor would affect how I was going to be perceived in the field. Unbeknownst to me, my sponsor had the reputation of being difficult. He was disliked by many people and soon by me as well. Instead of being my guide and protector, he became my liability. Thus, one of the selves I quickly had to create in the field was a person who could function independently of my sponsor. Obviously, I was not going to be able to divorce myself from him entirely; therefore, another self I had to develop was a person who could cope with this individual. Moreover, because he was my sponsor, his wife automatically became a kind of auxiliary sponsor. In conflicts between us, his wife had to take his side. Although I liked the wife, I realized that developing a separate relationship with her would be impossible.

In retrospect, I recognize that I actually benefited experientially from this exceedingly difficult relationship because most kibbutz members have at least one problematic tie: They live, work, eat, and do just about everything together. Even when relationships are severely strained, people have to be able to live with each other. On a kibbutz, people remain in deeply interdependent relationships even with individuals they despise. If it becomes truly unbearable, they may renounce their membership and leave. They may even be asked to leave, as occurred in the case of two individuals whose families were asked to leave by a vote at the town meeting during the year I spent on the kibbutz. The fact that many kibbutz members have dissatisfying relationships made me attractive to many people as a potential new friend. I suspect that I had no difficulty obtaining interviews, in part because people valued the chance to talk to someone who had not heard their story. I also suspect that I was particularly privy to negative comments about the kibbutz and about other people, for there were no interpersonal consequences telling these things to a stranger.

Because of my tense relation with my sponsor, I understood and empathized with kibbutz members who had interpersonal problems with other members. During the course of the year, I learned about who was currently not speaking to whom and which people were locked in a state of "permanent" hostility. A few individuals had become complete isolates. I observed many people fighting with one another verbally and a small number who got along with nearly everybody. I assumed that I would be able to get along with everyone, but I, too, could not.

My husband, daughter, and I had a "festive dinner" with my sponsor's family in the collective dining hall every Friday night along with the entire kibbutz community. Although my sponsor seemed to undermine my work as much as support it, we maintained our "public festive face" of sitting together because originally we had requested this seating assignment from the person who makes the Friday evening dining room arrangement.[20] To ask for a change would mean, in a sense, stating publicly that we dislike the very family that had invited me to the kibbutz. I could not bring myself to make such a "declaration" and so spent each week's ostensibly festive meal in extreme tension.

Being a Temporary Member

The kibbutz is run internally as a cashless economy—for example, members receive meals without paying for them and work without receiving a salary. As a "temporary member," my contract gave me a one-room apartment (with electricity and water) located in the section of member housing (as opposed to volunteer housing), all meals, laundry service, child care, health care (visits to a kibbutz doctor and all medications), health insurance, pocket money at the rate received by a member of my age and family status, telephone tokens,[21] an English-language newspaper subscription, haircuts,[22] and some research expenses such as audiocassettes, photocopying, and bus fare for travel within

Israel. The kibbutz provided me with rugged work shoes, sturdy work clothes, and a clothing and shoe allowance for my daughter.

My contract entitled me to use a kibbutz car for occasional research-related transportation. I also received lodging, meals, and laundry service for my husband when he visited me.[23] I was permitted to bring guests to the dining room and have overnight guests stay in my room. Using these necessary services compelled me to construct situationally created selves and both allowed and forced me to have many role relationships with a broad range of kibbutz members and institutions.

In exchange for this support and to enhance my research, I agreed to work in various kibbutz work branches, guided by the needs of the "women's work organizer" at the rate of 8 hours per day (6:30 a.m.-2:30 p.m.), 6 days per week (not Saturdays) required of kibbutz members my age. I also carried out all the service rotations considered appropriate for women members of my age,[24] including guarding the children's houses at night and taking care of groups of young children every fourth Saturday afternoon.

There are several categories of people who reside or spend time on a kibbutz—adult members over age 20 or so, children of members, nonmember parents of members, guests of members, long-term nonmember residents, hired workers (Arabs and Jews), volunteers, and special volunteers who take Hebrew language classes half-days. Volunteers usually are non-Jewish foreigners; special volunteers usually are foreign Jews, especially American Jews. My particular work obligations, Jewish religion, one-year residential status, ability to speak Hebrew, and status as a mother made me more similar (not identical) to the category of female kibbutz members my age than to any other category. I was unlike a guest who has no work obligation and unlike a volunteer who usually works in one branch only (typically requiring no Hebrew language skills—e.g., fruit picking), does no guard duty rotations, and usually stays less than a year. Although volunteers work hard, they are peripheral to the social life of the kibbutz (although because they are young and single they frequently become involved with young, single children of kibbutz members, and many marriages ensue). Being a temporary member with all these duties and assets brought me close to kibbutz members and thereby enhanced my ability to understand their experience.

Being a Worker

My work-formed self-in-the-field (just like my status as "temporary member") created role relationships with kibbutz members and institutions. It also made me acceptable in some members' eyes, as evidenced in this example from a transcribed interview with an elderly female kibbutz member:

> I always say, "The world belongs to the young; it's their kibbutz." I have to respect that this is how they want things. Except for one thing—work. I always tell young people, "Whatever you want to do, fine, but you have to earn your keep." I ask them if they work enough to make a living. They produce children, and in the afternoon they're already off the job. They only work a few hours. They're great socialists, but in the meantime, the Arabs are working, the volunteers are working, and the kids who go to the *ulpan* (study Hebrew) are working. What about the young kibbutz members? That's the one thing I can't tolerate. I could never forgive them for that.

After hearing what she had to say, I was relieved that I had chosen to work. In many ways, my working was the key to securing interviews. Only by working could I be sure that I would not be placed in the stigmatized category of "parasite." Not only did I have to *be* a worker, but I had to be *seen* working. Thus my first job, which consisted of serving food in the dining room, was ideal: Everyone in the kibbutz would have to interact with me to get their food. This job also reinforced my status as a woman—women were always being assigned to the kitchen. Thus the work I did helped form my identity in the field as did all the other ways I interacted on the kibbutz.

Being an Academic

About 2 months into my stay, there was a change in leadership on the kibbutz. The two elected kibbutz heads with whom I had negotiated the conditions of my research ended their term of office, and a new head assumed office. Kibbutz members told me that this man "had no patience for the academics who contribute 'nothing' to the kibbutz." The "academics" to whom he was referring were the four kibbutz members who were professors in Israeli universities. Hearing about his antipathy to "academics" made me wary about the kind of relationship we would have. After we met, however, I learned that he himself had an academic degree from the United States. It appeared that he would not dismiss me out of hand as long as I also worked at regular kibbutz jobs. To my surprise, he actually seemed to enjoy talking with me privately in my role as an academic. What he wanted to avoid, I soon realized, was any public acknowledgment of this shared interest that might highlight *his own outsider status*. Because he was not born in a kibbutz, the kibbutz-born members might not perceive him as a "real" kibbutznik. As a person with an academic degree who was not working in academia and had just become a *mazkir,* he expressed kibbutz members' historic ambivalence toward academic jobs.[25]

> 186:2: I met with the new "mazkir" in his office from 9:00 to 10:00 a.m. . . . . I asked him if a new social worker would start working at Emek (because I knew the current social worker had left). He told me that Emek has applied for a social worker from the main kibbutz movement, but there is a long waiting list(!). He doesn't think social work is such a great thing anyhow, except maybe for individual therapy which is simply "listening" and kind of "silly." The only social worker he is interested in accepting is a kibbutz member since otherwise it takes a year for them to figure out what a kibbutz is. . . . He agreed to meet on Thursday morning for a more "personal discussion." He set aside from 9 a.m. to noon, although I had asked for only an hour or two.

As it turned out, he was skeptical about me for another reason—he thought I would arrogantly assume that I understood the kibbutz. Since my accepting the role of "not knowledgable about the kibbutz" was clearly important to him, I was careful to let him explain things to me and to express few opinions of my own. At the same time, how could I sustain this "ignorant self" without becoming "silly"?

Later in our private discussion, he expressed considerable disdain for the United States because of the "crazy ideas Americans try to bring to Israel." He probably would have appreciated me more if I had been an Israeli social scientist, preferably an Israeli who was a member of one of the 200 kibbutzim. With him I had to downplay both being an American and understanding the kibbutz.

Fortunately, as a kind of bureaucrat, the *mazkir* accepted my presence as long as I was generally self-sufficient. As a new *mazkir,* he had a great deal to do and did not need superfluous burdens. We could be intellectually close about topics other than the kibbutz as long as I remained distant and did not make him look like an academic who likes Americans.

Being a Person Who Was Staying for a Year or Only a Year

The first thing that seemed salient to *non-office-holding* kibbutz members was that although I was going to be with them on a temporary basis, it would last a full year.[26] Thus, one of the initial categories I was put into by kibbutz members was a "temporary" person or nonapplicant for permanent membership. In this community, the temporary/permanence dimension was highly significant.

18:3: Nicole (a long-term nonmember resident) said about herself: I'm unimportant on the kibbutz. Everyone says I've got good ideas, but they aren't implemented. It's because I'm not a member.

Sociologically, the question arises as to how much a community will invest in a temporary person.

154: Me: Do you prefer to socialize with the people who live here, in contrast with the volunteers?

Tamar: It's not really a preference, it's knowing that the volunteers will be leaving soon. So, I should invite them? Every 3 months to start all over again the same story?

Me: So slowly, you turn away from doing that.

Tamar: The volunteers are not really connected, they are, "as if," "next to" the society. Volunteers are distributed among the members to be hosted, and I didn't know what to do with the last one since he spoke no Hebrew and I speak almost no English. People know Mindy (another volunteer) from work; she speaks Hebrew and has a kibbutz boyfriend, so I have gotten to know her. Also Laurie who is going to marry a kibbutz son.

A "temporary person" is someone who, by definition, usually has limited social value because a community's investment in him or her cannot pay off in terms of future interaction. A "temporary" person is someone the community knows in advance it will lose. Yet the temporary person has value as a stranger— a person who is exotic, can hear secrets, and provides a new perspective. This issue is very salient in the kibbutz because there are so many temporary people; so many people pass through. I would suggest that the two major social categories are in fact "members" and "temporary people" (ranging from one day to several years), and I was immediately part of the second category. For some people, my being "temporary" was the only salient thing about me. Because I would not stay and become a member, I automatically had diminished value. There was no compelling reason for anyone to get to know me.

The "temporary" category contained gradations. Some temporary people lived on the kibbutz for a few years and thus had *higher* social value than I. Some stayed only for a summer or 6 months and had *less* social value.[27] Some temporaries had permanent relations with kibbutz members (e.g., parent of a member). I found myself constantly being asked how long I would stay and reiterating endlessly that I would be staying for a year. This question expressed more than the kibbutz members' desire for information—it was, I believe, a way of placing me in the hierarchy of community value. I found myself emphasizing my difference from volunteers.

For me, one calendar year revealed the cycle of seasons that constitutes the agricultural, school, holiday, and fiscal year in a kibbutz. I could get sick and get better; I could anticipate future events and reminisce a bit with people about past events that we had experienced together. I could observe the way crises would come to a head, be brought to the town meeting for resolution, be debated all week long in every corner of the kibbutz, and then brought back for endless discussion and voting.

Living on the kibbutz day and night for a year meant that I was always "bumping into" people. Those individuals whom I sensed would be hard to approach for formal interviews I could interview informally in what I called "sidewalk interviewing." The views expressed on the sidewalks, which I immediately entered in my field notes in the privacy of my room, were spontaneous and thus perhaps even more authentic than the interviews that were scheduled, prepared, and tape-recorded.

> 305:3: On the way to the dining room, I bumped into S. We asked each other, *Ma nishma?* (How are things?), which was an invitation to talk. . . . It turns out that S is completely bitter. . . . She would like to leave.

Staying a year enabled me to reschedule canceled interviews, if needed. It allowed me to witness the kibbutz's collective joy when children were born (although it varied), how secrets about who is pregnant were kept or not, and how weddings were prepared and funerals conducted. A full year's stay enabled me to experience the cycle of moods as the kibbutz went through all the weather changes of the year and defined how people's behavior correlated with the weather.

> X:X: My sponsor said, "It's so hot, people don't visit each other."
>
> 38:6: She said, "People are a little edgy in August anyhow since it's so hot. Things will get better soon."
>
> 48:2: He said, "Things are a little difficult right now in the kibbutz, with the weather being so hot, so many people on vacation. There really are pressures."

Understanding these connections and the annual cycle generated ideas about years to come and years that have passed. As time went on, I anticipated situations and no longer had to ask so many questions, giving me confidence that I understood aspects of kibbutz life. I knew different people's tastes in food (97:3) and how they responded to each other. I soon could predict what would happen next at most events.

92:2: Breakfast.[28] I joined H. Everything was very quiet. . . . I knew it wouldn't take long for things to heat up. There is a certain rhythm to most of our breakfasts. Today's blow-up came over the *mazkir* who came by the table where the flower-arranging staff was eating and announced that he was going to present some flowers in the name of the *mazkirut* to R and to some of the actors in the kibbutz play. E was furious and said, "Why shouldn't the electricians get flowers too?" Everyone stopped eating to listen and then discussed the blow-up when they resumed their meal.

My problem here was that to be seen as really being part of the kibbutz and understanding kibbutz life I had to have an opinion. An opinion almost always meant taking one side or another. If I waffled, I would be seen as being "just an academic," or a "coward," or lacking "principles." There was no escape because kibbutz members were always looking for ways to judge each other's character or to use one's behavior as further proof of one's reputation.

In the eyes of some members of the kibbutz, the constant change that occurred made it seem ludicrous that a year was sufficient to understand kibbutz life. To these people, my plan to stay a year illustrated that my study was superficial.

85:4: I told her that my goal was to examine the situation of the elderly members and give the kibbutz some suggestions. She said I wouldn't be able to do that because the situation changes all the time. What is not happening today might occur tomorrow. The elderly are an "unstable population," in her view.

Although field researchers might say that one year is adequate for the kind of study I was doing,[29] some people in the kibbutz disagreed. People I considered to be insecure (e.g., recent kibbutz members) used their greater length of stay on the kibbutz relative to mine as a way of pulling rank on me and undermining my right to claim I understood the kibbutz.

101:1: Chana said that my (erroneous) beliefs probably reflect the fact that I have been here such a short time. She's been here 4½ years, so she knows!
Does that mean that being an outsider will leave me forever ignorant in the insiders' eyes? What about the objectivity they wanted? Or is it just Chana's way of pulling rank on me?

There were those who stressed the brevity rather than the length of the year I was devoting to this study. Even people who were very involved with me and helpful occasionally said that more time was necessary:

> 198:3: Z grabbed me by the arm and asked how things were going. I told him
> "Well," and he wished me good luck. But he said it would take at least 2 or 3
> years for me to learn about the kibbutz. [A *mazkir* told me it takes people a year.
> What does it take?]

Others stressed that the kibbutz was essentially unknowable regardless of the
time spent:

> 6:5: C said to me, "People who write about kibbutz are people who don't know
> about it."

It was unknowable even by esteemed researchers who have lived on a kibbutz
most of their lives:

> 57:1: Y thinks that one of the major sociologists of kibbutz life doesn't under-
> stand the kibbutz.

If the kibbutz was unknowable, or required enormous time before one could say
that one understood it, then, surely, it was completely inappropriate for me to
make recommendations to the kibbutz on the basis of a year or any amount of
time. I believe that the constant reminders by people of the near impossibility
of understanding the kibbutz functioned to motivate me to study it as well as I
could and to be cautious about what I claimed to know. These reminders were
the way that some kibbutz members expressed the "otherness" and special
quality of kibbutz life. After all, the kibbutz was founded, in part, to provide an
alternative to nonsocialist living. Could I, as an inhabitant of the capitalist world,
understand what it is like to live in a socialist society? Would I be arrogant and
assume I could take the ideas from "my world" and use them to improve "their
world"? Clearly, some members considered it presumptuous when outsiders
claimed to know what was going on and how to do things better. I also began to
discern condescension in social science's assumption that we can understand
worlds that people spend their whole lives trying to understand. This reciprocal
problem became a crisis for me at the end of the study.

Some kibbutz members pointed out the significance of my temporary status,
not in terms of adequate or inadequate knowledge but in terms of how I was
better off than permanent kibbutz members because my stay was shorter:

> 282:2: M explained to me that I'm happy here since I'm temporary.

Although this comment was made to me ironically, he may have been right in suggesting that being temporary allowed me to experience more pleasures than pains of membership. Experiencing the kibbutz as a visitor is utterly different from experiencing it as a member. I could walk away from conflicts. I did not participate in the essence of kibbutz life, a lifetime of mutual social obligations.

My announced intention to stay a year might have provided a convenient cover for delay in consenting to an interview:

> 16:3: When I said I'd like to invite her to talk sometime, she seemed pleased but said, "We have lots of time."

> 60:6: S cancelled for today, too busy.

And I did the same:

> 45:4: S asked me if I had read his book and I said, "No, I was too busy." He said, "There's no rush."

Thus, my temporary status was salient to kibbutz members and to me and was loaded with meaning about whether or not the community was knowable, what my rank was in the kibbutz, and what my/their knowledge of the kibbutz actually meant.

There were others, however, who felt that whether or not I could be said to "know" the kibbutz depended on people's willingness to speak with me and whether or not I worked on the kibbutz. It was not the length of stay but whether or not I was "integrated." There was a difference in members' eyes between being a member and being fully accepted:

> 305:3: T claims it took her 15 years to be integrated here. Earlier, she tried to move with her husband into the kibbutz in which he was born, realized she could never be integrated there, and "fled" within a week.

Clearly, people were telling me that despite the kibbutz having formally approved of my project I would have to pass additional tests of acceptance based on the way I did my work and who I was as a human being. In a sense, I was treated like all new "members"—although they had "voted me in," I had to prove myself. The running joke in the kibbutz was that if people had to be voted on once again (after having been members for years), most would *not* be accepted.

Kibbutz life consists of nearly imperceptible change, on the one hand, and dramatic events, on the other. Opinions grind against each other until a person's reputation becomes rigid or a policy becomes firm. Stories unfold; problems emerge; relationships change; decisions are made; people come; people go. Had I stopped at one point in the process, I might mistakenly have prejudged the outcome. Thus, a major factor in the study was my presence for a year, which allowed me to experience change. Of course, it was only one year, and only that particular year, so I wonder what I would have learned if I had stayed longer.

FINAL COMMENTS

The researcher does not know in advance what attributes will be meaningful in the field.[30] From the examination of my field notes, it appears that the attributes are those listed earlier in this chapter: the research-based selves, the brought selves, and the situationally created selves. These general categories can be applied to any field setting. The specifics within these categories, however, are related to the culture of the particular setting. The meanings related to these various selves are the basis of how the researcher is perceived. How the researcher is perceived, in turn, will affect how she or he understands him- or herself. And finally, this understanding will affect the way the study proceeds. Documentation of these processes is essential in fieldwork and does not consti-tute an unwarranted, narcissistic display. Quite the contrary: Understanding the self in fieldwork releases us from the epistemological tension between unre-flexive positivism, on the one hand, and navel gazing, on the other. It will help us document how and why the self is the key fieldwork tool.

NOTES

1. John Van Maanen, Peter Manning, and Marc Miller (1989), p. 5.
2. Pat Caplan (1993), p. 178.
3. Caplan (1993), p. 180.
4. Shulamit Reinharz (1992).
5. Oonagh O'Brien (1993), p. 235.
6. See Andrei Simic (1978), p. 9.
7. See Shulamit Reinharz and Graham Rowles (1987) and Shulamit Reinharz ([1979] 1984).
8. Adler and Adler (1987), p. 38.
9. His name was entered into the record. For the sake of his privacy, I refer to him as my sponsor.
10. The social worker and neurologist never materialized, nor did a parallel internal team.
11. Thus, my knowledge of Hebrew was defined in advance as salient and adequate. Perhaps this explains why people didn't want to see me as needing help in Hebrew and no one found time

to work with me systematically, although several discussed it with me a bit. People who wanted to learn Hebrew went to the *ulpan.*

12. In which a researcher could live. Members of a kibbutz live on a kibbutz. The members of this kibbutz were saying that they would have to provide the researchers with a place to live.

13. For a second researcher or family.

14. Every time a person is mentioned who is over age 65, I put an asterisk next to their name.

15. Kibbutz members must find housing on the kibbutz for soldiers after their release from the army. The kibbutz did not have a sufficient supply of rooms for all the soldiers who were expected to be released in the near future.

16. Areas within this kibbutz consisted of apartments in which certain groups lived (e.g., young couples, newly released unmarried soldiers, middle-aged couples, older people, volunteers, etc.).

17. When I left, I joked with one kibbutz member who was sad that I was leaving, "Don't be sad, now you'll have a room."

18. In other communities, the phases would take different forms, grounded in the structure of the particular community.

19. A "mazkir" is the kibbutz member elected to coordinate all kibbutz activities. *Mazkirim* is the plural form. This particular kibbutz was developing a pattern of electing two individuals—a man and a woman—to serve in this post.

20. Friday night dinner is the weekly festive meal. Most kibbutz members and their families eat as families in the large dining room at assigned seats that they select at one point and retain for a long time.

21. At the time of my study, most kibbutz members (except for high-ranking army officers) did not have telephones in their homes. Most calls were made from a public telephone, which required the use of tokens, or from a telephone that required the assistance of a kibbutz member who served as switchboard operator.

22. Having my hair cut on the kibbutz became a valuable source of observations and interviews with the hairdresser. My hair was cut on day 79, 150, 228, and 292 of my year in the field. Having my hair cut by the kibbutz hairdresser was a political statement that she was good enough for me!

23. During the week, my husband lived in Jerusalem; on weekends he came to visit me and our daughter on the kibbutz. Although he was not obligated to perform work on the kibbutz, he participated in the men's dishwashing rotation and in the grapefruit harvest.

24. Older women had different rotations, such as ironing clothes for soldiers who were home on leave.

25. Historic ambivalence refers to the fact that some socialist Zionists believed that to free themselves from anti-Semitism, Jews would have to change their preference for academic work and enter new lines of work to develop a proletariat. When Jewish youngsters in Europe reached late adolescence, they had to decide whether to go to the university to study (in which case they would be "lost") or learn to be a farmer who would immigrate to Palestine/Israel and be part of a kibbutz.

26. The kibbutz actually made a commitment to me that I could stay for half a year, renewable for another half. I assumed, in advance, that things would work out well and that I would stay for a year. That is how I always announced it to people when asked. I realize that many projects have undefined termination points, such as reported in Tamar El-Or (1997 [this volume]). She visited a particular woman "over a two-year period . . . 2-3 times per week" and ended her fieldwork after she realized she could continue only if she accepted some of their practices. Staying with them a long time implied incorrectly that she was accepting their beliefs.

27. Of course, the temporary/permanent distinction was not quite as certain as this statement makes it appear. Some "temporaries" married a kibbutz member and ended up staying perma-

nently. Other "permanents" suddenly got up and left—illustrating that they only seemed to be permanent.

28. In principle, all meals are eaten communally on a kibbutz. In this kibbutz, however, as in most kibbutzim, breakfast and lunch were eaten communally with co-workers from one's work setting, whereas families ate dinner on their own in their private apartments. Lunch is the hot meal of the day.

29. "What is the natural ending for a field work? My teachers used to say that one has to work for at least a year, to experience a full round of seasons, holidays, cycles of agriculture, and so forth. Some talk about an inner feeling signalling the right time to withdraw. Others have financial restrictions, like a limit on grant funds. Some say that, in a sense, most ethnographers never really leave their field" (El-Or 1997 [this volume]:169).

30. A previous researcher on this same kibbutz was completely discredited because he left the field during wartime. I was told the story about this researcher on my first day in the field and repeatedly thereafter. I knew how I would have to act should war break out if I wanted to retain the opportunity of studying this community.

REFERENCES

Adler, Patricia A. and Peter Adler. 1987. *Membership Roles in Field Research.* Qualitative Research Methods Series No. 6. Beverly Hills, CA: Sage.

Caplan, Pat. 1993. "Learning Gender: Fieldwork in a Tanzanian Coastal Village, 1965-85." Pp. 168-181 in *Gendered Fields: Women, Men and Ethnography,* edited by Diane Bell, Pat Caplan, and Wazir Jahan Karim. London: Routledge & Kegan Paul.

El-Or, Tamar. 1997. "Do You Really Know How They Make Love? The Limits on Intimacy with Ethnographic Informants." Reprint. Pp. 169-190 in *Reflexivity and Voice,* edited by Rosanna Hertz. Thousand Oaks, CA: Sage.

O'Brien, Oonagh. 1993. "Sisters, Parents, Neighbours, Friends: Reflections on Fieldwork in North Catalonia (France)." Pp. 234-247 in *Gendered Fields: Women, Men and Ethnography,* edited by Diane Bell, Pat Caplan, and Wazir Jahan Karim. London: Routledge & Kegan Paul.

Reinharz, Shulamit. [1979] 1984. *On Becoming a Social Scientist: From Survey Research and Participant Observation to Experiential Analysis.* New Brunswick, New Jersey: Transaction Books.

———1992. *Feminist Methods in Social Research.* New York: Oxford University Press.

Reinharz, Shulamit and Graham Rowles, eds. 1987. *Qualitative Gerontology.* New York: Springer.

Simic, Andrei. 1978. "Aging and the Aged in Cultural Perspective." Pp. 9-22 in *Life's Career— Aging,* edited by Barbara G. Myerhoff and Andrei Simic. Beverly Hills, CA: Sage.

Van Mannen, John, Peter Manning, and Marc Miller. 1989. "Editors' Introduction." Pp. 5-6 in Jennifer C. Hunt, *Psychoanalytic Aspects of Fieldwork.* Qualitative Research Methods Series No. 18. Beverly Hills, CA: Sage.

2 Parent-as-Researcher

The Politics of Researching in the Personal Life

Patricia A. Adler
Peter Adler

The ethnographic study of children has become a focus of growing sociological interest. Researchers undertaking such projects have attempted to bridge the gap between children and themselves by assuming roles in their settings that were compatible with participation in children's worlds. Discussing his research with preschoolers, Corsaro (1981:130) has argued that "becoming a participant in the children's activities was necessary for gaining insight into what *mattered most to them* in their everyday interaction" (emphasis in original). The physical and demographic differences between adults and children limit the range of partici-patory roles adults can take in children's settings. Most ethnographers have assumed the position of either friendly observers (Best 1983; Corsaro 1985; Eder 1995; Glassner 1976; Goodwin 1990; Kless 1992; Opie 1993; Thorne 1993) or observing friends (Fine 1987; Mandell 1988). Fine and Sandstrom (1988) have articulated four roles available to adult ethnographers: the supervisor, the leader, the observer, and the friend. With few exceptions, these roles are not naturally

EDITOR'S NOTE: This chapter originally appeared as an article in *Qualitative Sociology,* Vol. 19, No. 1, 1996. Reprinted by permission of Human Sciences Press, Inc.

existing in children's settings, but are researcher-created, imbuing them with a certain artificiality. Moreover, they have generally been constructed within institutionalized settings, such as schools, where children are most readily found.[1] Such sellings restrict the range of behavior available to researchers, limiting them from fully entering into the lifeworlds of children. As a result, researchers' understanding of children's culture and experiences may be lacking in both breadth and depth.

One research role that has been previously overlooked is the *parent-as-researcher* (PAR). Parents can readily gain entree to the world of children through their own children. They can then capitalize on this "complete membership role" (Adler and Adler 1987) by "opportunistically" (Riemer 1977) making the community of youth to which their children belong a focus of study. This approach offers several advantages over more conventional ethnographic roles and relationships. First, it is a naturally-occurring membership role with which children are totally familiar. Second, it spans children's participation in a variety of settings, offering access into their school, home, recreational, and social lives. Many scholars have fruitfully made their personal arena a focus of research (see Ellis 1995, Karp 1996, Krieger 1991, and Ouellet 1994, for just a few recent book-length examples). Among them, a smaller number have studied their own children, focusing primarily on socialization and development, including Charles H. Cooley, Jean Piaget, and Erik Erikson.[2] PARs integrate these foci, looking at their own children and those of others in the social worlds they inhabit. But rather than looking exclusively at developmental issues, PARs can follow Waksler's (1986) call to study children on their own terms, to stop looking at them as incomplete adults, and to examine phenomenologically the lived experiences of childhood. Parental research, like the work of many who draw upon their personal life arenas, encompasses a dual research-membership focus. Such role-fused postures have also been applied to the study of children through the approaches of the teacher-as-researcher (Carere 1987; Daiker and Morenberg 1990; Goswami and Stillman 1987; Pinnell and Matlin 1989) and the counselor-as-researcher (Cottle 1980; Moustakas 1990). Little reflection has been done, however, on the contours of these other dual approaches, leaving their advantages, their problems, and some of the solutions to their problems underinvestigated. The ethical implications of these role-fused approaches warrant particular reflection, as our society and its researchers forge new collective moral attitudes toward the definitions of public and private domains and the needs and rights of researchers versus those of the researched. When social scientists straddle the parental and research roles they may find themselves in situations where the distance between the researcher and the researched diminishes and their service to these two endeavors does not always easily coincide. Issues that have been particularly raised as sensitive include those of researchers' potential power over subjects (Corsaro 1981) and their responsibility for the knowledge they gain during the research (Fine and Sandstrom 1988; Glassner 1976; Mandell 1988). Further issues to consider include the moral and legal responsibilities of parental researchers and the ultimate consequences of this dual role for both the research and the researched.

In this chapter we offer such an exploration. We describe the research we conducted, detailing the community we studied, our relations with community members, and the specific types of empirical materials we gathered. We then outline some of the conceptual features of this research role, focusing on the specifics and implications of the role advantages, role location, and role relations. We conclude by addressing the ethical issues raised by this type of research.

METHODS

In this research project, we gathered data through longitudinal participant observation and interviews with preadolescents in the upper grades (third through sixth) of elementary schools. Over the course of seven years (1987-94) we observed and interacted with children both inside and outside of their schools. During this period we witnessed children progress from elementary through middle to high school, and we incorporated data about them as they matured. The children we studied came from seven public and five private schools drawing on middle- and upper-middle-class neighborhoods (with a smattering of children from lower socioeconomic areas) in a predominantly white university community with a population of around 85,000.

Studying circles in which our children broadly traveled greatly enhanced our research. Our membership role in the setting offered us a naturalness and ease of entree which we would not otherwise have had. We did not have to negotiate either formal or informal entree with setting members, we were already intimately familiar with the scene, and, as parents, we had access to a wide variety of different types of setting members.

In doing our research, we occupied several parental roles located in different arenas. We interacted with children, parents, teachers, and school administrators as *parents-in-the-school,* volunteering in classrooms, accompanying field trips, organizing and running school carnivals and other events, driving carpools, and serving on school committees. We interacted with children, parents, other adults, and city administrators as *parents-in-the-community,* coaching and refereeing youth sports teams, serving as team parents, being the team photographer, organizing and running the concession stand, and founding and administrating our own youth baseball league. We interacted with children, their parents, neighborhood adults and children, and adult friends and their children as *parents-in-the-home,* being a part of our neighborhood, having friends in the community, interacting with the neighborhood and friendship groups of our children, offering food and restroom facilities (our house bordered the neighborhood's playing field), nursing children through illnesses, injuries, and substance abuses, helping them with their school decisions and schoolwork (assisting with library research, editing their rough drafts, providing home computer and copying facilities), serving as mentors and role models, serving as friends and confidantes, bailing them out of jail and other troubles, and helping them talk to their own parents. We became the "cool parents" in the group, to whom our kids and their friends could turn.[3] These diverse roles built upon our natural parenting activities, contacts, interests, and style, taking us into locations and events populated by children. We undertook them both as they naturally presented themselves and as deliberate research strategies, sometimes combining the two as opportunities for interacting with children became available through familial obligations or work/school requirements. It helped, at times, that we were of different sexes, as there were occasions where children sought us out to talk about gender-related topics, and times where our gendered experiences and insights made us more interested in and helpful about discussing different subjects.

We also took a more explicit *parent-as-researcher* role, conducting audiotaped interviews with children in our home, at their homes, and in schools. We let these interviews flow out of and build on our participant observation. We generated research topics and conceptual questions about specific and general areas through our interactions and casual conversations with people in our parental roles. When we were ready to write about a particular subject we conducted focused, unstructured interviews. We selected theoretical samples (Glaser and Strauss 1967) of people to interview based on our knowledge of who might offer us a range of different points of view and experiences with regard to the topic at hand. In deciding on who to interview we relied on our own knowledge of people in the community, and got referrals from our children, their friends, parents, neighbors, and teachers we knew, and people whom we had already interviewed (Biernacki and Waldorf 1981). We contacted or were contacted by potential interviewees, arranged for parental consent, and interviewed them at the location they preferred. We also conducted interviews with children in schools, both individually and in groups. On several occasions, we did whole-class interviews with students in the third through sixth grades, at the invitation of their teachers (some who had taught our children). After obtaining parental consent, we asked their help with our research and moved through the topics on our interview schedule. This technique offered the advantage of bringing together children from a variety of social groups and asking them to resolve their different perspectives on sociological issues. In addition, we used this school base to conduct individual interviews with members of these and other classes. Instead of interviewing whole classes, we sometimes went into classes and talked about our current topic. We then solicited volunteers who wanted to be interviewed (and got recommendations from their teachers), and after obtaining informed consent conducted taped interviews with individual children in unoccupied classrooms or offices. We then conducted select interviews with seven teachers at three different elementary schools to get a broader overview of children's social lives and their dynamics from individuals whose experiences were more comparatively rooted in working with many different groups of children over the years.

We used this combination of personal life and school settings to generate a diverse pool of empirical materials. The informants we generated outside of schools, for both participant observation and interviewing, were influenced by our personal location in our community. We followed our daughter and son, their friends and enemies, the children of our neighbors and friends, and other children we met through our involvement in youth leisure activities through their school and extracurricular experiences. Our children inadvertently obliged us by occupying or passing through vastly different types of social groups and experiences. Our daughter moved through preadolescence in the popular group, surrounded (and occasionally overwhelmed) by a strong, although shifting, circle of friends. Her concerns included maintaining acceptance and popularity, tailoring group membership to suit her preferences, avoiding the conflicts engendered over status and power, and dealing with manipulative leaders. Our son's experiences spanned a broader spectrum of the social scale, as he grew up surrounded by a crowd that was popular but vicious, was expelled from and quit the group in a terrible fight that kept him hovering in and out of social isolate status for nearly a year, and finally made friends in a shifting and oscillating mid-level friendship circle. We thus used the different social locations of our children and their friends, other people we knew, and the children we gathered through our school interviews, to triangulate (Denzin 1989) our data, putting together a wide representation of people.

ROLE INVOLVEMENTS

The PAR role creates a number of unique arrangements that differentiate it from other approaches to field research. The greater involvement and overlap between researchers' personal lives and research role invoke methodological, epistemological, and ethical issues salient to contemporary ethnographers.

Role Advantages

There are several advantages afforded the PAR, as compared to more distanced or "objectified" research roles. These may lead to a greater understanding and deeper involvement in the lives of children.

Diminished Role Pretense

In traditional research roles, fieldworkers often enter their settings and forge identities that do not naturally exist there. They create a set of behaviors and meanings associated with studying the members, a concept that may, especially initially, be alien or forced. In forging a research role they may feel internal and/or external pressures to reciprocally offer something back to setting members in exchange for their research entree and assistance. This may lead them to assume contributory roles or to act interested in or committed to the setting in ways that they really are not. Ethnographers studying children may also find their role choices restricted by the institutional nature of the settings in which children are most easily found. To study children only in school settings, for instance, limits the types of interaction ethnographers can have and observe, and they have to forge roles that somehow bypass the authority of the adult-as-stranger[4] and construct the accessibility of the adult-as-friend (Fine 1987; Mandell 1988). This may be awkward or difficult. Even in more informal leisure settings, adult-researchers must forge roles, such as observer, supervisor, or friend (Fine and Sandstrom 1988), that carry with them certain limitations and artificiality. In contrast, the PAR role is recognizable and familiar to setting members. In our case, we had no need to pretend to be something we were not or to create some unwieldy research persona. Our presence and role in the settings were understood and expected by participants. Children, and the adults who surrounded them, interacted with us naturally, during the course of conducting everyday business. As parents we were expected to be in and have interest in these settings. Our parental attachments and responsibilities thus constituted our involvement in the settings, necessitating no further explanation or "contribution."

Role Immersion

Another advantage of the PAR role involved the totality of our participation in the setting. Unlike other researchers who can only interact with their informants at circumscribed times, the children we studied, particularly our own, were available to us all the time. We could observe them on the weekends as well as week days, in the evenings as well as day times, during the mundane periods of their lives as well as when crises periodically arose. The constancy of this role meant that we were always around children, not only in times when we had negotiated entree. For instance, in contrast to the method Eder (1995) employed in studying middle-school children where she and her team of researchers observed students in the cafeteria during lunch time, our house was "on limits" constantly. We prided ourselves on having the best snacks in town, thereby becoming a frequent waystation for children after school or when children congregated to play sports and games. We spent many hours observing them in the backyard park from our deck or living room, often without their paying attention, to see how they negotiated and compromised with each other. To our own children's bemused consternation, neighborhood kids would stop by to visit with us during the summer months, when our children weren't even home. Fully cognizant of our desire to know about the shifting social developments that commonly define the summer months, these children would give us updates on the latest news. This immersion increased the intensity and profundity of our research, enhancing its validity compared not only to less participatory depth interview studies, but to nonmembership participant observation as well.

Role Triangulation

A third advantage of the PAR role involved our greater ability to triangulate data in the setting. Rather than just coming into the scene and observing or asking subjects directly about themselves, we had many avenues by which we could access empirical information about people. Naturally, we relied on our own children as key informants since they were readily available, usually willing to talk (although this became more problematic as they neared adolescence), and understood the research process. However, they, like anyone else, had their own value judgments and their own data access limitations. Supplementing them, we had, as noted, many widely dispersed and varied contacts in our community.

These sources were all backed up by the foundation of our own observation. We gathered data formally, in taped interviews, or informally, as we stood around at sporting events and chatted with other parents and their children.

Role Location

Our PAR roles were strongly affected by our positioning in the setting. This influenced our outlook, our perspectives, and the way we were perceived by others.

Role Attachment

In cases where people assume dual research/membership roles, their involvement in and commitment to one aspect of this role may be stronger than to the other. As in any complete-member-research, our attachment was stronger to our parental membership role. We had a greater investment in this dimension because it was primary, deeper, longer lasting, and more central to our core identities and goals. This had the potential to affect our research and research relations. For instance, one Halloween evening, our son came home early from trick-or-treating because some of the neighborhood bullies had been picking on him. One, in particular, in whom we were extremely interested because of his clique background, was extremely manipulative, denigrating our son in an effort to aggrandize himself to other boys (who eventually "ditched" him themselves). Later that evening, when his worried mother called to see if we had seen or helped her "lost" son, we could not contain our anger. We strongly expressed our feelings, described her son's behavior, and told her how unwelcome he would be in our house. She, naturally, defended her son. The next morning, when calmer heads prevailed, we called the mother to apologize, but by this time the damage had been done. We feared that we had lost any future direct research access to this family.[5] In this case, our role as parental defenders superseded that of measured observers, temporarily jettisoning our research concerns. Actual conflicts with those we study is a serious problem arising from the PAR's role attachment that is less likely to occur in non-PAR research on children.

Role Obligations

At times, our membership role in the setting created obligations and responsibilities for us. Although we were often able to integrate our membership efforts into alignment with our research interests, this was not always the case. Membership role obligations occasionally ran independent and in opposition to the values and philosophies we developed and espoused in our research role. For instance, during the course of this research we founded, along with two other couples, our own competitive youth baseball organization. Although we had written about some of the detrimental effects associated with the adult control for youth recreation and the pressure this brought to young people, fostering highly competitive and goal-oriented attitudes toward sport at ever younger ages (Adler and Adler 1994), we tried to develop a program that incorporated the positive aspects while restraining the negative ones. Not surprisingly, however, we began to see some of the same disappointing aspects in our league as in other youth sports leagues. While we were frustrated and disappointed with the league, having already obligated ourselves to the other members of the Board of Directors, we could not pull out, and despite our protests about how things were run, we were committed to operating the new organization.

These membership role obligations worked the same way in our own household. We often heard children denigrate the importance of school, making fun of kids who did well, or distancing themselves from educational investment. While we could nonjudgmentally accept the decisions and attitudes these people made for themselves, talking about their lives and options within the parameters they had set, we could not take that same approach with our own children. Our responsibilities as parents necessitated that we uphold our family values and goals. There were also times when we were called upon by other parents to assume the parental mandate and join with them in enforcing membership obligations. We have been awakened in the middle of the night to hear that our daughter and friend had sneaked out of someone's house, and been enjoined to track them down; we have been alerted that a carload of our girls was seen filling up the trunk with beer and heading out of town, and been recruited to find and stop them at the city limits. In these kinds of cases we have held relationships with other parents, shared things from a parental perspective, and collectively enforced parental norms. The membership role, while offering the advantages of naturalness, ease, and entree, carried with it a set of responsibilities and requirements that could not be avoided.

Though these role obligations precluded some data from coming our way, at the same time, there were fewer obligations from artificially structured research bargains that we had to pay off. Often in field research, ethnographers must ingratiate themselves with setting members to equalize the moral exchange. Since our role was a naturally occurring one, we did not have to "pay back" people in this way. Our favors to others were done in socially expected venues, and when we did not reciprocate, it was because it was not expected. All meaningful field research relations carry within them the necessity for reciprocal exchange. The difference between ours, as a membership role, was that the nature of our obligations were clearly articulated, and part of our everyday life responsibilities, while for nonmember researchers they are negotiated or stipulated.

Role Identification

In contrast to other research roles, PARs have a greater relational identification by themselves and others with their children-as-subjects. This anchors their location in the setting and gives them a reflected identity.

Being affiliated with our children-as-subjects enhanced our ties to some setting members. For instance, our close ties to our children's friends led them to say things to us that they might never have revealed to other parents or researchers. We were fearful, for example, in our study of clique dynamics (Adler and Adler 1995), that we would never learn how powerful clique leaders actually felt about the way they acted towards others, or if they were consciously aware of their manipulations. Yet our daughter and her friends poured forth about these matters freely, speaking to us as they would only have to extreme insiders. Similarly, we had easy access to teachers in the local schools. Having made contacts with them when they taught our children, we were able to return to their classrooms for years following. They contacted parents for us, vouched to kids for us, and proudly hung up articles from the local newspaper about our work in their classrooms. We received help from other parents, too, who shared their inner feelings and frustrations about their kids with us, knowing that as parents we could understand and relate to their troubles and turmoils. Whole networks of people were also opened up to us through our role identification, particularly the afterschool activities in which our children participated. For years, when we needed more data, when we needed answers to particularly puzzling issues we were trying to sort out, or when we needed to triangulate data on people or events about which we were dubious, we had merely to walk down to the Little League fields on a Saturday and drift from group to group. By the end of several hours, we had harvested all the latest tidbits, scheduled a dozen interviews, and rounded up assistants who would search for the types of others we still needed. Being parents of children in the community even enhanced our ties to people who didn't know our kids. For instance, Patti was interviewing a third grade girl outside of her school one day about the stratification hierarchy of kids in her grade. The girl mentioned a particularly mean clique leader by first name, and later in the conversation pointed him out as he passed by. Patti recognized him as the younger brother of a mean bully who had given our son a black eye and acknowledged, to the girl, the acquaintance. Her eyes grew wide as she exclaimed, "Oh, you know him?" She subsequently turned toward Patti, confidentially, and revealed a whole array of secret, negative information that she had previously withheld.

On the other hand, our close identification with our children and their friends diminished our access to other setting members. People who disliked our children tended to avoid us as well. This included children who were our children's enemies, parents of children who they had treated badly, and those parents, noted earlier, with whom we had fought defensively on their behalf. Other times we had difficulty gaining direct information from people who thought ill of our children. In interviews with one of our son's former teachers and one of his former friends, these people had to delicately step around descriptions of behavior that they thought damaging because they found it embarrassing to say negative things that they believed applied to our son. Further, despite our promises of confidentiality, there were people who probably didn't want to say things to us that they feared would get back to our kids or to others, through our kids. Finally, there were others who tried to hide their marginal behavior, such as smoking cigarettes or having sex, because they thought it might affect the way we felt about them. These types of diminished access are less likely to occur in non-PAR research on children.

Role Relations

The PAR role places the individual in definite positions vis-à-vis others in the setting. These role relations, in part, dictate the outcome and effects that the researcher may have on others, and the types of empirical materials that are gathered.

Role Effects

Casting a research dimension onto a previously existing membership role may have numerous effects on the incumbent role and its associated relationships. This may, in some respects, be damaging. Studying their children and community may impinge upon researchers' relationships with their children or other community members. In pursuing depth information and feelings, researchers may intrude into people's personal lives and invade their private areas. There were times when our children resisted our interest in and curiosity about them. They were particularly sensitive about anything concerning their relation-

ships with members of the opposite sex. Adding the research role into the relationship also brought with it added responsibilities for our children. While at times they
relished our interest in their friends, they also tired of facilitating our search for
information and insight. Finally, the research relationship is characterized by an
informational exchange. To some, this may be seen as having manipulative
overtones that could negatively impinge on the relationships it touches.[6]

In other respects, the added role may enhance researchers' relationships with
their children and others by deepening their intimacy, involvement, and understanding. Our children grew up in the security that their parents were interested
and actively involved in their lives. We knew intimately about their inner
feelings and the vicissitudes of their social worlds. We took their questions and
problems as our own. When they needed help, our suggestions reflected our depth
immersion in their experiences. Our commitment to studying our children thus
afforded us the opportunity to invest time we might otherwise have had to divert to
other research settings into their worlds. We also developed an enhanced intimacy
with our children's friends. Several of them told us that they lacked the closeness
with their parents that our children had with us. They never tried to explain their
feelings and behavior to their parents, they said, because their parents were so
unfamiliar with their lives that they would never understand them. Not only our
own children, then, but these others, told us about their personal lives or came
to us for guidance. The addition of the research role thus deepened and enhanced
our involvement in the lives of our children and their friends.

Role Confusion

Using the dual roles of parent and researcher was occasionally a source of
confusion. In our case, this primarily occurred in two ways. First, there were
some people, usually acquaintances or distant others, who did not understand
our roles and questioned our behavior. Children who came into contact with us
or our children were sometimes surprised to find us so interested in their lives.
One time Peter and our son were out shopping one evening when they ran into
some acquaintances from our son's class. They stopped to say hello, and Peter
ended up engaging them in a long conversation, during which he chatted with
them about other kids at school and about themselves. When they saw our son
at school the next day they asked him why his father was so curious about their
friends and their lives. They were not used to talking to parents who knew so
much or were so interested in them. There were adults, too, who misunderstood
our relationship with their children when they glimpsed it superficially. For
instance, after our daughter and her friends got into trouble one evening, when

they were supposed to be at our house, one mother accused us of being too permissive. She claimed that the reason the girls hung around our house was because we allowed them to do things that others prohibited. This was not true, in fact, as we maintained the same curfew and behavioral standards as others. We knew, though, what the girls were generally doing, how and to whom they were lying, and when and where to balance liberty with control, rather than imposing strict unilateral rules. In contrast to this mother, who had to rely on rigid regulations that made her daughter hide everything from her and flee, we used our knowledge and our judgment to work within their culture, moderating its excesses. In these cases, people misunderstood the relationship between, and the way we integrated, our research and parental roles.

Other instances of role confusion were brought about by people, usually close others, who did not understand our seeming behavioral inconsistencies. These arose due to conflicts we had between our values as parents and our desire to watch children as they naturally behaved. We occasionally seemed to flip in our attitudes, as we struggled between the nonjudgmental value stance of the research role and the moral imperative of the parental role. For instance, our interest in popularity led us to discern that for some, academic achievement was not a trait salient to the hierarchy of popularity (Adler, Kless, and Adler 1992). When we would force our children to read challenging books, to edit and rewrite their papers, or to stay home to study, this confused some of their friends. While we seemed to understand (better than their parents) their needs for faddish clothes, their desire to see an R-rated movie, their obsession with a weekly television show, or the necessity of acquiring their own phone line, we also had strong moral judgments about time that robbed them of their academic focus.

Role Integration

The majority of the time we were able to integrate the research and the membership roles, engaging in them simultaneously. By making our personal lives a focus for research, we fused the commitment to time, place, and behavior between the two, bringing them together and fusing them. In this endeavor, the parental role served as the base and the research role flowed out of it. This is generally the case with opportunistic member-research, as the membership role precedes and is unlikely to be meaningfully transformed by the research addition. The shape and character of our research posture was influenced by our natural membership inclinations in several ways. We have always tried to follow a laissez-fairist parental posture (Adler and Adler 1984), avoiding intervention in children's disputes and letting them learn (wherever possible) from the "natural consequences" of their own experiences.

The integration of the research and membership roles offered several advantages for us. First, we could be simultaneously engaged in gathering data while living our everyday lives. Second, as noted, instead of having to ferret it out, data would come to us immediately and regularly as important events occurred. We were thus able to see people's initial, instead of reconstructed, emotional reactions and the way they individually and collectively forged their responses. Third, research questions arose for us in the pursuit of everyday life, which could then be addressed and answered in this same realm. Other setting members, both children and adults, were particularly helpful in this regard, as they found our questions fascinating and enjoyed discussing them with us. Fourth, when we entered settings exclusively for the purpose of gathering data (such as schools), we were able to apply our membership knowledge to facilitate rapport, as when we brought our own "Pogs" to elementary schools and played with kids on the playground in between interviewing them in their classes.

The PAR role thus represents an integration of self, enabling practitioners, in large part, to synthesize their work and play, their personal and professional dimensions. PARs can then focus their research lens on topics that have meaningful interest to their lives, at the same time as they use their research skills to pursue the understanding and analysis of personal interest.

Role Bifurcation

While these roles meshed comfortably most of the time, there were occasions when they were better separated or distinguished. The prompt to bifurcate these roles could come from either others or ourselves.

At times, we initiated this distinction ourselves, for the purpose of clarifying our interests or goals. We did this to people with whom we primarily shared a membership relationship, to indicate the emergence of a research interest. For example, our daughter and several of her friends had been invited to the "homecoming" dance of the rival high school by several boys with whom they were not "going," something that rarely occurred in their circle. Our queries about who these boys were and why they would invite our daughter's friends were met with a series of rebuffs and denials of knowledge. The morning of the dance, in unsuccessfully raising the question once again, Patti finally said to her, "Okay, I'm not asking as your mother anymore. I want to know as a sociologist." Suddenly a different expression crossed her face and she explained that these boys were the stars of the football team, the highest statused boys in the school.

She and her friends represented the cream of the popular girls' group at her school. But since her school held higher local status than their rival, these boys bypassed the popular girls at their own school to seek the highest status girls in town, even if it meant inviting girls with whom they were not romantically involved. It was as if this role was apart and separate from her relationship with us as parents. Similarly, one day at school we saw our son, who had trouble making friends, hanging out with a "nice" boy. When we asked him why he didn't invite this boy over to play, he informed us that this was a "school friend," not someone with whom he played at home. Intrigued, we asked him to explain this concept further, but he walked away annoyed. Exhortations that this relationship could prove of research interest were only met with further rebuffs. This shift in posture from parent to researcher, although not always successful in evoking data, was articulated to clarify a shift in goals that carried with it a rise in the confidentiality, impersonality, and generic interest of the communication.

At other times, the prompt to bifurcation came as the result of role conflict. Sometimes others tried to invoke our allegiance to one role over the other. This created dilemmas for us that we had to resolve individually, balancing our needs as parents, our children's needs, the needs of their friends, and our research needs. In some instances we allied with parents and the parental perspective. We responded to a call to join with other parents, for example, in holding a meeting with our son's basketball team to tell the boys that their collective behavior was inappropriately mean and hurtful. This was difficult because we had been pursuing noninterventionism as we gathered rich data, observing, interacting with, and carpooling the boys as they talked about each other and enacted their intricate clique manipulations. On another occasion, we responded to the direct query of a mother by informing her that her daughter had not arrived at our house by her curfew. This caused a breach in our trust relationship with the child, one that we were eventually able to recoup, but not without some difficulty. Nonparental researchers might not have had the same moral obligations to the surrounding adult community.

Occasionally, we sensed the role conflict ourselves and had to take a stance between research and membership pulls. We established standards to guide our conduct with children. In most cases we leaned toward the membership role, particularly in behavior involving our own children. We abandoned detachment and value neutrality when we felt that their welfare or moral development was in jeopardy. Yet, in others, we followed a policy of passive acceptance (but not active facilitation) of problematic behavior. We made it perfectly clear to our informants, for example, that while we would not seek out their parents to volunteer our knowledge, neither would we lie for them. When asked directly, as noted above, we would tell. We also drew the line between knowing about deviant behavior and enabling it. While we recognized that some people used alcohol and drugs, we neither permitted illicit substance use in our house, nor would we assist people in obtaining them. Finally, we refrained from engaging in any deviant behavior or consuming any illicit substances (including alcohol) with our informants. This culminated in our having to take the strongest membership stance of our research career: excluding a topic from study. While conducting interviews about clique dynamics, we were told by several people that we should interview them about drugs, that drugs were coming in and tearing their cliques apart, that drugs were salient to the hierarchy of status and the confines of group membership. We pursued the topic, obtaining a Certificate of Confidentiality from the Federal Department of Health and Human Services which would have protected the data we gathered from the curiosity of parents or the subpoena of law enforcement. After thinking about the project for a long time, however, we finally decided to abandon it because of the potential role conflict and ethical issues it might engender. We did not want to put ourselves in situations where we would feel too pulled by the research loyalty of protecting informants' confidences and the membership loyalty of protecting them and their families from dangerous behavior.

Role bifurcation occurred, then, when we deliberately detached one role from the other, drawing the distinction between the researcher and membership line. We stepped out of research/membership role fusion when we thought it would clarify our purpose, when we needed to assert authority and distance, or when we took an ethical stance with regard to a particular behavior.

Role Betrayals

As Lofland and Lofland (1995) and Punch (1994) have stated, any foray into the field may yield the sense of betrayal. When researchers gain intimate knowledge of people's lives and write about it, the subjects may feel as if they have been betrayed (Rochford 1985; Vidich and Bensman 1964). Subjects may also feel betrayed when researchers leave the field, especially if they have taken a membership role. In contrast to these "active" membership roles (Adler and Adler 1987) that researchers may quit, the parental research role is one that endures: Once the research is terminated, participants remain within the setting. Despite this, role betrayals can arise during complete membership research out of the dual role situation, done by researchers to others, and to others by researchers. When any party interacts through one role, they may betray the commitment of self and others to the alternate role.

The issue of role betrayal particularly arose in our interaction with our own children. We often expected them to treat their lives toward us as research, while we acted toward them as parents. They, in turn, wanted us to accord them the acceptance and value neutrality of the research stance (that we gave their friends), while they treated their lives toward us as personal. We were thus caught with them between the relationships of parent-child and researcher-friend. This often worked, making us friends with our children; it also occasionally created feelings of role betrayal toward each other. During the instances, then, when we applied our parental standards to them, as opposed to our research standards, they felt betrayed. On the other hand, when we felt obligated to apply our research standards rather than our parental standards, we felt impinged upon. This double standard was a confusing aspect of our dual roles.

Manipulation was another potential betrayal factor. We had to ask ourselves if our behavior was sometimes imbued with too great of an instrumental purpose. We reflected, at times, about whether we were treating the children instrumentally because of the "side-bets" (Becker 1960) we had with them, and wondered if they occasionally thought the same. We questioned our acceptance of friends and acquaintances our children brought home who were not to our liking, but whom we found empirically interesting. At the same time, we questioned their offerings to and requests from us.

ETHICAL ISSUES

The PAR role is a simultaneously potent and potentially explosive one in the eyes of the research community. It offers many strengths, from depth immersion and understanding to naturalness of data gathering and enhanced triangulation, making it one of the most internally valid research postures. Yet, at the same time, it raises several potential ethical problems for ethnographers researching in the personal life.

Power

The differential social power between researchers and their subjects has been a common charge leveled against ethnography. This can be more pronounced when researchers are studying children (Corsaro 1981). In our case, power differentials existed in the areas of age, status, education, financial resources, potential influence (over them through their parents) and occasionally direct authority (over our own children). Common to much of ethnography, power differentials, or "studying down" (Nader 1972), are oft-discussed forms of relations between researchers and their subjects (Gusterson 1993; Hertz and Imber 1993; Rosaldo 1989). Numerous examples of studying down appear in the literature, ranging from anthropological (colonial) studies, research on criminal groups, studies of the disenfranchised and disadvantaged, and nearly all research involving children and other vulnerable populations. However, in no other research relationship, with the possible exceptions of the teacher-researcher or counselor-researcher, does the question of direct authority over the researched stand out as critically as it does with the parent-researcher (PR) role.

In our role, power issues are primarily germane to problems associated with pressuring children to reveal data (the power of authority), or using data gathered through research to harm children in their personal life (the power of knowledge). Fine and Sandstrom (1988) have noted that preadolescence is the first age period where children develop the power to control or contain research over them, leaving researchers at their mercy. When researchers ask for entree or inquire about specific topics, their requests carry a certain weight merely by having been made, but preadolescents have a keen sense of their privacy and deflect unwanted prying. The role of adult, parental-friend, or friend's parent was not a sufficiently formal authority role to enable us to compel data from others' children. We had no more ability to compel these participants to divulge data or to harm them through the knowledge we gathered than researchers do about any subjects they study.

The power of PRs more centrally involves their relationships with their own children. This is a role conflict issue, arising when PRs tip the balance between research and membership excessively toward the former. In an imperfect world, it is possible to imagine researchers abusing, exploiting, or in some way harming their own children. However, we feel that the likelihood of this happening is remote. The emotional and familial primacy of the parental role dictates that the issues of protection, safety, and affection will take precedence over instrumental or career gains for the vast majority of researchers, as they did for us.[7]

Guilty Knowledge/Behavior

A second potential ethical issue arises when PARs possess guilty knowledge about the behavior of others' children. Such guilty knowledge may also be viewed as guilty behavior when it involves withholding information about, or nonreporting, potentially problematic incidents. Ethnographic researchers studying children frequently encounter this problem, as youth is a period during which people learn by experimenting and testing boundaries. Scholars of children's behavior must weigh the moral obligation associated with knowing secrets about children's norm and rule violations with the damage to trust that results when researchers inform on their subjects. In most cases, researchers studying children have located the ethical imperative in maintaining the confidence of their subjects (Fine and Sandstrom 1988; Glassner 1976; Mandell 1988). Fine and Sandstrom (1988:55) have argued that "children must be permitted to engage in certain behavior and speak certain words that the adult researcher finds distressing. Further, in some instances, the researcher must act in ways that are at least supportive of these distressing behaviors." Polsky (1967), in discussing research on the crime and deviance of adults, has taken this one step further. He has suggested that researchers studying such groups must be willing to engage in violations themselves, if only by not reporting these to the authorities, and must prove to their informants that these actions are consistent with their beliefs. This ethical issue is compounded when researchers' subjects are children, however, because behavioral standards for juveniles are different from those for adults, with morals issues added to legal issues. Although the morality of children is partly societally legislated, children also fall under the moral guidance of their parents, and each family's standards are *sui generis,* in a category of their own, that may differ from those of researchers. This leads to questions, discussed earlier, about how researchers should treat children whose parents have different standards and expectations for their behavior.

For researchers to turn to parental or other authorities whenever they witness a mean-spirited, deviant, or delinquent activity, would not only be impractical, but would bring the research process to a screeching halt. Such action, moreover, would violate the membership norms of parental behavior, as parents deem it inappropriate to report to each other everything they know. Yet researchers may find occasions where either reporting or intervention is appropriate. Here, the guideline of endangerment can serve as a rule of thumb. When researchers observe children engaging in behavior that could be harmful to either themselves or others, or when they encounter behavior committed by others that could be harmful to children, they should step out of the neutral posture and attempt to help. This can take the form of reporting such behavior to the appropriate person(s) and/or directly intervening themselves.

The responsibility for making this judgment can only lie with researchers themselves. No structure of bureaucratic regulations can substitute for the interpretive judgment of participating individuals, as children's behaviors are understood and given meaning within the context of their situations. If re-searchers deem that these behaviors fall within the parameters of children's "normal" deviance, then latitude can be invoked. Thus, we acquiesced to remaining silent about children's bullying, exclusion, and lying, just as Mandell (1988) permitted children to urinate in the corner without telling the teachers and Fine (1987) witnessed stealing without reporting it. When the younger boys we studied engaged in such antisocial behavior, we did not necessarily stop them or break up their fights, believing that such dominance plays were a common feature of male preadolescent culture. Yet, in other cases, we intervened directly with our informants about their behaviors, especially their alcohol consumption, sexual exploits, and binge eating, acting on the basis of our concern for their welfare. We advised them about safer techniques, health issues, and problematic behavioral patterns, but neither told on them to their parents nor severely chastised them. It was our belief that they would experiment with these acts anyway, and we felt that if we could gain their confidence, we could impart information that would, in effect, be more beneficial than stringent admonitions for abstinence. We never encountered behavior that warranted, in our opinion, reporting to either parents or authorities, such as Weiss (1994) found, for example, in her study of deformed children, when she observed these youngsters being mal-treated by their families and had to report it to the social welfare service.

Responsibility

A third issue concerns the moral and legal responsibilities of the PAR and how these differ, if at all, from those of the parent as nonresearcher and the researcher as nonparent. Whether or how the responsibilities and liabilities of parents change upon the addition of the research dimension has never been specifically addressed. Guidelines to these concerns are not clear, and can only be deduced through inference, if at all.

In reviewing our planned research, our Institutional Review Boards sug-gested that following our customary parental behavior was appropriate as long as we restricted ourselves to interacting naturalistically within the confines of the "parental role." Only when we moved outside of this to conduct taped interviews did we need to obtain formal review and parental consent. In so doing, we were carefully instructed about how to handle issues of disclosure, consent, and anonymity, and screened for areas involving sensitive topics, participants' law violations, and the ethical treatment of our subjects. We were told to refrain from addressing sensitive topics, either to avoid asking about or to inform subjects that we could not protect data they gave us about their law violations, and that we would have to inform the authorities if we witnessed any instances of abuse or maltreatment, even if it meant violating subjects' trust. Once we stepped out of the parental role, then, we were to act as agents of the state.[8]

Over the years we have seen the increasing expansion and bureaucratization of official behavior, encumbering greater numbers of people with formalized regulations and obligations. At the same time we have witnessed the rise in public intervention into people's private lives through the vehicle of government-mandated reporting. A host of people in different roles have been required to assume the responsibility of coming forward to reveal information where they might previously have avoided involvement, particularly in areas involving the potential physical or sexual abuse of women and children. This no longer applies only to medical and educational personnel, but now to social researchers as well. Parents, then, are asked to assume a different social and legal responsibility, even if their moral responsibility feels the same, when they bring the research enterprise into their lives.

Moral standards and concerns in the academy have shifted dramatically over the last decade. Heightened attention has been brought to bear on areas that might previously have been considered unproblematic, the concept of vulnerable populations has been brought to the fore, and a host of heretofore common practices have become morally questioned. This rise in the ethical imperative and movement toward interventionism reflects a general shift in the broader societal ethic away from an emphasis on the good and the rights of the individual, towards the benefit and needs of the collective. We are increasingly being asked to evaluate less strongly the interest of individual freedom and liberty against those of the collective welfare.

In deriving conclusions about the ethical responsibilities of the PAR, we get no assistance from those who have developed the corresponding roles of teacher-as-researcher and counselor-as-researcher. These practitioners have been less reflexive about their behaviors than traditional academics.[9] Parent-researchers operate in a research area where two sets of standards concurrently operate: the public arena of the research role and the private arena of the parental role. We are asked to find a balance between two, often conflicting, sets of guidelines: those of a social moral order that is changing and that of a personal moral order that holds constant; those of a social moral order that seeks elaborated rules and guidelines to protect the vulnerable from the potentially capricious judgment of the individual, and the personal moral order that seeks flexibility and discretion to uphold the traditional goals of family, reciprocal loyalty, and trust. Until such time as we develop clear, integrated norms that obviate the need for such tightrope balancing, we can only advise PRs to seek the good in both sides, to equilibrate, as best they can, the benefits intended by the moral collectivists with the loyalty and judgment that comes from the heart of the moral individualists.

NOTES

1. Notable exceptions to this trend include Goodwin's (1990) work on the language of neighborhood street children, Willis' (1977) work on the culture of working-class youth, and Wulff's (1988) work on the ethnicity of South London girls.

2. For discussions of the methodological approaches of these social scientists, see Erikson 1973, Evans 1967, and Maier 1965, on Erik Erikson; Evans 1973, Maier 1965, and Modgil 1976 on Jean Piaget; and Jandy 1942 and Reiss 1968 on Charles Cooley. It is interesting to note that the intellectual climate of their times was more receptive to the theories generated by their observational methods than to the methods themselves, which were often viewed as excessively subjective and not adequately methodologically rigorous.

3. We would like to thank Spencer Cahill for suggesting this concept to us. While the children never actually addressed us by the term "cool parents," they said such things as "I could never talk to my parents like this," "You guys are so much easier to talk to," and "I could never tell my parents about this."

4. One of the most common dilemmas faced by adults who enter school settings as strangers and attempt to establish ethnographic research roles is pressure from institutional gatekeepers to enforce school disciplinary norms. Such authoritative behavior distances researchers from their subjects, yet noncompliance risks alienating them from their adult sponsors (cf. Eder 1995; Mandell 1988; Thorne 1993).

5. Ironically, however, when doing interviews in the school the following year, a younger brother volunteered to be interviewed, and the parents spoke with us and gave us their consent.

6. Gary Alan Fine, personal communication.

7. Although we have found nothing specifically written about this subject, there is, however, discussion in some fields about negative effects of researchers' nonconsensual use of their children as subjects. In particular, the Child Language Data Exchange System, a compilation of parent-child transcripts donated by researchers (including some parent observers), is openly available to all language acquisition scholars. Stories of the subsequent resentment of children whose early language anecdotes have been written down, preserved indefinitely, and made accessible to hundreds of researchers have circulated informally in this field (James Morgan, personal communication).

8. This contrast is mirrored by the differential latitude afforded private investigators, who can enter locations and make inquiries relatively freely, while government officers, such as police, are bound by more restrictive investigative and evidentiary requirements.

9. One minor exception to this is the methodological reflection offered by Carere (1987) on the covert research she conducted while substitute teaching elementary school children.

REFERENCES

Adler, Patricia A. and Peter Adler. 1995. "Dynamics of Inclusion and Exclusion in Preadolescent Cliques." *Social Psychology Quarterly,* 58(3):145-62.

————. 1994. "Social Reproduction and the Corporate Other: The Institutionalization of After-School Activities." *Sociological Quarterly* 35:309-28.

————. 1987. *Membership Roles in Field Research.* Newbury Park, CA: Sage.

————. 1984. "The Carpool: A Socializing Adjunct to the Educational Experience." *Sociology of Education* 57(4): 200-9.

Adler, Patricia A., Steven J. Kless, and Peter Adler, 1992. "Socialization to Gender Roles: Popularity among Elementary School Boys and Girls." *Sociology of Education* 65:169-87.

Becker, Howard S. 1960. "Notes on the Concept of Commitment." *American Journal of Sociology* 66:32-42.

Best, Raphaela. 1983. *We've All Got Scars.* Bloomington: Indiana University Press.

Biernacki, Patrick and Dan Waldorf. 1981. "Snowball Sampling." *Sociological Research and Methods* 10:141-63.

Carere, Sharon. 1987. "Lifeworld of Restricted Behavior." Pp. 105-38 in P. A. Adler and P. Adler (eds.), *Sociological Studies of Child Development,* Vol. 2. Greenwich, CT: JAI.

Cottle, Thomas J. 1980. *Children's Secrets.* Garden City, NY: Anchor Press/Doubleday.

Corsaro, William A. 1981. "Entering the Child's World: Research Strategies for Field Entree and Data Collection in a Preschool Setting." Pp. 117-46 in J. Green and C. Wallat (eds.), *Ethnography and Language in Educational Settings.* Norwood, NJ: Ablex.

————. 1985. *Friendship and Peer Culture in the Early Years.* Norwood, NJ: Ablex.

Daiker, D. A. and M. Morenberg. 1990. *The Writing Teacher as Researcher.* Portsmouth, NH: Heinemann.

Denzin, Norman K. 1989. *The Research Act.* 3rd ed. Englewood Cliffs, NJ: Prentice Hall.

Douglas, Jack D. 1976. *Investigative Social Research.* Beverly Hills, CA: Sage.

Eder, Donna. 1995. *School Talk: Gender and Adolescent Culture.* New Brunswick, NJ: Rutgers University Press.

Ellis, Carolyn. 1995. *Final Negotiations.* Philadelphia: Temple University Press.

Erikson, Erik H. 1973. *In Search of Common Ground.* New York: Norton.

Evans, Richard I. 1967. *Dialogue with Erik Erikson.* New York: Harper & Row.

Evans, Richard I. 1973. *Jean Piaget.* New York: Dutton.

Fine, Gary Alan. 1987. *With the Boys.* Chicago: University of Chicago Press.

Fine, Gary Alan and Kent L. Sandstrom. 1988. *Knowing Children.* Newbury Park, CA: Sage.

Glaser, Barney and Anselm Strauss. 1967. *The Discovery of Grounded Theory.* Chicago: Aldine.

Glassner, Barry. 1976. "Kid Society." *Urban Education* 11:5-22.

Goodwin, Marjorie H. 1990. *He-Said-She-Said.* Bloomington: Indiana University Press.

Goswami, D. and P. R. Stillman, eds. 1987. *Reclaiming the Classroom: Teacher Research as an Agency for Change.* Portsmouth, NH: Boynton/Cook.

Gusterson, Hugh. 1993. "Exploding Anthropology's Canon in the World of the Bomb: Ethnographic Writing on Militarism." *Journal of Contemporary Ethnography* 22:59-79.

Hertz, Rosanna and Jonathan B. Imber. 1993. "Fieldwork in Elite Settings: Introduction." *Journal of Contemporary Ethnography* 22:3-6.

Jandy, Edward C. 1942. *Charles H. Cooley, His Life and His Social Theory.* New York: Dryden.

Karp, David. 1996. *Living with Depression.* Oxford, UK: Oxford University Press.

Kirby, Richard and Jay Corzine. 1981. "The Contagion of Stigma: Fieldwork Among Deviants." *Qualitative Sociology* 4:3-20.

Kless, Steven J. 1992. "The Attainment of Peer Status: Gender and Power Relationships in the Elementary School." Pp. 115-48 in P. A. Adler and P. Adler (eds.), *Sociological Studies of Child Development,* vol. 5. Greenwich, CT: JAI.

Krieger, Susan. 1991. *Social Science and the Self.* New Brunswick, NJ: Rutgers University Press.

Lofland, John and Lyn H. Lofland. 1995. *Analyzing Social Settings.* 3rd ed. Belmont, CA: Wadsworth.

Maier, Henry W. 1965. *Three Theories of Child Development: The Contributions of Erik Erikson, Jean Piaget, and Robert Sears.* New York: Harper & Row.

Mandell, Nancy. 1988. "The Least-Adult Role in Studying Children." *Journal of Contemporary Ethnography* 16:433-67.

Modgil, Sohau. 1976. *Piagetan Research.* Windsor: NFER.

Moustakas, Clark. 1990. *Heuristic Research: Design, Methodology, and Applications.* Newbury Park, CA: Sage.

Nader, Laura. 1972. "Up the Anthropologist: Perspectives Gained from Studying Up." Pp. 284-311 in D. Hymes (ed.), *Reinventing Anthropology.* New York: Vintage.

Opie, Iona, 1993. *The People in the Playground.* Oxford: Oxford University Press.

Ouellet, Larry. 1994. *Pedal to the Metal.* Philadelphia: Temple University Press.

Pinnell, G. S. and M. L. Matlin, eds. 1989. *Teachers and Research: Language Learning in the Classroom.* Newark, DE: IRA.

Polsky, Ned. 1967. *Hustlers, Beats, and Others.* Garden City, NY: Doubleday.

Punch, Maurice. 1994. "Politics and Ethics in Qualitative Research." Pp. 83-98 in N. Denzin and Y. Lincoln (eds.), *Handbook of Qualitative Research.* Thousand Oaks, CA: Sage.

Riemer, Jeffrey. 1977. "Varieties of Opportunistic Research." *Urban Life* 5:467-77.

Rochford, E. Burke. 1985. *Hare Krishna in America.* New Brunswick, NJ: Rutgers University Press.

Rosaldo, Renato. 1989. *Culture and Truth: The Remaking of Social Analysis.* Boston: Beacon.

Thorne, Barrie, 1993. *Gender Play.* New Brunswick, NJ: Rutgers University Press.

Vidich, Arthur J. and Joseph Bensman. 1964. *Small Town in Mass Society.* Princeton, NJ: Princeton University Press.

Waksler, Frances Chaput. 1986. "Studying Children: Phenomenological Insights." *Human Studies* 91:71-82.

Weiss, Meira. 1994. "Nonperson and Nonhome: Territorial Seclusion of Appearance-Impaired Children." *Journal of Contemporary Ethnography* 22:463-87.

Willis, Paul. 1981. *Learning to Labour.* New York: Columbia University Press.

Wulff, Helena. 1988. *Twenty Girls: Growing Up, Ethnicity, and Excitement in a South London Microculture.* Stockholm Studies in Social Anthropology, No. 21. Stockholm: University of Stockholm.

3 Ethnography and Anxiety

Field Work and Reflexivity in the Vortex of U.S.-Cuban Relations

Raymond J. Michalowski

This chapter examines how macro-social forces can influence the process of doing, interpreting, and representing ethnographic fieldwork. The context for this analysis is the tensions between the United States and Cuba that inscribed themselves on my fieldwork with legal professionals in Havana and on my efforts to interpret and represent this fieldwork to audiences in the United States. I will specifically focus on three things: (1) how micro-social interactions between myself and informants in Cuba were framed by geo-politics, in this particular case U.S.-Cuban hostilities, (2) how these geo-political forces influenced my relationships with professional audiences at home, and (3) how the eventual construction of ethnographic tales is influenced by dominant discourses as these are deployed in the narratives of informants and audiences.

My interest in these issues was initially animated by uncertainties that arose as I pursued an ethnographic study of lawyers and legal processes in Cuba. I eventually came to name these uncertainties *disciplinary anxiety* and *discursive*

EDITOR'S NOTE: This chapter originally appeared as an article in *Qualitative Sociology,* Vol. 19, No. 1, 1996. Reprinted by permission of Human Sciences Press, Inc.

anxiety. These anxieties were rooted in a growing awareness that my interactions with both Cubans in Havana and scholars in the United States were being framed as much by the political tensions between these two nations as they were by either my agency or that of my interlocutors. As I became more aware of the impact of geo-politics on my relationships in the field and at home, I became more concerned with interpreting just how this impact was shaping my efforts to construct ethnographic interpretations of law and justice in Cuba.

The discussion of disciplinary and discursive anxiety I present here is informed by contemporary theorizing about reflexivity in ethnography. It is also a modest attempt to focus the reflexive lens a bit more sharply on the macro-social aspects of the ethnographic process, and particularly on how politically positioned informants and audiences shape the eventual construction of ethnographic tales. Before engaging the question of reflexivity in ethnography more directly, however, I would like to contextualize the problem.

GEO-POLITICS AND
ANXIETY IN THE FIELD

I first traveled to Cuba in 1985 as part of a "political tour" designed to acquaint U.S. researchers with the Cuban justice system. Between then and the fall of 1988 I went to Cuba on four more occasions to interview attorneys and other justice system officials, acquaint myself with Cuban legal practices, and conduct interviews with youths involved in the currency black market (Michalowski and Zatz 1990). In spring of 1989 I returned to Havana to begin field work in a Cuban law collective (*bufete colectivo*) in central Havana. I subsequently returned in the fall of 1989 and the spring of 1990, 1991, 1992, and 1993 for additional follow-up work in the "*bufete,*" as it is called by the people who work there.

My fieldwork in the law collective was part of a larger project aimed at understanding the relationship between law and socialist construction in the Cuban context, which in turn, grew out of a long-standing interest in the relationships between social systems and legal systems (Michalowski 1985). Additionally, and very importantly, my Cuban research was also animated by twenty years of inquiry into questions regarding the political-economy of human social relations, and practical political engagement on behalf of various Leftist causes, including opposition to U.S. interventions against socialist governments and movements in the Western Hemisphere. Thus, I first went to Cuba in 1985 as a 40-year-old male leftist, with positive sympathies for the Cuban revolution, particularly its social welfare accomplishments, and with negative animus toward U.S. policies, particularly the economic and intellectual barriers the U.S. government had erected between the people of Cuba and the people of the United States.

In contrast to my pro-socialist sympathies, a lifelong attachment to liberal conceptions of human rights meant that I also bore uncertainties about the practice under actually existing socialisms—including Cuba's—of sacrificing individual freedoms in the name of collective economic well-being. I began my field work in the *bufete* hoping that, by hearing both legal professionals and people caught up in Cuba's justice system "speak for themselves" about law, socialism and human freedom, without the distorting filters of political argumentation within the United States, I could better resolve my own intellectual tensions between socialist and capitalist visions of human rights. When I first entered the law collective to begin field work I naively anticipated that I could engage Cubans in conversations that were not framed by the geo-political contest between my government and theirs.

I soon learned that any attempt at fieldwork in Cuba takes place within a vortex of geo-political conflict between the governments of Cuba and the United States. For three decades the relationship between the U.S. and Cuban governments has been a hostile one. The U.S. government has enforced an economic blockade against Cuba longer than it has against any other country in the world, including most recently the Torticelli bill which prohibits ships that have called at Cuba from docking in the United States for 180 days (Alarcon 1991). For its part, since the early 1960s Cuba's socialist government has maintained an anti-U.S. posture, repeatedly arguing that U.S. policies towards Cuba are naked proof of the U.S. government's imperialist designs on Cuba (D'Estéfano 1985). The Cuban government has also argued that U.S. counterrevolutionary designs on Cuba necessitate the militarization of Cuban society, the maintenance of an internal state security network, and limiting certain political freedoms, most notably those associated with forming independent political parties and developing organs of mass communications outside of government supervision (Halperin 1981).

It quickly became apparent that the geo-political tensions between the United States and Cuba were and would remain an ever-present part of my fieldwork in Cuba. It also became apparent that these geo-political tensions were influencing my relationship with audiences in the United States. Whether it was a casual conversation with an informant in Cuba, or giving presentations to audiences in the United States, few exchanges associated with my Cuban research were untouched by a political discourse rooted in the conflict between socialism and capitalism, (re)constructed as a morality play featuring the United States and Cuba in the key roles. Even if I wanted to forget that my field work was conducted in a space between the hammer of U.S. anti-communism and the anvil of Cuban anti-imperialism, neither my interlocutors in Cuba nor my audiences in the United States would permit this bit of selective amnesia. The constant presence of U.S.-Cuban relations within the context of my fieldwork situation kept the political nature of my work, if not always directly in my line of sight, clearly within my peripheral vision.

In this context I became increasingly discomforted by the feeling that my ethnographic endeavors were being shaped less by *my* subject position than the rhetorical moves of my informants in Cuba and my professional colleagues at home. These discomforts—which I termed *disciplinary anxiety* and *discursive anxiety*—signaled that I was feeling less in control of my fieldwork experiences and my interpretations of those experiences than I had initially expected.

By the time I had begun working in the law collective I had developed some familiarity with the concepts of ethnographic reflexivity and subject positioning. Based on this, I was prepared to consider how my positioning as a white, male, Polish-Italian, leftist, 40-something ethnographer from a privileged core nation shaped my ethnographic vision. I also was ready to be sensitive to how my privileged position as an ethnographer gave me the ability to transform human subjects into the written-about characters of ethnographic storytelling. I was, however, much less prepared to consider two other things: how the agency of both informants and audiences would affect my experiences and interpretations of them, and how all of us, ethnographers, subjects, and audiences, are always imbedded in a larger geo-political theater. Unraveling these relationships and their emotional impact on my fieldwork experience required more reflexive work than I had initially planned.

REFLEXIVITY IN ETHNOGRAPHY

In recent decades ethnographic fieldwork has been the subject of considerable effort to theorize the relationship between the ethnographer and the ethnography. This effort has had four interrelated foci: (1) the subject position of the ethnographer, (2) the privilege of the ethnographer, (3) the subject positions and agency of informants, and (4) the location of ethnographic narrative within larger dominant discourses.[1]

The Ethnographer's Subject Position. In one of the earlier challenges to the detached (and therefore presumably authoritative) voice of classical ethnography, Scholte (1974:438) noted that "the ethnographic situation is defined not only by the native society in question, but also by the ethnological tradition 'in the head' of the ethnographer." Later writers would expand this concern beyond the academic "ethnological tradition" to include all of the ways in which the socially positioned experiences that ethnographers bring to the field shape the "knowledge" and "facts" they derive from it. In this vein, Rosaldo (1989:19) observes that

> the ethnographer, as a positioned subject, grasps certain human phenomena better than others. He or she occupies a structural position or structural location and observes with a particular angle of vision. . . . The notion of subject position also refers to how life experiences both enable and inhibit particular kinds of insight.

The various approaches to understanding the origins, impacts, and alternatives to the ethnographer's "particular angle of vision" were the foundation of a concern with developing reflexive approaches to ethnography. The meaning of reflexivity in field work, however, has come to be interpreted in a variety of ways, and there is presently considerable debate over just what reflexivity might mean and just how it might be practiced (Dubisch 1995).

In general we can say that reflexivity is "consciousness about being conscious; thinking about thinking" (Meyerhoff and Ruby 1982:1). More specifically, however, reflexivity in ethnography is rooted in the awareness, first of all, that the ethnographer, as a positioned subject, constructs interpretations of experiences rather than simply reporting on the "facts" discovered during fieldwork (Rabinow 1986). As Bruner (1986:5) notes, every ethnographic tale represents the "imposition of meaning on the flow of memory, in that we highlight some causes and discount others; that is, every telling is interpretive." Thus, from a reflexive standpoint the ethnographer ceases to become the absent cause of written pages, slides on screens, or words spoken in professional settings, but rather the active *agent* of those pages, slides, or spoken words. As Karp and Kendall (1982:250) observe,

> Field workers do not observe subjects behaving: they interpret human actions. To recognize that field work consists of inferring the meaning of human activity is to acknowledge the role that the observers play in their own analyses . . .

This awareness that all ethnographies are interpretations of experience from the subject position of the ethnographer directed reflexive ethnographers to monitor how their biographies intersected with their interpretation of field experiences. Reflexivity, in this sense, constituted a continuous internal dialogue about how biography, and particularly the deeply invested standpoints arising from it, influences the assignment of meaning to the words and actions of informants in the field (Wasserfall 1993). Two expressions of this concern with unraveling the impact of biography on ethnography were highly subjectivist accounts of fieldwork, and attempts to construct polyphonous texts that presumably fractured the monopoly of the ethnographer's voice. Marcus (1994:569) suggests that these forms of reflexivity tend to dead-end in the self of the ethnographer, except where they are linked to more overtly feminist approaches. Okely (1992:2), however, suggests a more general, productive use of autobiography by noting that

> the concern for an autobiographical element in anthropology is to work through the specificity of the anthropologist's self in order to contextualize and transcend it.

This latter approach to the impact of biography on ethnographic interpretation is most fruitful when it enables the ethnographer to experience and interpret the *interaction* between host and home cultures as these cultures are deployed in the person of the ethnographer and the informant.

Ethnographic Privilege. Self-critical forms of reflexivity generated not only a concern with the biography of the ethnographer, but also with how these biographies often privileged the ethnographer vis-à-vis informants in the field. Barthes (1972) notes that the ethnographer stands at the margins between two cultures, decoding the host culture and recoding it for the home culture. In doing so, the ethnographer enjoys greater power than the members of the culture being studied, because it is the ethnographer who does the decoding and recoding, ultimately turning the living subjects of the host culture into written-about objects to be consumed by the home culture (Nader 1972). This attention to the privileged positioning of ethnographers emerged, in part, in response to Post World War II decolonization, and as a reaction against earlier "colonial" anthropologies (Rabinow 1977; Clifford 1986). Decolonization focused attention on the privilege imbedded in the subject positions of anyone, ethnographers included, who went out from imperial, neo-colonial, or metropolitan nations to spend time among peripheral worlds (Asad 1983).

The concern with the power of unexamined, privileged biographies to inform ethnographic writing was further fueled by the emergence of what could be termed a "feminist ethnography." This approach framed reflexive recognition of a privileged biography as an initial step toward using that privilege to confront and reframe the power imbalances between ethnographers and informants (Abu-Lughod 1990; Bordo 1990; Mascia-Lees, Sharpe, and Cohen 1989; Harding 1987), and/or to serve the larger cause of empowering women (Reinharz 1979). Reinharz (1992:51) characterizes this latter form of "feminist ethnography" as having three goals:

> (1) to document the lives and activities of women, (2) to understand the experience of women from their own point of view, and (3) to conceptualize women's behavior as an expression of social contexts.

Thus, feminist ethnography reached beyond simple awareness of the ethnographer's privilege to strategies for transforming or fracturing that privilege in the context of fieldwork.[2] In doing so, feminist ethnography leveled the most direct challenge to the classical notion of the ethnographer as the detached observer of other cultures.

Informant Agency. Initially, the interpretive shifts in ethnography described above focused almost exclusively on the ethnographer's power to interpret and to write. Eventually, however, they also led to greater attention to informants as *active subjects* in the ethnographic process. Rosaldo (1989:19, 50) again:

> So-called natives are also positioned subjects who have a distinctive mix of insight and blindness. . . . They can be insightful, sociologically correct, axe-grinding, self-interested, or mistaken.

With or without deliberate awareness, informants engage in rhetorical moves designed to shape the ethnographer's interpretation of the "facts" of the culture under study. By the faces and postures that they show, the emotions they reveal, and the things they choose to talk about, informants engage in a subtle co-authoring of the eventual ethnography. As Wasserfall (1993:33-34) notes about her Moroccan Jewish informants,

> My informants were not naive and in truth they bargained with each other (as well as with me) for a better representation of their action in public as well as in the written text . . . (they) had amazing capabilities in reading power relations and presenting themselves in different lights when needed.

To the extent that informants are understood as enjoying a degree of agency in the field work setting, ethnographers must then extend their reflexive routines to encompass the *intersubjective* relationships they share with informants, and the role of informants in shaping that relationship.

Somewhat less attention has been given to the relationship between ethnographers and real or imagined *audiences*. Nevertheless, as Meyerhoff and Ruby (1982:26) observe, part of the task of doing ethnography is reporting one's field work to professional audiences in ways that are deemed consistent with professional rules of representation. The constraints exerted by these rules will shape the eventual representations of field work to those audiences. I would suggest that the relationships between ethnographers and audiences, no less than those between ethnographers and informants, exerts powerful shaping influences on the eventual interpretation and retelling of ethnographic tales and needs also to become a routine topic of ethnographic reflexivity.

Dominant Discourses. Crapanzano (1986) notes that ethnography is the product of the historical moment of the encounter between ethnographers and informants (and I would add, between ethnographers and audiences). Thus, the characteristics of a given historical moment will inevitably enter into the ethnography. While an ethnographer's informants and audiences will maneuver to achieve a preferred writing of the story, the nature of the preference will be shaped by salient macro-social characteristics of the historical moment in which the ethnographic encounter occurs or is re-told.

Bruner (1986) argues that each historical moment is characterized by a dominant discourse, and this dominant discourse constitutes a frame within which a narrative structure emerges. This narrative structure, in turn, guides ethnographic inquiry and interpretation. Brunner seems to offer a quasi-structuralist interpretation of ethnography by suggesting that the ethnographer "appears not as an individual creative scholar, a knowing subject who discovers, but more as a material body through whom a narrative structure unfolds" (Bruner 1986:150).

Bruner's view of discourse and narrative structure in ethnography is based on his analysis of a *temporal* change in the dominant discourse and the typical ethnographic narrative about American Indians. In this telling, the dominance of the dominant discourses is relatively unproblematic. At one historical moment the dominant discourse of assimilation led to typical narratives of disorganized or disappearing Indian cultures. At a later historical moment, a dominant discourse of decolonization generated typical narratives of Indian resistance. For many ethnographers, however, the comparison between different discourses and narrative structures is not temporal, it is cultural. That is, the ethnographer must negotiate his or her way through several discourses, each of which may be dominant in their own setting. At one level this would seem to be nothing more than the problem of interpreting other cultures. Adopting Bruner's use of the term "discourse," however, helps focus attention on the macro-social political forces that shape ethnographic narratives. As Lutz and Abu-Lughod (1990:9) note, the concept of discourse reconfigures the ideas of "culture" and "ideology" into a single construct that does the theoretical work of both. On the one hand, the concept of dominant discourses politicizes our understanding of "culture," and on the other, it normalizes the circulation of ideology as a routine, collective social act rather than manipulation by elites. Ethnographers construct narratives by negotiating between the dominant discourses of home and host societies. These discourses carry considerable political freight. Thus, reflexive considera-tion of how they are deployed in the ethnographer's narratives helps foreground the ways in which macro-social forces inscribe themselves on the micro-social relations between ethnographers and their informants and audiences.

Reflexivity and Ethnography in Cuba. Inserting the concept of discourse into ethnographic reflexivity provides a frame for understanding how macro-social political processes exert an influence over the biography of the ethnographer, over what informants may intend, and over the narratives that real or imagined professional audiences will be willing to accept. In the case of my research in a law collective in Havana, the geo-political conflict between the United States and Cuba meant that I was subject to multiple discourses, each dominant in its own context, and each (in Bruner's terms) competing for my body as the vehicle of its expression.

When in the United States I experienced two powerful discourses regarding Cuba. One constructed Cuba as an oppressive, human-rights insensitive, pawn of the Soviet Union. The other framed Cuba as the only Western hemispheric example of a Third World nation effectively protecting its citizens from the ravages of monopoly capital. Although the former might be considered domi-nant in terms of the space it enjoyed within mainstream vehicles of communi-cation in the United States, the latter discourse exerted its own form of domi-nance within the academic Left of which I was a part. In Cuba these discourses were cast somewhat differently. One emphasized the venality of Cuban leaders who used socialism as a means to their own economic and political advantage. The other emphasized the courage of the Cuban people, in the face of U.S. resistance, to struggle for a more humane alternative to the competition and inequalities of the capitalist world.

The more time I spent with Cubans, the more I came to realize that the tensions between our two nations were unavoidably inscribed on all our inter-actions through one or other of these discourses. The more aware I became of this, the more I wanted to understand how we—American and Cubans—were framing each other, and were ourselves being framed by larger geo-political forces. I entered into the particular reflexive process Meyerhoff and Ruby (1982:19) characterize as the ethnographer looking at the subject looking at the ethnographer (to which I later added the ethnographer looking at the audience looking at the ethnographer). These reflexive endeavors produced an anxiety-provoking plunge into an Alice in Wonderland world of shadowy meanings, sliding interpretations, and multiple self-images that began to erode my belief that I could construct *any* interpretations or representations of my field work that I could trust.

It was my perceived imbededness in a struggle over the preferred reading of Cuban justice that generated the disciplinary and discursive anxieties I intro-duced previously and want to explore below. In doing so I want to consider how the geo-political hostility between the U.S and Cuban governments shaped (1) my standpoint toward field work in Cuba, (2) the kinds of rhetorical maneuvers pursued by my informants, and (3) how my "tales of the field" were shaped, not only by these forces, but by imaginary readers to whom I would tell these "tales" (Van Maanen 1988).

In pursuing these lines of inquiry I am also concerned with Foucault's (1980:96) claim that "Where there is power, there is resistance." Thus, I want to consider not only the power embedded in or bearing on ethnography, but also resistances to that power. Consequently, I will consider (1) not only the power of the United States to construct an information embargo around Cuba, but the ways in which my resistance to the embargo influenced the meaning I would ascribe to my field work, (2) not only my power to write about my fieldwork subjects, but their strategies to resist that power, and (3) not only my power to frame my tales of the field for imaginary readers, but the power of these imaginary readers to discipline my tale telling.

DISCIPLINARY AND DISCURSIVE ANXIETIES

My attempts at a reflexive ethnography of Cuban justice always take place in the company of those two unwelcome companions—disciplinary anxiety and discursive anxiety. The initial point of departure for naming these anxieties comes from de Certeu's (1984) suggestion that the culture-based exercise of power takes two forms, and each form generates its own type of pleasures. Exercising the power to shape the behavior of others produces *disciplinary pleasure*. Experiencing power over words, that is, exercising the ability to make meaning and participate in the circulation of meaning, generates *discursive pleasure*.

My efforts at being "conscious of my consciousness" while doing field work in Cuba and reporting that work in the United States frequently revealed less the pleasures of being the subject of these powers than a sense of being their object. If exercising power over others, or over the making and circulation of meaning, is pleasurable, what then is the subjective condition of feeling that one's power to do these things is being diminished or shaped by others? I call these inverse experiences disciplinary anxiety and discursive anxiety.

Disciplinary anxiety is characterized by an uneasy or vague sense that my actual behaviors are being controlled or shaped by others. I experience this concern in the form of anxiety to the extent that the source and/or the effect of this power is unclear. This disciplinary anxiety takes two forms: *surveillance anxiety* and *control anxiety*. Surveillance anxiety is the suspicion that I am being watched, that my behavior is being scrutinized and evaluated by unidentifiable others for unknown purposes. Control anxiety is the suspicion that the experiences I am being allowed to have in the field are being consciously shaped by others to conform to some hidden actor's political goals.[3]

Discursive anxiety is the product of social interactions where it becomes difficult to trust one's interpretations of the motives underlying the meanings that are being produced and circulated by others, or by oneself. Like disciplinary anxiety, discursive anxiety takes two forms: *interpersonal anxiety* and *audience anxiety*. I experienced interpersonal anxiety in situations where I could not be certain whether or not my Cuban informants were specifically framing their presentations in order to emphasize or conceal certain aspects of the topic at hand precisely *because I am a U.S. citizen*. Audience anxiety, on the other hand, is the concern that I am shaping my ethnographic representations in particular ways because I imagine audiences ready to reconstruct the meaning of my accounts in accordance with meta-narratives vastly at odds with my own.

Disciplinary Anxiety

As Control. The United States government places a number of difficulties in the path of any U.S. citizen hoping to undertake fieldwork in Cuba. These range from cumbersome travel restrictions to prohibitions against the use of any U.S. government funding for research in Cuba. The knowledge that I, along with everyone else traveling to Cuba, am the object of policies designed to limit my contact with that country, forces me to reflect on the extent to which the conduct of my field work and my interpretations of it have been shaped by my awareness of these special barriers. There are, first of all, practical matters that make access to my field work setting difficult. How have the administrative hoops I must jump through, having to work through the only travel agency that had a dispensation from the U.S. Department of Treasury to make arrangements for U.S. citizens to travel to Cuba, and the continual worry that any trip might be the last for a long while should the U.S. chose to prohibit academic travel to Cuba (as President Clinton threatened to do in September 1994) shaped my standpoint regarding law and socialism in Cuba. If I do not interpret certain conditions—such as the difficulty some Cuban academics have experienced in trying to obtain authorization from the Cuban government to travel to the United States—as serious restraints on individual liberties, is it because, being able to circumvent what I feel to be analogous restrictions, I minimize the problem. Or if I interpret such problems as evidence of Cuba's insensitivity to human rights, is it because of the felt limits on my own freedom? I do not have definitive answers for such questions, but I offer them as examples of how the macro-social conflict between the United States and Cuba inserts itself into my own reflexive processes, generates uncertainty about my own reflexive efforts, and begins to alienate me from my own interpretations of my experiences in the field.

Then there is the matter of *resistance*. Insofar as the U.S. government has placed barriers in my path to field work in Cuba, to what extent is my standpoint toward that research shaped by a sense of participating in an act of resistance to those barriers, and more broadly to the policies that brought them into being? I do know that every time my flight landed at the Jose Marti Airport in Havana I experienced a sense of excitement and relief that formed itself in the thought: "Yes!! I've made it back—despite all their damn restrictions." How are my ethnographic interpretations affected by the (romantic?) sense that studying Cuba's justice system is an act of political resistance? Does this feeling influence my interpretations of what I observe and hear? Given my initial standpoint as a leftist, do these experiences increase the already existing potential danger of arriving at positive interpretations of things I would view negatively in other contexts? Does my sense of engaging in a (small) act of resistance create an affinity for those pro-socialist Cubans who see themselves as likewise engaged in a large act of resistance toward the U.S. government's avowed goal of eliminating socialism in Cuba? Conversely, in a reflexive doubling back on myself, do my fears that I might be overly sympathetic to Cuban socialism lead me to downplay or question my positive interpretations, and to be less reflexive about my negative ones?

In Cuba, there were also times when I wondered whether my behavior might be the object of control efforts. At times I wondered if my inquiry was being consciously facilitated in certain directions and away from others. I never experienced any obstacles to obtaining information regarding the day-to-day activities in the *bufete*. I sat in on attorney-client discussions, read case documents, enjoyed free run of the law collective's archives, followed attorneys to court and to consultations with other attorneys and with judges, and met with clients without their attorneys present. The attorneys with whom I worked, the administration of the law collective, the faculty at the Law School of the University of Havana, and officials of the Ministry of Justice were always exceedingly helpful and remarkably prompt in insuring that I obtained whatever access I asked for. On the other hand, my efforts to obtain quantitative data about rates of crime in Cuba were less successful. Although I obtained aggregate national crime statistics for the years 1986 to 1988, I was unable to obtain comparable data for more recent years. I had never been told that I could not obtain the data that I requested. Quite to the contrary, when I initially asked for crime data, the answer was the typical "*Si, como no?*" ("Sure, why not?"). When the data were not forthcoming and I persisted, I was told that there was no real problem obtaining the data, but it would be best if I submitted a formal request detailing what I needed. Contrary to the ease of access I enjoyed to the everyday life of the law collective, I ultimately failed to obtain the official crime data I sought.

Do my Cuban associates prefer that I write about attorneys and their clients primarily from first-hand experience in the law collective rather than attempting to situate their work in the context of the overall Cuban crime problem? Is someone (anyone?) consciously making decisions to limit my access to Cuban crime data? If this is the case, and if I persist in pursuing this information, will it compromise the open *entre* I have been given to other areas of Cuban legal life? The politically charged nature of the situation—including years of exposure to U.S. government claims about the tendencies of "communist" countries to control access to sensitive social data—tempts me to interpret my difficulty in obtaining detailed crime data as emanating from political sources. It is equally plausible that my lack of success in obtaining aggregate crime data resulted from little more than normal bureaucratic barriers to unplanned demands, or the relatively low priority given my requests by busy administrators. (To briefly preempt my later discussion regarding audience anxiety, I assumed that some who have read the previous passage will be inclined to agree I was unable to obtain detailed crime data for political reasons, while others will be more inclined to believe that it was apolitical bureaucratic forces that led to these difficulties.)

Whether or not my access to detailed crime data resulted from political or bureaucratic sources, my experience in the field was conditioned by the uneasy sense that political factors *might* be at work. This awareness, rooted in Cold War propaganda battles, becomes part of the reflexive baggage I carry around as I attempt to do and report field work in Cuba.

As Surveillance. Both when I am inside the United States and when I am in Cuba it is difficult not to wonder if I am the object of some official form of surveillance. There is ample evidence of the size and scope of the U.S. government's surveillance over its citizens and the existence of millions of government files detailing the political behavior of Americans (U.S. Congress 1976). The United States according to Agree (1976) kept, and may very well still keep, records of the passenger lists of all flights into Cuba that do not originate in the United States, with particular attention to identifying the U.S. citizens among the passengers.

For flights that originated in the United States this process was more direct than CIA scrutiny of passenger manifests. In 1977, President Carter liberalized U.S. travel* restrictions to Cuba. The Reagan administration, despite intensifying the Cold War with Cuba, did not fully reinstate the former travel ban. It did, however, limit the travel of U.S. residents to Cuba. Since the early years of the Reagan administration, until 1996, U.S. residents could travel to Cuba if they were: visiting immediate family, gathering news, conducting research that has some reasonable expectation of publication, or were hosted entirely at the expense of the Cuban government. Citizens who traveled to Cuba outside of these restrictions were subject to the aforementioned penalties for violating the Trading With the Enemy Act.

When I was conducting research in Cuba, charter flights between Miami and Havana operated regularly. Every passenger on these flights was required to complete a document specifying the purpose for travel and the amount of U.S. currency they were carrying. These forms were then collected by U.S. immigration upon departure. Whether or not these forms were actually put to any surveillance purpose, they gave a clear message that the U.S. government was monitoring who travels to Cuba more closely than to any other country.

In addition to the sense of being under surveillance at the moment of departure, it is also difficult for me to avoid wondering if I am under U.S.

---

*Since the early years of the Reagan administration until 1996, U.S. residents could travel to Cuba. Due to changes in travel policies, the information above is no longer current.

government surveillance while in Cuba. The U.S. Interests Section in Cuba, like any embassy, is fundamentally an information-gathering agency, that is, a nest of spies.[4] To what extent is it likely that someone in the U.S. Interests Section either directly or through Cuban "assets" keeps tabs on the activities of U.S. citizens in Cuba, particularly those such as myself who are frequent visitors and who stay for long periods of time? Given what I think I know about U.S. intelligence gathering, would I be naive to assume that my comings and goings in Cuba are not under surveillance by some component of the U.S. government? Or is it paranoid and/or pleasurable to assume that my activities are of any interest to the U.S. intelligence community?

If I accept that I am the target of U.S. government surveillance, does that belief affect the way I conduct my field work? Foucault (1979) has argued that the surveillance of behavior and the control of bodies are synchronic processes. If I believe I am under U.S. government surveillance do I become more inclined to accept Cuban claims regarding U.S. imperialism, and consequently more ready to accept arguments that limitations on certain political liberties in Cuba are a necessity of the struggle against U.S.-fostered counterrevolution? Or does it in some way subtly limit the range of the things I might do or the things I might say? Am I less publicly critical of U.S. policy toward Cuba when I am in Cuba, than when I am in the United States? Or do I see the imagined surveillance as an opportunity to further my resistance to U.S. policy? My inability to answer these questions in any definitive way can send me into dangerous reflexive spirals.

It is not only my own government that I wonder about. Several Cuban informants have told me that every work group in Cuba has at least one member who works for the state security system (*la seguridad*). One of the key tasks of these state security informants is supposedly to keep track of the activities of foreigners and the interactions between foreigners and Cubans. Cubans who are strong supporters of the revolution explain this surveillance of foreigners and their relationships with Cubans as a necessary evil in a country with a long and demonstrable history of CIA-inspired counterrevolutionary activity. Dissident Cubans, on the other hand, claim that the extensive state security system is just another manifestation of the government's mistrust of, and control over, its citizens.

As a consequence of my informants' claims, it is hard for me to escape the feeling that at least some of what I do in Cuba is scrutinized by agents of the state security system, and that some of the people I do it with are themselves the agents of this surveillance. How does this awareness influence my interactions with Cubans and my subsequent reflections on those interactions? When I first visited the *bufete,* for instance, the director arranged a meeting for me with several of the law collective's criminal law specialists because the initial focus of my project had been the role of attorneys in criminal law processes. One of these attorneys was more affable and open than the others. He offered particularly interesting insights on criminal processes, and seemed to have a particular interest in my project. Very quickly we established a close rapport. This attorney became one of my best informants, facilitating access to cases, clients, and trials, and devoting time to my questions whenever I had them. We also became friends sharing much about our lives, and our personal problems. After about three months, in a conversation with another attorney in the *bufete,* I learned that my friend was the head of the Communist Party nucleus in the *bufete.*[5]

Once I learned of his role in the Party leadership within the *bufete* I queried him at some length about the Party and its role in the *bufete,* to which he responded (appeared to respond?) quite candidly. I felt fortunate that one of my best informants was someone who could unravel the complexities of Party operations at the base level. Nevertheless, it became difficult not to wonder if our seemingly spontaneous early rapport and his willingness to devote time to my research was linked to his Party position in the *bufete.* Was he part of the surveillance network? In this case, my problem was rooted in the inherent ambiguity of friendship in the field. As Richardson (1975:521) says of friends in the field:

> The ethnographer must ask probing questions; he cannot, as one does with friends, accept the informant as the person he is, but the ethnographer must find out, he has to find out, why the informant believes what he does.

Yet I never asked the probing question that was on my mind once I learned my informant/friend was the head of the Party nucleus in the *bufete.* This unasked question was: "Was I right in thinking we were naturally *simpatico,* or were you directed to become my friend in order to keep tabs on me and/or to insure I got the *right* impression about the law collective." I recognized that if my suspicions were wrong, this question would be hurtful, and if they were correct I would have to accept that a friendship that I wanted to believe was somehow "real," would now seem like a choreographed *pas de deux* in a ballet of surveillance—this, even though my own relationship with him had the instrumental motivation of wanting "data." I subsequently found myself weighing and measuring his responses to my questions in new ways, shaped by the uncertainty of whether or not this particularly "good" informant was acting exclusively on his own motivations, or as part of some larger plan to discipline my research.

Discursive Anxiety

Discursive anxiety concerns relationships with informants and with audiences. It arises when something in the relationship leads one to be uncertain of the motives that animate the meanings being produced and circulated by others, *or by oneself.*

Informant Anxiety. The presence of a U.S. citizen changes the nature of almost any conversation in Cuba. For the vast majority of adult Cubans, both the political and personal understandings that they will articulate to a North American researcher about living in revolutionary Cuba are inevitably imbedded in a discourse, however subtly, about the relative merits or demerits of Cuban socialism as compared to U.S. capitalism. For many of the Cubans I talked with at length, the discursive point of departure is usually some comparison between social equality in Cuba and social inequality in the United States.[6] They counterposed the universal access of Cubans to health care with the injustices and lack of access to health care that resulted from a health care market in the United States. Or Cuba's commitment to racial equality was contrasted to U.S. racism. Or the relative safety of Cuban cities was compared to the problems of drug gangs, violent crime, rape, homelessness, and public poverty in major urban centers in the United States.[7]

These same sets of facts could receive quite another interpretation if my informant was disaffected with the Cuban revolution. For these latter Cubans, the United States was not the land of social problems, but the land of individual freedoms and consumer possibilities, while Cuba was a place where the conditions of material existence and material culture were dictated by the government. "The stores here are empty," or "There is nothing to eat in this country" were common complaints of those striking an anti-government, and sometimes, although not always, an anti-socialist posture.

These tales of Cuba's accomplishments or its failures under socialism were not reserved for specific political discussions. They inserted themselves into even the most apolitical moments. In one instance I was in a bar drinking beer with a friend. We discussed the merits of several Cuban beers, and we shared embellished stories of youthful days as beer-swilling carpenters. At one point he asked how much it would cost to buy a comparable beer in an American bar. When I told him about two dollars—double the price of the Cuban beer we were drinking—he observed that workers fared twice as well under Cuban socialism than under U.S. capitalism because Cuban workers could buy beer for half the price.

Every Cuban has a story to tell the *norteamericano*. Repeatedly, between 1985 and 1991, I had Cubans tell me that "Here everyone gets enough to eat. There is no hunger in Cuba."[8] Or conversely, "Here there is nothing to eat. The government sends all the food abroad so you wait in long lines and when you get in the store there is nothing to buy." In a politically charged situation such as that between Cuba and the United States, the U.S. visitor is never approached as a neutral listener. Rather, the *norteamericano* must be convinced either of the wrongheadedness of U.S. policy, or of the failings of Cuban socialism. For the ethnographer this means that the ideological contest between socialism and capitalism inscribes itself on nearly every conversation as informants negotiate to ensure a particular, eventual *writing* of the Cuban story.

When informants are university educated professionals such as lawyers, their sensitivity to shaping the tale that will be told is even greater. As products of the world of books and writing, the attorneys with whom I worked were well aware that they were in the process of becoming the written-about. Indeed, they often asked me "Will you write about me in your book?" or "Do you think this will be important for your book" Unlike Ellis' (1994) informants who learned to be guarded only after they read her ethnographic portrayal of them, the Cuban attorneys and other officials with whom I worked closely, were aware at the outset that I had the power to write about them, and to do so for audiences in an enemy nation. Consequently, they sought to shape our discussions in ways that would promote their being written about according to their particular standpoint regarding the geo-politics of U.S.-Cuban relations, standpoints which are themselves products of larger discourses about socialism and capitalism.

Most (although not all) of the Cuban attorneys I know lived lives that were invested in socialism and socialist forms of organization. The majority were in their early forties or younger, educated mostly after the revolution, and imbued with the ideology, and often the ethic, of Cuban socialism. At a more pragmatic level, they owed their relatively prestigious occupational positions to a socialist system of occupational selection and career development.

Those in more advanced positions of authority were more typically in their fifties and sixties. These people, for the most part, had histories of close involvement with, and intense commitment to, the revolutionary process. Many had been active participants in the early stages of Cuba's revolutionary transformation, and had risen to their current positions, in part, because of their demonstrated commitment to the development of socialism in Cuba. This investment in, and commitment to, a socialist order on the part of both the young beneficiaries of socialism and older revolutionaries provided added motivation for them to consider carefully how and what they communicated to me as a potential (re)teller of their tales.

I am not talking about misrepresentation or falsification by these attorneys and government officials. To the contrary, most of the attorneys and government officials with whom I worked were insistent that I understand the problems and failures, as well as the accomplishments and successes, of both the Cuban revolution in general and Cuba's socialist legal system in particular. Several officials with whom I spent considerable time emphasized that past writings about Cuba by sympathetic U.S. observers who overplayed the successes and overlooked the problems of the Revolution did more political harm than good by presenting an easily-discredited picture of Cuba. I was often told by my interlocutors that they hoped that what I would write about Cuba and its legal system would be objective (*objetivo*). From their point of view this meant writing about them from neither an anti-socialist bias nor from a perspective shaped by overenergetic solidarity politics, but rather one that balanced successes and failures in some mix that reflected what *they* understood as the actual experience of Cuba under socialism. It was clear, however, that they understood that my project also had potentially positive or negative ramifications for the academic discourse about Cuba in the United States. In addition, because their understanding of the relationship between scholarship and political processes was shaped by the close linkages between the universities and the government in Cuba, I suspect they tended to overestimate the possible political impacts that my work might have in the United States. These perceptions made them understandably interested in shaping my eventual writings in accordance with their understanding of the truth. The very fact that they could articulate their desires for an objective ethnography indicates they were quite aware that our relationship included negotiating what would constitute the preferred form of an "objective" report on socialist legal practices. They consciously recognized my power to write and consciously exercised their powers to shape the nature of our discourse and ultimately what I would write.

When even the most casual discussion is laden with contentious political implications, it becomes difficult to discern the motives underlying what is being said. Do people actually believe things are as good (or as bad) as they claim? How would the tale they tell differ if it was being told to another Cuban? Or perhaps to a Brazilian? Or even a Canadian? And if each of these tales would be different, how do I interpret and incorporate the tales I've been told into my writing? From what standpoint?

Audience Anxiety. Audiences play an important role in shaping the process of ethnographic interpretation and writing. The ethnographer must not only engage in field work, but must also report that fieldwork in some acceptable form to disciplinary colleagues at home. The power of disciplinary (in both senses of the word) audiences resides in their impact on the imagination of the ethnographic writer. White (1984) says that every writer imagines an "ideal reader," the one who will decode meaning exactly as the writer imagines having encoded it, and for whom one writes. Although I can imagine those who might fit White's notion of the "ideal reader" I also imagine others who will be less-than-ideal readers.

Audience anxiety grows out of reflexivity regarding how presentation of my Cuban research to academic audiences in the United States is shaped by my knowledge of the politically charged nature of the dominant discourses on Cuba. Among Cuban specialists in the United States there is a tendency to identify researchers as either "for" or "against" socialism in Cuba, and as either "for" or "against" the government of Fidel Castro. This is evidenced, among other things, by the constant attention to the question of whether or not Cuban socialism "works" (Zimbalist 1990). Classical ethnographers of the past were not expected to tell us whether or not the social systems of Trobriand islanders or African pastoralists "worked" in some judgmental sense of the word. More contemporarily we do not expect those who study India, or Japan, or Greece to tell us whether these social systems "work" in the same way those who focus on Cuba are expected to make pronouncements about the success or failure of Cuban socialism. But Cuba is different. It is not India, or Japan, or Greece, or some far removed tribal society. The Cuban revolution has lodged itself firmly as a bone in the throat of U.S. political discourse, and research on Cuba always finds itself imbedded in political conflict within the United States.[9]

Given these factors, I can readily imagine one group of less-than-ideal readers who will view my work on Cuban legality through a lens of suspicions regarding Marxist-Leninist societies, particularly given their now-demonstrated lack of staying power. Some will suspect that the Cuban government would never really allow a foreign observer such as myself to witness the real truth about Cuba's legal system. For these readers my work will lack sufficient attention to inadequacies, inefficiencies, and brutalities of socialism and socialist legal systems. One actual (rather an imagined) part of this audience, a U.S. sociologist, suggested to me that the entire *bufete* where I was a participant observer was little more than a Potemkin village created specifically to mislead people like me.

In contrast to the suspicious, anti-socialist audience, I also imagined another group of "readers" who would interpret my work through a lens of solidarity with the Cuban revolution.[10] For these less-than-ideal readers my work would either lack sufficient praise for socialism, or would inappropriately touch upon topics that could be considered unsympathetic to the revolution. This audience consists characteristically of those, like myself, whose political consciousness was born in the social movements of the 1960s, and for whom Fidel Castro and the Cuban revolution stood as a symbol of hope for a new world. Many of these progressives hoped to find evidence for the viability of a Western-hemispheric socialism in the Cuban revolution. Among academics who shared this New Left vision of Cuba, there were often tensions between the ideals of research and those of solidarity with "the Revolution." My first field work endeavor in Cuba, for instance, was an exploration of Cuba's currency black market that involved interviewing young men who exchanged Cuban *pesos* for U.S. dollars with tourists. Several colleagues suggested that while research on the currency black market might be interesting, there were more important *positive* aspects of the revolution that could (and should) be studied. As one said: "There are many good things about Cuba. You don't have to write about money changing." Several other accomplished researchers reacted with shock to the idea that my colleague and I planned to present this research at a social science conference in Havana. They suggested that, not only was this contrary to solidarity with Cuba's struggle against the United States, but doing so would brand me an ideological opponent of the Revolution in both Cuba and the United States, and would probably result in a curtailing of research access in Cuba.[11] While I continued with my inquiry into the illegal currency market, it was hard to ignore the criticisms from valued colleagues that I lacked "sensitivity" to political realities, and it is even harder to know how these criticisms affected my eventual interpretations of what I observed in the currency black market.

Concrete experiences of criticism give substance to imagined readers. For one imagined audience I am a dupe of Communist lies. For another I am either an academic mystified by the hegemonic discourse, or a careerist who puts professional goals ahead of solidarity with a people's revolution. My awareness of these less-than-ideal readers raises bothersome questions. Do I re/interpret my experience or re/write my tales of Cuba with greater criticism or greater defense of the Cuban legal system and Cuban society in order to answer imagined critics to the Right or the Left? How would I tell these tales if they did not feel the need to engage politicized criticism? While imagined audiences are not actual audiences, we begin with imagined audiences when we write. How do I come to some peace with my own "writing" when attempts to be reflexive about that writing continually raise unanswered questions about the degree to which imagined political criticisms are the muse at my shoulder?

CONCLUSION

By now it should be clear that my reflexive efforts to understand the impact of geo-political forces on my Cuban research has produced a "messy text" (Marcus 1994:567). There are far more questions here than answers. While I can describe the disciplinary and discursive anxieties associated with conducting fieldwork in Cuba and reporting that work to audiences in the United States, I cannot account with certainty for their impact.

Reflexivity has led me to question the motives of my interlocutors, the impact of my audiences, and ultimately the validity of my interpretations of Cuban justice. While an essential component of self-aware ethnographic writing, reflexivity is not an automatic formula for greater clarity. On the other hand, the messiness of my text and the provisionality of my analysis has, I hope, a certain utility. Specifically, it provides an example of how ethnographic research can become a conversation between conflicting political discourses, and how anxieties about the impact of those discourses on the research process can provide a frame for analyzing them.

My focus here has been on how geo-political conflict inscribed itself on the micro-social process of relating to informants in Cuba and audiences at home. I suggest, however, that similar dynamics affect most, if not all, field work endeavors. Politics is not limited to geo-politics. Geo-politics are only more public, and their impacts perhaps more readily observable. The development of interpretive ethnographies of all types, however, may benefit from increased attention to the ways in which informants and audiences, no less than the ethnographer, are bearers of political discourses and make rhetorical moves that reflect those discourses and are designed to influence the ethnographer's interpretation of ethnographic experience. In sum, I suggest that greater attention to how macro-social forces bear on ethnography through the actions of informants and audiences, as well as through the biography of the ethnographer, will provide added richness to our ethnographic interpretations.

ACKNOWLEDGMENTS

I would like to thank Jill Dubisch, Joseph Schneider, and Neil Websdale for helpful comments on earlier drafts of this chapter.

NOTES

1. In contrast to these foci for reflexivity Marcus (1994) identifies four "styles of reflexivity": (1) self-critique and personal quest, (2) "objective" reflexivity—*a la* Bourdieu—designed to preserve and perhaps improve the empirical quality of analysis, (3) reflexivity as a "politics of location," and (4) feminist reflexivity as the analysis of "standpoint epistemologies" and the acceptance of the provisionality of all texts. This taxonomy of reflexive styles is useful for understanding different *forms* of reflexivity. While it parallels somewhat my concern with ethnographers, informants, and audiences, I am more interested here with how each of these can become the objects of the ethnographer's reflexivity more than the style of reflexivity that is brought to bear on them. If I were to identify my own style of reflexivity, in Marcus' terms, I would characterize it as some hybrid of a "politics of location" combined with Haraway's (1989:579) vision of a feminist reflexivity simultaneously concerned with standpoint epistemologies and a kind of small-"t" truth that makes possible "a no-nonsense commitment to faithful accounts of a 'real' world."

2. I want to make it clear that I am making a distinction here between feminist *ethnography,* as characterized by Reinharz and feminist *anthropology.* The former is consciously animated by a commitment to using ethnography to tell women's stories and to empower women. The latter is more concerned, as Okely (1992) notes, with using a reflexive analysis of one's gendered position as an analytical strategy to transcend one's own gendered position in order to understand another culture and establish fruitful relationships with representatives of that culture. For a more detailed discussion on the distinction between feminist ethnography and feminist anthropology see Abu-Lughod (1990) "Can there be a feminist ethnography," and Dubisch (1991) "Gender, Kinship, and Religion: Reconstructing the Anthropology of Greece."

3. While it can be argued as has Foucault (1979) that surveillance *is* control, I separate them here for the heuristic benefit of being able to examine several different ways in which I suspect my behavior might have been shaped.

4. The United States government broke diplomatic relations with Cuba in January of 1961. In 1977, as part of the Carter opening toward Cuba, the United States and Cuba established "interests sections" in each others countries. Interests sections lack an ambassador, and thus maintain the formal status that Cuba and United States do not have diplomatic relations. They, however, perform most of the functions of an embassy including the exchange of information between governments, consular functions, and spying.

5. Every workplace in Cuba has a Communist Party nucleus consisting of those workers who are members of the Party. The nucleus is responsible for maintaining Party discipline in the workplace, disciplining Party members who fail to fulfill their responsibilities as workers and exemplars of Communist virtue, and organizing the recruitment and evaluation of potential Party members.

6. These conversations took place before the deep economic crisis that began in Cuba in 1992. Prior to this time, while few Cubans were able to acquire many hard consumer commodities,

nearly all had access to basic food, housing, health care, education, and recreation through various state subsidy programs.

7. By 1992 the social peace that I had come to take for granted in Havana and elsewhere during my work there between 1985 and 1990 was increasingly threatened by rising crime in response to the deteriorating economic conditions brought about by Cuba's loss of its socialist trading partners.

8. When I returned to Cuba in 1991 the effects on the Cuban economy of the collapse of the socialist trading block were noticeable. The claims that "here we have enough" had been silenced by decreasing availability of many basic commodities. Additionally, the informal economy had become extensively "dollarized" which meant that while those with access to U.S. dollar could obtain almost anything they wanted, those limited to Cuban *pesos* were finding it increasingly difficult to maintain the consumption patterns they had become used to.

9. This situation is further intensified by the fact that many of the leading Cubanologists in the United States are themselves first or second-generation Cuban-Americans.

10. I say "until recently" because with the collapse of Soviet and Eastern European socialism the number of progressives who claim solidarity with socialist Cuba, or who are willing to admit they once acted in solidarity with Cuba, has declined substantially.

11. As far as I know, my research access did not suffer the predicted limitations. It was after the work on the currency black market was presented that I obtained the authorization from Cuban authorities to begin my fieldwork in the law collective.

REFERENCES

Abu-Lughod, L. 1990. "Can there be a feminist ethnography?" *Women and Performance* 5(1):7-27.

Agee, P. 1976. *Inside the Company: CIA Diary*. New York: Bantam Books.

Alarcon, R. 1991. Speech before the United Nations General Assembly. November 13.

Asad, T. (ed.). 1973. *Anthropology and the Colonial Encounter*. London: Ootheca Press.

Bordo, S. 1990. "Feminism, Postmodernism, and gender skepticism," in *Feminism/Postmodernism,* Nicholson, L. (ed.) New York: Routledge, pp. 133-156.

Bruner, E. M. 1986. "Ethnography as narrative," in V. Turner and E. Bruner (eds.), *The Anthropology of Experience*. Chicago: University of Illinois Press, pp. 139-148.

Burawoy, M. et al. 1991. *Ethnography Unbound: Power and Resistance in the Modern Metropolis*. Berkeley: University of California Press.

Clifford, J. and Marcus, G. (eds.) 1986. *Writing Culture: The Poetics and Politics of Ethnography*. Berkeley: University of California Press.

Clifford, J. 1988. *The Predicament of Culture*. Boston: Harvard University Press.

Crapanzano, V. 1986. "Hermes dilemma: The masking of subversion in ethnographic description," in Clifford, J. and Marcus, G. (eds.), *Writing Culture*. Berkeley: University of California Press, pp. 51-76.

de Certeu, M. 1984. (Rendell, S., trans.) *The Practice of Everyday Life*. Berkeley: University of California Press.

D'Estefano M. (ed.) 1985. *Agresiónes de Estados Unidos a Cuba Revolucionaria*. Habana: Editorial de Ciencias Sociales.

Dubisch, J. 1995. *In a Different Place*. Princeton, NJ: Princeton University Press.

Ellis, C. 1994. "Emotional and ethical quagmires in returning to the field." Paper presented at the American Sociological Association.

Foucault, M. 1979. *Discipline and Punish*. New York: Pantheon Books.

Foucault, M. 1980. *The History of Sexuality, Vol. 1.* New York: Vintage.

Halperin, M. 1981. *The Taming of Fidel Castro.* Berkeley: University of California Press.

Harding, S. (ed.). 1987. *Feminism and Methodology.* Bloomington: Indiana University Press.

Karp, I. and Kendall, M. 1982. "Reflexivity in field work," in P. Secord (ed.), *Explaining Human Behavior: Consciousness, Human Action, and Social Structure,* Secord, P. (ed.). Beverly Hills, CA: Sage, pp. 249-273.

Lutz, C. A. and Abu-Lughod, L. 1990. *Language and the Politics of Emotion.* New York: Cambridge University Press.

Mascia-Lees, F., Sharpe, P., and Cohen, C. B. 1989. "The postmodernist turn in Anthropology: Cautions from a feminist perspective." *Signs,* Vol. 15, No. 1:7-33.

Marcus, G. E. 1994. "What Comes (Just) After 'post'? The case of ethnography," in N. Denzin and Y. S. Lincoln (eds.), *Handbook of Qualitative Research.* Thousand Oaks, CA: Sage, pp. 563-574.

Meyerhoff, B. and Ruby, J. 1982. "Introduction," in J. Ruby (ed.), *A Crack in the Mirror.* Philadelphia University Press, pp. 1-35.

Michalowski, R. 1985. *Order, Law, and Crime.* New York: Random House.

Michalowski, R. and Zatz, M. 1990. "The Cuban second economy in perspective," in (Los, ed.) *The Second Economy in Marxist States.* New York: MacMillan, pp. 141-156.

Okely, J. 1992. "Anthropology and autobiography: Participatory experience and embodied knowledge," in J. Okely and H. Callaway (eds.) *Anthropology and Autobiography.* New York: Routledge, pp. 1-28.

Rabinow, P. 1977. *Reflections of Fieldwork in Morocco.* Berkeley: University of California Press.

Rabinow, P. 1986. "Representations are social facts: Modernity and post-modernity in ethnography," in J. Clifford and G. Marcus (eds.), *Writing Culture: The Poetics and Politics of Ethnography.* Berkeley: University of California Press, pp. 234-261.

Reinharz, Shulamit. 1979. *On Becoming a Social Scientist.* San Francisco: Jossey-Bass.

Reinharz, Shulamit. 1992. *Feminist Methods in Social Research.* New York: Oxford University Press.

Richardson, 1975. Quoted in Karp, I. and Kendall, M. 1982. "Reflexivity in field work." in *Explaining Human Behavior: Consciousness, Human Action, and Social Structure,* Second, P. (ed.). Beverly Hills, CA: Sage, p. 258.

Rosaldo, R. 1989. *Culture and Truth: The Remaking of Social Analysis.* Boston: Beacon Press.

Turner, V. and Edward M. Bruner (eds.). 1986. *The Anthropology of Experience.* Urbana: University of Illinois Press.

U.S. Congress. 1976. *Senate Select Committee to Study Governmental Operations with Respect to Intelligence Activities,* Washington, D.C.: U.S. Government Printing Office.

Van Maanen, John, 1988. *Tales of the Field.* Chicago: University of Chicago Press.

Wasserfall, R. 1993. "Reflexivity, Feminism and Difference." *Qualitative Sociology,* Vol. 16, No. 1:23-40.

White, James B. 1984. *When Words Lose Their Meaning: Constitutions and Reconstitution of Language, Character, and Community.* Chicago: University of Chicago Press.

Zimbalist, A. 1990. "Does the Economy Work?" *NACLA: Report on the Americas,* Vol. 24, No. 2:16-19.

4 | A Feminist Revisiting of the Insider/Outsider Debate

The "Outsider Phenomenon" in Rural Iowa

Nancy A. Naples

A feminist perspective on community studies offers a critically valuable lens through which to view the debate contrasting insider and outsider ethnographic research. The "insider" versus "outsider" debate, i.e., whether it is more effective to conduct fieldwork as an insider or an outsider to the communities you study (see Aguilar 1981; Messerschmidt 1981; Pollner and Emerson 1983), challenges those of us who use ethnographic methods in our research in our "home" country to reexamine our taken-for-granted assumptions about what constitutes "indigenous" knowledge and how we use both our commonalities and differences to heighten sensitivity to others' complex and shifting world views. In this feminist revisiting of the insider/outsider debate, I argue that the insider/outsider distinc-

EDITOR'S NOTE: This chapter originally appeared as an article in *Qualitative Sociology,* Vol. 19, No. 1, 1996. Reprinted by permission of Human Sciences Press, Inc.

tion masks the power differentials and experiential differences between the researcher and the researched. The bipolar construction of insider/outsider also sets up a false separation that neglects the interactive processes through which "insiderness" and "outsiderness" are constructed. "Outsiderness" and "insiderness" are not fixed or static positions, rather they are ever-shifting and permeable social locations that are differentially experienced and expressed by community members. By recognizing the fluidity of "outsiderness"/"insiderness," we also acknowledge three key methodological points: as ethnographers we are never fully outside or inside the "community"; our relationship to the community is never expressed in general terms but is constantly being negotiated and renegotiated in particular, everyday interactions; and these interactions are themselves located in shifting relationships among community residents. These negotiations simultaneously are embedded in local processes that reposition gender, class, and racial-ethnic relations among other socially constructed distinctions.

In this chapter, I explore the relevance of findings from an ethnographic study of two rural Iowa towns for the insider/outsider debate. The study was designed to examine how economic and social restructuring is reshaping the lives of rural residents in the midwest (see Naples 1994b). One theme pervading the data gathered in the field is the extent to which residents with a diversity of social, economic, and demographic characteristics experienced feelings of alienation from the perceived community at large. In fact, most people interviewed in-depth said they were "outsiders" to the community for a variety of differing reasons. My own "outsiderness" became a resource through which I was able to acquire an "insider" perspective on many residents' perception of alienation from others in their community. This finding appears to support Georg Simmel's (1921) contention that people will share confidences with a "stranger" that they may not share with friends and acquaintances. Yet the parallel findings that many residents also felt themselves outside the community led me to reexamine the insider/outsider debate and to identify what I have come to call the "outsider phenomenon." Simmel's analysis was based upon a rigid conception of social life which assumed an unchanging distinction between the "stranger" and the "insider"; an inattention to power in encounters between the "stranger" and "insiders"; and a belief in the stranger's greater "objectivity." In this feminist revisiting, I highlight the fluidity of "outsiderness" and "insiderness"; center attention on power in ethnographic encounters; and challenge reductive and essentialist notions of "standpoint." Rather than view insiderness/outsiderness as identifiable and relatively fixed social locations, the concept of "outsider phenomenon" highlights the processes through which different community members are created as "others"—a process in which all members participate to varying degrees—and by which feelings of "otherness" are incorporated into self perceptions and social interactions. The identification of the "outsider phenomenon" is especially noteworthy given the continued salience of *gemein-schaft* found in accounts of rural small town life offered by residents and nonresidents alike (see Naples 1994b).

The "outsider phenomenon" does not describe a specific social identity as in Simmel's construct or set of statuses as in Robert Merton's (1972) formulation; rather it refers to the interaction between shifting power relations in this rural context and the personal and interpersonal negotiations adopted by residents to resist further differentiation from the perceived community. As another "new-comer" to these towns, I am drawn into these processes and inevitably become a party to the renegotiations as I and my research assistants interact with different residents over time. A feminist approach to fieldwork includes a sensitivity to issues of power and control in the research process and argues for a self reflexive practice (see Reinharz 1992). Furthermore, the materialist feminist approach utilized in this analysis draws upon "postmodern notions of the subject in conjunction with a theory of the social which is congruent with feminism's political goals" (Hennessy 1993:3-4). This approach challenges the perspectives derived from attempts to identify outsiders and insiders with reference to historically ascribed or achieved social identities as in Becker's (1963) or Simmel's (1921) conceptualizations or to externally identifiable statuses as in Merton's (1972) classic argument.

REVISITING A CHAPTER IN
THE SOCIOLOGY OF KNOWLEDGE

The insider/outsider debate is simultaneously a contestation over divergent epistemological assumptions, methodological strategies, and political claims making. Merton's analysis of this debate appeared in 1972 and addressed issues raised by Black scholars who were challenging the dominance of white intellectuals in academic institutions and disciplinary knowledge production by claiming epistemic privilege for Black intellectuals. Merton believed that when Black scholars posited such privilege, this "Insider doctrine" would lead to a polarization of claims and a more entrenched ethnocentrism in intellectual activity. He also feared that by ". . . affirming the universal saliency of race and by redefining race as an abiding source of pride rather than stigma, the Insider doctrine in effect models itself after the doctrine long maintained by white racists" that judged a person's value on the basis of his or her "racial pedigree" (p. 20).[1] The more effective intellectual position to strive for, he argued, is one that allows for assessment of the "distinctive contributions . . . to social knowledge" offered "in our roles as Insiders or Outsiders" (p. 41).[2]

Merton (1972:11) characterized the insider/outsider debate as "the problem of patterned differentials among social groups and strata in access to certain types of knowledge." Drawing upon his role theoretical framework, Merton argued that since we each hold multiple statuses, ". . . we are all, of course, both Insiders and Outsiders, members of some groups and, sometimes derivatively, not of others" (p. 22). While recognizing the multiplicity of statuses upon which people could feel part of one group or another and, when a part of a particular group, further differentiate from one another on the basis of these contrasting status sets, Merton does not provide the framework through which to analyze how statuses become differentially valued, how power differentials influence conflicts among members who share a particular status, and how statuses could be revalued or reassigned. More importantly for the purposes of this analysis, his approach does not offer a methodological strategy through which to explore how these processes are embedded in community contexts and how individual members actively participate in their construction.

Since Merton firmly believed that "criteria of craftsmanship and integrity in science and learning cuts across differences in the social affiliations and loyalties of scientists and scholars," (p. 42) he did not deal with the fundamental challenge brought by Black intellectuals of the early 1970s. Black scholars who argued for the epistemic privileging of Black intellectual perspectives accurately pointed out how white privilege and racist practices infused the academic enterprise. Merton never directly responded to their claim. He did recognize that the structure of racial inequality which segregated whites and Blacks generated more systematic opportunities for Blacks to observe whites while "the highly visible whites characteristically did not want to find out about life in the black community and could not, even in those rare cases where they would" (p. 30). He also agreed with Kenneth Clark's (1965) powerful point that "privileged individuals" will "shield themselves from the inevitable conflict and pain which would result from acceptance of the fact that they are accessories to profound injustice" (quoted in Merton 1972:39). Despite his recognition that racial inequality placed Blacks and whites in different social locations to generate different knowledges in their everyday lives and that whites may not want to address structures and processes of inequality, Merton failed to apply this analysis to the structure of academic institutions and disciplinary knowledges. He assumed the value neutrality of intellectual activity and believed that "[c]ommitment to the intellectual values dampens group-induced pressures to advance the interests of groups at the expense of these values and of the intellectual product" (p. 42).

In contrast, feminist scholarship has been particularly effective in identifying the processes by which power and "relations of ruling" are embedded in disciplinary practices (see especially Smith 1987; 1990). Smith (1987: 2) defines the "relations of ruling" as a term "that brings into view the intersection of the institutions organizing and regulating society with their gender subtext and their basis in a gender division of labor." The term "ruling" is used to identify "a complex of organized practices, including government, law, business and financial management, professional organization, and educational institutions as well as the discourse in texts that interpenetrate the multiple sites of power." For Smith, power is woven in and through the institutions that contour women's daily activities as well as in the academic disciplines that shape official knowledge about them. Women and others who are not typically found in positions of power within educational institutions are objectified in academic practices and constructed in ways that distort or render invisible the organization of their everyday activities (also see Collins 1991; Harding 1991).

Feminist analysts further contest the firm belief expressed by Merton (1972:42) that adherence to "intellectual values" inevitably lead to a more objective, value neutral "intellectual product" (see Acker, Barry and Esseveld 1991; Collins 1990; Harding 1991). Of course, this issue is not a uniquely feminist one. For example, Gary Fine (1993:286) writes: "Objectivity is an illusion—an illusion snuggled in the comforting blanket of positivism—that the world is ultimately knowable and secure." Feminists take this critique further when they argue that a belief in the value neutrality of social scientific and other intellectual practices, in fact, serves to mask the relations of ruling embedded in the production of knowledge in the academy.

Situating Knowledges and Modes of Inquiry

The feminist theoretical commitment to explicate the intersections of gender, race-ethnicity, class, and other social structural aspects of social life without privileging one dimension or adopting an additive formulation (see Lorber 1994; Naples 1992) has influenced the development of diverse feminist standpoint theories which are exemplified by the different approaches of Patricia Hill Collins (1990, 1991) and Dorothy Smith (1987; 1990). Collins (1991) offers a contemporary analysis of the value of "outsider within" theorizing that mirrors the claims of Black scholars contested by Merton. Drawing upon Simmel's assertion that strangers "see patterns that may be more difficult than those immersed in the situation to see" (Collins 1991:36), Collins argues that "personal and cultural biographies [are] significant sources of knowledge" for "outsiders within" the academy (p. 53). She explains that since working class Black women are "much more inclined to be struck by the mismatch of [their] own experiences and the paradigms of sociology itself" (p. 50), they are more likely to identify "anomalies" between their experiences and those represented by normalized, yet distorted, sociological accounts (p. 51; also see Haraway 1988; Sandoval 1991). Collins' argument parallels, to a certain extent, Smith's (1987) analysis of women's "bifurcated consciousness." Yet there are significant differences between Collins' and Smith's standpoint theoretical perspectives.

Dorothy Smith, who differentiates her theoretical framework from Collins' as well as Sandra Harding's (1986) with whom she is often linked, argues that her approach "does not privilege a knower" (or subject of research) whose expressions are disconnected from her daily activities and social relations (Smith 1992:91). Rather, Smith starts inquiry "with the knower who is actually located: she is active; she is at work; she is connected with particular other people in various ways. . . . Activities, feelings, experiences, hook her into extended social relations linking her activities to those of other people and in ways beyond her knowing" (p. 91). This mode of inquiry calls for explicit attention to the social relations embedded in women's everyday activities as well as the deeply felt expressions of "outsiderness." However, it does not end at the level of individual women as "knowers" but is "directed towards exploring and explicating what [they do] not know—the social relations and organization pervading [their] world but invisible in it" (p. 91). Yet such an inquiry also involves the researcher's engagement with individual knowers who are shaping and reshaping the researcher's own understanding. As Smith (1992:94) asserts: "The project of inquiry from the standpoint of women is always reflexive. Also, it is always about ourselves as inquirers—not just our personal selves, but our selves as participants."

Neither Smith nor Collins offers guidance on how a researcher interested in exploring women's differing standpoints should navigate relationships with the different individuals she encounters. Each theorist does highlight the significance of dialogue for the development of knowledges that more accurately capture the "nature of the matrix of domination" (Collins 1990:236) or "relations of ruling" (Smith 1987; 1991). Not surprisingly, their approaches to the nature of this dialogue differ. Collins (1990:236) emphasizes the "partial, situated knowledge" of groups like African American women, Latina lesbians, Puerto Rican men and "other groups with distinctive standpoints" who together can contribute to a broadened understanding of "the nature of the matrix of domination" through dialogue across their different standpoints. In contrast, Smith stresses ongoing dialogue between the inquirer and the subjects and objects of inquiry where " . . . the inquirer is always exposed to the discipline of the other—sometimes the others' direct response, but more often how people's activities are actually coordinated." Both Collins and Smith agree that the goal of such dialogue is to decenter dominant discourse, and to continually displace and rework it "to 'get it right' " (Smith 1992:93). On a few occasions, I participated in group discussions that brought together people from diverse social locations within the two towns which were more similar to the dialogic strategy Collins recommends. However, the dialogic strategy that formed a central component of the method I employed to gather and assess ethnographic information is closer to Smith's representation.

Yet two questions remained when I considered how to proceed to "get it right" in my research with rural residents in Iowa. First, whose perspectives should be privileged in a dialogic process when I encounter the competing, and sometimes overlapping, viewpoints of groups represented within the towns—single mothers working in the factories, single mothers on public assistance (two of many overlapping categories), newly arrived Mexican factory workers, longer term Mexican American residents, low income white European American women married to Mexican men, full time homemakers, full time family farmers, low income elderly residents, etc. The second and related question relates to how to locate myself in relationship to different residents.

One key aspect of Collins' (1990:215-215) analysis of Black feminist thought that does offer a partial methodological strategy is found in her discussion of the "ethic of caring." She describes the "ethic of caring" with reference to three interrelated dimensions: an emphasis on "individual uniqueness"; "the appropriateness of emotions in dialogues"; and "the capacity for empathy." These dimensions of the "ethic of caring" spoke directly to my own partial solutions to the questions raised above. Yet, as the following analysis will illustrate, emphasizing the uniqueness of individuals within a particular context, valuing emotions in dialogues designed to "get it right," and using empathy with different residents as methodological strategies further demonstrate the challenge of feminist standpoint theories when applied within a specific context. As Donna Haraway (1988:590) argues: "Situated knowledges are about communities, not about isolated individuals. The only way to find a larger vision is to be somewhere in particular."

I will illustrate the "outsider phenomenon" through excerpts from the narratives of a small, but diverse subset of women interviewed in order to problematize the notion of "women's standpoints."[3] Standpoints within the "outsider phenomenon" are rooted in material conditions that are structured by class divisions, gender and racial inequality, among other dimensions of inequality. By shifting the standpoint to those who are marginal to the mythic community "insider," certain less visible features of daily life are brought into view (see Harding 1991). Furthermore, from a materialist feminist perspective, "standpoints" are simultaneously constructed in discourse which, in turn, contributes to a more fluid conceptualization of "standpoint" than offered in certain standpoint theoretical frameworks or, more typically, in misappropriation of standpoint methodologies. Drawing upon Michel Foucault's (1984) analysis, discourse is defined here as "historically variable ways of specifying knowledge and truth—what is possible to speak of at a given moment" (Ramazanoglu 1993:19). Discourses are not merely "groups of signs (signifying elements referring to contents or representations) but [are] practices that systematically form the objects of which they speak" (Foucault 1974:49).

Materialist feminism, as I reconstruct its intellectual history, has its roots in sociologist feminist theories (for example, Barrett 1980; Eisenstein 1979; Hartmann 1981) and has been particularly influenced by the theoretical critiques of African American and Third World feminists (for example, Joseph 1981; Spivak 1987) which in turn contributed to the development of diverse feminist standpoint epistemologies such as offered by Nancy Hartsock (1986); Sandra Harding (1986); Dorothy Smith (1987); Mary Hawkesworth (1989); Chela Sandoval (1990); and Chandra Mohanty (1991), just to name some of the most frequently cited theorists (see Hennessy 1993).[4] Contemporary formulations of materialist feminism are also informed by Michel Foucault's analysis of discourse (Hennessy 1993; Landry and MacLean 1993). Smith's (1990) "everyday world" perspective is closest to the approach I invoke here, although she differentiates her theoretical framework from Foucault's in significant ways. In fact, Smith (1993: 183-184) argues that: "Those of us who have written what Sandra Harding (1986) has explored as 'standpoint epistemologies' learned that there are indeed matters to be spoken of that discourse does not yet encompass."

Smith's (1987:147-148) institutional ethnographic approach focuses on how women's actual everyday experiences are mediated and defined by text-based sociological and other institutionally related discourses. I apply her framework to this ethnographic study by broadening the understanding of text-mediated discourses to include oral historical narratives and related field notes constructed in the course of research. In particular, I question the sociological construction of outsider/insider often used without question in descriptions and analyses of ethnographic field methods. I also draw upon materialist feminist perspectives by exploring how local discourses hold material consequences for social, cultural, political, and economic processes and how locally constituted material structural conditions contribute to shifts in discursive constructions. These embedded processes are implicated in the social construction of inequality. In my analysis of the "outsider phenomenon," I explore the material processes through which "outsiderness" is constructed as well as the material effects this discursive construction has on the residents in these two rural towns.

For clarity of presentation and space considerations, I am forced to present the analysis of the "outsider phenomenon" and its implication for ethnographic field work in this rural setting in separate sections. Although separating the description of the "outsider phenomenon" from methodological considerations does not do justice to the process by which I identified and subsequently analyzed this construct (and was personally implicated in its construction), I must now utilize just such a false division in the following presentation.

"NEWCOMERS" AND "OUTSIDERS": THE DYNAMICS OF GENDER AND CLASS

Contrary to popular belief, residents of rural communities frequently experience the sense of alienation and fragmentation often attributed to urban life. The growth in industrial capitalism revealed a variety of political perspectives, social statuses, and perceived "outsiderness" within the supposedly "egalitarian" rural communities. Adams (1992:372) found in her historical study of agrarian activism in Southern Illinois that: "Although this society is frequently charac-terized as egalitarian, differentials in wealth, status, and political power existed" (also see Fink 1992). The diversity of political perspectives and economic circumstances evident among rural residents as documented in historical studies continues to typify rural communities in contemporary America. Changes in the rural economy enhance the variety of perspectives and experiences among residents. Three significant shifts are evident: change in women's work from on-farm to factory and from part-time nonfarm to full-time nonfarm labor which, in turn, contributed to and accompanied a restructuring of gender roles and household composition; a growing disparity between the few wealthy farmers and business owners and those who are living on the economic margin of the rural economy; and increased racial-ethnic diversity in small rural communities in certain areas in the Midwest (Naples 1994b; Monney 1988). The two towns,

Southtown and Midtown (pseudonyms), chosen for this study illustrate these three patterns.

Southtown and Midtown are located 20 miles apart in one of the most rural counties in Iowa. Each town has a population of less than 1,500 residents. Racial-ethnic diversity varies between the two towns. Southtown's population is comprised almost entirely of white European Americans. Midtown, on the other hand, experienced an increase in the number of Mexican and Mexican American residents who moved to the area for employment in a locally owned and recently expanded food processing plant. The social, demographic and economic changes reshaping the experiences of residents in these two towns contribute to the salience of the "newcomer" status in their ethnographic accounts (also see Fitchen 1991). The category of "newcomer" was used by residents to refer to a wide array of individuals and groups including those who had resided in these communities for a decade or more. Recipients of Aid to Families with Dependent Children and food stamps in both towns, many of whom had lived in these communities for extended periods of time, were frequently defined as "newcomers" as were nonwhite residents regardless of their length of residency.

Perceived "newcomer" status is only one aspect of "outsiderness." Martha Brand moved to Southtown over a decade ago and continues to feel like an outsider. Residents who were born in the area and left only later to return as adults to raise their children in these towns also described themselves as "outsiders." Barbara Drake was born in Southtown, married someone from another area in Iowa and returned to Southtown after her children were born. Barbara explained that "when you're an outsider, which is what we basically are, moving into a different community . . . you have no name there, even . . . though the kids' grandparents live here, their last name isn't the same." While Martha moved to Southtown as an adult and Barbara left for a number of years, Amy Grove lived in Southtown her entire life. But Amy also expressed that she "always had the feeling of being the outsider, of being inferior" because, she explained:

> We just grew up on a farm and we didn't have much . . . And then when I got out of 8th grade, out of country school and went to high school, well, I was a country bumpkin, and it was . . . very difficult because here were all these kids that knew one another, and here you were coming in from a country school. And you knew your one classmate. So I would have to say it was really difficult!

Women in both towns, regardless of "newcomer" designation, who did not adhere to traditional gender roles also reported feelings of "outsiderness." They sensed disapproval from neighbors and other community members that increased their sense of rejection and isolation. Women whose marital status changed from married to single frequently described themselves as "outsiders." As Jenny Sands, who divorced from her husband after ten years of married life in the community explained: "It's not a place for a single parent really . . . 'cause it's very couple- or family-oriented." Jenny's feelings of isolation mirrored those expressed by many women, married and single, on public assistance.

Residents who worked at the local factories all reported feeling marginal to the more economically secure town residents they defined as "insiders." However, economic security formed but one dimension of a broader more fluid category of "prestige" which in turn formed another dimension by which some community members were defined by others as "insiders." Not all those perceived to have secure and middle class incomes were viewed as having "prestige" within the community. Barbara Drake who works in a Southtown sewing factory explained that in Southtown those with "prestige" in the community could "get by with a lot of things where others don't." Barbara thinks that the "prestige" carries "privileges" such that certain families are protected from exposure in the local media if they are involved in any transgressions. According to Barbara, those with "prestige" are those who have lived in the area "forever," whose "folks were raised around here" along with their grandparents, "and on down the line." These community members could "do no wrong," Barbara said. Drawing upon her own standpoint analysis, she believed that she is more aware of the power differences within the community because she is a relative newcomer. She said that as an outsider "when you sit back and kind of look, you can see probably things that the people that lived here for a long time don't see."

Overall, a majority of the community residents interviewed, especially women, reported feelings of alienation from the perceived wider community. Women were particularly affected by the discursive construction of "outsiderness" as their interactions in the community were most likely to reveal family household form, gender behavior, and class position. Men were rarely found in the role of single parent or expected to secure household provisions by using food stamps or going to the food pantry. Even when men stepped outside the traditional family form and divorced or lived openly with a woman who was not their wife, they did not report experiencing the same sanctions described by the women who were in similar situations. Women working at the local factories, growing up in poverty, receiving public assistance, moving to those communities as adults, leaving and returning as adults after marriage to a local farmer, living as a single mother or otherwise living in a nontraditional family form all expressed feelings of isolation and "outsiderness." Ironically, those who were defined by others as "insiders," also said they felt like "outsiders" who will never be accepted. I often left Midtown and Southtown after a field trip asking: "Who are the insiders here?" I have yet to meet a community resident who feels completely like the mythical community "insider" although several people presented themselves as more "legitimate" members of the community than others. Those named as "insiders" such as the owners of the food processing plant and the local bankers, also felt like "outsiders" as they perceived other community residents' resentment of their economic success and political clout. Erin Landers, one of the plant owners and longtime resident of Midtown, reported that she felt a number of community members, particularly older residents who knew her and her husband as children, resented their financial success. She also perceived hostility from community members who were displeased with the number of Mexican and Mexican Americans who had moved to Midtown for employment in their plant.

Yet embedded in the "outsider phenomenon" were the patterns of inequality that shaped social life in these two rural towns. While those with more political and economic resources also felt "outside" for reasons often associated with their power and wealth, those with less resources were more disadvantaged by the social control processes associated with the "outsider phenomenon." The mythic construction of a *gemeinschaft*-like "community" fed into the "outsider phenomenon." The idealized construction of what it meant to be a part of the "community" and of who were "legitimate" community members served as both an internalized and externalized means of social control. When someone spoke up to challenge the construction, they were formally silenced or ostracized. Others silenced themselves for fear that they would disrupt the fragile sense of community. Consequently, many members walked around feeling alienated from the mythic "community" yet were careful not to share their feelings with others who they perceived were more connected to the "community." As long as those on the margins felt silenced by the "outsider phenomenon" they would not challenge the power base and definition of the situation that privileged a small elite who controlled town politics and economic development (see Naples 1994a). The Mexican and Mexican American residents offer further insight into the dynamics of social control embedded in the "outsider phenomenon." On the other hand, a number of events and discursive shifts identified during the field work highlighted the fluidity of the "outsider phenomenon." This is most evident when we examine the process of racialization in Midtown.

RACIALIZATION PROCESSES IN MIDTOWN

Mexicans and Mexican Americans were most likely to fit into the taken-for-granted definition of "newcomer" as they were among the most recent arrivals in Midtown. However, the term "newcomer" was also used to differentiate between "Americans" and others viewed as temporary and, oftentimes, "illegitimate" residents. Under this formulation Mexican Americans were frequently categorized along with undocumented Mexican workers as illegal and posing numerous problems for the so-called "legitimate" members of the community. However, the process of racialization in Midtown demonstrates that such a totalizing conceptualization of the Mexican and Mexican American residents was unstable and, consequently, quickly fell apart in the face of interactions with different agents of the state—a process I will illustrate below. The totalization was further compromised as young Mexicans and Mexican Americans entered the school system, were adopted by local families, dated white European teenagers, or married local white residents.

Whiteness formed an unspoken, but powerful backdrop to the construction of "community" in both towns. As the number of Mexican and Mexican Americans increased in Midtown (the percentage grew from less than one percent to almost ten percent during the four years of field work) residents became increasingly vocal about the threat the increased racial-ethnic diversity posed to their quality of life (see Naples 1994b). Racial formation theory helps capture "the processes by which racial meanings are attributed, and racial identities assigned" and infused in material practices and institutional arrangements in a particular society (Winant 1994:23; also see Frankenberg 1993; Hyde 1995; Omi and Winant 1986). "Racialization," the process by which racial formation proceeds, is fluid and multifaced and provides an analytic tool that allows us to map the changing and contested negotiation of different racial-ethnic groups and subgroups as they insert themselves and are inserted into new social, political and economic environments. This conceptualization counters the tendency found in certain standpoint theoretical frameworks to treat standpoints as fixed in time and space and unproblematically attached to specific and identifiable individuals or groups (Hennessy 1993). Yet, as in this case study, race-ethnicity remains a powerful marker through which "outsiderness" is further constructed and experienced.

Workers of color, especially Mexican and Mexican American workers, have always been overrepresented among the migrant agricultural workers in the Midwest, yet, for the most part, they have not remained as permanent residents in the rural communities. The shacks and trailers of the migrant labor camps huddled at the edges of rural communities remain a symbol of the migrant laborer's marginal status as a nonresident of the communities that employ them. As permanent residents, Mexicans and Mexican Americans continue to face discrimination and harassment from neighbors, business owners, and health care providers as they attempt to make a home in the small towns. Newly devised housing segregation strategies in Midtown placed Mexican and Mexican American residents in the trailer park at the edge of town or in the least desirable rental properties and further highlighted their marginal and presumed temporary status.

The ethnographic research revealed three separate enclaves among the Mexican and Mexican Americans in Midtown: those who moved to Midtown from Mexico City, those who were from rural Mexican towns, and those who moved from Los Angeles or other urban areas within the United States. The fragmentation within the Mexican and Mexican American community enhanced the feelings of alienation expressed by the different residents. On the other hand, the Mexican and Mexican Americans were treated as one separate and homogeneous community within Midtown despite differences in immigration status, citizenship, and region of birth. As Anna Ortega, a United States citizen in her 30's who moved from Texas to Midtown with her family, explained:

> But a lot of the Americans think that because we're brown everybody comes from Mexico and it's not like that you know. Because you can be Mexican, Hispanic, and you can come from Texas; you can come from Chicago . . . You can be born and raised in California . . . [They think]: "They're from Mexico. They're all illegals."

Ortega distinguished herself from the white European American residents who she defined as "Americans." The process of racialization creates a boundary between "real Americans" (read: white European Americans) and other Americans. These boundaries are maintained by ideological constructions as well as material practices and institutional arrangements (see Naples 1994b; 1994c). Those who do not fit the narrow definition of "American" feel themselves outside the category despite their legal status as citizens.

Racialization is an ongoing process through which patterns of inequality are reshaped and resisted. Racialization formed one of the most salient processes embedded in the "outsider phenomenon." The dynamic racialization process shaped my relationships with different community members as my ethnographic identity was repositioned by shifts in constructions of "community" that accompanied ongoing social, demographic, and political changes. The ongoing community efforts to incorporate or resist incorporating the Mexican and Mexican American residents was further revealed when I hired bilingual Chicano graduate student Lionel Cantú to assist me in Midtown.

A key event that helped reorganize racial formation in Midtown followed a raid of the community by agents from the Immigration and Naturalization Service (INS). The INS had been contacted about the possibility that illegal workers were employed in the food processing plant. Competing stories arose blaming, respectively, an older white resident, the police, "outside" complaints, and a disgruntled worker. Informants report that as many as 100 Mexicans were arrested and a large percentage were discovered to be undocumented and subsequently deported. The INS raid served as a crucial event in the process of racialization in Midtown and contributed to a reshaping of "outsiderness" as expressed by many residents interviewed after the raid. Many Mexican and Mexican American as well as white European American residents witnessed the deportation of co-workers and neighbors when the INS "raided" the town in the Spring of 1992. The tension created by this and other "raids" in Midtown generated a sense of anxiety among many Latinos including those with United States citizenship and legal working papers. Since legal residents had also been picked up in the raids and driven to INS regional headquarters in Omaha before they were released without transportation home, their fears were well-founded. The consequences of this anxiety was experienced by Mr. Cantú who on his first trip to Midtown drove into town in a four-door sedan with Omaha plates. Initially he could not find many Mexican and Mexican Americans willing to talk with him until word-of-mouth confirmed that he was not an INS agent. INS intervention also made visible the contradictions in the construction of the "outsider" in Midtown. While INS activities served to confirm white European American residents' fears that there were, at least initially, many undocumented Mexican workers in the plant, it also highlighted the fact that many other workers were "legal," even "legitimate" members of the community. In addition to the reported growing acceptance of the Mexicans and Mexican Americans on the part of some white European American residents, several white residents also reported an increased awareness of the oppressive features of INS interventions.

A similar, and in many ways, more interesting shift in perception occurred in response to perceived unfair treatment of the Mexican and Mexican American residents by the local police. Here the local police, all of whom are residents of the town, were constructed as separate from "the community" in much the same way as the INS agents. The fear of deportation by INS officials was embedded in ongoing harassment by local police. Even many white European American residents reported that the police targeted Mexican and Mexican Americans to a greater extent than the white youth who were often the cause of certain problems. Some reported that the Mexican and Mexican Americans were arrested for drinking when white residents would be escorted home or ignored. As the contact between the white European Americans and Mexican and Mexican Americans increased, the awareness of the police harassment grew. Sympathetic white residents have complained about the unfair treatment and established alliances with some of the Mexican and Mexican American residents.

The documented shift in discursive constructions of "outsiderness" with regard to the Mexican and Mexican American residents as well as the illustrative material changes (also see Naples 1994c) highlight the fluidity of "standpoints" when viewed over time. Yet the tension between white European American and Mexican and Mexican American residents remain. As my field investigations focused increasingly on the experiences of the Mexican and Mexican American residents and the process of racialization in Midtown, I was also repositioned by formerly receptive informants, especially those who held positions of power in the town. This repositioning was furthered when Mr. Cantú joined the project. Where I found no difficulty moving freely about the town, Mr. Cantú reported being followed by the police, having his mail tampered with, and fearing for his safety. Mr. Cantú's hire coincided with my move from Iowa State University to the University of California. With this move, I lost one key component of my "insider" designation which, in turn, further revealed the fluidity of this status. Since both factors occurred simultaneously, it is difficult to identify which one contributed more to a new mistrust expressed by previously receptive informants.

On the other hand, Mr. Cantú quickly won the trust of many Mexican and Mexican American residents, a trust that would have been harder for me to gain as an Anglo non-Spanish-speaking researcher.[5] In fact, when Anna Ortega was concerned with increasing police harassment in the town, she phoned Mr. Cantú in California for assistance. After some deliberation, we decided to mobilize my network of contacts in Iowa who were working as advocates for Latino residents in other parts of the state. My hesitation in connecting her with these advocates related to fear of exposing her position as an "informal" recruiter of numerous Latino workers and their families. When Mr. Cantú returned her call and asked if we could give her name to several people whom we thought might be able to assist her in dealing with the town officials, she agreed. In her role as recruiter and as a Latina, she felt more responsible for the well-being of those she brought to Midtown than was evidenced by the plant owners who initially sponsored her activities.

THE PERSONAL POLITICS OF FIELDWORK

Incorporation into the racialization process in Midtown and my dilemma over how to negotiate a more activist involvement in the town formed but two key tensions I confronted. The racialization process was illustrative of the ways in which the ethnographic field shifted over time and limited my ability to take one unchanging position on any methodological dilemma. Returning to the strategies adopted in response to these dilemmas, I will highlight how "the ethic of caring" [an emphasis on "individual uniqueness"; "the appropriateness of emotions in dialogues"; and "the capacity for empathy" (Collins 1990:215-216)] in ethnographic encounters helped deepen my understanding of "outsiderness" as well as raised further dilemmas.

The more I elaborated the diverse experiences of "outsiderness," the more I recognized the futility of privileging any particular perspective. Yet each strategy I adopted to counter a reductionist standpoint analysis revealed the limits of such efforts. For example, one strategy I used to gain a broader understanding of the social construction of community included gathering in-depth information from diverse perspectives—a commonplace field work method. With the help of my four research assistants, I gained access to a diversity of residents, many of whom we interviewed in-depth. However, in an effort to "get it right" I also utilized group discussions with selected community members where they helped set the agenda, to a certain extent, and maintained watch over the research process. This technique is typically used in collaborative or activist research projects (see, for example, Elden and Levin 1991; Light and Kleiber 1988; Maguire 1987). In these small group discussions, I posed specific questions about the two towns that were generated from my interviews and other data gathering efforts. Responses from the group helped clarify my "findings" (or "hunches") and, in some instances, redirected my investigations. These discussions often occurred in the course of other activities and sometimes included residents of nearby communities as well as Midtown and Southtown. These often impromptu discussions were enriched by the presence of nonresidents as they further highlighted the differences between nonindigenous but contiguous perspectives and indigenous constructions. However, never did any one group include the wide variety of perspectives found within the two towns. Mexicans and Mexican Americans seldom met informally with non-Spanish-speaking white residents. Low income residents rarely spoke openly about their perceptions and experiences in a group discussion with those they perceived as more economically secure.

Such dialogic strategies with particular knowers within the communities also overlapped with a second, more traditional ethnographic strategy—residing with local families during field trips. Entry into the field and, more particularly, the choices I made regarding where each member of the research team should reside inevitably placed each of us in dialogue with certain members of each town more than with others. I stayed with a local social service worker and her family on their family farm in Southtown. Ms. Perry stayed in Southtown with a local minister and her family. Ms. Schwebach stayed with a young single woman on a small acreage she rented just outside of Southtown. Mr. Cantú and Ms. Bornstein resided with a couple who ran a bed and breakfast on their large farm at the edge of Midtown. All four households provided safe and rich places in which to discuss some aspects of the research and to further explore indigenous views on the economic and social changes reshaping their communities. Not surprisingly, these four families did not present a full range of perspectives on social life in these two towns despite their differences in political, economic, and social locations. I depended upon the reflections of those with whom we stayed, yet I also viewed the more extended dialogues with them as further data—not as more accurate representations. Since each member of the team had differing angles of vision through which to observe and interact with certain residents, each of us inevitably formed somewhat contrasting views of social life in these towns. During the so-called "debriefing" sessions I held with members of the research team after each field trip, I often was amazed by the differing perceptions. These sessions also highlighted for me that the growing familiarity and empathy with different residents did shape what each research team member identified as the most significant questions to pursue.

This strategy of "passionate detachment" (Haraway 1988:585)—in this study, developing close relationships with residents and reflecting upon these relationships after each field trip—was somewhat successful. However, I found this strategy challenging to sustain as field work roles and relationships shifted over time. Two of us developed friendships with women in whose houses we stayed plus several other community members.[6] In addition, a number of the Mexican and Mexican Americans began to perceive the role of the Spanish-speaking member of our research group, who stayed in Midtown for only a short time, as advocate more than researcher or friend. These shifts in perception and relationship raised additional dilemmas that often led to the necessary privileging of one social identity over the other (also see Ellis 1995; Stacey 1988). Building relationships is, of course, a necessary part of gaining trust and access in ethnographic encounters (C. Smith and Kornblum 1989). Less acknowledged in much of the field work literature is the emotional consequences for the researcher when, over the course of field work, more distanced relationships are transformed into friendships (see Johnson 1983). During "debriefing sessions" each member of the research team expressed personal concerns for the well-being of different community members and debated how to intervene effectively to assist them in their personal crises or to help in their fight against discriminatory practices. Such growing identification with the personal troubles and political tensions in the two towns developed directly out of the feminist methodological strategies I adopted for this study.

Emotions are always present in personal interactions in ethnographic work. Here the feminist perspective is useful in reminding us that emotions can form an important basis for understanding and analysis (Ellis 1991; also see Kleinman and Copp 1993). Collins' reports (1990:215) that for Black feminist thought "[e]motion indicates that the speaker believes in the validity of an argument." To extend her argument to field work strategies, by "developing the capacity for empathy" (p. 216), a feminist researcher broadens the grounds upon which individuals will share deeply felt experiences. Rather than attempt to keep a distanced stance in an effort to achieve more "objective" analyses, feminist scholars acknowledge that power is infused in social relations including in relationships between researchers and "informants." On the one hand, the "ethic of caring" forms one strategy to break down power differentials and experiential differences between the researcher and the researched. On the other hand, the limits of such an approach must also be acknowledged for, as Sondra Hale (1991:134) cautions, " . . . in the 'feminist interview,' the closeness and inter-subjectivity remain artificial and temporary" (also see Oakley 1981).

As I gathered data in Midtown and Southtown and identified the "outsider phenomenon," I further explored the notion of "outsiderness" to get underneath residents public presentations of self that typically masked the dynamic processes and experiences of exclusion. I shared my own feelings to a certain extent and explored the similarities and differences between mine and those of the community residents interviewed using the multiple strategies just illustrated (also see Ellis 1991; Krieger 1985; Williams 1990). This intersubjective approach coupled with my methodological reflections and personal experience of the "outsider phenomenon" reinforced my already critical stance towards reductionist analyses of "insider" and "outsider" standpoints.

By drawing upon the "ethic of caring" as a methodological strategy, I further revealed two major limits of the outsider/insider debate: the neglect of the interactive processes through which "insiderness" and "outsiderness" are constructed and the illusive search for the most objective position from which to assess truth. Both Collins and Smith argue that certain standpoints provide a more reliable vantage point from which to assess "how things work" (Smith 1990:34) especially with regard to "the matrix of domination" or "relations of ruling." Collins and Smith offer two contrasting views of "standpoints." For Collins, standpoints are analogous to diverse social locations organized by gender, race, and class among other dimensions. For Smith (1992:90), "[t]o begin with the categories [such as gender, class, or race] is to begin in discourse." In contrast, her approach is designed to shift the standpoint from "text-mediated discourse or organization" to the "actual site of the body" where a woman as knower is "actually located" in order to discover "the social relations and organization pervading her world but invisible in it" (p. 91). Since a primary goal of feminist research is to uncover how inequality is reproduced and resisted, how we draw upon our capacity for empathy and dialogue is directly related to a deep commitment to this political project. The use of dialogue, emotion, and empathy helped clarify the relationship between individual narratives and broader processes like racialization and the "outsider phenomenon" that are hidden from an individual knower's direct sight.

CONCLUSION

This materialist feminist analysis challenges the false divide between "insider" and "outsider" research and between so-called "objective" or scientific knowledge and indigenous knowledge. Smith's (1992:88) conceptualization of "standpoint" as a place to begin to explore "how things are put together" and as "a *method of inquiry,* always ongoing, opening things up, discovering" offered a broad methodological strategy designed to avoid reducing "standpoint" to the expressions of a particular knower. Collins' analysis of the "ethics of caring" in Black feminist thought reflects the interpersonal methodological strategy I adopted to negotiate my relationship with different "knowers" in the encounters in Midtown and Southtown. These methodological strategies were incorporated into a broader materialist feminist analysis that explored the construction of "standpoints" in discursive as well as materialist practices. The discursive construction of "outsiderness" served to control who felt entitled to speak out and who could be trusted to hear. The discursive shifts in the notion of "outsiderness" were woven in and through material practices and simultaneously had material effects on individual expressions and interpersonal experiences—both of which became empirical resources for our understanding of the "outsider phenomenon."

This materialist feminist revising of the outsider/insider debate demonstrates
the limits of Simmel's, Merton's, and other "standpoint" analyses that neglect
the interaction between shifting power relations in a community context.[7] As
"newcomers" to these rural towns, I and my research assistants were implicated
in these processes and inevitably became a party to the renegotiations as we
interacted with different community members whose "positions" were shifting
over time. Identification of the "outsider phenomenon" and my methodological
reflections on the interactions between my own "outsider" feelings and those of
community members highlighted for me how processes of inequality and
resistance shaped social life in these small towns.

In particular, the process of racialization documented in the course of the field
work demonstrated how insider/outsider positions were ever-shifting and permeable social locations. Furthermore, "standpoints" within the "outsider phenomenon" are informed by material processes that organize class divisions and
gender and racial inequality, among other dimensions. By highlighting the
material as well as the discursive processes in and through which "outsiderness"
was constructed and reconstituted, this materialist feminist analysis reveals how
as ethnographers we are never fully outside or inside the "community." We
negotiate and renegotiate our relationship to the community through particular
and ongoing everyday interactions which are themselves influenced by shifting
relationships among community residents. Individual as actors and knowers
within these small communities do not embody a particular and unchanging
"standpoint." What we choose to define or locate as "standpoints" must also be
open to interrogation throughout the course of field work. Donna Haraway
(1988:584) argues that " '[s]ubjugated' standpoints are preferred because they
seem to promise more adequate, sustained, objective, transforming accounts of
the world" but also cautions that:

> Subjugation is not grounds for an ontology; it might be a visual clue. Vision
> requires instruments of vision; an optics is a politics of positioning. Instruments
> of vision mediate standpoints; there is no immediate vision from the standpoints
> of the subjugated.

By viewing "standpoint" as a mode of inquiry and utilizing an "ethic of caring"
in ethnographic encounters, I was able to identify and analyze a phenomenon of
"outsiderness" that was hidden from the view of individual knowers within the
community. This materialist feminist revisiting of the insider/outsider debate
focuses careful attention on the "instruments of vision " we use in ethnographic

encounters and acknowledges the powerful role we play in shaping what can be seen.

NOTES

1. See Bat-Ami Bar On (1993) for a critique of "epistemic privilege" for socially marginalized groups claimed by contemporary feminists.

2. William J. Wilson (1974:333) supports Merton's position and further argues that: " . . . although it may be safe to hypothesize a connection between one's race and one's approach to race-related matters today, no sharp lines can be drawn between the writing of black and white scholars, and there is no guarantee that what is taken to represent the black perspective today will not be rejected by a new group of Insiders tomorrow." He argues that "the field of race relations be free to develop like any other substantive area in sociology, with the discovery and codification of knowledge, with the search for truth, and with the absence of arbitrary barriers imposed by Insiders and Outsiders doctrines" (p. 334).

3. A total of 175 residents, both men and women, were interviewed in the two towns. See Naples (1994b) for more detailed discussion of the methodology.

4. Many theorists whose work has been identified with "standpoint epistemologies" contest this designation. Dorothy Smith (1992:91) has been particularly vocal about the limits of this classification. She writes: "If I could think of a term other than "standpoint," I'd gladly shift, especially now that I've been caged in Harding's (1986) creation of the category of 'standpoint theorists' and subjected to the violence of misinterpretation, replicated many times in journals and reviews, by those who speak of Hartsock and Smith but have read only Harding's version of us (or have read us through her version)."

5. Trust is only one dimension through which understanding proceeds as Riessman (1987) demonstrates. Culturally specific experiences and narrative forms through which these experiences are expressed interfere with understanding between researchers and informants who share gender characteristics but differ according to class, cultural, racial, ethnic, or generation.

6. Susan Stern (1994) argues that friendship is an underexplored basis and rich arena for generating indigenous knowledge (also see Johnson, 1983; Lugones and Spelman, 1983).

7. Of interest here is the fact that Simmel (1921:323) equated the "stranger" with the European Jew who he then defined unproblematically as trader and "no landowner." Nowhere does Simmel explore the long history and processes of exclusion and anti-Semitism that constricted the European Jew's landowning and other economic and politics claims to "rootedness."

ACKNOWLEDGMENTS

Support for the research reported in this chapter was provided through a National Institute of Mental Health grant to the Center for Family Research in Rural Mental Health at Iowa State University and a Faculty Senate Grant from the University of California, Irvine. Thanks are due to Erica Bornstein, Lionel Cantú, Morgan Perry and Kristine Schwebach for their diligent research assistance. Appreciation also to Rosanna Hertz and three reviewers of *Qualitative Sociology* for their careful reading and valuable comments on previous drafts of this chapter.

REFERENCES

Acker, J., K. Barry, and J. Esseveld. (1991). Objectivity and truth: Problems in doing feminist research. In M. M. Fonow and J. A. Cook (Eds.), *Beyond methodology* (pp. 133-153). Bloomington: Indiana University Press.

Adams, J. (1992). 1870s agrarian activism in Southern Illinois: Mediator between two eras. *Social Science History* 16(3): 365-400.

Adler, P. A. and P. Adler. (1987). *Membership roles in field research.* Newbury Park, CA: Sage.

Aguilar, J. L. (1981). Insider research: An ethnography of a debate. In D. A. Messerschmidt (Ed.), *Anthropologists at home in North America* (pp. 133-149). London: Cambridge University Press.

Bar On, B. (1993). Marginality and epistemic privilege. In L. Alcoff and E. Potter (Eds.), *Feminist epistemologies* (pp. 83-100). New York: Routledge.

Barrett, M. (1980). *Women's oppression today.* London: Verso.

Becker, H. A. (1963). *Outsiders.* New York: Free Press.

Collins, P. Hill. (1990). *Black feminist thought.* Boston: Unwin Hyman.

Collins, P. Hill. (1991). Learning from the outsider within: The sociological significance of Black feminist thought. In M. M. Fonow and J. A. Cook (Eds.), *Beyond methodology* (pp. 35-59). Bloomington: Indiana University Press.

DuBois, W.E.B. (1989/1903). *Souls of Black folk.* New York: Bantam Books.

Eisenstein, Z. R. (Ed.). (1979). *Capitalist patriarchy and the case for sociologist feminism.* New York: Monthly Review Press.

Elden, M. and M. Levin (1991). Cogenerative learning: Bringing participation into action research." In W. Foote Whyte (Ed.), *Participatory action research* (pp. 127-42). New York: Sage.

Ellis, C. (1991). Sociological introspection and emotional experience. *Symbolic Interaction* 14(1): 23-50.

Ellis, C. (1995). Emotional and ethical quagmires in returning to the field. *Journal of Contemporary Ethnography* 23(1): 68-98.

Fine, G. (1993). Ten lies of ethnography: Moral dilemmas of field research. *Journal of Contemporary Ethnography* 22(3): 267-294.

Fink, D. (1992). *Agrarian women: Wives and mothers in rural Nebraska 1880-1940.* Chapel Hill: University of North Carolina Press.

Fitchen, J. M. (1991). *Endangered spaces, enduring places: Change, identity and survival in rural America.* Boulder, CO: Westview Press.

Foucault, M. (1972). *The archeology of knowledge.* New York: Harper & Row.

Frankenberg, R. (1993). *White women, race matters.* Minneapolis: University of Minnesota Press.

Hale, S. (1991). Feminist method, process, and self-criticism: Interviewing Sudanese women. In S. Berger Gluck and D. Patai (Eds.), *Women's words* (pp. 121-136). New York: Routledge.

Haraway, D. (1988). Situated knowledges: The science question in feminism and the privilege of partial perspective. *Feminist Studies* 14(3): 575-599.

Harding, S. (1986). *The science question in feminism.* Ithaca: Cornell University Press.

Harding, S. (1991). *Whose science? Whose knowledge?* Ithaca: Cornell University Press.

Hartsock, N. (1983). *Money, sex and power.* Boston: Northeastern University Press.

Hartmann, H. (1981). The unhappy marriage of Marxism and Feminism: Toward a more progressive union. In L. Sargent (Ed.), *Women and revolution* (pp. 1-41), Boston: South End Press.

Hawkesworth, M. E. (1989). Knowers, knowing, known: Feminist theory and claims of truth. *Signs* 14(3): 533-57.

Hennessy, R. (1993). *Materialist feminism and the politics of discourse.* NY: Routledge.

Horowitz, R. (1986). Remaining an outsider: Membership as a threat to research rapport. *Urban Life.*

Hyde, C. (1995). The meaning of whiteness. *Qualitative Sociology* 18(1):87-95.

Joseph, G. (1981). The incompatible menage a trois: Marxism, feminism, and racism. In L. Sargent (Ed.), *Women and revolution* (pp. 91-108). Boston: South End Press.

Johnson, J. M. (1983). Trust and personal involvements in fieldwork. In R. M. Emerson (Ed.), *Contemporary field research.* Prospect Heights, IL: Waveland Press.

Kleinman, S. and M. Copp. (1990). *Emotions and fieldwork.* Newbury Park, CA: Sage.

Kreiger, S. (1991). *Social science and the self.* New Brunswick: Rutgers University Press.

Landry, D., and G. MacLean. (1993). *Materialist feminisms.* Cambridge, MA: Blackwell.

Light, L., and N. Kleiber. (1988). Interactive research in a feminist setting: The Vancouver Women's Health Collective. In D. A. Messerschmidt (Ed.), *Anthropologists at Home in North America: Methods and issues in the study of one's own society* (pp. 185-201). New York: Cambridge University Press.

Lorber, J. (1994). *Paradoxes of gender.* New Haven: Yale University Press.

Lugones, M. C., and E. V. Spelman. (1983). Have we got a theory for you! Feminist theory, cultural imperialism and the demand for "the women's voice." *Women's Studies International Forum* 6: 573-581.

Maguire, P. (1987). *Doing participatory research: A feminist approach.* Amherst, MA: The Center for International Education.

Merton, R. K. (1972). Insiders and outsiders: A chapter in the sociology of knowledge. *American Journal of Sociology* (Vol. 77): 8-47.

Messerschmidt, D. A. (Ed.), (1981). *Anthropologists at home in North America.* London: Cambridge University Press.

Mohanty, C. T. (1991). Under western eyes: Feminist scholarship and colonial discourses. In C. Talpade Mohanty, A. Russo and L. Torres (Eds.), *Third world women and the politics of feminism* (pp. 51-80). Bloomington and Indianapolis: Indiana University Press.

Monney, P. H. (1986). Class relations and class structure in the Midwest. In A. E. Havens, with G. Hooks, P. H. Mooney, and M. J. Pfeffer (Eds.), *Studies in the transformation of United States agriculture* (pp. 206-251). Boulder, Colorado: Westview Press.

Naples, N. A. (1994a). Contested Needs: Shifting the Standpoint on Rural Economic Development. Paper presented at the Fifth Conference on Rural/Farm Women in Historical Perspective, Chevy Chase, Maryland, December 3.

Naples, N. A. (1994b). Contradictions in agrarian ideology: Restructuring gender, race-ethnicity, and class in rural Iowa. *Rural Sociology* 59(1): 110-135.

Naples, N. A. (1994c). Widening the Lens on the State: Shifting the Standpoint to Mexican and Mexican American Migrants in the Midwest. Paper presented at Annual Workshop of Research Network on Gender, State, and Society, Social Science Historical Association, Atlanta, Georgia, October 13.

Naples, N. A. (1992). Activist mothering: Cross-generational continuity in the community work of women from low income communities. *Gender & Society* 6(3): 441-463.

Oakley, A. (1981). Interviewing women: a contradiction in terms. In H. Roberts (Ed.) *Doing feminist research* (pp. 30-61). London: Routledge & Kegan Paul.

Omi, M., and H. Winant. (1986). *Racial formation in the United States from the 1960s to the 1980s.* New York: Routledge.

Pollner, M., and R. M. Emerson. (1983). The dynamics of inclusion and distance in fieldwork relations. In R. M. Emerson (Ed.), *Contemporary field research* (pp. 235-252). Prospect Heights, IL: Waveland Press.

Ramazanoglu, C. (1993). Introduction. In C. Ramazanoglu (Ed.), *Up against Foucault: Explorations of some tensions between Foucault and Feminism* (pp. 1-25). New York: Routledge.

Reinharz, S. (1992). *Feminist methods in social research.* New York: Oxford.

Riessman, C. Kohler. (1987). When gender is not enough: Women interviewing women. *Gender & Society* 1(2): 172-207.

Sandoval, C. (1991). U.S. Third World feminism: The theory and method of oppositional consciousness in the postmodern world. *Genders* 10: 1-24.

Simmel, G. (1921). The sociological significance of the 'stranger.' In R. E. Park and E. W. Burgess, (Eds.), *Introduction to the science of sociology.* Chicago: University of Chicago Press.

Smith, C. D., and Kornblum, W. (Eds.), (1989). *In the field.* New York: Praeger Publishers.

Smith, D. E. (1987). *The everyday world as problematic.* Toronto: University of Toronto Press.

Smith, D. E. (1990). *Conceptual practices of power.* Boston: Northeastern University Press.

Smith, D. E. (1992). Sociology from women's experience: A reaffirmation. *Sociological Theory* 10(1): 88-98.

Smith, D. E. (1993). High noon in textland: A critique of Clough. *The Sociological Quarterly* 34(1): 183-192.

Spivak, G. C. (1987). *In other worlds.* New York: Methuen.

Stacey, J. (1988). Can there be a feminist ethnography? *Women's Studies International Forum* 11(1): 21-27.

Stern, S. (1994). Social science from below: Grassroots knowledge for science and emancipation. Unpublished Ph.D. dissertation, City University of New York.

Williams, A. (1990). Reading feminism in fieldnotes. In L. Stanley (Ed.), *Feminist praxis* (pp. 253-261). New York: Routledge.

Wilson, J. (1974). The new black sociology: Reflections on the "insiders" and "outsiders" controversy. In J. E. Blackwell and M. Janowitz (Eds.), *Black Sociologists: Historical and contemporary perspectives* (pp. 322-338). Chicago: University of Chicago Press.

Winant, H. (1994). *Racial conditions.* Minneapolis: University of Minnesota Press.

5

Studying One's Own in the Middle East

Negotiating Gender and Self-Other Dynamics in the Field

Hale C. Bolak

INTRODUCTION: THE PROBLEMS OF LOCATION AND KNOWLEDGE IN FIELDWORK

The process of doing and writing about fieldwork poses particular dilemmas for researchers. How these dilemmas are experienced, problematized and negotiated depends on the positionality of the researchers and the geographical location of the project. In the past decade, questions of politics and epistemologies of location have become increasingly central to readings of social science research. Postmodernist and feminist theorists have incisively challenged universal knowledge claims. The emphasis on the close connection between personal and representational process has framed the common ground of new

EDITOR'S NOTE: This chapter originally appeared as an article in *Qualitative Sociology,* Vol. 19, No. 1, 1996. Reprinted by permission of Human Sciences Press, Inc.

ethnography and feminist research: our representations are only partial truths and descriptions; furthermore, how we represent and account for others' experiences is intimately related to who we are, and the connections need to be spelled out.[1] It is within this common ground that I anchor my self-reflexive account of the study I did of urban working class households in Turkey.

Postmodern anthropology calls for an attention to the constructed nature of cultural accounts and asks for a "specification of discourses" in ethnographic writing (Clifford 1986). In a similar vein, Haraway (1988) has argued forcefully that "Feminist objectivity is about limited location and situated knowledge, not about transcendence and splitting of subject and object. It allows us to become answerable for what we learn how to see" (p. 583). This position calls for a self-reflexivity—both in *doing* and *writing* about research. Indeed, feminist anthropologists, sociologists and to a much lesser extent psychologists have been increasingly responsive to this plea, exploring the implications of self-understanding and self-assessment for doing social science in general and fieldwork in particular, and making the connections between their self-understandings and theoretical accounts of what they hear and observe (Altorki & El-Solh 1988; Acker, Barry & Esseveld 1983; Bhavnani 1993; Chodorow 1989; Daniels 1983; Fine 1989; Krieger 1985, Scheper-Hughes & Clark 1983; Reinharz 1983; Stacey 1988).[2] For example, Harding (1991) has asked what it would mean to activate her identity as a white in seeking antiracist feminist understandings. Chodorow's (1989) theorization of "gender salience" was grounded in her realization that she was asking "seventies" questions to "thirties" women psychoanalysts:

> The pervasiveness of gender as a category to me simply did not resonate with their own life experiences, and I began to realize how much my perceptual and analytic categories have been shaped by my coming of age in the women's movement and my immersion in the recent literature of gender theory. (p. 217)

In a very stimulating piece, Collins (1986) has made the argument that intellectuals can enrich and strengthen their disciplines by learning to "trust their own personal and cultural biographies as significant sources of knowledge" (p. 29). Addressing the question of how to use location or position as a source of knowledge, Collins identifies a researcher's "outsider within" status as particularly informative. As a case in point, she associates Afro-American women's "outsider within" status with a "creative marginality" which she contends has not only provided a special standpoint on self, family and society for Afro-

American women, but has also broadened the sociological paradigms of how work and family are conceptualized.

As anthropology evolved to be more than a study of "others," the concept of the "outsider within" has become more salient. For example, the literature on indigenous research has addressed the problems of location, emphasizing the difficult task native researchers face in creating enough distance between themselves and their own cultures. In the account of her fieldwork about women's reproductive process, Martin (1987) contrasts her indigenous experience with doing fieldwork elsewhere, describing her "anguish" at home over the "obviousness" of what women were saying: "That women's responses in our interviews were obvious to me is a way of saying that I felt as much at home hearing them as a fish in water. As an anthropologist, my problem was to find a vantage point from which to see the water I had lived in all my life" (p. 11). While a foreign researcher runs the risk of being culture blind, an indigenous researcher runs the risk of being blinded by the familiar.

The positions of "insider" and "outsider" are obviously relative and exist on a continuum. Based on a life history project with her own family, Kikumura (1981) has argued that a researcher's relative positioning on this continuum is informed by the definition used by the participants.[3] As an alternative to the implicit model that characterizes all researchers as absolutely inside or outside a homogeneous socio-cultural system, Aguilar (1981) has proposed a more realistic model which would view the local ethnographer as relatively inside (or outside) with respect to a heterogeneous system. Furthermore, indigenous researchers can enjoy both insider and outsider status by being strategic in their selection of demographic locations and research topics, thereby regulating "the degree of their social involvement and cultural immersion" (p. 25). In fact, an indigenous researcher working with a community with which s/he may not have had much previous contact may assume or be ascribed the role of "marginal native" (Freilich 1977).

Bi-cultural researchers have also commented on the connections between their "outsider within" status, and their fieldwork experiences.[4] For example, as an Arab American researcher, Joseph's (1988) research in Lebanon raised the question for her of the difference in the Western and Middle Eastern constructions of personhood and self, thereby advancing her research on the self. It was as a result of her fieldwork that she understood her ability to merge and separate as "a unique vantage point" associated with her bi-cultural experience. Her insider/outsider status brought with it a relationship to herself as subject/object, the experience of which became relevant to her subsequent research on the self.

Similarly Abu-Lughod's (1988) experience of learning to live as a "modest daughter" within the Bedouin community also generated data at an experiential level, which became essential to the development of her analysis of modesty and women's veiling:

> It was at this moment, when I felt naked before an Arab elder because I could not veil, that I understood viscerally that women veil not because anyone tells them to or because they would be punished if they did not, but because they feel extremely uncomfortable in the presence of certain categories of men. (Abu-Lughod, 1988, p. 155)

Abu-Lughod (1993) makes explicit and explores her own positionality in her recent experiment with feminist ethnography. In her introduction, she notes that feminist scholarship has "encouraged a heightened consciousness of two issues—standpoint and the power dynamics of self and other—that dovetailed with anthropologists' increasingly sophisticated attention to reflexivity in fieldwork and writing" (p. 6). These are some of the concerns that anchor my self-reflexive account of the fieldwork process as well.

This chapter is based on a project that evolved out of my interdisciplinary and cross-cultural interest in gender, and more specifically in the connections between gender as a socio-cultural system of organization on the one hand, and as subjective experience on the other. My primary goal was to understand the implications of a woman's status as major provider and her husband's inability to bring in a family wage for the construction of gender and household dynamics among married couples in a traditional context. In Turkey, expectations about gender are still rigidly defined with less than 20% of urban women in gainful employment. At a broader level, the project aimed to contribute to a comparative effort towards understanding the linkages between gender, class and culture and their role in mediating the construction of gendered subjectivities and the negotiation of work and family responsibilities at the household level.

Through comparisons across households and over time, I showed how cultural scripts explain the diversity in how couples negotiate the cultural ideology about gender. I also showed how the developmental trajectories of men and women as well as the cultural construction of gender reinforce differential positionings vis-à-vis the "male provider discourse," making women more competent in coping with the changing realities of work and family life; men are more defensive of their prerogatives and less resilient in coping with the disjunctions between the economic realities of their households and the cultural ideal of the traditional family. My analysis challenged the "household strategies" model and suggested the need to look at hierarchical divisions in the working class household along gender and generation.[5]

While doing the field research, my status was simultaneously that of an insider and an outsider. I was a relative insider by virtue of my indigenous cultural status; I had lived in Istanbul—where most of my extended family was—until I was twenty-five when I left to pursue a doctoral program in the United States. At the same time, I was also a relative outsider to working class communities by virtue of my middle class professional status. My family lived on my father's moderate salary as a university professor and placed the highest priority on the three children's education; hence, I had been able to attend bi-lingual schools which was still a privilege at the time, and did not work for pay except as a research assistant during my undergraduate years. Finally, my personal, cultural and intellectual biographies were informed by five years of living and studying in the United States; due to my experience abroad as an "outsider within" both in the culture and in my discipline, I had become a natural boundary spanner in how I think and function.

In the remainder of this chapter, I focus on my own experience of doing indigenous research in a metropolitan context in the Middle East as a woman, and on the shifting boundaries in the self-other relations in the field. Two arguments frame my discussion. I contend that for researchers who are positioned as relative "insiders," whether indigenous or bi-cultural, such aspects of the researcher identity as gender, class, professional and relationship status are made especially salient, perhaps even more so in Middle Eastern contexts.[6] I illustrate the fluid and situated constructions of gender and professional identity in my interactions with male and female participants in the field, focusing particularly on the crossing of gender boundaries. I also argue that while indigenous status can be both empowering and restricting, the insider/outsider position can be employed vantage point for "rethinking the familiar" (Reinharz 1994). I discuss with examples how this position informed my researcher role and my perspective on what is "traditional." I conclude with a couple of questions about how we know and write about women and gender in Middle Eastern contexts.

FIELD RESEARCH ON WORKING-CLASS HOUSEHOLDS IN TURKEY

Selection of Households

The absence of ethnographic work on blue-collar marriage (and couples data in general) guided my decision to do a small scale in-depth study of married female blue-collar workers and their households.[7] Initial interviews at the factories where women worked gave me a chance to talk with them one on one and to assess their potential as collaborators as well as their situation at home. Households in which the women had carried out the major responsibility for the livelihood of their families in the recent past were selectively oversampled. The final selection of 41 households was partly based on my initial rapport with the women and the willingness of their husbands to cooperate.

The data collection was carried out over a period of 18 months. The study was qualitative in nature and was based on individual and family histories gathered from a series of separate tape-recorded intensive interviews with women and their husbands. In looking at the current household dynamics, the emphasis was on negotiations around paid work and family work, couple and kin relations, parenting and finances, and particularly on the processes by which such negotiations were carried out. In addition, I took field notes at the factories and at people's homes, where, with a few exceptions, the depth interviews took place. The process journal I kept during the process provided most of the data for this chapter.

Constructing a Professional Identity

As a *sine qua non* of one's professional identity, the role of fieldwork upon the "budding" anthropologist has been likened to the role of the training analysis in the development of the psychoanalyst.[8] As I continue to work with the material, I keep noticing more issues, although I am probably still not able to identify all the psychological dynamics that were relevant to my fieldwork. I am most aware of how my professional status, education, age and relationship status interacted with my gender and indigenous status in influencing how I went about doing my research.

At the same time that I was studying the diversity of ways by which the dominant gender ideology was negotiated in the working-class households, I was negotiating a gendered professional identity in the field.[9] For example, my professional middle-class position in the social system affected my self percep-tion as a researcher and made me self-conscious about my reputation. Once during the first few months of conducting screening interviews with women workers, I ended up getting stuck in a marsh on my way to the factory, arriving at the door in a horrible mess. As I walked with a union representative to the workers' restroom to clean up, I prayed that I would not run into the owner of the company whom I had gone to college with. Both my appearance and my preference in this instance to seek entry through the union would have made the encounter awkward in a cultural context where evaluations of one's professional status depend heavily on such concerns.

The particular manner by which I negotiated my relationships in the field stirred up personal and professional issues that were not easy to articulate in the field. Reflecting on my approach to the relationship between the researcher and the researched, and my preference for empathy and relative symmetry in my research relationships, I wondered if my values were confounded with the questions I had about professionalism, and struggled for a while with the task of negotiating a professional identity. For example, I treated working-class respondents as collaborators rather than as mere "subjects," and wanted to make sure they did not feel pressured to participate. This feminist concern was often surprising to the administrators who constructed me as a "cultural other" by drawing attention to my being too "Western" either in my research agenda or in my approach to the workers. In one of the factories, even some women workers told me that my "thoughtful" style was a pleasant surprise that they had not expected of a psychologist, and encouraged me to not worry so much about people's willingness to talk with me.

Every now and then, an encounter with another professional woman in the field provided an occasion for a comparative appraisal of self-other relationships. At one point, I was introduced to a dentist who was giving check-ups to workers in the plant. I remember observing her image—tough-looking with a cigarette holder in hand, wearing tight jeans and red lipstick—and contrasting it with mine. I watched her interact with the workers in a very down-to-earth way, and observed the mutual recognition of the status and liberties she had as a doctor. Envying her apparent lack of concern with her image or her authority over them and her ability to offer her expertise, I wished that I also had something to offer. Doing indigenous research heightens ethical issues around lack of reciprocity and other inherent inequalities in the field relationships, as well as one's sense of responsibility towards policy makers and participants for doing "useful" research (Morsy 1988; Stacey 1988). For example, while in the field, Morsy wished she had studied medicine instead of anthropology. Although I had gone to the field believing that not all research on gender had to be for emancipatory reasons, once I was there, I was confronted by a problem centered discourse, shared by workers, management and professionals alike. Regardless of what I told people about my research, they reconstructed it as investigation of "working people's *problems.*" One woman asked me if the reason I was doing my research in this particular plant was because the workers there had the most problems! Although there were times when I was affected by this discourse, I held on to my insistence on seeing working-class men and women as not just victims of their circumstances, but as "actors" negotiating their options, albeit limited, and making choices (Ortner 1984).

Negotiating Entry/Negotiating Gender

I spent the first several months of my research in the factories. Although formally doing a study of family life, the first stage of entry entailed promoting my project, establishing credibility, and structuring my role as a fieldworker with male administrators who were in a position to give me permission to do screening interviews with women factory workers during work hours. From the very beginning of my field research, I was made aware of how easy it was to be perceived as both an insider and an outsider, the difference it made, and the connection with the construction of my researcher role. This role is negotiated jointly by the researchers and the participants in the field and determines how one gains access to data. Very early in the research process, I began to note how my researcher role was facilitated by my perceived *difference* from the women workers. At my first appearance before the head of the production unit at a tobacco plant, I was able to "pass" as one of the workers. Although the supervisor was expecting me, and had been given orders to be helpful, he was not prepared to see me in plain black boots and coat with no make-up on. He automatically assumed I was the "girl" who had been sent to him for a possible transfer to another plant. When I told him who I was, he jumped up, buttoned his jacket and apologized profusely for the mix up.

My experience with the managers' paternalistic and offhand manners taught me the importance of accentuating my difference from the women workers in the way I presented myself. In addition, in a society where marital position is a clear status and boundary marker, both my adult status and sexual availability were open to negotiation. Throughout the research, I developed a survival kit of counter strategies to men's efforts to challenge my authority as a single and relatively young professional woman: having the right references, being "properly" dressed and sometimes made-up, and holding my own while also bolstering their egos. My efforts culminated in a particular construction of professional identity that consolidated the culturally valorized attributes of *masculinity* and *femininity*. I was a curiosity as a "single" professional woman, and how I navigated the interaction determined whether or not they helped me with the project.

There was a ritual involved in my encounters with the male administrators. They would start by sizing me up to see if I deserved their attention. The ritual would continue with personal queries. They would then test my perseverance by questioning whether it was worth my time as well as the company time to do this research. Historically, educational status in Turkey has been a gateway to enhanced social status, and often to upward mobility. The men would end this ritual by talking about their own academic histories and projecting mixed feelings about academics, in an effort to compensate for the difference in our educational backgrounds. Their eventual decision to help me would be based on my "pleasant personality" and "good references." Sometimes, paternalistic control was cloaked as helpfulness: instead of issuing me a permit, a manager told me that I could call him from the gate whenever I needed to enter the factory.

How I negotiated my gendered behavior with the male gate keepers was somewhat variable, but at all times, critical for entry. With the highest ranking authorities, it worked to be just professional and well poised. With the lower level management, with whom I had more interaction, I was encouraged to be "relaxed" and conversational. For example, I am quite certain that my initial determination to be just businesslike (and hence "unfeminine") made the bureaucrat at the unemployment office decide not to help me. In a culturally characteristic way, however, he never told me directly that he would not cooperate; he just kept saying he was waiting for the central office to give permission, an easy excuse that I could not dispute.[10] On several occasions, I was conscious of managing my gender and professional status as a strategic way of getting the managers to reveal their uncensored beliefs and attitudes concerning workers. For example, a middle manager gave me a lengthy discourse about his preference for hiring women workers: "Despite all the problems, they make good workers because they are subservient and easy to command" he said. It was only by playing up my difference from the women who worked there that I could gain access to this kind of information.

Those who accepted me started treating me as they would treat a man. Because of my higher educational and professional status, I was given the status of an "honorary male," and my latitude to cross norms for appropriate gender behavior was acknowledged.[11] The production manager at the tobacco plant who facilitated my work by letting me use his room—in exchange for the "cultured" conversation he longed for—said "I'm talking to you as if you were a man!" He referred to me with some of the dictionary synonyms for "manly"—courageous, honest and true, doesn't lie or gossip—while some of the references he made to the women workers on the shop floor suggested that these terms would not apply to them. He claimed that there were only a few among them with whom he could joke without becoming an object of gossip. After I returned to the United States, I sent him a catalog as I had promised. A few months later, I got a letter from him telling me how pleasantly shocked he was to receive my gift, and that "I never respected any woman like I respected you—except mothers, of course—all mothers are sacred!"'

Women workers themselves communicated a class based construction of womanhood. Joseph (1988) remembers from her research with working-class women in Lebanon feeling caught between the participants' expectations that she be both like them and different from them. In my case, they may have expected me to be even more different, since unlike Joseph, there were no kinship or other ties connecting me with the community. In a response to my question about how my use of the male manager's office would be interpreted by the workers, one woman said: "If you were one of the workers, it would be a problem; but with your education and status, you are like a man now!" All these interactions were quite revealing of the cultural assumptions regarding gender, and made me see my gender as a negotiated rather than a given status during the research process.

INTERVIEWS WITH WORKING CLASS MEN AND WOMEN

The major part of my fieldwork involved separate interviews with the blue-collar women and their husbands. In this section, I talk about how I negotiated self-other relations with my interviewees. I address the interactive construction of my researcher identity, the dynamics of empathy, and the shifting boundaries of self and other in the research relationship with women workers and their husbands. The experiential approach (Reinharz 1983) integrates attention to the self, substantive concerns of the research project and the methods used. On the basis of my pre-interview and interview self-assessments (Krieger 1985), I tried to identify and differentiate between any preconceptions I may have brought to the interview, personal agendas I may have had during the interview, interview dynamics, and my subsequent interpretations.[12] I also focused on what women and men were choosing to talk or not talk about. Reality was negotiated for therapeutic and creative purposes, as Early (1985) observed in the informal narratives of the traditional Cairene women. There were parallel processes going on in the self-presentations of the informants. On the one hand, their stories referred frequently to husbands' and wives' expectations of one another. At the same time, since they were not often asked to self reflect, they looked to me for validation as they navigated through their stories.[13]

In a cultural context where people rarely come into contact with mental health services unless they are severely disturbed, an in-depth interview may provide an occasion for a therapeutic encounter. Women and men both wanted to offer their explanations for why things happened the way they did, vent their frustrations and feelings of alienation, and elicit my reading of their experiences. One of my most vivid memories of field work is of my interview with a young religious man who believed in total gender segregation and in different "roles" for women and men; he was depressed over having to "let" his wife work in the factory among men, which meant daily humiliation for him. Unable to communicate with his wife, he used the interview to confide in me as a professional who might be able to help with what he saw as an unbearable situation. This was another example of blurred gender boundaries which meant that I was not as clearly marked as "woman" in the same way that his wife was.

Empathy in the Research Relationship

Most of my interviews were with women. In fairly intimate exchanges, they used me as a sounding board in an attempt to understand what they saw as puzzling and unappreciative behavior by their husbands. Oppressed by a jealous husband who gave her a hard time about working outside the home, a woman asked me if she seemed "normal" and if I would be willing to talk to him. Another woman wondered what her husband meant when he told her she wasn't a "real woman," and whether his lack of sexual interest in her may be out of a concern for her or because he was "satisfying his natural urges" somewhere else. When I asked her if she ever talked to him about this, she replied "I haven't; you see, we're married, but it's very formal between us." If they were in the process of rethinking their own marriages, or at least engaged in an internal dialogue about their own situation, using stories about other women was a safer way to elicit my reaction than being direct. They presented me with narratives about women asking their husbands to take care of them, or women who were beaten by their husbands for demanding more power as breadwinners. It was only on our third encounter that a woman I developed a good rapport with asked me point blank: "My neighbor tells her husband: 'You have to provide for me.' What do you think of that?"

Before the field research, I was not sure whether the shared category of womanhood was going to make it easy for me to establish a good enough rapport with the working-class Turkish women and vice versa. The status hierarchy among women is quite ingrained in Turkish society, because of the rural-urban cleavage, and most of these women were of rural origin. I left the field very positive about the connection I made with the majority of women, sustaining Aguilar's (1981) contention that shared frames of reference and consensual meanings make interaction more natural and rapport more thorough in insider research.[14] In general, women assumed I would expect them to observe the traditional norm of deference towards their husbands, while sharing their perceptions of women as more competent and responsible than men. The following is a quote from a woman who asked me to empathize with the difficulty she had respecting a husband who was too "incompetent" to take his own son to the bathroom:

> For example, he can help set the table, make the salad, pick up around the house, these are things that a man can do; he can even vacuum, it's indoors, nobody would see him! Even if they did, so what? We both work and earn money and I even make a bigger contribution to the household budget. These are normal things, he shouldn't even make me have to talk about them. Okay, let's say he doesn't want to do those things; the other day, I'm cooking, my hands are greasy and my little boy wants to go the bathroom—my husband walks in the door and I tell my son to ask his father to help—I assume that he did, only to find out that he didn't. The boy is still waiting to go the bathroom and my husband has gone and sat down. He was right there; would he have fallen from manhood had he helped him to the bathroom? This is a perfectly reasonable expectation. Now what can I do when something like this happens? What can I possibly do but get frustrated and yell. He says "A man can't do it, wash your hands and you do it." I know that a woman should respect her husband, but this is too much! Can he be that incompetent that he cannot even take his own kid to the bathroom? What kind of backwardness is this?

With *women,* my empathy was unbridled, and my account occasionally more partial in their favor. In response to men's vulnerability, I felt torn between wanting to respect their subjectivity and wanting to avoid colluding with them against their wives.[15] This ambivalence was most salient at times when I perceived my presence as evoking comparisons with the wife. My indigenous status made such a comparison viable for them. Addressing the different power dynamics intrinsic to the depth interview, Ribbens (1989) draws attention to the potential dilemma of a woman interviewer who feels that her silence may imply consent and thus reinforce the objectionable views of a powerful male interviewee. In my interviews with men, I struggled to achieve a balance between my desire to allow them a space for their experience to come out, and my wish to avoid legitimizing their inclination to favor me over their wives, something which would probably not have been an issue had I been a foreigner.

Ribbens also raises the question of what is meant by empathy or "empathetic listening": "Does it mean the suspension of judgment and the endeavor to see things from the other person's view, or does it mean more than this, with an active emotional engagement with the interviewee" (p. 586)? An empathetic listener most of the time, there were times during the interviews with men that I felt myself wearing a poker face which I did not need to wear when I talked with women. There were also instances in which I found myself getting impatient with men's stories about themselves or with their evasiveness. In Turkey, gender interacts with class and professional status. To compensate for the class differential, men wanted to impress me with self enhancing life stories of hard work, accomplishments and ambitions for the future. At times when this was not easy to do, they drew attention to their family of origin or their reputable acquaintances. Unable to do either, an unemployed man told a typical story of a self made man and his perseverance.[16] After I turned the tape recorder off, he turned to me and asked: "Don't you want to know how I brought this family this far?" Seeing him make himself so emotionally vulnerable, I wondered how empathic a listener I had been during the interview.

Negotiating Self-Other Boundaries

I noticed negotiating my researcher identity differently with my male and female respondents. For example, I insisted on addressing both men and women with the formal pronoun "siz" rather than the informal "sen" (which some women used to address me) until a close relationship was established. Whereas this form of address seemed natural with men, it introduced some formality to the encounter with women. In turn, women acknowledged my researcher identity by asking me to come and visit them again as a "guest." I was caught in a dilemma, especially in the initial stages of the research, between wanting to recognize the demands of the situation for mutuality and informality and wanting to make the interview not just another conversation but a special occasion for them in which they would feel respected. I feel that if I were doing the research with the same group now, I would be more secure in my researcher role and less concerned with boundary setting.

Coming from the same cultural background seemed to counteract the class barrier for women; class *difference,* thought was acknowledged, more explicitly in some cases than in others, as women voiced their appreciation for being "treated as human beings rather than as workers," and for "being taken seriously." Although I assured them of the value of their interview a few women did tell me how they wished they had been more articulate.[17] Paradoxically, my linguistic competence may have contributed to this power differential, whereas a foreigner's lack of a comparable competence might have possibly made the research relationship more equitable. The value of education was made salient as women ruminated on their missed opportunities to stay in school. In only one case did this difference elicit open resentment: a woman who became downwardly mobile and had to drop out of adult education when she got married said: "See, you got educated and now you can do all these things; and your father won't let you work for strangers." Such encounters with some of the more traditional women of longer rural background accentuated the power differential as well as my apprehension about exploiting them.

Not having children of my own interfered in my relationships with women only when I allowed it to do so. In a few cases where the presence of children made it impossible to have an uninterrupted interview with women, I became frustrated and thought of ways to keep the children away. Being childless myself colluded with my (feminist) desire to see women's individual identities as separate from their roles as mothers. Unwittingly, I contributed to the maternal guilt that women were already suffering from, an issue that, again, a more humble foreigner would have been more sensitive about. In a cultural context where motherhood is a status marker, I was a status inferior, trying to equalize the situation in my favor.[18] I justified my interest in constructing a woman as her own person and my attempt to isolate her from her children on the grounds that she would enjoy alone time as special.

Being able to read verbal and non-verbal cues of embarrassment and discomfort enabled me to adapt my style to the demands of the situation, serving at the same time as a self protective buffer against the possibility of a culturally inappropriate encounter. For example, I proceeded gingerly when sexual matters were raised with women. My awareness of gendered expectations for women at different points in the life cycle made me cautious about engaging in a detailed dialogue about sexuality, since my professional status only partly moderated the difficulty of gaining access to marital issues as a "single" woman. After describing her husband's "strange" behavior, one of the women asked me if I thought he might be having an affair. Then, realizing that this might be an inappropriate question to pose to a single woman, she asked "I guess you're not married?" However, most of them projected their sexuality as a "duty" to their husbands—a distanced stance which made it easier to talk about it.

Negotiating a professional identity with the male interviewees involved a different set of dynamics. First of all, observing the social code against a one-one-one encounter between a single (albeit a professional) women and a married man, in the privacy of his home (Dorn 1986), I had a male assistant accompany me to the interviews with men. The repertoire of symbols for men to interact with women in one-to-one encounters is still limited due to the tradition of relative gender segregation. Traditionally, the available categories have been: loose woman, kin or guest (Kiray 1984). Initially, some men's use of kinship terminology (bacim = sister) to address me made me anxious for my professional credibility; this fear soon turned out to be unfounded, however, as I realized both that traditionally sisters are men's most intimate confidants, and that I was already one-up with my upper middle-class status. The effect of the class difference was most pronounced in my interviews with men.

As with the gate-keepers, my credibility as a researcher with these men was facilitated by my perceived *dissimilarity* with the women workers. In general, the men saw themselves as more urbanized/worldly/educated than their wives and hence compatible with me. Most attempted to appear nonsexist, as they expected me to have liberal views. For example, they told me they would "help" their wives more with housework if they only knew how or if they had more time. Their perception of me as not in the same category of women as their wives, made them feel free to use a double standard. Some of them even seemed uncomfortable with their marital status as if they wished to be able to shrug it off. They showed me photos from their bachelor days, and talked about their expensive hobbies. For most of the men, the interview and their association with me seemed to serve as another means of status enhancement. On the other hand, to compensate for the salience of class in my interactions with men, I played one-down, especially in sensitive areas such as breadwinner responsibility, as when they saw themselves employed when they were not, and did not challenge them when they contradicted the information I had received from their wives concerning their employment history, income, or marital relations. When they looked for my reaction to their control over their wives, I tried not to threaten their expectations vis-à-vis powerful patriarchal norms. While listening to the interview tapes, I hear my ambivalence about eliciting more information than they seemed comfortable revealing.

Joseph (1988) reports that with men, she was more businesslike and the boundaries were clear, whereas with women, she felt herself as a "woman more than as a researcher," and in her more "passive" Middle Eastern mode. The following example will illustrate how my experience of negotiating self-other boundaries was different with men and women. My personal beliefs were questioned twice by the informants, and both times around the issue of religion. One encounter involved a woman whose religious conviction made her "sick with the desire to not work outside the home." At the end of our interview, she told me she could see why I had to dress the way I did, but could I still not find a way to do my ritual prayers during the day? Her feeling of pity for me for not being a true believer made me feel vulnerable and resentful, but I sustained my dialogue with her instead of running away. Not knowing how we could handle the difference and retain the same rapport, I avoided openly admitting that I did not observe Islam. Another time, a man of Kurdish origin engaged me in a debate over women's use of the head scarf at the work place. Expecting the educated viewpoint to also be the *secular* one, he was surprised to hear me entertain the notion of individual freedom to do so. Being from an ethnic minority made him overly defensive of nationalism and the secular state. In retrospect, I am fascinated by the difference of tone in the two encounters: the feelings of engulfment by the emotional demands of my interaction with the woman were in stark contrast to the rational model I employed in my exchange with the man. My ability to stay relatively separate seemed to be gendered.

Gender and Insider/Outsider Dynamics
in Research in the Middle East

My status as insider/outsider in the culture as well as the problematization of my gender had various implications for the dilemmas I experienced, the ways in which I negotiated them, and the information that I gathered. For example, most respondents told me they would not discuss family matters with outsiders, *and* proceeded to tell me about them. Pride before "outsiders" (Friedl 1970) and fear of moral judgments by the "insiders" (Altorki 1988) may prevent people from self disclosure. My in-between status as well as the associations with my profession as a psychologist may account for their lack of apprehension. I was not a part of their everyday world, and thus did not pose a threat as a potential gossiper. The same advantage may have been lacking had I attempted to be a total participant in the working-class community. On the other hand, I was able to ask relevant and meaningful questions to tap into their experiences, which made them feel understood and validated. Some of my richest informants were relatively marginal in their own networks—family, neighborhood, shop floor— and saw themselves as potentially closer to me by virtue of their perceived distance from those in their immediate environment.

For the relatively focused inquiry I was engaged in, being a semi-distanced insider with baseline cultural understanding facilitated my work as well as revealing a middle-class self. I was able to both "notice" and "problematize" the familiar and obvious. Having been abroad for so long, and formulating some of my theoretical concerns while I was still in the United States helped mitigate the problem of not noticing that which is too familiar, a problem indigenous researchers face. Instead of total immersion in the field, I structured ways of distancing myself so that the setting never became too familiar. One of the ways I used to counteract this difficulty was to problematize some of the common assumptions about the working-class world, doing what Reinharz (1994) identifies as "rethinking the familiar" from a position of healthy feminist distrust.

For example, instead of assuming that workers have internalized the dominant gender ideology, I probed to see who they thought should take on breadwinning responsibility and why the men did not participate in domestic chores. Although these women worked long hours at unskilled jobs, I did not assume that they would rather "sit at home" or that they worked solely to help support their households. In one of the factories, I noticed a sizable percentage of couples alternating shifts for child care reasons. When I asked the psychologist at the plant's child care facility whether she had any ideas about how this was working, she told me the situation aggravated the already existing problems that the families had, and did more harm than good. My desire to understand the variations in how individual men and women coped with the demands of their situation and negotiated their options sensitized me to question the obvious and to transcend the "problem" framework. I was probably more cognizant of complexity and variation than an outsider would have been.

Implicit and embedded in this discussion is also the dimension of geographical location which I want to touch on briefly. As I reflect on my fieldwork experiences and on the debate about the representations of women in the Third World, my thinking revolves around two different yet related questions which I would like to pose as avenues for future research. One question that calls for a comparative appraisal is whether any generalities exist in the patterning of self-other relations in the field in the Middle Eastern context, and if so, what are their implications for research?

The more relational construction of the self in the Middle East (Joseph 1993) may bear on the self-other relations in the field. If, as the above discussion about religion suggests, difference can easily be perceived as "betrayal," how we indigenous and bi-cultural researchers negotiate self-other boundaries becomes critical. To give another example, I revealed my age if asked because I wanted people to know I was old enough to understand and empathize with them; I was also aware, however, of challenging their normative expectations for a woman my age (heterosexual, married with children), and found myself providing excuses for my single status and having a hard time saying "No" when asked whether I would get married sometime. The vulnerability that came with their compassion for my single and childless state was hard to bear. I found it fortunate that there were others who admired and envied my autonomy and mobility, and for whom education was a good enough reason to be "single."

A Middle Eastern researcher's relationship with her family seems to be particularly important in the community's construction of a social identity for her (Dorn 1986). For example, Abu-Lughod's (1988) adoption of the role of a "dutiful daughter" facilitated her researcher role. To the participants in the field, I also situated myself in familial terms, and provided such welcome details as that I was living in my aunt's flat, that she was away in another city taking care of her granddaughters while her daughter worked, and that I had a nephew and a niece for whom I frequently babysat, all of which was true and facilitated my researcher role and rapport. Similarly, as a "single" female researcher with no apparent obligations, my legitimacy was probably comparable to, albeit different from that of a married woman with children. Having a husband and children waiting for me at home might have made hanging around the factory at late hours appear questionable. I do not want to suggest, however, that there is homogeneity among Middle Eastern contexts in terms of the construction of the female professional role. For example, in the secular republic of Turkey, a legitimate and visible category of professional women has evolved in the metropolitan areas in the last seventy years that does not exist among the Bedouins.

Writing About Women in the Middle East:
Towards Situated Understandings

My second question relates to the politics of understanding and accounting for how people construct their lives and identities: Morsy (1988) contrasts the account of the fieldwork experience of an indigenous or bicultural female anthropologist with anthropology's "traditional focus on the alien others," drawing an analogy between the latter and the androcentric practices in anthropological research. How do we locate ourselves vis-à-vis this analogy as feminist researchers—from within or outside the Middle East—studying women and men in the Middle East? How do we position ourselves vis-à-vis the women we study in societies with deep seated cleavages along class or urban/rural differences? How *do* our accounts compare with those of men?

Indigenous and bi-cultural researchers are not impervious to 'existential bias.' Understanding gender within the fabric of people's lives and giving voice to women's subjectivity without contradicting the feminist project are challenges that cut across the boundaries of cultural membership. For example, if I were to do an ethnography of Islamic fundamentalism among college age women in Turkey, my personal and professional experience abroad might potentially allow me the distance to be more empathetic than a resident Turkish feminist, while a foreign researcher with less investment in secularism might be even less threatened and hence, more open. During her study of upper-class volunteers in the United States, Daniels (1983) had to face her "sexism" about non-employed women. Chodorow (1989) assumed "gender salience" for women who grew up in the thirties.

I experienced an initial uneasiness with women who expected their husbands to be the sole providers. My interest in seeing women primary breadwinners as having changed their self perceptions made me resistant to hearing their complaints about how "oppressive" their situations were. Just as Joseph's (1988) personal and professional investment in secular identity prevented her from seeing the emotional grounds for ethnic prejudice in Lebanon, my curiosity about the informants' use of gender in constructing their situation made me look for its salience. Similarly, I had to learn to hear how positive feelings about working outside the home could be congruent with traditional attitudes about family.

Atkinson (1982) argues from a contextualist position that feminist ethnography should address the sociocultural patterning of male and female experience. The social relations which inform everyday experiences are not always available within people's experiences. The work of a sociologist is, in Smith's (1987) own words:

> . . . to develop a sociology capable of explicating for members of the society the social organization of their experienced world, including in that experience the ways in which it passes beyond what is immediately and directly known, including also, therefore, the structure of bifurcated consciousness. (p. 89)

In the studies concerned with non-Western women, how this contextual understanding is articulated becomes critical. The feminist project—whether indigenous or not—may be overly determined by "Western" conceptualizations. Ong (1988) is quite justified in arguing that "the non-Western woman as a trope of feminist discourse is either non modern or modern; she is seldom perceived as living in a situation where there are deeply felt tensions between tradition and modernity" (p. 86). She asserts the urgency of locating indigenous cultural politics as well as constructions of gender and sexuality for a more contextual understanding of non-Western women's lives. For example, a recognition in this study of women's identification of their individual interests with those of their families is not incompatible with a focus on the gendered conflicts and asymmetrical relationships in the working-class household and the larger cultural processes within which women's subjectivities are embedded. Critical reflection grounded in a self-reflexive account may be one way of bridging the roles of researcher/researched as well as insider/outsider. As Gordon (1988) points out:

> Studies of Third World women by Third World women suggest rich possibilities for linking Western and Third World feminist writers who are embedded in and

wish to speak to diverse audiences . . . [linking indigenous and feminist ethnography] is what attention to ethnographic form should be about—insights and knowledge into global relations among people directly located and vying for power. (p. 21)

The work of bi-cultural ethnographers is particularly revealing of the shifting boundaries between self and other, and the interconnections between multiply-constituted identities, knowledges and representation. If feminist knowledge is constrained by its relationship with its audience (Kawar 1991), and if as Haraway astutely states, "we do not seek partiality for its own sake but for the sake of connections and unexpected openings situated knowledges make possible" (p. 590), collaborative projects between feminist ethnographers at different points on the insider-outsider continuum in Turkey and elsewhere in the Middle East may enable them to speak to and about each other, as well as facilitate the emergence of other voices. My study suggests that such collaboration would be particularly welcome in rethinking the "traditional" in our projects.

ACKNOWLEDGMENTS

Parts of this chapter were originally presented on the panel "Shifting Boundaries of Self and Other" at the annual meeting of the Middle East Studies Association, Nov. 2-5, 1988, Los Angeles, CA. The field research resulting in this chapter was made under a dissertation fellowship granted by the Joint Committee on the Near and Middle East of the American Council of Learned Societies and the Social Science Research Council, with funds provided by William and Flora Hewlett Foundation and the Ford Foundation. Dr. Deniz Kandiyoti of the University of London, was a collaborator in a wider project carried out as an extension of my dissertation research. This project was funded by the MEAwards of the Population Council. I am grateful to Nancy Chodorow, Deniz Kandiyoti and Brewster Smith for their comments on an earlier version of this chapter. I also thank the three anonymous reviewers for *Qualitative Sociology* and Rosanna Hertz for her valuable editorial help.

NOTES

1. In earlier discussions, Stacey (1988) and Strathern (1987) have provided overviews of how the two genres treat the self-other issues, pointing to the existing parallels and divergences, as well as the lack of a fruitful dialogue between them, agreeing at the same time that the

relationship is an "unavoidably ambivalent" one. The special issue of *Inscriptions,* nos. 3/4 (1988) and Mascia-Lees et al. (1989) provide critical appraisals of the relationship between post-modernist anthropology and feminism which build on earlier dialogues.

2. This increased interest in addressing issues around the "self" in the research process crosses interdisciplinary boundaries although it is most lively in anthropology and to a lesser degree sociology. Despite a decade of feminist challenges to the use of "context stripping" methods relying on a strict separation between subject and object (Parlee 1979; Fine & Gordon 1989), Sherif's (1979) charge concerning the lack of awareness of self in relation to others in orthodox psychology's assumptions or methodology is still valid; for example, researchers still aim to eliminate "interviewer bias" rather than integrate it as useful data.

3. Although she was a member of the family she was studying, the generational difference that separated her from her mother gave her an outsider status as well, enabling her to proceed with "the objectivity of the outsider's perspective, but with the benefits often available to the insider" (p. 140). She believes that her study could not have been carried out by a "real outsider" who, according to her first generation Japanese immigrant mother, would be anyone not related to the family.

4. For the purposes of this chapter, I identify "indigenous researchers" as those who are natives to the society that they are studying, such as myself. I use the term "bi-cultural" to refer to those researchers whose families of origin reflect more than one cultural membership, or who are of mixed heritage.

5. For a discussion of the findings of the study, please see Bolak (1995).

6. Several pieces in a recent anthology by Arab women researchers (Altorki & El-Solh 1988) attest to this arguments as well. Two other excellent works on the role of gender in fieldwork are Warren (1988) and Whitehead & Conaway (1986), both reviewed by Hondagneu-Sotelo (1988).

7. I located my households through those factories that had a high percentage of women workers. Through a chain of contacts ranging from union leaders to company president, I eventually gained access to five factories, each representing one of the five branches of the manufacturing subsector of the industry in which women workers are most concentrated. In 58% of the households I studied, wives were the major providers; they were the only stable providers in 68% of the households. Women's ages ranged from 22 to 38, and had been wage workers for an average of 13 years. They and their husbands were mostly rural migrants. In general, husbands were a little older, with longer residence in the city, and relatively more schooling.

8. Buckley (1993) noted the stark contrast between the abundance of theoretical material on the nature of conducting an analysis with the paucity of comparable development on the psychological nature of fieldwork.

9. The development of a gendered professional identity is discussed extensively in Reinharz (1984).

10. My heightened sense of femininity echoes Josephs' (1988) experience in Lebanon. In her study of women garment workers, Gannage (1986) was similarly advised by the male gate-keepers to be more "feminine" in her approach. See also Daniels's (1983) accounts of resorting to a "feminine presentation of self" for purposes of persuasion in her research on military officers.

11. It is not uncommon for women fieldworkers to assume or be given this status (Golde 1986).

12. My self assessments revealed quite an array of emotions. I saw myself reciprocating with empathy and occasional "feminist tips" as women reflected on their lives, respecting them for being hard workers and holding their own; being somewhat surprised at the readiness of some to see me as their friend; being drawn to those who combined respect with eagerness to talk. There were also those emotions that were not so pleasant, such as feeling exploitative of people's need for empathy and appreciation; fear of falling into the therapist trap, knowing at the same time that it is unavoidable; boredom with hearing cliches; uneasiness about stealing from family time; discomfort with power differences or their difficulty with narration that hindered an interactive interview.

13. I am not suggesting that my respondents were presenting themselves to me in any strategic way. In contrast to Goffman's "self-presentational" model, students of the Middle East (Abu-Lughod 1988; Joseph 1993) argue for a more relational construction of the self in the Middle East. I observed in my own study that people organized their self descriptions around how they related to others; a primary source of frustrations was the ingratitude and perfidiousness of kin; women's depictions of men as generally irresponsible and incompetent did not detract them from acknowledging their husbands as "elders" to be heeded.

14. Familiarity with the culture—socialization experiences, linguistic abilities, etc.—could make it easier for an indigenous researcher to gain access and attach cultural meanings to the words and acts by the participants (Ohnuki-Tierney 1984; Stephenson & Greer 1981). For example, sharing of local assumptions about what makes sense or is acceptable for a male or female, youth or adult, a single or married person, or one who is high or low in socio-economic status can mitigate the problem of selective perception and interpretation in the field (Clark 1983). Furthermore, the "covert culture" of the insider can lend psychological reality (or cultural validity) to ethnographic analysis (Aguilar 1981).

15. Feminist therapists have written extensively about power dynamics in their work with heterosexual couples (Hare-Mustin 1989).

16. Bertaux-Wiame (1981) identified a different "social logic" underlying migrant men's and women's lives, which she claims was manifested both in the life stories and in the way they were told. Men presented their life stories as a series of self-conscious acts, and mostly talked about jobs, which was true for the most part in my research as well.

17. It was for this reason that I discontinued using TAT cards after a while. Although I employed an interactive procedure, most women had difficulty making up stories, and felt inadequate.

18. I am indebted to Nancy Chodorow for bringing this to my attention.

REFERENCES

Abu-Lughod, L. (1988) "Fieldwork of a 'dutiful' daughter." In S. Altorki & F. El-Solh (Eds.), *Arab women in the field.* New York: Syracuse University Press.

Abu-Lughod, L. (1993). *Writing women's worlds: Bedouin stories.* Berkeley: University of California Press.

Acker, J., Barry, K. & Esseveld, J. (1983) "Objectivity and truth: Problems in doing feminist research." *Women's Studies International Forum, 6,* 4, 423-435.

Aguilar, J. (1981) "Insider research: An ethnography of a debate." In D. A. Messerschmidt (Ed.), *Anthropologists at home in North America: Methods and issues in the study of one's own society.* Cambridge: Cambridge University Press.

Altorki, S. (1988). "At home in the field." In S. Altorki & F. El-Solh (Eds.), *Arab women in the field.* New York: Syracuse University Press.

Atkinson, J. M. (1982) "Anthropology: A review essay." *Signs: Journal of Women in Culture and Society, 8,* 2, 437-458.

Bhavnani, K. (1993) "Tracing the contours: Feminist research and feminist objectivity." *Women's Studies International Forum, 16,* 2, 95-104.

Bertaux-Wiame, I. (1981) "The life-history approach to the study of internal migration." In D. Bertaux (Ed.) *Biography and society: The life-history approach in the social sciences.* Beverly Hills: Sage Publications.

Bolak, H. (1995) "Towards a conceptualization of marital power dynamics: Women breadwinners and working class households in Turkey." In S. Tekeli (Ed.), *Women in modern Turkish society.* N.J.: Zed Press.

Buckley, P. (1993) "Observing the other: Reflections on anthropological fieldwork." *Journal of the American Psychoanalytic Association, 42,* 2, 2, 613-635.

Chodorow, N. (1989) "Seventies questions for thirties women: Gender and generation in a study of early women psychoanalysts." In N. Chodorow, *Feminism and psychoanalysis.* New Haven: Yale University Press.

Clark, M. H. (1983) "Variations on themes of male and female: Reflections on gender bias in fieldwork in rural Greece." *Women's Studies, 10,* 117-133.

Clifford, J. (1986) "Introduction: Partial truths." In J. Clifford & G. E. Marcus (Eds.), *Writing culture: The poetics and politics of ethnography.* Berkeley: University of California Press.

Collins, P. H. (1986) "Learning from the outsider within: The sociological significance of Black feminist thought." *Social Problems, 33,* 6.

Daniels, A. K. (1983) "Self-deception and self-discovery in fieldwork." *Qualitative Sociology, 6,* 3, 195-214.

Dorn, P. (1986) "Gender and personhood: Turkish Jewish proverbs and the politics of reputation." *Women's Studies International Forum, 9,* 3, 295-301.

Early, E. A. (1985) "Catharsis and creation. The everyday narratives of baladi women of Cairo." *Anthropological Quarterly.* Self and Society in the Middle East (Special Issue), 172-181.

Fine M. (1989) "Coping with rape: Perspectives on consciousness." In R. Unger (Ed.), *Representations: Social constructions of gender.* Amityville: Baywood Publishing.

Fine, M. & Gordon, S. M. (1989) "Feminist transformations of/despite psychology." In M. Crawford & M. Gentry (Eds.), *Gender and thought: psychological perspectives.* New York: Springer.

Freilich, M. (Ed.) (1977) *Marginal natives: Anthropologists at work.* New York: Harper & Row.

Friedl, E. (1970) "Fieldwork in a Greek village." In P. Golde (Ed.), *Women in the field.* Chicago: Aldine.

Gannage, C. (1986) *Double day, double bind: Women garment workers.* Toronto: The Women's Press.

Golde, P. (ed.) (1986) *Women in the field: anthropological perspectives.* Berkeley: University of California Press.

Gordon, D. (1988) "Writing culture, writing feminism: The poetics and politics of experimental ethnography." *Inscriptions, 3/4,* 7-24.

Haraway, D. (1988) "Situated knowledges: The science question in feminism and the privilege of partial perspective." *Feminist Studies, 14,* 3, 575-599.

Harding, S. (1991) *Whose science, whose knowledge? Thinking from women's lives.* Ithaca, NY: Cornell University Press.

Hare-Mustin, R. (1989) "The problem of gender in family therapy theory." In M. Goldrick, C. M. Anderson & F. Walsh (Eds.), *Women in families: A framework for family therapy.* N.Y.: W. W. Norton & Co., Inc.

Hondagneu-Sotelo, P. (1988) "Gender and fieldwork." *Women's Studies International Forum, 11,* 6, 611-618.

Joseph, S. (1988) "Feminization, familism, self and politics." In S. Altorki & F. El-Solh (Eds.) *Arab women in the field.* New York: Syracuse University Press.

Joseph, S. (1993) "Gender and relationality among Arab families in Lebanon." *Feminist Studies, 19,* 3, 465-486.

Kawar, Amal. (1991) "The intersection of gender and politics: Revising a political science course." *Women's Studies International Forum, 14,* 305-309.

Kikumura, A. (1981) *Through harsh winters.* Novato, CA: Chandler and Sharp.

Krieger, S. (1985) "Beyond 'subjectivity': The use of the self in social science." *Qualitative Sociology, 8,* 4, 309-324.

Martin, E. (1987) *The woman in the body: A cultural analysis of reproduction.* Boston, MA: Beacon Press.

Mascia-Lees, F. Sharpe, P. & Cohen, C. B. (1989) "The postmodernist turn in anthropology: Cautions from a feminist perspective." *Signs: Journal of Women in Culture and Society, 15,* 11, 7-33.

Morsy, S. (1988) "Fieldwork in my Egyptian homeland." In S. Altorki & F. El-Solh (Eds.), *Arab women in the field.* New York: Syracuse University Press.

Ohnuki-Tierney, E. (1984) "Native anthropologists." *American Ethnologist, 11,* 3, 584-586.

Ong, A. (1988) "Colonialism and modernity: Feminist re-presentations of women in non-Western societies." *Inscriptions, 3/4,* 79-93.

Ortner, S. (1984) "Theory in anthropology since the sixties." *Society for the Comparative Study of Society and History, 26,* 1.

Parlee, M. B. (1979) "Psychology and women." *Signs: Journal of Women in Culture and Society, 5,* 1, 521-533.

Reinharz, S. (1983) "Experiential analysis: A contribution to feminist research." In G. Bowles & D. Klein (Eds.), *Theories of women's studies.* London: Routledge & Kegan Paul."

Reinharz, S. (1994) "Rethinking the familiar: Developing a healthy distrust of implicit messages, presumed fairness and benign neutrality." Distinguished Publication Award Invited Address, Association of Women in Psychology.

Ribbens, J. (1989) "Interviewing—An 'unnatural situation'?" *Women's Studies International Forum, 12,* 6, 579-592.

Scheper-Hughes, N. (1983) "Introduction: The problem of bias in androcentric and feminist anthropology." *Women's Studies, 10.*

Scheper-Hughes, N. & Clark, M. (Eds.) (1983) *Women's Studies, 10.* Special Issue.

Sherif, C. (1979) "Bias in psychology." In J. Sherman & T. Beck (Eds.), *The prism of sex: Essays in the sociology of knowledge.* Madison, WI: University of Wisconsin Press.

Smith, D. (1987) "The everyday world as a problematic: A feminist methodology." In D. Smith (Ed.), *The everyday world as a problematic: A feminist sociology.* Boston: Northeastern University Press.

Stacey, J. (1988) "Can there be feminist ethnography?" *Women's Studies International Forum, 11,* 1, 21-27.

Stephenson, J. B. & Greer, L. S. (1981) "Ethnographers in their own cultures: Two appalachian cases." *Human Organization, 40,* 2, 123-130.

Strathern, M. (1987) "An awkward relationship: The case of feminism and anthropology." *Signs: Journal of Women in Cultural and Society, 12,* 2, 276-292.

Warren, C. A. (1988) *Gender issues in field research.* Newbury Park, CA: Sage.

Whitehead, T. L. & Conaway, M. E. (Eds.) (1988) *Self, sex and gender in a cross-cultural fieldwork.* Urbana: University of Illinois Press.

6

Interactive Interviewing

Talking About Emotional Experience

Carolyn Ellis
Christine E. Kiesinger
Lisa M. Tillmann-Healy

A few minutes late, as usual, I [Carolyn] rush into Applebee's Restaurant. "I assume you put in our names," I say as I wiggle my way through the crowd toward Lisa and Christine. As they nod affirmatively, I tell them, "Of course, people who like to eat would know to do that." We laugh, but I wonder if I should have made a joke about their love of food.

A young male waiter, about mid-20s, seats us. "Welcome to Applebee's. How are you lovely ladies tonight?"

"We're fine," we reply in tandem. "You're busy tonight," I add to be polite.

"Yes, every night." Then noting the folders and books we carry, he says, "Surely you're not going to work while you're here. You should be having fun."

"We'll have fun while we work," I reply.

"Let me show you to your table."

AUTHORS' NOTE: We thank Arthur Bochner for assistance at every stage in this project and Rosanna Hertz for helpful editorial comments.

His words sound flirtatious, but more than that I notice his manner. He seems to preen for us as he stands up straight and tall, slicks back his hair, and motions for us to follow him to our seats. When he pulls out a chair for Lisa and then rushes around the table to help Christine and me as well, his movements are exaggerated and attention getting. He stands close to our table, looking directly at one of us and then another as he describes the specials, offers to get us drinks, and tells us that Sue will be our waitress.

Lisa and Christine make small talk with each other, politely but briefly smiling and nodding when he demands their attention. They don't seem to notice his interest.

I notice. Waiters no longer flirt with me, but this scene reminds me of how they used to respond when I was 25 and how I sometimes flirted back, enjoying that I could catch their eyes.

I glance at Christine and Lisa. No wonder the waiter flirts. They are attractive young women with striking figures, straight postures, and perfectly applied makeup. The smell of their perfume alerts the senses. Christine's long, flowing black dress and Lisa's short, form-fitting denim dress call attention to their bodies yet conceal them at the same time. Every hair is sprayed and in place.

How different I am from them. In this moment, I become aware of the heaviness of the extra 10 pounds that I long ago allowed my now 45-year-old body to settle into. I am dressed casually in comfortable, cotton pants and an oversized T-shirt belted at the hips; wearing glasses and no makeup; untamed curly brown hair framing my face; slouching comfortably in my chair. Attractive perhaps, but not a head turner.

Their perfection covers up a lot of "mess," I muse, as I think about why we are eating dinner together tonight. We are here to talk about our joint project on interactive interviewing and bulimia. Christine and Lisa are considered bulimic. Christine, age 30, has periodically binged and purged with laxatives for 8 years; Lisa, age 25, has binged and purged by vomiting for 10 years. If they had not allowed me into their private worlds, I would never have suspected. Not only are they attractive and poised, they also are professionally successful. Christine earned her Ph.D. in Communication from the University of South Florida, and Lisa is working on her dissertation in the same program.

I am a professor at USF. I do not have an eating disorder, although I have struggled with the same cultural stereotypes of thinness as Lisa and Christine. I used to diet constantly, my weight fluctuating wildly. Although I haven't dieted for years, I exercise diligently to maintain my current zoftig level. Sometimes in my complex mentor-friend-mother role, I wish Lisa and Christine could relax about their looks and feel better about themselves. How do they deal with the conflict between a feminist consciousness and obsessing over appearance? Why isn't being respected for their intelligence enough? But occasionally, like tonight, I catch myself envying the way they look—and are looked at.

INTERACTIVE INTERVIEWING

In this chapter, we introduce interactive interviewing as an interpretive practice for getting an in-depth and intimate understanding of people's experiences with emotionally charged and sensitive topics, such as childbirth, illness, loss, and eating disorders, the case we will consider here. Other researchers have discussed the interactive nature of interviewing. For example, McMahan and Rogers (1994) in their work on "interactive oral history interviewing" emphasize the communicative processes that occur in an oral history interview. Additionally, Laslett and Rapoport (1975) describe "collaborative interviewing and interactive research," involving multiple interview situations where researchers and respondents engage in a joint sense-making endeavor. In their view, interviewers should attend to their own feelings and experiences and to the interactive character of the interview in order to address validity and bias in research.

Similarly, we view interviewing as a collaborative communication process occurring between researchers and respondents, although we do not focus on validity and bias. For us, interactive interviewing involves the sharing of personal and social *experiences* of *both* respondents and researchers, who tell (and sometimes write) their stories in the context of a developing relationship. In this process, the distinction between "researcher" and "subject" gets blurred. We also view researchers' disclosures as more than tactics to encourage respondents to open up. The feelings, insight, and stories that researchers bring to the interactive encounter are as important as those of respondents. Thus, our work focuses on the interview process, the stories and feelings that both respondents and researchers share in the interview, and the understandings that emerge during interaction.

Interactive interviewing requires considerable time, multiple interview sessions, and attention to communication and emotions. It also may involve participating in shared activities outside the formal interview situation. Our approach is flexible and continually guided by the ongoing interaction within the interview context (Bird 1995). Participants engaged in this kind of research must be open to vulnerability and emotional investment while working through the intricacies of sensitive issues. In some cases, research roles may overlap with caretaking and therapeutic ones.

Interactive interviewing reflects the way relationships develop in real life: as conversations where one person's disclosures and self-probing invite another's disclosures and self-probing; where an increasingly intimate and trusting context makes it possible to reveal more of ourselves and to probe deeper into another's feelings and thoughts; where listening to and asking questions about another's plight lead to greater understanding of one's own; and where the examination and comparison of experiences offer new insight into both lives. This intersubjective process provides a contextual basis for a level of understanding and interpretation (Mishler 1986) that is not present in traditional hierarchical interview situations, where interviewers reveal little about themselves, aloofly ask questions in one or two brief sessions, and little or no relationship with respondents.

Interactive interviewing differs from life history research in its emphasis on the researcher as well as the respondent and the attention paid to the dynamics of the interview situation (but see McMahan and Rogers 1994). It also differs from the therapeutic interview in that intervention and change are not primary goals (although they may be achieved). Further, the relationship of interviewer and respondent is not as distinctly hierarchical or as guided by a set of rules as the relationship between therapist and client (Bar-On 1996). Instead, all participants are expected to probe both self and other.

Many practical and ethical questions arise in doing interpretive interactive interviewing: Who can do this kind of research? What are some of the considerations that should be taken into account? What procedures should be followed? How do participants provide a supportive context that encourages talk about intimate experiences? What precautions should researchers take to avoid doing harm to themselves and to respondents? How might participants handle the silences—what is not talked about—in the interview? How might participants respond if the interview becomes emotional? Is it feasible/desirable to merge the goals of therapy and research?

Many of these questions have been addressed in the past two decades by interpretive social scientists who have challenged traditional interviewing practices. These writers have paved the way for the evolution of interactive interviewing, and their work is important to acknowledge and examine before turning to our case study.

PAVING THE WAY TO
INTERACTIVE INTERVIEWING

Interpretive scholars, particularly feminists, have debunked the myth of value-free scientific inquiry (Cook and Fonow 1986; Reinharz 1992; Roberts 1981) and have called for researchers to acknowledge their interests and sympathies. They also have questioned the separation of the researcher from the respondent and viewed research as properly ascribing to goals of empowerment, consciousness raising, and improvement of life circumstances.

Interpretivists who write about interviews often view them as communicative events with their own norms and rules (Briggs 1986; Kvale 1996). They examine the collaborative interview process—the practices of interviewers and interviewees—rather than focus solely on the outcome—the words spoken by interviewees (Chase and Bell 1994; Futrell and Willard 1994; Hertz 1995; Jorgenson 1995; Langellier and Hall 1989; Miller 1996; Mishler 1986; Suchman and Jordan 1992).

Interpretivists also view as important the relationships between respondents and researchers in terms of their similarities and/or differences in gender, social class, race, and ethnicity (Bergen 1993; Collins 1986; DeVault 1990; Edwards 1993; Finch 1984; Riessman 1987). Many acknowledge the relational aspects of the interview and note the interactional construction of meaning (Holstein and Gubrium 1995; Langellier and Hall 1989; Oakley 1981). This interaction, of course, occurs in the context of an ongoing relationship where the social identities of both interviewers and interviewees continually change as each responds to the other (Jorgenson 1991, 1995). Thus, interpretive scholars note the "double subjectivity" (Lewis and Meredith 1988) that abounds in interviewing: how each participant's attitudes, feelings, and thoughts affect and are affected by the emerging, reciprocal relationship.

Moving away from a traditional research model, interpretivists encourage self-disclosure on the part of the researcher. Researcher involvement both helps respondents feel more comfortable sharing information and closes the hierarchical gap between researchers and respondents that traditional research encourages (Bergen 1993; Cook and Fonow 1986; Douglas 1985; Hertz 1995; Oakley 1981), thus promoting dialogue rather than interrogation (Bristow and Esper 1988). In this interactive context, interviewees become narrators who improvise stories in response to researchers' questions, probes, and stories (Bruner 1986; Chase and Bell 1994; Holstein and Gubrium 1995; Mishler 1986; Myerhoff 1992; Riessman 1993).

Clearly, interpretive interviewers must listen empathically (Mies 1983; Stanley and Wise 1983), identify with participants, and respect them as emotional beings (Mies 1983). Unlike traditional research where feelings and private realms of experience often are avoided, interpretivists assume that emotions and personal meanings are legitimate topics of research (Anderson et al. 1987). As a result, scholars now explore sensitive topics that are intimate, discrediting, or incriminating (Renzetti and Lee 1993). When doing so, they pay close attention to ethical issues as they try to listen "around" and "beyond" words to get to experience (DeVault 1990), exploring the unsaid as much as the said (Ochberg 1996).

Research on sensitive and emotional topics has raised questions about the boundaries between research interviewing and psychotherapy (Lieblich 1996; Miller 1996). Writers ponder how a researcher should respond if a respondent asks for help (Lieblich 1996; Miller 1996), and they question the morality of withholding information and assistance (Cook and Fonow 1986; Oakley 1981; Reinharz 1992). Some researchers have voiced concern about the emotional harm that can be done to participants with whom we develop personal relationships (Stacey 1988) and about the emotional load this kind of relationship can place on the researcher who is not trained as a psychotherapist (Brannen 1988; Edwards 1993). On the other hand, some writers suggest that there are therapeutic benefits for respondents and interviewers participating in research interviews (Bloom 1996; Hutchinson, Wilson, and Wilson 1994; Langellier and Hall 1989; Rosenwald 1996).

More and more, interviewers express concern about participants' responses to what they write (see Agronick and Helson 1996; Apter 1996; Chase 1996; and Josselson 1996). Many researchers, especially those doing participatory and action research (Stringer 1996), now suggest a more collaborative approach, which gives interviewees an opportunity to respond to and change what gets reported (Belenky et al. 1981-1982; Duelli Klein 1983; Tripp 1983). They heed the call for research that articulates and proves useful for the lives of respondents and others, rather than research that merely creates data for restricted academic audiences (Bochner and Ellis 1996; Finch 1984; Oakley 1981). Consequently, interviewers are being asked to consider how their research affects subjects on both personal and policy levels (Bergen 1993).

Interviews offer opportunities for self-conscious reflection by researchers as well as respondents. Some interviewers now discuss how they feel during interviews (Bar-On 1996; Miller 1996) and how they use their feelings, experiences, and self-analysis to understand and interpret the experiences of others

(Douglas 1985; Griffith and Smith 1987). Rothman (1986), for example, writes poignantly about the pain she suffered as she took on the feelings of women who had undergone amniocentesis. By immersing herself in their emotional worlds, she was able to understand and write about women's experiences in a more powerful and empathic way than she could have by keeping emotionally distanced. Other researchers discuss how they gained insight into themselves and were changed in the process of interviewing others (Miller 1996). For example, Yerby and Gourd (1994) show how interviewing a nontraditional family led to reflections on their own marital relationship. Langellier and Hall (1989), moreover, report that their research on mother-daughter storytelling strengthened their relationships with their own mothers.

Some researchers now advocate interviewing peers with whom one has an already established relationship (Platt 1981) and making use of everyday situations in which one is involved (Stanley and Wise 1983). Qualitative researchers have coconstructed narratives with family and friends (Austin 1996; Ellis and Bochner 1992; Fox 1996; Kiesinger 1992; Yerby and Gourd 1994), included themselves in their studies of others (Abu-Lughod 1995; Behar 1995; Krieger 1991; Linden 1993; Mykhalovskiy 1997 [this volume]; Ponticelli 1996; Richardson 1992, 1997; Zola 1982), and introspectively written about their own experience as the focus of research (Ellis 1993, 1995; Ellis and Bochner 1996; Gray and Geist forthcoming; Jago 1996; Kolker 1996; Payne 1996; Perry 1996; Quinney 1996; Robillard 1997 [this volume]; Ronai 1992, 1995; Shostak 1996; Tillmann-Healy 1996a). For us, interactive interviewing is the next step along the interpretive trail these writers have blazed.

OUR PROJECT

Our project started with Christine writing her own history as a bulimic woman in a class Carolyn taught on "Sociology of Emotions" in 1992. In her coconstructed narrative (for a discussion of the methodology, see Bochner and Ellis 1992), titled "Writing It Down: Sisters, Food, Eating, and Body Image" (Kiesinger 1992), Christine and her sister showed the connection of their bulimia to family relationships. They focused on their aversion to heavy bodies and their fear of becoming obese like most of their extended family. In 1994, Arthur Bochner assigned Christine's paper in his course, "Narrative as Social Inquiry." In response to reading this piece, Lisa, a student in the class, composed an emotional and graphic journal entry that described aspects of her own bulimic experience.

Lisa continued working on her own story of bulimia (Tillmann-Healy 1996a) and, at the same time, agreed to participate in Christine's dissertation on women with eating disorders. In her dissertation, Christine wrote separate stories of four women with eating disorders, including Lisa, and wove her own story among their accounts (Kiesinger 1995). Later, their roles reversed when Lisa interviewed Christine and wrote about Christine's struggles with body and food (Tillmann-Healy 1996b). In both cases, Lisa and Christine wrote from interview transcripts, field notes of their sessions, and introspective materials (poems and diary entries) written by the interviewee.

As a critical reader of Christine's and Lisa's work, Carolyn concluded that these projects could form the basis for a study in interactive interviewing, an extension of her work on systematic sociological introspection and emotional sociology (Ellis 1991a, 1991b). To discuss interactive interviewing and bulimia, the three of us met approximately every three weeks from January through May 1996, taping and then transcribing our two-hour discussions. On one occasion, we had dinner together at Applebee's Restaurant, which provided the opening scene in this chapter.

What follows are four stories written from transcripts of each of our interview settings—two dyadic interviews between Christine and Lisa, the interactive sessions in which all three of us participated, and our dinner at Applebee's written as a narrative ethnography. These accounts tell the story of the development of our interactive interviewing project, with each story adding another layer to the approach.

In writing these stories, we have stayed close to the transcripts of recorded conversations and interviews. However, we have taken narrative license in selecting and arranging these materials and in adding dramatic detail to make our story convincing and evocative. After telling the stories, we return to the questions we raised earlier about doing this kind of research and discuss briefly the ways our narratives address them.

CHRISTINE'S STORY

[In this narrative, Christine shows her attempt as a researcher to get past Lisa's controlled public face to access the "mess" underneath. Christine's reflections highlight how her own experience impacts the questions she asks.]

Lighting the last candle, I lean in close to its flame. I feel the warmth of its light and hear the crackle of the wick as fire meets the wax. The wax warms, then begins to melt. The doorbell rings. I take a deep breath, pick one last spot of lint from my black sun dress, and rush to the door. Lisa has arrived.

I open the door, invite her in, and ask her to sit where she feels most comfortable. Appearing fresh and radiant, she chooses the large chair near the love seat. I offer her a glass of iced tea and take my time squeezing lemon into the tall glass. We chat at length about the summer teaching shortage. We could go on like this forever. I wonder if she is as nervous as I am. When there is a brief break in the conversation, I look to her and ask if we should get started.

"Let's do it," she replies. Hands trembling, I reach over and press "record."

* * *

It took months for me to muster the courage to formally schedule an interview session with Lisa about her life and history as a bulimic woman. In retrospect, I realize that my fear about asking her to participate in my dissertation project was twofold. First, Lisa, a few years behind me in her program, was becoming interested in interpretive and narrative studies. I, however, was now "doing" what she was learning, and I feared she would scrutinize my ethnographic practices.

Second, although Lisa was a peer and colleague, we didn't know each other that well. I began thinking about how much of myself I would reveal to her and what parts of my story I would conceal. I made a conscious decision to hold back certain aspects of my experience. I feared the depths of my own story I'd have to share to get at the emotionality of hers. I knew that by revealing I would facilitate a connection between us. I also knew that by concealing certain aspects of my story I could protect myself. For whatever reason, I felt a strong urge to protect myself.

* * *

Lisa and I are masters at intellectualizing bulimia. Through our conversations, I have moved beyond a literal interpretation of bulimia as being only about thinness to thinking about how eating disorders also speak to personal longings. But, it always has been hard for us to focus on emotional issues. I have come to see this as a relational problem to which we both contribute. I don't know why we do this, but I can guess.

Bulimia is about mess. Lisa and I talk about it, study it, analyze it, and WE DO IT! As perfectionists, as two "well put-together women intellectually and physically," we craft exteriors that contradict the mess in our lives. Still, I know what goes on "behind the closed doors" in Lisa's life, because I know what goes on behind my own closed doors. How can we open those doors? How can we get in and stay in awhile? How can we get behind the analysis of the experience to feel it, see it, and face it? To do this, we must drop the perfection and control. Ironically, we must "be" a mess in order to understand it. But how?

* * *

I struggled through my first interview with Lisa. I asked questions, shared some experiences, probed her for more information, and still the conversation fell flat. I noted that we connected in a lot of ways. We spoke at length about our mothers, adolescence, self-destructive streaks, and our tendency toward wild times, dangerous situations, and "bad boys." I hesitated to move on to what has been a very significant issue in my life and history as a bulimic woman—my relationship with my father. When accounting for my bulimia, I can't help but place it within the context of an abusive relationship in which I bore the brunt of my father's violent blows and degrading verbal attacks. I hesitated to ask Lisa about her father because I feared that in this area a connection between us would *not* be made.

"So, tell me about your father," I said eventually, with great care and hesitation. Lisa smiled.

We didn't connect.

* * *

Listening to Lisa speak of her father, I am disappointed and ashamed. I feel much like I did in elementary school when my friends bragged about their "daddies." I fear that she will turn the question back on me and I will lie, much like I did in third grade, proclaiming, "My daddy is the greatest!" My cheeks flush with shame. "Please, God, don't let her ask me," I pray.

Lisa talks of the great relationship she and her dad share. She says they "flirt." I imagine Lisa as a little girl charming her dad. He scoops her up in his arms. She throws her head back, giggling. The image is too much to bear. Inside, I shrink. Lisa had a "daddy." I feel ashamed because . . . I did not. Later, I write:

A daddy has strong warm hands and a soft, gentle smile. A daddy dries his daughter's tears, makes his daughter laugh, keeps her secure. A daddy takes away his daughter's pain; he is not the cause of it.

My father indeed had strong hands, but he used them to hurt me. He offered his smile only during long apologies. "I'm sorry," he'd grin shyly. "I only hit you because I love you." My father never made me laugh.

Since I make sense of my bulimia in terms of my relationship with my father, one question burns inside as I listen to Lisa speak of her dad. If Lisa had a "daddy," how does she have bulimia too?

After our session ends, I am confused. I reflect, noting the ways we are so different. Her life seems tidy, perfect. What is responsible for the mess that bulimia currently makes in her life? Am I stretching for "the cause"? I know better. I remind myself that I am in search of the story, and the story must stand on its own. Admittedly, my quest for the cause of Lisa's bulimia is more about me than her. Confronting the neatness of Lisa's life forces me to delve more deeply into the mess of my own. Searching for her cause forces me to come to terms with the depth of the multiple events in my life that may have led to my bulimia. As I listen to Lisa's story, I find myself remembering other things: a string of less-than-healthy romances, an abortion at 17, and an isolated and lonely adolescence. When I listen to Lisa's story, my own story deepens and takes new shape.

✳ ✳ ✳

Months after our interview, I received a 30-minute, life history tape Lisa had recorded for her narrative class. I immediately rushed to my player in hopes that I would find clues to her "mess." The taped version of her story was perfectly spoken. It supplied me with dates, chronological details, and some insights into her parents' childhoods. Nothing else. She exhibited careful control over the story she told. How would I get past that kind of control? I wondered. Did I want to? Did I want to see what was beneath her exterior—to really know her? Or, did I fear that in doing so I might be forced to know myself more deeply?

We agreed to meet for lunch months later at a nearby German café. I told Lisa that the purpose of our meeting was to probe for the details of her experience. My real goal was to probe for the "mess." I sought the literal mess: I wanted her to take me into the bathroom, to describe the deep heaves and the vomit. I wanted to get into her emotional mess: the shame she feels upon flushing the toilet, the guilt she experiences in keeping this secret from her parents. I wanted access into the metaphorical mess: What emptiness does the food fill? What pain does she rid herself of each time she kneels over the toilet to purge? I wanted to push her a bit, and I feared I might not have another chance.

* * *

In the German café, our relationship both as scholars and as friends changes.

"Lisa," I start, "I once asked you how you feel when you're about to purge. You told me you felt like a little girl. Do you remember that?"

"No, no, I don't remember saying that," she replies softly, almost shyly. She talks then about being a little girl, carefully watching her mother anguish over weight and dieting. Then she pauses, looks at me quizzically, and asks, "I don't know. What do you make of my saying that—of my saying that I feel like a little girl?"

The silence between her question and my response is long and uncomfortable. I begin to stumble into an answer—maybe not an answer but a justification for my asking the question. "I don't know," I respond. "I was hoping you might talk about it some more."

She says nothing.

Hesitantly, I continue. "Compared to the other women I have interviewed about anorexia and bulimia, your story has been the most difficult to write. You are not debilitated by bulimia. You are a successful, functioning woman. I think that all stories that involve this disorder are tragic in their own ways, but I can't seem to isolate your tragedy. It has been hard for me to get at your emotions. With the other women I interviewed, I saw and felt their pain, but you don't show pain. I wanted to see if you had anything to say about your private side."

"Tell me . . . show me how it feels," I ask. There is a long pause.

"Um, well, I think that . . . well for me, I think that, you know . . . in the bathroom there is usually a mirror . . . and you know what you look like—tears coming down your face, vomit on your lips and chin, vomit on you. And I have thought, 'if people could see me like this . . . right now.' She pauses. "Oh, God! What a difference there is between my public and private personas." She pauses again. "I think that I have always been insecure about how I look or about not measuring up. I think bulimia is part of that fear." She stops, taking a long sip of the Diet Coke that sits before her.

Lisa has stumbled through her response, and I realize that putting emotionally laden feelings and experiences into words is not easy. Yet in the moments that have just passed, I have stepped behind the "closed door."

LISA'S STORY

[In this story, Lisa demonstrates the interactive nature of her work and how her own story takes on a new form when she interviews Christine.]

The tables have turned. In preparation for my first interview of Christine, I place a tape she made of her life history into the recorder and press "play." As I ease into my reading chair, Christine's soothing voice directs me to a long poem enclosed in a sealed envelope. I hit "pause," tear open the packet, and pull out several loose pages. Before reading the title, "Without Daddy," I smile in anticipation of the childhood I imagine Christine had, a childhood of recitals and girlish crushes—the childhood I remember having.

Eagerly, I take in each word. But almost immediately, something thick begins to seep into the pit of my stomach, and I scan the pages more and more quickly. "The beatings . . . I remember," she writes of her father. The beatings? My gaze locks on that line for a few moments before I force myself to continue. "They began with the unbuckling . . .

> how I hated that sound,
> the unbuckling of your belt
> you'd pull it out of the loops of your pants
> and then fold it over so that it was taut—tight
> so that it would sting
>   sting, sting, bare, young skin."

And it's only the beginning. A cruel father. An unprotective mother. A teenage pregnancy and abortion. Oh my god! Who is this woman I thought I knew? I stare into the corner of the room for 10 minutes before returning to the tape.

Her story jolts me again and again. Depression. Panic disorder. Laxative abuse. I try to write notes for interview questions, but my hands won't stop shaking. At last, the tape clicks off. Slumping back, I wonder, "What have I gotten myself into?"

* * *

I take a deep breath before ringing the bell to her apartment. I've had a few days to muddle through what Christine shared, and I feel privileged to have been invited inside her despair. Given the emotional and relational turmoil she described, it makes sense that Christine would use food to fill the voids in her life. But when I turn that lens back on myself, I don't find any such voids. Having grown up in a stable, loving home, how can I explain my bulimia to her and to myself? Is it a mess I've created out of nothing?

The door opens, and our brown eyes meet. "Hey, Christine," I say.

"Hi! Come in."

We reach the top of the stairs, and she offers an iced tea. As Christine strides to the kitchen, her black dress flows about her long, graceful legs. I marvel at the beauty and poise undiminished by her often difficult circumstances. She brings two glasses to the living room, and we sit down to talk about school. We spend a few minutes sipping and chatting before I ask if we can begin. Christine nods, and I turn on the recorder.

Still nervous, I don't immediately offer my reactions to her life history tape and poem. Instead, I begin with a question that will permit her to talk for some time without interruption. "Christine," I say, "we've spoken often about this, and you've written much about eating disorders, but I wonder, if you were going to recount the history of your bulimia, what story would you tell today?"

She begins with subjects we've discussed before—obese relatives and a weight-conscious mother—and the experiences Christine delineates resonate strongly with my own. Our conversation flows comfortably, too comfortably perhaps.

Christine pauses. Then, for the first time in a face-to-face encounter between us, she ventures into an area where our histories truly diverge. Christine speaks of her pregnancy, quickly and matter-of-factly. She seems determined to, at last, get it all out. The prospect of opening so fully to each other both excites and frightens me. Part of me wants to understand her and, in turn, understand myself. Another part finds solace in the mystery that allows us to skirt deep emotion. Still, it seems we've crossed a threshold—no turning back now.

When Christine finishes describing the abortion, which prompted her first binge, I ask about another step in her progression toward bulimia. "Can you tell me about the first time you took laxatives?"

"I remember that vividly," she says, and then walks me through the process—buying the Ex-Lax, hiding them in a desk drawer, and, eventually, taking a double dose. "Have you ever taken laxatives?" she asks.

Her question catches me off guard. "Never," I say, not admitting how often I'd considered it.

"I can remember blowing out my system that first time," she tells me. "You get a lot of cramping. I was sick for a week. Every time I went to the bathroom, I had diarrhea—really intense."

As she speaks, I think of my own experiences with stomach flu and food poisoning. I recall the abdominal pressure, the dashes to the bathroom, and the sounds and pungent odors associated with emptying.

I try to imagine Christine inviting such awful, ugly effects. As we sit here in her tasteful, spotless living room, I note her manicured nails, her shiny, smartly styled hair, and her soft, flawless makeup. In light of all I see, her bulimia is almost unthinkable. Then again, I suppose Christine has equal difficulty picturing me kneeling in front of a toilet with my finger down my throat and vomit dripping from my mouth.

Her chronology continues. She talks at length of her sister's struggles with bulimia. "When Julie told me," Christine says, "I really started to recognize that I had a problem, too."

She then recalls telling her family of her eating disorder. I want to ask Christine how she told her parents, what words she used, and how they reacted, both at the time and since the disclosure. I'd like her guidance in divulging this to my own parents, who remain unaware of my 10-year struggle with binging and purging. This secret haunts me like nothing else in my life. I know Christine would be understanding and caring, but my role as interviewer and my ever present need for self-control prevent me from opening this emotional discussion.

So we talk about something "safer"—significant others. We share stories of continuing to engage in covert behaviors and of "you don't ask/I don't tell" pacts between partners that enable bulimia to go on behind the scenes.

After we finish that exchange, she tells me about her success with Zoloft, an antidepressant. Christine says, "I wasn't on it very long before I had no desire whatsoever to overeat, no desire to purge. For the first time, I remember feeling this incredible freedom."

No desire whatsoever to overeat. The phrase sticks in my mind. That's what I want: no desire to overeat. But then she says, "Unfortunately, that has not lasted. I binged and purged after I found out a childhood friend died." So much for a window out.

"That must have been a painful loss." I hesitate, then ask, "Was that the last time you binged and purged?"

"Yes," she responds. "Like the recovering alcoholic who returns to the bottle, I ruined six months of 'sobriety.' "

I wait for her to inquire about my most recent binge/purge cycle. If she asks, what will I say? Hers happened months ago, mine only days. Christine beats herself up for a rare slip; what will she think about my repeated self-destruction? Is mine a more grave situation than I've led myself to believe? Do I need to see a therapist? Should I be in a 12-step program? Is bulimia a disease I can't control? Christine doesn't ask how I'm doing now, and despite how desperately I want to share these fears, I can't quite bring myself to do it.

Again, we return to a place we feel comfortable connecting, this time around our mothers. Fighting the urge to remain in that buffer zone, I find the strength to inquire about the disclosure. "What, what has been . . . your parents' response to your eating disorder?" I ask her. "How did you come to tell them?"

I don't want to hear what follows. "My mother said, 'You're too smart for that!' and 'You have such a wonderful imagination!' She's really in denial about the whole thing." Wham! Christine's experience adds yet another "worst-case scenario" into my already vast repertoire.

At this point, I'm feeling overwhelmed. There's so much I want to say and ask, so much twisting and swirling inside me. Although I'm still afraid of losing control, I begin down a scary path. "Christine, before I read your poem and listened to your life history tape, I assumed, probably for my own self-preservation, that you and I were more similar in our experiences. I want to read you the last part of a response I wrote after the tape clicked off."

But something overcame me as I read and listened to Christine's life history, something unexpected and frightening. Bulimia, in the context of Christine's life, made *perfect* sense to me. She used addictions as means of coping with her disordered life. I responded to her account by thinking, "Ah, yes. So *that*'s why." At the same time, my own story began to make less and less sense. What reasons could I offer to explain my bulimia? What empty spaces?

"I guess what I'm saying is, I no longer feel like I have a plausible account for my eating disorder." My eyes fill with tears, but I blink them away.

We sit in silence. Finally, Christine says, "Yours was the hardest story for me to write. The thing that bothered me the most was that the bulimic women I know have had troubled relationships with their fathers. You have not." She pauses, searching for the right words, "And I get really uncomfortable with people who had daddies. You had a daddy."

Her words take me aback, and I spend a few seconds collecting my thoughts. "Yes," I begin tentatively, "I suppose that's true, but my relationship with my father is also extremely one-sided. It's very easy to share the brighter moments of my life with him but very difficult to share the darker ones. Your father may not have been a daddy, but he *knows* you, Christine."

She processes what I have said. "In the beginning," she tells me, "I was worried about working on this project with you. Your story of your father is the story that I thought I wanted. But now I'm getting a somewhat different picture."

In this moment, I feel connected to her like never before. Although our stories diverge, talking through the divergence offers each of us new understanding of our struggles, each other, and our deepening relationship. We talk on for several minutes until I ask, "Are you hungry, Christine?"

"Starved. Should we get lunch?"

"Absolutely," I say. The food that afternoon tastes better than any I'd had in a long time.

CAROLYN'S STORY

[In this story, Carolyn writes about the group discussions, adding her own reflections as a participant who does not engage in the bulimic behaviors they all are seeking to understand. She shows how, as an "outsider," she considers the problems and risks in this kind of interview situation, how she attempts to get inside a world she knows little about, and how Christine and Lisa move her to consider her own relationship with food.]

Scurrying, I hide the "mess" in my house. I stack old newspapers neatly in the magazine rack and shove piles of books into the closet in my office. Following my directions, my spouse, Art, puts yesterday's dirty dishes into the dishwasher. I call our four dogs into the bedroom, pitch in their bones and toys, and close the door, confining them and hiding the basket of dirty laundry and unmade bed at the same time.

Only then do I look into the mirror at my haphazard appearance—no bra, baggy running shorts, and a stained white T-shirt. I change shirts and put on a bra. As I comb my hair and imagine the "perfect" appearances of Christine and Lisa, I quickly rub concealer under my eyes. I consider changing shorts, then think, "This will have to do. I'm not trying to be like Lisa and Christine. It'll be good for them to see me this way."

Just as Christine and Lisa walk up the driveway, Art yells that our puppy has had diarrhea all over the bedroom carpet. "What a mess," I say quietly, when I look in. "Close the door. Don't say anything," I command. "Will you clean it up after we go to the study?" I ask, as I rush to greet my visitors.

I glance discreetly past their perfect exteriors to note that Lisa has lost yet more weight, but I'm delighted to see that Christine looks healthy—"with a little meat on her bones," as my mother would say. They accept my offer of Diet

Cokes. "What about some bean dip and Fritos?" I ask. "They're left over from the party last night," I say to explain their presence. Christine and Lisa look at each other while I dig into the dip. Their hesitance makes me wonder if I should have offered, and I feel conflicted between being a good hostess and honoring their problems with eating, between always taking their bulimia into account and treating them like "normals." "There are pretzels too," I say, "they're low-fat." Of course, they know that. They each eat one chip with a small amount of dip, "to be polite" I think. I decide not to take the food upstairs to my study where we will work.

A few minutes later, we begin by turning on the tape recorder. First, I ask them to talk about the transcripts from the session before. I then take on the role of interviewer, asking and probing Christine and Lisa about bulimia. I listen as they construct and reconstruct their stories, taking in each other's comments, all the time seeking coherence and sense making. They portray bulimia both literally—as the purging of food to lose weight—and metaphorically—as an attempt to "fill the self" followed by the "destructive efforts to bankrupt it" (Tillmann-Healy 1996b). They compare fathers, weight-conscious mothers, aversion to fat, the connection of self-esteem to reactions from men, adolescent struggles, control issues, emphasis on perfection, and exercise obsessions. They talk about how much they love to eat. Bulimia, they agree, occurs when they're stressed and doubting themselves. Food grounds them, binging and purging calms them, they tell me. Bulimia also has elements of play and rebelliousness, they add, like "getting away with something." I can't help but think this attitude trivializes the issue, but I don't say so. Later, I realize that bulimia as rebelliousness may connect to the desire of a child to escape from being seen, or the illusion of freedom that may result from maintaining a secret self.

Initially, I do not understand that I am fashioning my story as well (Parry 1991). I hesitantly add my thoughts about food—how I too love to eat and am a "sugar junky," how I try to remember to pause after one helping to wait for fullness cues. I also speak of our differences: how my generation enjoyed adventure and being out of control while theirs seems to want to have it all—adventure and control, fullness and thinness.

Next we discuss binging and purging, vomit and shit. I've read before, many times, their graphic descriptions of purging. We talk now much less graphically than they write; still, our face-to-face conversation about their practices seems intimate and disclose. Later, they acknowledge they feel more comfortable when they write their own stories and present their own materials than when they are interviewed. In an interview, they feel potentially out of control.

"What might I be asked?" each wonders. "How might I respond? What will she think of me?"

Although they never say as much, I know this fear applies to how I might react to them as well. I try to be honest in my responses, yet also kind and caring. "How would this talk be different if I weren't 'their professor'?" I wonder. Perhaps the hierarchical role constrains me as well. What might I reveal if they were my peers? What risks might I take if they were not a part of my life outside this context?

They say that going out to dinner is their favorite activity. I admit it is mine too. They say they obsess about food. I deny that I do but then think about how much food enters my consciousness on any given day. Like Christine and Lisa say, working on this project makes me think more about food and my body. Is it healthy to concentrate so much on these details? "There's too much to accomplish to become consumed by these issues," I think—for me perhaps but not for young women like Christine and Lisa whose lives are intertwined so intricately with the subject. I wonder how our research can help us refashion personal and cultural scripts about women's bodies.

Sometimes, I think I understand their world so well it frightens me. I imagine being them and purging and then admiring my thin body. Then I recoil, knowing I won't engage in such an unhealthy activity. At 45, health is more important than appearance. What about when I was 20? What if someone had suggested purging to me then? Were the diet pills I occasionally took so different? Not having answers to these questions keeps me from feeling judgmental.

I understand the desire to be physically attractive. In my sophomore year in college I lost 47 pounds by eating 500 calories a day. I wore contact lenses, even when I had to take Excedrin each time I inserted the lenses into my watery, itchy, red eyes. What really separates me from Lisa and Christine? Twenty years? Growing up in an earlier decade where those in my cohort rebelled against gender stereotypes and were less inclined to take on cultural labels? Coming of age in a decade where the thrill of "getting away with something" involved drugs and sex, not binging and purging? We all have our temptations.

Being thin is less important to me now than ever. Is that because other issues have my attention now, and I have a career I enjoy and a mate who loves and accepts me? Or is it only because a "beautiful" body is less attainable now? I remember a scene that I've never described to anyone. At a conference a few years ago, I wore a bathing suit to the hotel pool and ran into Christine and her sister, their perfection moved me to wrap my body in a towel. I guess at some level I still want to be thin.

All these thoughts abound as I try to enter their worlds, become their bodies with their concerns. I neither can nor want to distance myself from this intimate, interactive situation. I try to normalize what they do, to take away some of the stigma of shit and vomit. That doesn't mean I support their self-destructive behaviors; it means I am willing to consider that they are not so different from the rest of us. All women are affected by cultural messages of abundance and thinness.

But sometimes I am horrified, absolutely horrified by what they do to themselves!

I don't say as much. Instead, I probe gently into the stories Christine and Lisa tell, attending closely to their discomfort and sadness. It is important to me that our sessions do not harm them. My main concern, I tell them, is their welfare, not the information I can pull from them.

As we interact, Lisa, Christine, and I go far beyond traditional interviewing practices, and still there are unexplored silences. "We never talk about what's going on now," said Christine during one of our early sessions. I assumed her willingness to bring up the subject meant she was not purging. Perhaps she feared she would start again. Lisa, who was thinner than I have ever seen her, said nothing; her eyes blinked away tears.

A few months later, I return to Christine's question and hesitantly suggest that we talk about how they're doing now. Lisa's eyes again fill with tears, while Christine's widen expectantly. But she says nothing. Is she concerned about Lisa? About herself? I feel invasive, yet wonder if they want me to push. Retreating, I say, "This is a conversation we should have when we have a long time to talk. Now we have other places to go and commitments to keep."

"We never cry in front of each other," Lisa says, "yet I cried a lot when I read what you [Christine] wrote about me, and I cried when I wrote about you."

"Always when you were alone?" I ask.

"Always alone," Lisa answers. Still, Christine says nothing, and I don't probe. Later, when alone, Christine will write poignantly about how she sobbed when confronting herself in the story Lisa wrote about her.

"You are colleagues," I say, "and you have a need to present yourselves to each other and the academic world as in control." ("And to me," I think, but don't say.) I have intellectualized past the moment. Perhaps I don't want to cry, or see them cry, or risk the breakdown in the definition of the situation as a "research" project. I feel like I want to cry, to cry for their pain, the pain that young women go through trying to contort themselves into thinness. Maybe I even want to cry for myself because I'm not thin.

We are almost done, and Art yells up, "I got chicken salad. Tell Lisa and Christine they can have lunch with us before they go."

"Great," I reply. "Can you stay?" I ask, turning to the two women.

"Thanks," they respond, and we return to our work. But then when we're done, they say they have something they have to do instead. I'm not surprised.

When they leave, I wonder how we can get at their "messes" without making a larger one. Then, before I join Art for lunch, I open the bedroom door and once again confront my own mess. As the dogs jump all over me demanding affection, my mess recedes into the background.

EATING OUT

[To demonstrate some of the ideas discussed in each of our stories above, we now return to our dinner at Applebee's. Here we show the impact of bulimia on how we think, feel, and relate as we share a meal. We integrate our multiple versions of what unfolds, basing our joint account on introspective field notes each of us wrote immediately after the event, upon realizing the narrative possibilities this occasion provided.]

Lisa is starving by the time she arrives at Applebee's to have dinner with Christine and Carolyn. Waiting 15 minutes for a table has made her ravenous. Christine has spent the day thinking about the dinner she will eat out. Arriving at the restaurant, she promises herself that she will eat light and focus on the conversation to lessen her awareness of the food. When Carolyn sits down across from her, Christine instantly is aware that they have never eaten together. Since she tends to synchronize her eating pattern with others, she panics. Will Carolyn eat quickly or slowly? Does she talk while eating? Is she a sharer? Will Carolyn, a seasoned ethnographer, be watching her every move?

Lisa's stomach growls continuously as they sit talking without picking up their menus. Why don't they order? When the waitress at last stops to ask if they want an appetizer, Carolyn looks questioningly at Lisa and Christine. Lisa can almost taste the salty-greasy choices—oozing processed cheese nachos, fried mozzarella sticks, and hot chicken wings. But she's not feeling particularly "bad," and she knows Christine almost never eats appetizers. They shake their heads "no" simultaneously. Carolyn considered ordering some for the table, but after their response, she thinks that she really shouldn't have them either.

Carolyn takes one of the menus tucked behind the salt and pepper shakers. Immediately, Christine and Lisa reach for menus as well. It seems they have been waiting for Carolyn to make the first move. Right away Carolyn knows what she wants. But Christine and Lisa grasp their menus tightly, immersed, reading line by line. For what seems like minutes to Carolyn, they say nothing. Carolyn continues holding her menu in front of her face so they don't feel rushed. She'd like to know what they're thinking. Minutes go by.

Craving a cheeseburger and fries, Lisa scans the menu for a low-fat selection. Christine feels she should be making table conversation but, instead, pays attention only to the descriptions of each dish. Finally she asks Lisa, "What are you getting?"

Carolyn offers, "I always get the lemon chicken. It's light."

The word "light" catches Christine's attention. Light is something she feels after a purge. She feels the heaviness of her own body in contrast to Lisa's thinness. "That sounds good. Everything else, just about, has cheese."

Carolyn replies, "Can't you eat any cheese at all?"

"No, I'm lactose intolerant," Christine responds. "It'll make me sick." She doesn't want Carolyn to think she is avoiding cheese because of the calories. That thought does not cross Carolyn's mind.

After Carolyn and Christine order lemon chicken, Lisa feels constrained. Even getting the chicken with sun-dried tomatoes, most likely packed in oil, seems decadent. Besides, the dish is not listed under light entrees, so it must have more than 17 grams of fat. And the marinade on the Italian chicken also might contain a lot of oil. "What about the Italian chicken dish?" she asks Carolyn, who seems to know the menu well.

"I don't like the dressing they put on it," Carolyn answers. Coming up with a plan, Lisa orders the Italian chicken but instructs the waitress to leave off the dressing.

Lisa waits impatiently for her meal to come, turning to look each time a server passes by with food. She finds it difficult to focus on the conversation. Christine is enjoying the talk, although her need to urinate is interfering. Since she fears how going to the bathroom will be interpreted by her friends, she crosses her legs and holds it.

Carolyn does not notice that the food takes a long time to come. When it appears, she watches Christine's and Lisa's eyes grow large and happy. During the six years she has known Christine, she has never seen her eat a meal; she has eaten several times with Lisa and always appreciates her healthy appetite. They all dig in.

The relief Lisa feels when dinner comes dissipates as she realizes she is eating more quickly than the others, who seem content to chat and nibble. Overcome with one of those "don't look at me, don't talk to me, can't you see I'm eating?" moods, she tries to slow her pace by rolling her pasta around her spoon, chewing bites into mush, and taking sips of wine in between. Then she becomes obsessed with the notion that she also has more food on her plate than the others. The difference is two small, butter-slathered slices of garlic toast.

With each bite, the discomfort in Christine's bladder increases. She imagines excusing herself from the table and her friends whispering to each other when she is out of hearing range—"Do you think she's okay?"—or their internal conversations—"God, I hope she's not purging." She crosses her legs the other way now, and her thoughts drift from the talking and laughter to bulimia. "Why don't we talk about it?" she wonders. Do we fear asking because we fear "knowing"? Do we fear opening a conversation about it because of how dreadful it is to live with? She wants to say to Lisa and Carolyn, "Hey . . . I'm really having a hard time with this lately. I'm really trying." But, even with them, she can't say the words.

Carolyn does much of the talking. She thinks little about the food she eats, except to note that it is light and tasty, a rare combination. At the end, she leaves a little on her plate, something she seldom does.

When the waitress picks up Lisa's empty plate, Lisa is distressed to see that Carolyn has what appears to be a mound of pasta remaining on hers and that Christine has a similar pile and several florets of broccoli and cauliflower. She hates the way they both sit with food on their plates and is glad when a waiter finally comes to take them away.

They order coffee and tea. Since Lisa had announced earlier that she might want dessert, Carolyn hands menus to Christine and Lisa. Carolyn glances quickly, while the others again pour over the selections. Carolyn doesn't really want dessert—another rare occurrence—because she doesn't like Applebee's selections, and she's full. But what if they order? Should she too? How will they feel if she doesn't? She realizes that these are not concerns she usually has. "I'll just have a bite of theirs," she thinks. But what if they are protective of their desserts and want all of them? What if they need the whole dessert to be full? She doesn't know the rules for eating with them.

As she looks at the menu, Lisa realizes she really has no room for dessert. At the same time, she doesn't want Christine to feel like she's one-upping her by restraining.

Christine would never order dessert if no one else did. But she knows Lisa always does, so she feels permission tonight. It's an arrangement they have when eating together, Christine admits later.

Lisa decides to compromise by ordering the low-fat sundae. When she asks about it, Carolyn replies, "I've had it twice. It's okay, but not mouth-watering." As Lisa is finalizing her decision, Christine suddenly orders the high-fat apple cobbler. Again fearing being seen as competitive, Lisa then moves to match her but compromises by ordering the cobbler with low-fat yogurt instead of the ice cream it comes with. Too late she realizes that Christine's cobbler sans dairy product is still lighter than hers. Then Carolyn outdoes them both by asking only for Christine's unwanted ice cream. "What nerve," Lisa thinks.

For Carolyn, asking for the ice cream that Christine can't have because of her lactose intolerance feels like a good compromise. After all, the ice cream is included in the price. And she always likes a bite of ice cream after a meal. Will they think she is cheap?

Lisa impatiently waits for her cobbler to arrive, all the while pondering the possible calories and fat grams and admonishing herself for ordering a dessert she wasn't hungry for in the first place. Yet when it comes, she eats the cobbler at the same quick pace she had eaten dinner, monitoring Christine's progress out of the corner of her eye. When she scrapes the bottom of the bowl, she notes that Christine stops before she finishes hers. And, Carolyn, saying that she doesn't like the ice cream, leaves most of her dessert untouched.

After dinner, they talk about relationships, of old boyfriends, current partners, and the importance of physical attraction between lovers. The conversation makes Christine think about her body, about wanting to be a beautiful woman for a man. Lisa thinks about how important it is that she see *herself* as attractive. Carolyn identifies with the importance of physical attraction, but after listening to Christine and Lisa speak, she thinks that her definition of what's attractive is much broader than theirs.

"How come we never talk about *it*?" Christine asks during a lull, feeling comfortable now to reveal what has been on her mind during most of dinner. There is silence, followed by Carolyn's smile, as she appreciates the risk that Christine takes. Christine explains how self-conscious she has felt throughout dinner about using the restroom. The others laugh and tell her to go now, which she does. Carolyn and Lisa say nothing about Christine while she is gone.

When Christine returns, Carolyn mentions her discomfort about not knowing the others' rules or patterns of eating. She tells them the thoughts she had while ordering dessert, how she had wondered if they were sharers. In response to Carolyn's remarks, Christine worries that Carolyn is a sharer, which makes her embarrassed that she didn't offer any of her cobbler.

Carolyn suggests that they write about this dinner but doesn't ask them if they are currently in control of their bulimia or how they feel now. They never return to Christine's question.

On the ride home, Lisa thinks about how much she enjoyed the conversation after dinner, once she got eating out of the way. Christine drives away, noticing how strangely hungry she is. In her car, Carolyn turns off the radio to contemplate the silences.

RETRACING OUR STEPS TO INTERACTIVE INTERVIEWING

Our goal in this chapter has been to illustrate the self-consciously reflexive process of interactive interviewing, which we used to probe the emotional experiences associated with how women relate to food. We do not present ourselves as experts on interactive interviewing methods; indeed, our exploratory research has raised as many questions as it has answered. Instead, we hope this work stimulates a continuing dialogue about the possibilities and concerns raised by our approach. In closing, we begin to address some of these practical, personal, and ethical issues.

As our work suggests, interactive interviewing is emotionally demanding and time-consuming. Certainly, we recognize that the approach has its limitations. Ideally, participants should have an already formed relationship or be willing to work to develop a strong affiliation. They also should have personal experience with the topic under investigation or be willing to "take on the life" of other participants. Christine, for example, tells how she listened repeatedly to her taped interview of an anorexic woman to try to step into the woman's emotions and body before writing her story. Established relationships and an ability to role-take emotional experiences helps participants reach a level of intersubjectivity that facilitates a truly collaborative and reflexive atmosphere. Of course, status and power differentials among the participants cannot be eliminated or disregarded, but the emphasis on sharing and collaboration should override the hesitancies compelled by these inequities.

There are no set procedures to follow in doing interactive interviewing. Although our study offers guidelines, it is neither possible nor desirable to stipulate precise steps or rules. Interactive interviewing evolves reflexively during participation, in consideration of the emerging interaction and developing relationships of participants. Indeed, each unique combination of participants, topics, and goals will require its own set of concerns and modified procedures. In our case, for example, Carolyn, the senior researcher, is not bulimic. Thus she exercised considerable caution in the questions she asked and the comments she made. Lisa and Christine talked more openly and graphically with each other about binging, purging, and physical appearance than they did when Carolyn was part of the conversation. We were aware of these differences, and they became part of the content of our conversations.

Although we had an initial sense of what we wanted to achieve in our project—a greater understanding of bulimia and a reflexive account of the interactive interviewing process—at each point we stopped to consider how to proceed next. In each three-person session, we began by reviewing works we had read on interviewing and by discussing the transcript of our previous session, allowing our interpretations to build on what we had discussed before. Only then did we talk about the next step in the project. We also examined unplanned research opportunities that arose, such as our casual interaction regarding food that occurred prior to each taped session and during the dinner at Applebee's Restaurant.

We constantly felt the dialectical oppositions operating within our intimate conversations as we moved back and forth between expression and protection and between disclosure and restraint (Bochner 1984). Taking into account the feelings of all participants was a major concern during our research. We were eager to understand each other and the issues we addressed more deeply; at the same time, we wanted to protect one another from distress and harm. With these goals in mind, we tried to develop trust by openly sharing our lives, but we also had to respect each other's needs for privacy and restraint. Verbal responses, nonverbal cues, and our own feelings guided what we said and asked, which sometimes meant holding back comments until they seemed more appropriate. We probed gently, listened attentively, and let interaction flow "naturally" in an atmosphere that grew more candid, open, and trusting. For example, it was not until the last draft of this chapter that Carolyn felt sufficiently comfortable to disclose that Lisa's and Christine's purging sometimes horrified her and to express her "horror" in writing. Only then did she feel confident that her forthrightness would not devastate her collaborators. And, as would be true in any research of this kind, she asked their consent before expressing those feelings here.

As our relationship became more intimate, we revisited previous discussions to probe what we had been feeling and thinking earlier in the process. These conversations (and conversations about the conversations) stimulated us to talk about when to let go of a topic, when to protect the other's silence, and how to handle emotional topics in other contexts with interviewees who may not have research training. These discussions raised questions about what responsibilities we have for our subjects in any research situation (Ellis 1995; Richardson 1996), for the questions we ask them, for the stories we tell about them, and for the lives our stories represent.

Although we gained considerable understanding of how bulimia is experienced through our open revelations, our stories also show silences and unanswered questions that are usually concealed from awareness in other research contexts. We may pursue these silences in future sessions or write individually about them. Or we may leave them alone. As our narratives demonstrate, Christine and Lisa felt they could be more candid in writing than in a face-to-face encounter. From this, we learned that if respondents seem reticent about a topic or find it too emotionally disturbing, they can be offered another means of expression—for example, the opportunity to write or tape their stories in private. Discussing pictures in photo albums or participating together in leisure activities are other alternatives that might produce a comfort level for personal disclosure. We now understand more fully that people have different modes of and different comfort levels for expressing their lives.

We have been careful not to open up conversations that we were unprepared for emotionally or that we did not have time to address sufficiently. In our desire to let communication flow naturally, we have not attempted to stop emotional catharsis from happening nor moved eagerly to make it take place. Thus far, our conversations have not reached the peak of emotional intensity that might take place in psychotherapy; still, on several occasions, it has been appropriate to offer emotional support and advice to each other. Although we have acknowledged the potential awkwardness of emotional purging and counseling within a research context, we are receptive to our conversations moving further in those directions.

The reflexive quality of our interactive research has forced us to question the hard-and-fast boundaries traditionally erected between therapy and research. Both Christine and Lisa have commented on the personal understanding they have gained from this research and the therapeutic value of writing for each other as an audience. Keeping the welfare of each other in mind, they admit to giving the stories they write about each other hopeful, albeit narratively coherent and "true," endings (Fisher 1984). Their experience leads us to posit "personal understanding," "hope," and "helping each other live useful lives" as reasonable factors in determining which of the many stories we decide to compose from "our data" (Bochner and Ellis 1996). To the extent that research makes a difference in people's lives, it always has a therapeutic dimension; to the extent that people want to understand emotional and bodily practices, such as eating disorders, and even work to change personal and cultural constructions of these experiences, interactive interviewing provides an avenue for reflexively exploring those possibilities.

REFERENCES

Abu-Lughod, L. 1995. "A Tale of Two Pregnancies." Pp. 339-49 in *Women Writing Culture,* edited by R. Behar and D. Gordon. Berkeley: University of California Press.

Agronick, G. and R. Helson. 1996. "Who Benefits from an Examined Life? Correlates of Influence Attributed to Participation in a Longitudinal Study." Pp. 80-93 in *Ethics and Process in the Narrative Study of Lives* (vol. 4), edited by R. Josselson. Thousand Oaks, CA: Sage.

Anderson, K., S. Armitage, D. Jack, and J. Wittner. 1987. "Beginning Where We Are: Feminist Methodology in Oral History." *Oral History Review* 15:103-27.

Apter, T. 1996. "Expert Witness: Who Controls the Psychologist's Narrative?" Pp. 22-44 in *Ethics and Process in the Narrative Study of Lives* (vol. 4), edited by R. Josselson. Thousand Oaks, CA: Sage.

Austin, D. 1996. "Kaleidoscope: The Same and Different." Pp. 206-30 in *Composing Ethnography: Alternative Forms of Qualitative Writing,* edited by C. Ellis and A. P. Bochner. Walnut Creek, CA: AltaMira Press.

Bar-On, D. 1996. "Ethical Issues in Biographical Interviews and Analysis." Pp. 9-21 in *Ethics and Process in the Narrative Study of Lives* (vol. 4), edited by R. Josselson. Thousand Oaks, CA: Sage.

Behar, R. 1995. "Writing in My Father's Name: A Diary of Translated Woman's First Year." Pp. 65-82 in *Women Writing Culture,* edited by R. Behar and D. Gordon. Berkeley: University of California Press.

Belenky, M. F., B. Clinchy, N. Goldberger, and J. M. Turule. 1981-1982. "Listening to Women's Voices." *Newsletter, Education for Women's Development Project,* no. 2. Great Barrington, MA: Simon's Rock of Bard College.

Bergen, R. K. 1993. "Interviewing Survivors of Marital Rape: Doing Feminist Research on Sensitive Topics." Pp. 197-211 in *Researching Sensitive Topics,* edited by C. Renzetti and R. Lee. Newbury Park, CA: Sage.

Bird, S. E. 1995. "Understanding the Ethnographic Encounter: The Need for Flexibility in Feminist Reception Studies." *Women and Language* 18(2):23-27.

Bloom, L. 1996. "Stories of One's Own: Nonunitary Subjectivity in Narrative Representation." *Qualitative Inquiry* 2:176-97.

Bochner, A. P. 1984. "The Functions of Communication in Interpersonal Bonding." Pp. 544-621 in *Handbook of Rhetorical and Communication Theory,* edited by C. Arnold and J. Bowers. Boston: Allyn & Bacon.

Bochner, A. P., and C. Ellis. 1992. "Personal Narrative as a Social Approach to Interpersonal Communication." *Communication Theory* 2:165-72.

————. 1996. "Talking Over Ethnography." Pp. 13-45 in *Composing Ethnography: Alternative Forms of Qualitative Writing,* edited by C. Ellis and A. P. Bochner. Walnut Creek, CA: AltaMira Press.

Brannen, J. 1988. "The Study of Sensitive Subjects." *Sociological Review* 36:552-63.

Briggs, C. 1986. *Learning How to Ask: A Sociolinguistic Appraisal of the Role of the Interview in Social Science Research.* Cambridge, UK: Cambridge University Press.

Bristow, A. R., and J. A. Esper. 1988. "A Feminist Research Ethos." In *A Feminist Ethic for Social Science Research,* edited by Nebraska Sociological Feminist Collective. New York: Edwin Mellen.

Bruner, J. 1986. *Actual Minds, Possible Worlds.* Cambridge, MA: Harvard University Press.

Chase, S. 1996. "Personal Vulnerability and Interpretive Authority in Narrative Research." Pp. 45-59 in *Ethics and Process in the Narrative Study of Lives* (vol. 4), edited by R. Josselson. Thousand Oaks, CA: Sage.

Chase, S. and C. Bell. 1994. "Interpreting the Complexity of Women's Subjectivity." Pp. 63-81 in *Interactive Oral History Interviewing,* edited by E. McMahon and K. L. Rogers. Hillsdale, NJ: Lawrence Erlbaum.

Collins, P. H. 1986. "Learning from the Outsider Within: The Sociological Significance of Black Feminist Thought." *Social Problems* 33:14-32.

Cook J. and M. M. Fonow. 1986. "Knowledge and Women's Interests: Issues of Epistemology and Methodology in Feminist Sociological Research." *Sociological Inquiry* 56:2-27.

DeVault, M. 1990. "Talking and Listening from Women's Standpoint: Feminist Strategies for Interviewing and Analysis." *Social Problems* 37:96-116.

Douglas, J. 1985. *Creative Interviewing.* Beverly Hills, CA: Sage.

Duelli Klein, R. 1983. "How to Do What We Want to Do: Thoughts about Feminist Methodology." In *Theories of Women's Studies,* edited by G. Bowles and R. Duelli Klein. London: Routledge & Kegan Paul.

Edwards, R. 1993. "An Education in Interviewing: Placing the Researcher and the Research." Pp. 181-96 in *Researching Sensitive Topics,* edited by C. Renzetti and R. Lee. Newbury Park, CA: Sage.

Ellis, C. 1991a. "Sociological Introspection and Emotional Experience." *Symbolic Interaction* 14:23-50.

———. 1991b. "Emotional Sociology." Pp. 123-45 in *Studies in Symbolic Interaction* (vol. 12), edited by N. Denzin. Greenwich, CT: JAI.

———. 1993. " 'There Are Survivors': Telling a Story of Sudden Death." *Sociological Quarterly* 34:711-30.

———. 1995. *Final Negotiations: A Story of Love, Loss, and Chronic Illness.* Philadelphia: Temple University Press.

Ellis, C. and A. P. Bochner. 1992. "Telling and Performing Personal Stories: The Constraints of Choice in Abortion." Pp. 79-101 in *Investigating Subjectivity: Research on Lived Experience,* edited by C. Ellis and M. Flaherty. Newbury Park, CA: Sage.

———. 1996. *Composing Ethnography: Alternative Forms of Qualitative Writing.* Walnut Creek, CA: AltaMira Press.

Finch, J. 1984. " 'It's Great to Have Someone to Talk To': The Ethics and Politics of Interviewing Women." Pp. 70-87 in *Social Researching: Politics, Problems, Practice,* edited by C. Bell and H. Roberts. London: Routledge & Kegan Paul.

Fisher, W. 1984. "Narration as a Human Communication Paradigm: The Case of Public Moral Argument." *Communication Monographs* 51:1-22.

Fox, K. 1996. "Silent Voices: A Subversive Reading of Child Sexual Abuse." Pp. 330-47 in *Composing Ethnography: Alternative Forms of Qualitative Writing,* edited by C. Ellis and A. P. Bochner. Walnut Creek, CA: AltaMira Press.

Futrell, A. and C. Willard. 1994. Pp. 83-105 in *Interactive Oral History Interviewing,* edited by E. McMahon and K. L. Rogers. Hillsdale, NJ: Lawrence Erlbaum.

Gray, J. L. and P. Geist. Forthcoming. "Elation and Devastation: Women's Journeys through Pregnancy and Miscarriage." In *Women's Words, Women's Worlds,* edited by L. A. M. Perry and P. Geist.

Griffith, A. and D. Smith. 1987. "Constructing Cultural Knowledge: Mothering as Discourse." Pp. 87-103 in *Women and Education,* edited by J. Gaskell and A. T. McLaren. Calgary, Alberta: Detselig Enterprises Limited.

Hertz, R. 1995. "Separate But Simultaneous Interviewing of Husbands and Wives: Making Sense of Their Stories." *Qualitative Inquiry* 1:429-51.

Holstein, J. and J. Gubrium. 1995. *The Active Interview.* Thousand Oaks, CA: Sage.

Hutchinson, S., M. Wilson, and H. S. Wilson. 1994. "Benefits of Participating in Research Interviews." *IMAGE: Journal of Nursing Scholarship* 26:161-64.

Jago, B. 1996. "Postcards, Ghosts, and Fathers: Revising Family Stories." *Qualitative Inquiry* 2:1 495-516.

Jorgenson, J. 1991. "Co-Constructing the Interviewer/Co-Constructing 'Family.' " Pp. 210-25 in *Research and Reflexivity,* edited by F. Steier. London: Sage.

———. 1995. "Relationalizing Rapport in Interpersonal Settings." Pp. 155-70 in *Social Approaches to Communication,* edited by W. Leeds-Hurwitz. New York: Guilford.

Josselson, R. 1996. "On Writing Other People's Lives: Self-Analytic Reflections of a Narrative Researcher." Pp. 60-71 in *Ethics and Process in the Narrative Study of Lives* (vol. 4), edited by R. Josselson. Thousand Oaks, CA: Sage.

Kiesinger, C. 1992. "Writing It Down: Sisters, Food, Eating, and Body Image." Unpublished manuscript, University of South Florida.

Kiesinger, C. 1995. "Anorexic and Bulimic Lives: Making Sense of Food and Eating." Unpublished dissertation, University of South Florida.

Kolker, A. 1996. "Thrown Overboard: The Human Costs of Health Care Rationing." Pp. 133-59 in *Composing Ethnography: Alternative Forms of Qualitative Writing,* edited by C. Ellis and A. P. Bochner. Walnut Creek, CA: AltaMira Press.

Krieger, S. 1991. *Social Science and the Self: Personal Essays on an Art Form.* New Brunswick, NJ: Rutgers University Press.

Kvale, S. 1996. *InterViews: An Introduction to Qualitative Research Interviewing.* Thousand Oaks, CA: Sage.

Langellier, K. and D. Hall. 1989. "Interviewing Women: A Phenomenological Approach to Feminist Communication Research." Pp. 193-220 in *Doing Research on Women's Communication,* edited by K. Carter and C. Spitzack. Norwood, NJ: Ablex.

Laslett, B. and R. Rapoport. 1975. "Collaborative Interviewing and Interactive Research." *Journal of Marriage and the Family* 20:968-77.

Lewis, J. and B. Meredith. 1988. *Daughters Who Care: Daughters Caring for Mothers at Home.* London: Routledge & Kegan Paul.

Lieblich, A. 1996. "Some Unforeseen Outcomes of Conducting Narrative Research with People of One's Own Culture." Pp. 151-84 in *Ethics and Process in the Narrative Study of Lives* (vol. 4), edited by R. Josselson. Thousand Oaks, CA: Sage.

Linden, R. R. 1993. *Making Stories, Making Selves.* Columbus: Ohio State University Press.

McMahan, E. and K. L. Rogers, eds. 1994. *Interactive Oral History Interviewing.* Hillsdale, NJ: Lawrence Erlbaum.

Mies, M. 1983. "Toward a Methodology for Feminist Research." In *Theories of Women's Studies,* edited by G. Bowles and R. Duelli Klein. London: Routledge & Kegan Paul.

Miller, M. 1996. "Ethics and Understanding Through Interrelationship: I and Thou in Dialogue." Pp. 129-47 in *Ethics and Process in the Narrative Study of Lives* (vol. 4), edited by R. Josselson. Thousand Oaks, CA: Sage.

Mishler, E. 1986. *Research Interviewing: Context and Narrative.* Cambridge, MA: Harvard University Press.

Myerhoff, B. 1992. *Remembered Lives.* Ann Arbor: University of Michigan Press.

Mykhalowskiy, E. 1997. "Reconsidering Table Talk: Critical Thoughts on the Relationship Between Sociology, Autobiography and Self-Indulgence." Pp. 229-251 in *Reflexivity and Voice,* edited by R. Hertz. Thousand Oaks, CA: Sage.

Oakley, A. 1981. "Interviewing Women: A Contradiction in Terms." Pp. 30-61 in *Doing Feminist Research,* edited by H. Roberts. London: Routledge & Kegan Paul.

Ochberg, R. 1996. "Interpreting Life Stories." Pp. 97-113 in *Ethics and Process in the Narrative Study of Lives* (vol. 4), edited by R. Josselson. Thousand Oaks, CA: Sage.

Parry, A. 1991. "A Universe of Stories." *Family Process* 30:37-54.

Payne, D. 1996. "Autobiology." Pp. 49-75 in *Composing Ethnography: Alternative Forms of Qualitative Writing,* edited by C. Ellis and A. P. Bochner. Walnut Creek, CA: AltaMira Press.

Perry, J. 1996. "Writing the Self: Exploring the Stigma of Hearing Impairment." *Sociological Spectrum* 16:239-61.

Platt, J. 1981. "On Interviewing One's Peers." *British Journal of Sociology* 32 (March): 75-91.

Ponticelli, C. 1996. "The Spiritual Warfare of Exodus: A Postpositivist Research Adventure." *Qualitative Inquiry* 2:198-219.

Quinney, R. 1996. "Once My Father Traveled West to California." Pp. 349-74 in *Composing Ethnography: Alternative Forms of Qualitative Writing,* edited by C. Ellis and A. P. Bochner. Walnut Creek, CA: AltaMira Press.

Reinharz, S. 1992. *Feminist Methods in Social Research.* New York: Oxford University Press.

Renzetti, C. and R. Lee, eds. 1993. *Researching Sensitive Topics.* Newbury Park, CA: Sage.

Richardson, L. 1992. "The Consequences of Poetic Representation: Writing the Other, Rewriting the Self." Pp. 125-37 in *Investigating Subjectivity: Research on Lived Experience,* edited by C. Ellis and M. Flaherty. Newbury Park, CA: Sage.

———. 1996. "Responses to Whyte: Ethnographic Trouble." *Qualitative Inquiry* 2:227-29.

———. 1997. *Fields of Play: Constructing an Academic Life.* New Brunswick, NJ: Rutgers University Press.

Riessman, C. K. 1987. "When Gender Is Not Enough: Women Interviewing Women." *Gender & Society* 1:172-207.

———. 1993. *Narrative Analysis.* Newbury Park, CA: Sage.

Roberts, H. 1981. *Doing Feminist Research.* London: Routledge & Kegan Paul.

Robillard, A. 1997. "Communication Problems in the Intensive Care Unit." Pp. 252-264 in *Reflexivity and Voice,* edited by R. Hertz. Thousand Oaks, CA: Sage.

Ronai, C. R. 1992. "The Reflexive Self through Narrative: A Night in the Life of an Erotic Dancer/Researcher." Pp. 102-24 in *Investigating Subjectivity: Research on Lived Experience,* edited by C. Ellis and M. Flaherty. Newbury Park, CA: Sage.

———. 1995. "Multiple Reflections of Child Sex Abuse: An Argument for a Layered Account." *Journal of Contemporary Ethnography* 23:395-426.

Rosenwald, G. 1996. "Making Whole: Method and Ethics in Mainstream and Narrative Psychology." Pp. 245-74 in *Ethics and Process in the Narrative Study of Lives* (vol. 4), edited by R. Josselson. Thousand Oaks, CA: Sage.

Rothman, B. K. 1986. "Reflections: On Hard Work." *Qualitative Sociology* 9:48-53.

Shostak, A. B., ed. 1996. *Private Sociology: Unsparing Reflections, Uncommon Gains.* Dix Hills, NY: General Hall.

Stacey, J. 1988. "Can There Be a Feminist Ethnography?" *Women's Studies International Forum* 11:21-27.

Stanley, L. and S. Wise. 1983. " 'Back Into the Personal' or: Our Attempt to Construct 'Feminist Research'." In *Theories of Women's Studies,* edited by G. Bowles and R. D. Klein. London: Routledge & Kegan Paul.

Stringer, E. 1996. *Action Research: A Handbook for Practitioners.* Thousand Oaks, CA: Sage.

Suchman, L. and B. Jordan. 1992. "Validity and the Collaborative Construction of Meaning in Face-to-Face Surveys." Pp. 241-67 in *Questions about Questions: Inquiries into the Cognitive Bases of Surveys,* edited by J. Tanur. New York: Russell Sage.

Tillmann-Healy, L. 1996a. "A Secret Life in a Culture of Thinness: Reflections on Body, Food, and Bulimia." Pp. 77-109 in *Composing Ethnography: Alternative Forms of Qualitative Writing,* edited by C. Ellis and A. P. Bochner. Walnut Creek, CA: AltaMira Press.

———. 1996b. "Bulimic Biographies: Through a Shared Silence." Unpublished manuscript, University of South Florida.

Tripp, D. 1983. "Co-Authorship and Negotiation: The Interview as Act of Creation." *Interchange* 14:32-45.

Yerby, J. and W. Gourd. 1994. "Our Marriage/Their Marriage: Performing Reflexive Fieldwork." Paper presented at the annual Couch and Stone Symposium, Society for the Study of Symbolic Interaction, University of Illinois, Urbana-Champagne.

Zola, I. K. 1982. *Missing Pieces: A Chronicle of Living with a Disability.* Philadelphia: Temple University Press.

7

Reflexivity, Feminism, and Difference

Rahel R. Wasserfall

This chapter addresses the relation of feminist methodology to political commitments. The claim of commonalities among women conflates enormous differences among varied groups of women. These differences—of power, culture, belief, political commitments, ethnicity, class—cannot be easily transcended. Even if those differences are more and more becoming a topic of controversy in feminist studies (Moore 1988, Ferguson 1991), there is still a struggle over the meaning of commonality stemming from gender and an assumption that being a woman conducting research among women will help overcome the tensions stemming from these differences. For example, Rebecca Klatch working in "politically resistant communities," found that she had difficulties juggling the contradictory beliefs and values of her informants. Nevertheless, feelings of empathy toward informants based on shared gender identity arose and changed her way she would not have believed before she began the study (1982:82-85).[1]

Feminist theory and feminist methods generally include in their definitions a reference to reflexivity or self-reflexivity as a method to translate the types of differences noted above (Stanley and Wise 1990). Lately, feminists scholars such

[handwritten margin notes: "LJt is a politically resistance community", "identifications", "feelings + understanding another's situation"]

EDITOR'S NOTE: This chapter originally appeared as an article in *Qualitative Sociology*, Vol. 15, No. 1, 1993. Reprinted by permission of Human Sciences Press, Inc.

as Stacey (1991) have called for a dialogue between reflexive, self critical ethnographic literature and feminist methodological reflections. This response is much needed in feminists' work against what Patai (1991) calls the New Orthodoxy in feminist scholars engaging in ethnographic research. The kind of reflexivity proposed by postmodern literature could help prevent raising expectations and making wrong assumptions in ethnographic research and help promote a more ethical approach to social scientific research. Indeed, the underlying assumption in some post-modern ethnographic literature is that by being reflexive in one's field work, one may deal successfully with difficult issues of the difference in the research project as well as in the written text.

This stance toward reflexive methods has been recognized as useful in anthropology since the 1970's (Rabinow 1977, Kaplan 1984, Clifford 1986) as a reaction to a classical, and thus, "colonial" anthropology. It emphasizes the researcher as compassionate and reflexive forming nonexploitative relations with one's informants (see P. Golde 1986). With the "Interpretive Turn" in the social sciences, when objectivity is being questioned and the issue of the power involved in the process of knowledge is recognized, the ethnographer herself comes under scrutiny. What she brings to her field and how her specific social self and background influences the ways she gives meanings to her informants' lives and represents them becomes part of the methodological questions being raised in anthropology. Some argue that the researcher has become the instrument of his/her search (Storper and Wasserfall 1988) and so reflexivity has become one of the most important tools for controlling the acquisition of knowledge, by providing a monitor over the problem of subjective influences of the researcher on her topic. Yet, reflexivity is still ill defined (Watson 1987) and its meanings and underlying assumptions taken for granted.

The use of reflexivity can be characterized by a "weak" and a "strong" reading. Very broadly, what may be called the "weak" reading of reflexivity is a continued self-awareness about the ongoing relationship between a researcher and informants, which is certainly epistemologically useful: the researcher becomes more aware of constructing knowledge and of the influences of her beliefs, backgrounds and feelings in the process of researching.[2] Reflexivity is a position of a certain kind of praxis where there is a continuous checking on the accomplishment of understanding. (See among the many social scientist, using the weak reading of reflexivity Reinharz 1983, Shostak 1981, Rabinow 1977). The "strong" reading, on the other hand, contains certain assumptions or the deconstruction of the authority of the author and/or of the power difference in the field. These assumptions gloss over difficult theoretical and political tensions in which ethnographic knowledge is produced and consumed (See Mies

1983: Stanley and Wise 1990: Duelli Klein 1983 for feminists social scientists and Marcus and Fisher 1986, for the new ethnography-post modernist anthropologists).

In this chapter I will offer an analysis of some aspects of these assumptions and argue that reflexivity cannot be easily called upon to ease some of the tensions existing in doing feminist fieldwork. Reflexivity is not in itself a process for overcoming distortion or exploitation. More specifically I argue that the careful monitoring of one's own subjectivity, which is at the core of any use of the term, does not have in all situations a potential to keep distortion away. When one finds oneself doing research with people one basically likes and finds a sharing of basic fundamental principles, the uncovering of these premises—via reflexivity—can reinforce the idea that only through the process of reflexivity can one conduct an ethical study. However, in case of conflicts regarding basic political stands or fundamental principles, difference becomes marked and difficulties may arise.

THE PROMISES AND PROBLEMS
OF THE STRONG READING

A) Deconstruction of the Authority of the Author

Concentration v — mind
Careful consideration of oth
Chg self constantly

Catch more— According to Myerhoff and Ruby (1982) reflexivity is the process by which
flies w/ money an anthropologist understands how her social background influences and shapes her beliefs and how this self awareness pertains to what and how she observes, attributes meanings, interprets action and dialogues with her informants. Reflexivity is a process by which an ethnographer while engaging in her fieldwork becomes more aware and produces a "better representation,"[3] more in tune with
Reflexivity the reality she encounters. According to this position the use of reflexivity during
brings a fieldwork can mute the distance and alienation built into conventional notions
closer of "objectivity" or objectifying those who are studied. The research process
relationship becomes more mutual, as a strategy to deconstruct the author's authority. But as
(friends) many anthropologists recognized in the past ten years, authors, when they
but — subject present competing world views and how these views are embedded in the life
is always experiences of the actors, ultimately control the representations of those studied.
aware of Even "multivocal" ethnographies are controlled by the ethnographer as some of
an authority · the essays of *Interpreting Women's Lives* (1989) strongly acknowledged. The issue of interpretive authority is particularly problematic for feminist ethnographers, for our work often involves a tension between, on one hand the agenda

of empowering the women we work with by revealing the meanings they give to their lives; and on the other hand our political vision of the structural conditions that lead to the choices they made, a vision they themselves may not recognize as valid.[4] A second strategy used by reflexive feminists in deconstructing their own authority is to identify and contextualize oneself, but as Patai (1991 p. 149) strongly states, "those rhetorical maneuvers . . . are rapidly acquiring the status of incantations." While they may contextualize the study they do not erase the tension stemming from the fact that the ultimate responsibility toward the written work lies with the ethnographer. At best these identifications construct another frame of authority, another story, they do not erase it. Authority is an unavoidable ever if difficult issue for feminist ethnographers.

They may be contented happy. ie Culture

But it does minimize it.

I don't agree but I'm two faced resulting I like you but I don't understand you better. U attitude Social Works + - Welfare recipient.

B) Difference and Power

Prevalent in or peculiar to a particular locality or people

The second assumption of those advocating the "strong reading" of reflexivity is that the issues of difference and power—endemic to researcher/subject relationship—could be directly confronted and worked through via reflexivity. For feminists do not want only to learn about reality but they also want to help change the social reality in which women live their lives (Mies 1983, Stacey 1991, Stanley and Wise 1990). For example, in their critique of Postmodernism, Mascia-Lees, Sharpe and Cohen (1989) make the point that while sharing some of the agenda of Postmodernism as feminists they strongly differ from it because postmodernism precludes the possibility of liberating political action.

On closer scrutiny, this political agenda of feminists scholars reveal a tension between knowing and changing. Acknowledging the political agenda of feminism and calling for self-reflexivity and exposing biases does not in itself ease the tension of power difference between the researcher and her informants. What exactly can a feminist ethnographer do to help change her informants lives while conducting her research according to the canons of her own discipline (Patai 1991)? Some ethnographers like Berger Gluck (1991) will certainly choose to solve this tension by becoming the advocate of the people they study. Some others like Gorelick (1989) and myself once believed in the power of methodology to make them very sensitive to their informants needs and feelings, while not becoming alienated by the tension itself. This is why, I believe reflexivity is so important but it can also be misleading in its strong reading for the researcher.

But it adds a deeper dimension of understanding & bonding w the informant. They comes wn wn informed resources.

Oakley (1981), Finch (1984), Stanley and Wise (1990) and many others in feminist social science believe that "knowing" will help change the lives of informants. Certainly knowing is a form of empowerment, of changing, but for whom? Ethnographers have recognized for a long time the discrepancy between their "goals" and the desire of their informants. It is usual for an ethnographer to struggle with her informants to explain what "good" will come out of a study "for them" as Laura Nader (1986) recalled of her field work in 1957 among Zapotec Indians. Will it be possible that not only "roads, trains" can help informants' lives but that by being very sensitive and using reflexivity of the process of gaining knowledge itself, insights gained by the scholar will not only empower the scholars but also the informants? In the tension between knowing/changing which is part of the theoretical apparatus of a critical and engaged social scientist, lies the need for the "strong" reading of reflexivity as a way to ease questions of difference and power.[5]

For Myerhoff reflexivity was a process that made the researcher as well as some key informants conscious of both the frame and the contents of social life; thus reflexivity was for her at the core of grasping the "broader" meaning of one's life and social action (Myerhoff 1979). A reflexive mode implies a distance and unity at once, and because of that, can make one aware of oneself as subject and object as well as of the process that creates the consciousness of both. As ethnographers we want to learn about our informants but as reflexive ethnographers we also learn about our own lives in the process of grasping how the lives of others could teach us something about all lives (Prell 1989). Here lies that potential for change inherent in the reflexive stance—the learning itself—is viewed as empowering the scholar while the recording is a political act, and thus may help change the informants' lives. Further, the political capacity embedded in the "strong" reading of reflexivity is the assumption that the "uplifting" the scholar feels when suddenly grasping both herself and the frame could be shared by the informant and empower her.[6]

However, reflexivity in its "strong reading" did not help me with my goals of being a compassionate and a non-exploitative researcher. When I found myself in a field situation where I shared citizenship with my informants but found myself in strong conflict regarding the content of "Israelness" and the future of the country, reflexivity in its strong reading did not help. The issue of power difference led to the following salient question: How do I represent a group of people with whom I had strong conflict, whom I disliked and from whom I felt alienated? I studied a Moshav (cooperative village) of Moroccan Jewish and focused on their ways of constructing their gender and national identities. Let me explain some of the multiple dimensions of the differences between myself and my informants. I am a French Israeli citizen, ethnic Ashkenazi and a Jewish woman who differed strongly from my informants, fellow Israeli citizens, in my attitudes toward the Palestinian question, how to achieve peace, and the future of Israeli society. While I actually believed that plurality was at the core of the construction of Israeli society, I also counted on my reflexive praxis to deal in compassionate and non-exploitative ways with our difference. I will argue on the basis of my field experience that reflexivity has its own limits (a shared belief system). In a situation of intense conflict, reflexivity did not provide me with the necessary tools to overcome my subjectivity but may even have "helped" me select certain aspects of "reality" and reinforce a stereotype of a certain image of aggressiveness in the Moroccan Jewish community. I believe that a "weak" reading is even more necessary in the case of a discordant belief system in order for the researcher to try to understand her own perspective, and to understand the informants from their "own point of view." However, ethnographers cannot pretend to present fully their informants' voices: they have to take responsibility for their intrusions both in their informants' lives and the representation of those lives. This stance also cannot ease political tensions. I still wonder what impact my descriptions had on the perpetuation of certain images of the Moroccan Jews in the Israeli context.

JUDAISM, FEMINISM
AND ETHNICITY IN ISRAEL[7]

It is extremely difficult to untangle Judaism, Feminism and Ethnicity in Israel; those are in fact interactive and linked to each other in more than one way. In regard to Judaism, intense struggles over the meanings of Jewishness which is collective identity leave little room for any other more particular category of identification, special gender. For example, it is difficult to build solidarity between Jewish-Israeli women and Palestinian women on the basis of shared gender, the inter-ethnic and national conflicts are overriding. Between Jewish women (myself and my informants), as I argue in this chapter, issues pertaining to the definitions of Jewishness may have undermined a commonality based on a shared gender.

Since the 1980's in Israel, several grass roots movements of feminists working for peace goals have arisen (e.g., as Women in Black, Sheni = Women against the Occupation; Women for Women Political Prisoners, Women for du kiuom; Umbrella for Women for Peace) (Deutsch 1990). Israeli society has a history of women's movements as well as a women's worker movement under the umbrella of the labor party. Although some women did organize for membership in parliament, their lists had no success in the different elections. This notwithstanding, political and public participation of women in Israel is low. It is generally acknowledged that Israeli Jewish women are very tolerant of inequality and that feminist goals are weak in Israel (Izraeli and Tabori 1986 and Izraeli 1987).

For the Jewish Moroccan population, women and men have generally accepted the traditional distribution of inequality. In this context, committed as I was to empowering the lives of women, my study focused on the lives of women in order to study their beliefs and meanings, to describe their own ways of being what they are, how they solve their dilemmas, and finally, to bring back to the university, a sum of knowledge about women that previously was not ever considered worthy of academic research.

Massive emigrations of Jews from Muslim countries, commonly called by the Israeli public Sephardi Jews,[8] took place in the 1950's. The people who emigrated were mostly religious, Zionist-messianic and generally poor, and were perceived by Israelis (most of whom at that time were from Ashkenazi origin) as traditional at best and generally backward and in need of "modernization' (becoming Israeli = becoming Ashkenazi, i.e., shedding their cultural heritage, changing food habits, etc.). The relation between Ashkenazi Jews, who formed the political cultural and economic elites, and Sephardi Jews has been the topic of many studies over the years. Generally scholars agree that there was stereotyping from both sides, and Swirski, S. (1981 and 1989) even argues that Israel in the 1970's and early 1980's, developed into Ethno-classes with the Moroccan Jews at the bottom, a "second Israel" (second class) with a second generation of poverty.

The political ascendance of the right wing parties (Herut, Gahal and now the Likud), is generally associated with an influx of Sephardi voters in their rank, raging against the old paternalistic Ashkenazi establishment. One of the results of the right wing ascension was a renewed process of reevaluation of the Moroccan culture which had been stereotyped as aggressive and backward. Moroccan Jews came to be seen as more nationalistic than the Ashkenazi, less willing to withdraw from Gaza and the West Bank in exchange for a peace settlement with the Arab countries and the Palestinians. ˡⁱᵏᵉ ᶜⁱᵛⁱˡ ᴿⁱᵍʰᵗˢ

To give an example of everyday life of this process of reevaluation of the Jewish Moroccan beliefs and mentality, in 1983 during my field work, one young man became proud of his traditional behavior which was coined by the Ashkenazi as "primitive." He proudly attested that he thought of himself as 'primitive' with regard to women's work. In traditional Moroccan Jewish culture, women are not supposed to work outside the home, as it reflects poorly on the masculinity of their husbands (see Wasserfall 1990). This self-labelling,

I believe, would not have been possible before the ascension of the right wing and its reevaluation of the Jewish Moroccan culture.

EVERYDAY LIFE OF THIS PROCESS

The mood in Israel during and after the Lebanon war (1982) was that of polarization between two "Israels," between two politically incompatible views which were also perceived in ethnic terms. This was the context in which I began my fieldwork in 1983 on gender identification. I was on the political left of Israeli society, but my commitment to anthropological analysis led me to believe that harm had been done to the Moroccans and that their value orientation was an outcome of their historical position in Israeli society. I was sure that I would find a common language with my informants as I did with the previous ones.[9] I was sure that the common Jewish heritage would overcome any difference I would encounter and that my feminism (i.e., sympathy for women's hardship) would help me deal with difficult situations. What I did not and could not take into account was the terrible polarization that occurred in Israel after the Lebanon war. The government led by Menachem Begin and Ariel Sharon tried to delegitimize any critical position of the "Peace Now" movement and those opposing right wing positions were labelled as traitors. The political debate rapidly lost its rational content and became heated by feelings of hatred toward those (the young and not so young Ashkenazi intellectuals who formed and were the bulk of the movement) who did not hold right wing positions and were seen as leading Israel to doom. The streets of Jerusalem were very "heated," people were losing their patience, political disagreement often turned violent, and I found myself (as did my friends) becoming aware that I was slowly hiding my feelings and political opinions in public: the streets in those days belonged to the right.

REFLEXIVITY IN PRAXIS

Having now sketched the broader Israeli context which fueled my sense of difference and undermined any feeling of commonality, let me present the event that catalyzed all those feelings. As I noted briefly, my informants were traditional and in a very difficult economic situation. They also held right wing political commitments (the Moshav was part of the right wing association of Moshavim). This did not become an issue for me until a peace movement activist was killed by a right wing person in a peaceful demonstration in Jerusalem. My

informants were "understanding" (mevinim) of the murder and kept calling the
peace activists with whom I identify "traitors."

I was listening to the news in the company of my landlord and his wife when
the murder was covered on the evening news. While I was terribly upset and
tried to call friends to learn who the casualty was, my hosts were not at all
shocked and seemed to enjoy the whole issue. The next morning I made my
usual morning visit to the only grocery shop in the moshav. There some men
and women stood discussing the event and not only "understanding" the event
but saying that the peace movement had brought it on itself with their traitorous
political positions. "Magia lahem" "they deserve it" was the common attitude.
I burst into tears and asked one older man with whom I was very friendly, "if I
would have stood there would you have thrown the grenade?" They laughed and
he did not answer; it was a very difficult moment. A few days later the same man
commented on my behavior by saying that I was too emotional; " . . . what can
you expect from a woman!" He called on our Jewish-commonality by saying
that we ought to make peace between us. Hate was to blame, he added and by
loving each other we would overcome the difficulties. By calling on my
emotionality as a woman, I believe, he moved the potential political threat of
our different positions into a gender issue and so could misread my political
commitments. He could again relate to me as Rahel the Jewish anthropologist
perhaps a bit too emotional, but a friend nevertheless. By calling on our shared
Jewishness he put forward what he thought as the ideological cement of Israeli
society. Jewishness is called upon without questioning its content and assuming
that everybody involved accept the speaker's view of what kind of Jewish life
one should lead. This helps re-establish if only for the moment the feeling of
commonality so much needed by Israelis.

I also had an interest in playing down the event. I was in the midst of a crisis
concerning my commitment to my study and was becoming ever more aware of
the emotional difficulties some of my informants' behavior stirred in me. What
should I have done in this situation? Where did my feminism stand when my
other political commitments were questioned? I flirted with the idea of leaving
the village but I had too much already invested in the research. I stayed and went
on with my initial project; I did not try to reshape my interest for example and
study their political commitments. Instead, believing in the power of reflexivity,
I tried to analyze the ways we handled the difficult situation, but until this
chapter, I never tried to incorporate these events into my anthropological work.
My analysis of the situation helped me to clear my feelings, I understood but
could not help my harsh feelings against my informants. I became more goal
oriented and decided to further my own goals without taking my informants'

needs and desires into consideration. In fact, this event had a terrible influence on my relations with my informants. It catalyzed the negative feelings I had tried to hide. For example I suffered from the verbal aggressiveness I experienced in the moshav, verbal aggressiveness between spouses, with their children and also with me. I was at some point the target of verbal sexual aggressiveness by some of my male informants (see Storper and Wasserfall 1988 for an analysis of one of those incidents of verbal aggression). After the murder of the peace activist I more consciously disliked my informants as a group but found solace in the company of certain individuals whose positions I could ignore in private.

When interviewing in the privacy of their homes, I found myself facing individuals with whom I could relate on the basis of our shared human-beingness (e.g., gender, difficulties in struggling for meaningful lives, jewishness . . .). In those cases, I could relate to my informants' life struggles as an individual and as such find in my personal repertoire, resource of empathy as Klatch did when she interviewed women from a "resistant community" (1988). When I used participant observer methods in public, I found myself facing a collective as a member of a different collective with different or opposite values to the community studied. As a participant observer, I used a more holistic approach placing myself at times in situations where my public appearance triggered my (leftist, feminist) group identification. Then I had in front of me not only individuals struggling with their lives but also members of a certain group with its very specific values and norms. When I used participant observer methods it was much more difficult to forget our different groups identifications, than when I interviewed women on a one-to-one basis. It was thus much more difficult to trigger feelings of empathy in situations of conflicting values, and being reflexive about it did not help ease the feeling of alienation.

What is interesting to ask is whether my study would have been different without the tragic murder in Jerusalem? This is a difficult question, but my relations with my informants did change and this in itself may have changed the course of my study. My informants, particularly the men, must have felt some of my dislike and reacted to it. This may explain the curious phenomena that occurred in the field. After this incident, I was permitted to continue my field work in intimate family life, but I was not allowed to observe the public faces of the Moshav. I was asked by different people (men and women) from both political factions to leave some meetings which took place during the last months of my stay. At that time I interpreted this as an outcome of the very intimate knowledge I was accumulating on family life. My knowledge of their private lives in a context of strong political bargaining for honor in the public realm (Wasserfall 1990) may have stirred feelings of uneasiness in public. But according to this current analysis, the closing may have been caused by my social commitments which showed in my feelings toward my informants. Personally I was still able to enter intimate situations because my social self was less an issue just as their social selves were less an issue for me, but in public the content of my identities as a woman and a leftist could have been perceived as offensive. *It was*

In another example of the changing relation with my informants after the murder, one day I found one of my informants terribly upset. She thought she was pregnant and did not want a fourth child at that time. She was hysterically calling her sister and was particularly upset because her sister kept telling her that if she had an abortion she would bring bad luck on one of her living children who might even die. I just sat there trying to remember exactly who said what very coldly, all the time thinking, "oh what great material for my study!" I am sure this behavior of mine was an outcome of my sense of alienation from my informants. I just wanted at that time to get as much material as I could. I did not see the woman and her suffering. *selfish, forgot purpose*

I never went back to the moshav and I am not sure that my study changed anything in their lives. As one informant put it "another study on the moshav and what for us?" I may have been naive concerning the struggle over the construction of images and identities included in any dialogue between us or in the written text. My informants, however, were not naive and in truth they bargained with each other (as well as with me) for a better representation of their action in public as well as in the written text. They wanted to have a say in the book, being very much aware of the power of the written text. One woman, for example kept reminding me of my debt to her by saying that my book is not a docto-rate (Ph.D dissertation) but a docto-Ruth (her name). My informants had amazing capabilities in reading power relations and presenting themselves in different lights when needed (Wasserfall 1990). Perhaps I am still naive, but I ask "what are the responsibilities to the people who open their doors and life and share with us their daily lives for a long period of time, even if we do not like them?"

REFLEXIVITY AND POLITICAL ACTION

How did this sad experience influence my rethinking of the place of reflexivity for a feminist ethnography? My use of reflexivity helped me reveal my pre-conceptions and taught me that reciprocity is not enough to avoid exploitation. Giving gifts and listening carefully to one's informants while sharing with her my own struggles as a woman could have masked the difficult purpose of the

bribery to get wt u want. Be reflexive

research and the power of the written text as defining and perpetuating a certain vision of reality. Also while reflexivity helped reveal certain conceptions, it clouded others. Since any attempt at reflexivity is always phrased in terms of certain perspectives, this same reflexivity inevitably blocked other perceptions. In other words, reflexivity theoretically is the interface including the two sides that constitute it. But practically, I wonder how much can one in the praxis of field work be able to grasp both sides of the interface?

At this time, reflecting on the experience, I am led to ask if a feminist researcher should not only be aware of the power of images conveyed in the written text (interpretive authority), but whether she should use this power in conformity with the will and the desire of her informants (power and difference)? When she does not, because of political or other conflicts, does she perpetuate negatives images of the population studied in a wider context of ethnic, political or racial conflicts, and is she exploiting her informants?

More to the political issue, my attempt at a strong reading of reflexive methods did not help me overcome my political dilemmas. Understanding is not in all situations a guide to praxis. We may tend as scholars to put too much emphasis on understanding as a way to solve emotional, practical and political issues. While I understood and was very aware of the power of the image of aggression and right wing views of my informants (portrayed in the Israeli media as well as in the social sciences), did I portray my informants truthfully? So, the question remains to what extent a reflexive methodology can help in difficult issues such as the power included in the process of privileging certain images (power and difference and interpretive authority). In my case of intense political conflict, when I had to balance between my different commitments, political (to feminism and to a certain future of Israel), professional (to cultural anthropology), my political commitment to a certain future of Israel took the fore. My identity as an Israeli citizen struggling for a certain vision of society was more marked than my identity as a feminist. I could not find in my feminist repertoire enough resources to evoke feelings of empathy and identification. At that point reflexivity reached a certain limit, it could not help me balance my commitments. My reflexivity did not erase my uneasiness when confronted with aggression (or what from my culture is considered aggressive behavior), nor did it reduce my feelings of alienation from my informants. It did not smooth the conflict concerning the future of Israel. My study reinforced my views that the Moroccan Jews in the Moshav right wing behaved aggressively toward each other. The conflict was stronger than my feminism. Maybe in that, I do belong to Israeli society where struggling over the definition of the collective takes precedence over issues of inequalities between Israeli groups.

From this experience I am not so sure that my being aware of the impact of my dislike on my informants could have changed my positions which stemmed from a political opposition to the content of Israeliness they represented. It may have eased my anxiety about being banned from public meetings, and reinforced my study of the inter-personal realm of intimate issues. These issues were from the beginning my main interest, so I may not have tried at all to observe public events and confined myself to the intimate. I do not believe that a feminist anthropologist should study only what she likes, but I see that awareness of one's social category and commitments is not in itself a guarantee to achieve one's goals when confronted with strong political conflicts one could not foresee.

Moroccan Jews are portrayed as aggressive (Shokeid 1982). Part of my study does strengthen this perception. Am I correct? I did experience what I experienced and was very careful in taking notes, but my highlighting of certain phenomena has the power to perpetuate those images. While I kept using reflexivity during my field work to make sure I was not giving too much weight to this issue, I cannot be sure that some of my focus on aggressive behavior was not an outcome of our political conflict. In this strong context of political conflict my being reflexive, could have ironically reinforced certain negatives images. By making me so sensitive to my feelings against aggressiveness, I may have consciously looked for more details to reinforce my position and this in itself may have produced aggressiveness in my informants. My feminism could not bridge the overwhelming sense of political difference which issues of death and life carry with it in Israel. After the murder, I was not able and did not want to deny my own beliefs and values, consequently my identity as a leftist woman were even more marked in the Moshav than elsewhere in Israel. A certain sense of objectification and separation from one's informants may not only be inevitable but indeed may be also desirable in research such as mine, where I faced strong political conflicts and experienced negative feelings toward my informants.

However, the process of reflexivity in both its readings certainly helps minimize the potential of exploitation in situations where the informants and the researcher share and highlight some basic commonalities (e.g., gender, race, class, a political or religious vision of life . . .). In those cases, as Cesara (1982) claims, active recognition of the dialogue between informants and researcher can overcome the dichotomies between subjectivity and objectification, understanding and explanation. By acknowledging that "meaning" is created through a combined effort by researcher and subject one cannot only free scientific research of its "objective" limitations, but also, I thought take responsibilities for the influences her study has on her informant's life.

In situations of commonality, informants become subjects and the researcher needs to take into account how she influences, willingly or not, her informants' lives. In these cases, reflexivity makes the research process enjoyable for the researcher. For example, Steier (1991: 8) notes that scientists working in a constructionist and reflexive approach "may become surprised and enjoy being surprised by their informants shaking their understanding of what's going on." Perhaps in the classical definition of the anthropological project where the ethnographer studies the "other" from a totally different "metaphysical stand," reflexivity can minimize exploitation. I would argue, following Abu-Lughod (1986: 6) that even in those cases "the outsider self never stands completely outside." In a changing anthropology where more and more ethnographers may choose to work in their home countries, the boundaries of shared values and beliefs are no longer fixed, and problems stemming from shared but conflicting beliefs and values are becoming more salient. (Ginsburg 1989; Crapanzano 1985; Klatch 1988).

One of the ways to ease the conflicts some American ethnographers face when working with "resistant communities" (Klatch's wording) is intentionally or not, to build upon the commonalities the author finds with her informants. For example, Stacey (1990) finds in her feminism the resource "to respect and understand some of the social appeals and widespread nostalgia for eroding family forms even though (she) opposes conservative, gender class and sexual politics of the profamily movement" (p. 5). The author learned to appreciate the innovation of her informants in a "postmodern family." She could identify with the crisis of those lives because she also was undergoing a similar crisis in her own family under the same postmodern circumstances she identifies in her book. Circumstances which she argues, leaves so many people struggling under the strain of rapidly changing social reality toward what she calls an "uncertain future." She could see that the values and life strategies of her informants have been "profoundly influenced by feminist ideology while they hold their distance from feminist identity or politics" (p. 19). Stacey, despite the difference between herself and her women informants, was also part of this post-modern family which she describes, and she could find and identify with basic commonalities between them and cope with their political difference: they were all part of a changing "postmodern America."[10]

When I started my field work, I could not take into account the polarization that happened in Israeli society and its influence on marking difference, which previously could have been overlooked, between myself and my informants. I ended up needing the "distance" and objectification to complete my project. For when I attempted to converse with my informants I found myself in a deep

conflict with them over our respective political and ethical positions. In fact, by
the end of my stay one informant who was not happy with my way of handling
different disputes in the community, told me "if we knew what anthropology
meant we would not have allowed you in the village."

No but we must let them be who they are

Does this mean that a researcher should always study people she likes, she
identifies with? Do our reflexive methods work only in contexts where the
researcher "likes," sympathizes and identifies with her informants? When more
and more studies are being done by anthropologists whose identity or part of it
is shared by informants (for example see Lila Abu-Lughod's terminology to refer
to her own identity as a "halfie" [1989]), the possibility of emerging conflicts is
growing. These emerging conflicts between the researcher and her informants
over shared social, political issues (Ginsburg 1989) or collective identity (as in
my case) may well impinge not only on the ways we conduct our research and
on the relations with informants but also on the interpretations we propose in
our books. When the researcher finds herself as a citizen in profound opposition

leads to un own understand & interpretd

to the beliefs and actions of her informants, what happens to the "exploitative"
situation? What are the commitments of a feminist researcher to her informants?
I believe this set of problems is emerging as an important issue on the anthropological agenda.

The question that stems from those reflections is for whose sake do we
accumulate the knowledge? What of the feminist commitment to empower
women? Which women, the informants? The scholars? I do not want to sound
as if I am "throwing away the baby with the bath water." I still believe that

limits to all things

reflexivity is a very important tool but that we must be aware of its limits. The
content of awareness may shift with experience and is not in itself a guarantee
for action. In addition to these issues, I believe that a re-examination of our
critical ethnographic consciousness—reflexive methods—will also shed important light on the currently debated issues of cultural difference and feminism.
How do feminists ethnographers confer a sense of commonality stemming from
a feminist ideology amidst the cultural, social, racial and political differences

Our ways are not all ways

found in studying women from all over the world? Are those differences leaving
us with a fragmented topic and are women as a research category dissolving into
thousands of realities without the possibility of theorizing? (see Moore 1988 and
J. Flax 1990). This issue is not only the problem for an Israeli-Ashkenazi-left-
ist-woman anthropologist studying Israeli-Sephardi-rightist fellow citizens
(women and men). With the trend of "coming home" this problem of shared but
conflicted collectives could become central to the anthropological project.
Likewise, with modern-postmodern societies both more inter-related but also
more fragmented, one cannot assume the total otherness of foreign countries.

The "We" and the "Them" of the anthropological project are shifting positions, as we as well as our informants, incorporate into our selves, according to different social projects, political agenda, racial and gender identities. Here however, instead of focusing on ethical issues, I have focused on some of the tensions and political problems inherent in the choice of methodology used in the field. On a more theoretical level, rejoining Strathern (1987) and Stacey (1991), I wonder if a contradiction exists between a feminist anthropological project which seeks to understand and to empower women from different classes and races and the reflexive methodology in its strong reading which implies a certain political sameness, communality or identify in order to succeed.

NOTES

1. I would like to thank Connie Sutton, Don Handelman, Marie Heller, Shula Reinharz, Harvey Goldberg, Antonia Burrow, Adam Seligman and my "reading group" in Budapest especially Susan Arpad, for their careful readings, critical views and much needed encouragement.

2. This meaning given to reflexivity is somewhat different to the one Giddens is using in his "Modernity and Self-Identity." According to Giddens (1991: 20): "The reflexivity of modernity has to be distinguished from the reflexive monitoring of action intrinsic to all human activity. Modernity's reflexivity refers to the susceptibility of most aspects of social activity and material relations with nature, to chronic revision in the light of new information knowledge".

3. For a discussion of the current debate and so called crisis of anthropology concerning postmodernist's position of evocation versus interpretation of reality(ies) see Birth, 1990.

4. For an interesting example of this tension see Katherine Borland 1991, " 'That's not what I said': Interpretive Conflict in Oral Narrative Research," whose informant disapproved strongly of her feminist interpretation of her struggles.

5. Reflexivity is becoming a topic of queries in other social sciences disciplines. While I concentrate here on feminist work, other scholarship is also struggling with the tension stemming from the use of reflexivity in what I call the "strong reading," as a way to evade the "knowledge-power" issue. For example, Soderqvist, an historian, asks "is it possible to evade knowledge-power when writing reflexive biography?" The wording of the problem in terms of Reflexivity and the deconstruction of the "knowledge-power," parallels a similar tension I am identifying in this article as one of the promises and problems of the strong reading of reflexivity. Soderqvist (1991:155) writes: "Stories about the situated and embodied nature of the construction of knowledge claims to counterbalance the contribution of knowledge-power claims exerted by these claims. At the same time, however, the very ideas of a true story of a life—even a story that includes the situation and embodied character of its intellectual, is just another version of that same old knowledge-power."

6. I realize that this is a somewhat controversial statement but I believe that beneath the emphasis put on "dialoguing" by some feminists ethnographers, lies an assumption about its potential for changing not only the ethnographer's but also the informant's vision of her own life (see Finch 1984, Oakley 1981, Cesara 1982).

7. I am aware that feminism is not a monolithic category, the ranges of ideas found under its heading are very different and cover all the political range. I use feminism here as a very broad category including research done with the intention to empower women. Sure, the venues to

empowerment are as many as the different "feminisms." See among others Flax, 1990, Moore, 1988 for a discussion of these differences.

8. Israel is a highly stratified society where Moroccan Jews were at the bottom of the hierarchy at the time of this study. The terms used for categorizing Jews from Arab countries are all politically loaded as any categorization generally is. For a history of the term Sepharad see Goldberg, for a discussion of the political aspects of those categories see Dominguez, 1989. The term Mizrahi from the East, is sometimes used to refer to Sephardi Jews. I am not taking into account the emigration of Ethiopian Jews in the 1980's as well as of Russian Jews which started in 1991. The impact of these new emigrations on the system of stratification of Israeli society is the topic of various Israeli publications.

9. I had a previous field experience with Jewish Moroccan women when I studied a moshav in 1981. This was before the Lebanon war. The women were traditional, middle class, born in Morocco and accepted their place in the social order. I learned to appreciate their wit, their coping and their strong sense of accomplishment and I could easily identify with them on the basis of our shared gender. On the strength of this previous experience, I was confident that I could handle my differences (see Wasserfall 1992).

10. Another example of the building upon commonalities as a way to ease political difference between researcher and informants can be found in Ginzburg's *Contested lives.* Ginzburg (1989) analyzes discourses of pro-lifers and right to lifers grass roots activists in a small American town. While she started by mistrusting her own findings, with time she found that amidst their obvious difference, her informants activists shared concerns for women. Concerns she could identify with. The concerns stemmed from a particular frame she identifies as: "the resistance of women to the imposition of what they see as male cultural forms that corrupt and exploit women, if left unchecked" (p. 11). I believe that Ginzburg could steer feelings of empathy toward her pro-life informants because she, as a feminist shares and could relate to this cultural form; as an American feminist she is also part of the same cultural form; see also her epilogue significantly titled "Pro-dialogue."

REFERENCES

Abu-Lughod, L. 1986. *Veiled Sentiments.* Berkeley: University of California Press.

Abu-Lughod, L. 1989. "Writing against culture." Paper presented at the Seminar in Meta-Ethnography, School of American Research, Santa Fe, June 5-9.

Berger Gluck, S. 1991. "Advocacy Oral History: Palestinian Women in Resistance" in S. Berger Berger Gluck and D. Patai (eds.), *Women's Words.* New York and London: Routledge.

Birth, K. 1990. "Reading and the righting of writing ethnographies," *American Ethnologist,* Vol. 17, No. 3: 549-58.

Borland, K. 1991. " 'That's Not What I Said': Interpretive Conflict in Oral Narrative Research," in Berger Gluck and Patai (eds.), *Women's Words.* New York: Routledge.

Cesara, M. 1982. *Reflections of a Woman Anthropologist.* London, Academic Press.

Clifford, J. 1986. "Introduction: Partial Truths," in J. Clifford and G. Marcus (eds.), *Writing Culture,* pp. 1-26. Berkeley: University of California Press.

Crapanzano, V. 1985. *Waiting: The Whites of South Africa.* New York: Vintage.

Dominguez, V. 1989. *People as Subject, People as Object.* Madison: University of Wisconsin Press.

Deutsch, Y. 1990. "Israeli Women Organize Against Occupation and For Constructing a Culture of Peace" (in Hebrew). Unpublished article.

Ferguson, K. 1991. "Interpretation and Genealogy in Feminism." *Signs,* Vol. 16, No. 2: 322-40.

Finch, J. 1984. " 'It's Great to Have Someone to Talk To': The Ethics and Politics of Interviewing Women," in C. Bell and H. Roberts (eds.), *Social Researching: Politics, Problems and Practice.* London: Routledge & Kegan Paul.

Flax, J. 1990. *Thinking Fragments.* Berkeley: University of California Press.

Giddens, A. 1991. *Modernity and Self-Identity.* Palo Alto, CA: Stanford University Press.

Ginsburg, F. 1989. *Contested Lives.* Berkeley: University of California Press.

Goldberg, H. 1977. "Introduction: Culture and Ethnicity in the Studies of Israeli Society." *Ethnic Groups,* Vol. 1.

Golde, P. (ed.) 1986. *Women in the Field.* Berkeley: University of California Press.

Gorelick, S. 1989. "The Changer and the Changed: Methodological Reflections on Studying Jewish Feminists," in A. Jaggar and S. Bordo (eds.), *Gender/Body/Knowledge.* New Brunswick, NJ: Rutgers University Press.

Izraeli, D. 1987. "Introduction to Special Issue: Women in Israel." *ISSR,* Vol. 5, No. 1-2: 1-5.

Izraeli, D. and Tabori, E. 1986. "The perception of women's status in Israel as a social problem." *Sex Roles,* Vol. 14, No. 11-12: 663-78.

Klatch, R. 1988. "The Methodological Problems of Studying a Politically Resistant Community." *Studies in Qualitative Methodology,* Vol. 1:73-88.

Kaplan, A. 1984. "Philosophy of Science in Anthropology." *Annual Review of Anthropology* 13:25-39.

Klein, R. D. 1983. "How to Do What We Want to Do," in G. Bowles and R. D. Klein (eds.), *Theories of Women Studies.* London: Routledge & Kegan Paul.

Marcus, G. and Fisher, M. 1986. *Anthropology as a Cultural Critique: An Experimental Moment in the Human Sciences.* Chicago & London: Chicago University Press.

Mascia-Lees, F., Sharpe, P., and C. B. Cohen. 1989. "The Postmodernist Turn in Anthropology: Cautions from a Feminist Perspective." *Signs,* Vol. 15, No. 1.

Mies, M. 1983. "Towards a Methodology for Feminists Research," in G. Bowles and R. D. Klein (eds.), *Theories of Women Studies.* London: Routledge & Kegan Paul.

Moore, H. 1988. *Feminism and Anthropology.* University of Minnesota Press, Minneapolis.

Myerhoff, B. 1979. *Number Our Days.* New York: Simon & Schuster.

Myerhoff, B. and Ruby, J. 1982. "Introduction," in J. Ruby (ed.), *A Crack in the Mirror.* Philadelphia University Press, 1-39.

Nader, L. 1986 (1970). "From Anguish to Exultation," in Golde (ed.), *Women in the Field.* Berkeley: University of California Press.

Oakley, A. 1981. "Interviewing Women: A Contradiction in Terms," in H. Roberts (ed.), *Doing Feminist Research.* London: Routledge & Kegan, 30-61.

Patai, D. 1991. "U.S. Academics and Third World Women: Is Ethical Research Possible?" in S. Berger Gluck and D. Patai (eds.), *Women's Words.* New York and London: Routledge.

Prell, Riv-Ellen. 1989. "The Double Frame of Life History in the Work of Barbara Myerhoff," in Personal Narratives Group (ed.), *Interpreting Women's Lives.* Bloomington: Indiana University Press.

Rabinow, P. 1977. *Reflections on Fieldwork in Morocco.* Berkeley: University of California Press.

Reinharz, S. 1983. "Experiential Research: A Contribution to Feminist Research," in G. Bowles and R. Klein (eds.), *Theories of Women's Studies.* London: Routledge & Kegan Paul, 162-90.

Shostak, M. 1981. *The Life and Words of a !Kung Woman.* Cambridge, MA: Harvard University Press.

Shokeid, M. 1982. "The Regulation of Aggression in Daily Life: Aggressive Relationship Among Moroccan Emigrants in Israel." *Ethnology* 11(3):271-81.

Soderqvist, T. 1991. "Biography or Ethnobiography or Both? Embodied Reflexivity and the Deconstruction of Knowledge-Power" in F. Steier (ed.), *Research and Reflexivity*. London: Sage..

Stacey, J. 1990. *Brave New Families*. New York: Basic Books.

Stacey, J. 1991. "Can There Be a Feminist Ethnography?" in S. Berger Gluck and D. Patai (eds.), *Women's Words*. New York and London: Routledge.

Stanley, L. and Wise, S. 1990. "Method, methodology and epistemology in feminist research process," in L. Stanley (ed.), *Feminist Praxis,* New York: Routledge.

Strathern, M. 1987. "An Awkward Relationship: The Case of Feminism and Anthropology." *Signs,* Vol. 12, No. 2.

Steier, F. (ed.) 1991. *Research and Reflexivity*. London: Sage.

Storper, D. and Wasserfall, R. 1988. "Methodologie de la Raison, Methodologie de la Resonance: d'un devenir femme de la recherche?" *Revue de l'Institut de Sociologie,* Université Libre de Bruxelles, Vol. 1-2: 188-207.

Swirski, S. 1989. *Israel's Oriental Majority*. London: Zed Books.

Watson, G. 1987. "Make Me Reflexive—But Not Yet: Strategies for Managing Essential Reflexivity in Ethnographic Discourse." *Journal of Anthropological Research,* 28-41.

Wasserfall, R. 1990. "Bargaining for Gender Identity: Love, Sex and Money in an Israeli Moshav." *Ethnography,* Vol. 29: 327-41.

Wasserfall, R. 1992. "The Meaning of Niddah for Moroccan Women Immigrants to Israel," in Eilberg-Schwartz. (ed.) *People of the Body: Jews and Judaism from an Embodied Perspective*. Albany: Suny Press.

8

Do You Really Know How They Make Love?

The Limits on Intimacy With Ethnographic Informants

Tamar El-Or

"Hey, that sounds great, living with an orthodox family. How did they let you in? Isn't this type of Hassidism kind of closed? Do they know you're an ethnographer, or are they hoping you're a newly religious Jew? Tell me, is it true they have intercourse through a hole in a sheet? I bet you it's only stories. I wonder if their women are happier than we are, knowing their position in life and accepting it, are they?"[1]

Conducting field work five minutes from my home in a small community of Gur Hassidim in a suburb near Tel Aviv, I heard these sorts of questions very often. Bearing in mind the history of "deep penetration" into the field in the craft of ethnology, I was frustrated when I had no answers to these questions. As time went on, the frustration grew. I knew that good ethnographers were supposed to

EDITOR'S NOTE: This chapter originally appeared as an article in *Qualitative Sociology,* Vol. 16, No. 1, 1992. Reprinted by permission of Human Sciences Press, Inc.

deliver authentic and exotic material. I also knew that the women I was observing are considered by my people—my family, friends, and most colleagues—as primitive, similar to people from the lower classes, the third world and deviants. The anticipations of revelation and "hot" information was taken for granted.

My remoteness from this attitude, coupled with my desire to learn in a modern society, complicated the task. A research study of a known, observable and much discussed community demands a fresh analysis, or the treatment of a new or hidden problem.

The community of Gur Hassidim I studied is physically observable and fairly accessible, since Gur Hassidim is a major sect of ultraorthodox Jews that dominates the orthodox political parties of Israel. The sect originated in the town of Gur near Warsaw and today some 7000 Gur Hassidic families live in Israel. Unlike other fundamentalist groups, Jewish ones do not live in isolation in remote places, but prefer to live in communities in large cities. While they play a significant role in Israeli politics and culture, they are deeply prejudiced and are integrated into the larger society through limited channels. The sect is largely absent from the media. The self-segregation of the orthodox communities—an isolation they maintain on a daily basis within the fairly open society of Israel—serves their need to preserve their lifestyle and particular view of Jewish law and tradition, but at the same time intensifies curiosity about their private lives. This "magic circle" they draw around themselves denies the researcher both the treatment afforded a more exposed society, and the classical holistic approach taken to an unknown one.

HOW CLOSE CAN ONE GET?

The present chapter addresses the potential for a woman ethnographer who presented herself as a nonreligious Jew, and an ultraorthodox woman informant who was a member of an ultrareligious Hassidic sect, to become close: to bridge the distance between their different cultures within a mutually accepted context; to traverse the gap separating them without having to violate the other's beliefs and boundaries of intimacy. The work follows the dynamic development of their relationship over a two-year period, with visits to the field 2-3 times a week. It focuses on several methodological problems inherent in the situation. It examines how close the ethnographer need get in order to deliver the sense of "being there" (Geertz 1988), how close the ethnographer may get without creating a gap between him/herself and family, friends, and everyday reality. How close will one get before turning the work into a personal adventure?

These methodological questions are approached through the topic of intimacy. While intimacy is not the central issue in the study, the different meaning it holds for the researcher, her audience, and the informant will emerge.

On the theoretical side, the meaning of intimacy during field work, and its impact on possible ways of working within one's own society, joins a broader set of methodological debates that have always occupied ethnographers, and is currently receiving fresh treatment in the literature (Clifford & Marcus 1986; Marcus & Fishcher 1986; Sangren 1988; Shokeid 1988).

THE ILLUSION OF INTIMACY

Novels (Bar-Yosef 1985, 1989) and magazine articles have distorted the image of orthodoxy, and strengthened prejudices. Journalistic research (Harris 1985; Levy 1988) and academic studies (Berger-Sofer 1979; Friedman 1982 1986a, 1986b; Jayanti 1982), which could correct some misconceptions, are rare and less accessible to the public. Torn between the expectations for peeping that ethnology sometimes satisfies, and our major task to deliver a clear, well-founded description, I remember very clearly the first conversation I had with Hanna, my main informant.

It was two weeks before Passover and Hanna was preparing the house for the holiday, which includes removing all traces of food containing yeast. Hanna's daughters, 5 and 9 years old, were already home from school for the holiday, while the boys, 3 and 7 years old, would stay in school until the holiday. Boys and girls go to separate schools in the Gur Hassidic sect, and in fact in all orthodox groups. Boys attend a heder and then a Yeshiva, religious schools; one-third of them remain in the Yeshiva after their mid-twenties and two-thirds eventually drop out and go to work. Girls go to separate schools through the 12th grade and, unlike the boys, learn secular subjects in addition to religious ones. Many go on to attend two-year teacher training seminars.

Hanna's daughters' women teachers needed time to clean their homes, and the daughters were expected to help in this task. It was a busy morning. Hanna was washing the plastic toys and cleaning the children's bedrooms. At that time she had 5 children, ranging from 12 months to 9 years old, and was pregnant. The children were ordered not to enter their rooms with any kind of food. I followed her around the tiny flat, trying to be useful. I had so much to ask, but only a vague concept of what, how, and when.

One of my teachers, a modern orthodox man, had told me beforehand that the *mikva,* the public ritual bath where women purify themselves following a menstrual period, would be a good place to start. He assumed that there I would be able to see women in the company of other women sharing some private or intimate moments. Taking his cue, I asked Hanna whether she too thought it would be a good place to start. She led me to a bookshelf-lined living room, with a large dining table in the middle of the room. She closed the door behind us, leaving the noise of the children on the other side, didn't offer me a seat and didn't take one herself, and said:

I always do that when I talk about family purity or other matters they shouldn't hear. They're used to it. Look, the women of this community tend not to go to the *mikva* next door. They see it as a very private act and prefer to go some place where no one will recognize them. Especially us in Gur. We treat these matters very modestly. The Sephardim [Jews of Asian and North African origin, as distinguished from Ashkenazic Jews of European origin] are completely different. With them it's natural. The other day I went to see my Sephardi friend. I called her from the street below her flat, and her daughter came to the window and shouted down that her Mom was not home because she had gone to the *mikva,* and would be back soon. I was shocked. To yell out loud that a woman went to the *mikva* as if she had gone to the supermarket. On the other hand I admired it. They treat it so naturally. There's no shame in going there—it's a *mitzva* [a religious commandment or good deed], and after all what can someone gather by knowing it? That you're not pregnant? Some women need to go even when they are, if they have a heavy discharge. That you are permitted to your husband? Well, everyone knows you are two weeks every month, so actually there is nothing to hide. Still, the women do hide it.

Men are much more open about it, so they use the *mikva* next door. Still, they are ordered not to look at each other when they bathe—it is forbidden. Men bathe communally in a large pool, whereas women bathe privately in a smaller one. These matters of privacy and intimacy are more problematic for men. They are taught from an early age to refrain from looking at girls. At the age of 13 a boy goes to the *yeshiva* and lives only with boys. At home he stops playing with his sisters, and he won't play with girls in the playground at that age or even younger. So, when he is about to get married, usually between 20 and 24, there are a lot of difficulties to be overcome. He has to accept the idea that he is going to live with a woman, that he will have to take the lead and be the initiator, and that it can be done. Well, this is very complicated, but now, thank God, we have special counselors who take care of it. They talk with the young men before the wedding and explain their duties. They are such experts they make everything clear to those young men, and they do it gently. With girls it's altogether different. They get this guidance at home from their mothers. They don't need it at school. Thinking about it, maybe it isn't so good, because my mother never told me anything. I was lucky to have had an older sister, and when I got my first period

I ran to her and she told me all about it. For sure I will talk to my girls when the time comes, I definitely will.

A knock on the glass door interrupted our conversation. It was Hanna's youngest daughter. Hanna went out to her, and I was left in the living room, quite surprised. I never expected this kind of intimacy in the first conversation. It seemed too easy. A talk like that should have taken place, according to my professional calculations, much later. I left that room satisfied, like a successful hunter. I had something solid in my notes, facts that everyone would like to hear, information that came out of deep storage. Although a slight blush covered Hanna's cheeks once or twice, she seemed rather calm during this conversation. I took it as a hint, a promise of a very intimate future.

REDEFINING INTIMACY:
AWAY FROM MY PERCEPTION
AND INTO HANNA'S

Months went by and Hanna and I saw a great deal of each other. I visited her two to three times a week, helping her with the laundry, the house cleaning, and baby care. We went to town together to do errands, and took several religious classes in and outside the neighborhood together. The deeper the relationship between us grew, the farther we got from those "hot" intimate subjects. Most of the conversations centered around topics of everyday life: what to do about Yitzhak's thumb sucking or Rebbeca's loneliness and lack of suitable girlfriends, and where to have the leaking water tank repaired.

Sometimes, usually on Wednesdays when her mother visited, we shared opinions and feelings about family ties. Being the same age and married for a similar period we found much in common, although at that time she had five children and was pregnant, and I had two children and no plans for more. Topics like religious beliefs, the status of women, fulfillment of the Jewish commandments, and relations between men and women were hardly mentioned as such. We built our friendship very much like most other relationships I knew, and felt very close. On the intellectual level, women's literacy emerged as an interesting issue, and brought me much further into the study of the intellectual sphere and the access of women to "men's knowledge" in today's orthodoxy.

My entry into Hanna's home was not driven by curiosity about the women's intellectual life. I went there wanting to know "how they actually live," and while pursuing and developing those almost normal, personal contacts and stimulating intellectual discussions, everything was accompanied by a sense of failure. By that time I already knew that Hanna had not gone through any emotional conflict when she spoke with me about personal matters in our first conversation. In fact, she hadn't said anything personal at all. The information I took to be intimate was technical for her. She cited books or certain religious precepts and *Halakhot,* a translation of the Jewish laws and commandments into practical do's and don't's, and parroted her teachers from school, the Rabbi's wife, or other important women to whom she listened. An important woman is one valued by the community. She can be the wife of a well-known Rabbi, an outstanding teacher, a successful charity worker, or an active volunteer in social organizations. Knowing that she is accustomed to meeting newly religious women from time to time, I realized that she had already delivered this kind of information many times before. The significance attributed by me to that first talk rested solely on my perception of intimacy as a nonreligious woman, and on my expectations as an ethnographer. Later, on, I heard other women talk pragmatically and quite freely about these subjects, and I slowly came to realize that intimacy might lie elsewhere. I couldn't free myself from the desire to observe a young couple at home when no one else was there to watch them, when they would be free of the critical eye of the orthodox community. I wanted to know "what is actually going on," to use Berger's and Luckmann's terminology (1966). In my own society, literature, media, and art satisfy this kind of curiosity. In primitive societies and among deviants, anthropology is counted on to do this for us.

I never led a conversation with Hanna towards the topics that dominated our first one till the very end of my field work. Then, as it will be clear later, those topics reemerged on a different level. On the one hand, I presumed that there must be a real intimate level to these themes, while on the other hand I was afraid to get more proclamations, pamphlets, and impersonal views. As time went on, I experienced several events in which some of the deeper levels emerged. I became resigned to the idea that the only information I would get would be indirect, and that no frank and open discussions would take place between us about what I define as intimate. I settled for what was there in our intense ties: I didn't take it as less than it was, and didn't try to manipulate the dialogue. Rather, I simply went along the way with Hanna, her female neighbors, her family, and her everyday reality. Amongst these, I found what I was looking for. It came in bits and pieces—as slips of the tongue, in talks in the hospital shortly after she gave birth to her sixth child, and in a rare loss of temper like she had the other night.

It was late September, a week before the Jewish New Year and the High Holidays, a time of feverish activity and preparations in the Gur community.

Hanna was expecting her sixth baby any day. Her husband was studying in a *yeshiva* in Tiberias, a town in northern Israel about two hours from Tel Aviv on the sea of Galilee, and came home only on the weekend. Studying far from home is not unusual among Hassidim; it is, however, a sign of recognition of a man's intellectual prowess that he will choose to study in a more advanced *yeshiva* far from home.

At that time Hanna had no telephone at home and important messages were left for her at the neighbor upstairs. The end of a typically hot, humid summer night brought a fresh breeze, and Hanna and I were strolling home from a class she had given to some neighborhood women on the laws of festival meals. She was heavy and restless, as women tend to be in her situation.

So Hanna, where are you planning to be this New Year? Are you going to your in-laws in Bnei-Brak or will you stay home?

Eh, I really don't know yet. My husband was supposed to call and tell me, but he hasn't called yet. I really don't know what to do. Should I shop for the Holidays? Should I start cooking? It's going to be a long holiday because it's followed immediately by Shabbat. I really don't know where I'm at.

Then why don't you call him and ask? You must have his phone number at the *yeshiva,* don't you?

Well, yes I do, but he ordered me not to call him there unless it's an emergency.

Well, isn't it?

He said he'll let me know what he decides, and I'm sure he will. But here I am, six days before the holidays, expecting any minute, and knowing nothing. I can't figure out whether to start packing the kids' clothes for a long stay at my in-laws, or to prepare Rebecca to run the house in case we stay home and I go to the hospital. Shall I leave food for them here, or will it all spoil because we won't be here? Ooh . . . I wish he would call.

Knowing Hanna's forms of expression, I could tell that she was pretty mad at her husband. I also knew that she wouldn't express it, but in that moment of intimacy I tried:

Are you mad at him?

Sure I am! How could I not be? Here I am with 5 kids at home, expecting a baby any moment, and I'm paralyzed. He should know better, at least he could have called and said he hasn't decided yet.

Hanna got very red—she tended to blush in certain situations. I could tell she was quite ruffled, as if she had come close to a boundary she usually tries to stay

away from. It didn't take her long to regain her composure and she quickly
added:

> I'm sure he has good reasons for not calling, he knows what he's doing. It's me,
> I'm too tired, I have no patience, things are just a little too much for me now. I
> must rely on his good sense and let it be the way he planned. Ooh . . . see when
> I'm tired I talk too much.

Hanna was embarrassed. It appeared that she wasn't at all used to this sort of
emotional outburst. The society in which she lives, and her social position as a
very strict orthodox woman among ultraorthodox people, do not permit a wife
to complain about her husband to an ordinary member of her community. She
may, and does, in indirect ways, like jokes, double entendres, or small gestures.
When a Gur woman suffers from a serious problem in her marriage or family,
she will turn to a confidant. She might bring her troubles to a Rabbi, a counselor,
or a teacher she respects. Hanna's little outburst, which she presumably did not
treat as a minor one in my presence illustrated the paradox in our relationship.
On the one hand it showed that she felt quite open with me, pointing up our
closeness. On the other hand it indicated that she allowed herself to do certain
things around me that she wouldn't do in front of someone from her own
community, pointing up the gap between us. In my eagerness for shreds of
intimacy, I took what would be considered in my society as trivial anger towards
a life partner, to be a glimpse of a suppressed feeling in Gur and therefore a kind
of intimacy.

Other events of this nature strengthened these fragile bits of intimacy I
learned to listen to unspoken words, to look for hidden gestures, the slight
blush on the cheeks, to understand intimacy the way Hanna experiences it. A
visit to the nearby town of Bnei-Brak one morning deepened this understanding. It was a sunny winter morning, one of a few that year. Most mothers
hurried outside with their small babies and sat on the stone fences that
surround the houses of the Hassidic neighborhood. When I reached Hanna's
flat she was ready to leave to catch the first bus to town. She held Frieda-Lea
in one arm and tried to put Tzirale to bed with the other.

> Will you leave her asleep here all by herself?
>
> Oh yes, no problem, I just fed her. She'll be fine until we come back. It'll only
> take us a couple of hours.
>
> Come on, Hanna, how can you do that, aren't you afraid? What if she cries? What
> if no one hears her?

She'll do all right, she can't get out of her bed, so she'll cry for a while and fall asleep again.

I already knew that Hanna had her own methods of child-rearing. Some of them were irregular or even bizarre in the eyes of her community. A few of the women (who felt close enough to me) tried several times to engage me in gossip about Hanna and her husband. They all criticized her child-rearing methods. Most of them thought she was Spartan, rough and merciless. The more delicate ones said she was obeying her husband's orders, and since this is a basic role which can't be disputed in public, they saw her as a sufferer along with her children.

Hanna's marginal position in the community, her status as "the most orthodox woman around," and her relationship with her husband deserve a separate discussion. With regard to the question of intimacy, Hanna knew she was criticized. She knew that the women downstairs on the fences stopped talking when she approached because they were gossiping (not necessarily about her), and she is a reminder to them that they are violating the rule of the community against gossip and small talk, a rule especially directed towards women. She had no one to share her feelings with, and no means of reacting or explaining herself to her community. Her compensation was her high status on the religiosity scale, and the greater freedom her extreme religiosity gave her within the confines of the community.

Hanna's and her husband's extreme orthodoxy allowed them to do things others were not permitted. Hanna's husband consulted people other than the Gur Rabbi, attended a *yeshiva* outside the community, and worked to convert Sephardic Jews to orthodoxy whom others in the sect were not interested in or were even alienated from.

Hanna's husband is among the one-third of Gur Hassidic men considered talented enough and ready to continue studying in the Yeshiva beyond his twenties. Hanna and her husband and family are supported by the Yeshiva, and their ultraorthodoxy is further signified by Hanna's choosing not to supplement their meager income by working. Hanna knew and worked with women from neighboring communities, with whom the other Gur women had no contact. She was the only one who could let me into her home without threatening her reputation.

On several occasions Hanna justified her methods of child-rearing to me. They were based on the idea that most people treat their children according to the expectations of society, whereas she tries to ignore some of these so her children would go beyond those expectations. During the scene in question, she wanted to prove to herself that a well-fed baby can stay at home alone and that, with God's help, nothing will happen to her. Hanna used to "play games with God" to check how much love and attention she and her family receive for their religiosity. The reasons for and implications of these games can not be analyzed here, but leaving the baby alone at home is an example of such behavior.

Bearing all this in mind, I gave up the warnings about possible dangers of such an attitude and took another strategy:

> Look at the beautiful morning outside. Isn't it a shame to leave her inside after so many days of rain? I'll take Frieda-Lea in the stroller and you carry Tzirale in your arms. I bet you we'll manage.
>
> O.K. we'll do that. That way I'll be able to take care of some more errands and won't have to rush back home. See Tzirale, you've gained a trip to town, you are lucky today.

I followed Hanna in town. We had to change some dollars her husband received in the *yeshiva* into Israeli currency. This is not done in the bank where one gets the legal rate, but through dealers who give a higher one. Hanna tried several before she found a rate that satisfied her. Later we entered a bank where her husband maintains a saving account. The bank had notified him by mail that he must either withdraw the money or renew the account. Hanna's husband asked her to withdraw the money. We waited in a long line and the girls began to get restless. The little one wanted to nurse, and the older one kept trying to climb out of the stroller.

> I'm sure they won't let me withdraw the money, only he can do it, it's in his name, they'll never let me withdraw it.
>
> Did you tell him that?
>
> Of course I did, but he still said I should go.

When our turn finally came the clerk said it couldn't be done. Hanna told him that her husband studies in a distant *yeshiva* and can't come to the bank himself. He said the only way to withdraw the money in his absence is to obtain a written order signed before a lawyer. Outside the bank, after a wasted 40 minutes, she said:

> I knew it, I told him so, but he wouldn't listen. He put it on my list anyway [every weekend, Hanna and her husband prepare a list of things he wants her to do while he is away. She writes down the outcome of her activities and they discuss it the

next weekend]. I was sure they wouldn't let me draw the money out, but he wanted it. I did it and now it can be marked off the list.

For some time I had the feeling that Hanna was treated like a child. She was given orders to obey, and had to report her movements. Her own common sense and knowledge didn't count. The rumor of the "list of tasks" circulated around the neighborhood. People were critical of the way her husband treated her, pitying her for having to put up with him, thereby minimizing the resentment she aroused as the "perfect obedient wife."

Coming out of the bank that morning I saw it all differently. Hanna treated her husband like a child. It reminded me of a child asking for sweets he claims are "up there." The mother keeps telling him that "there is nothing up there," but he won't take her word for it. The mother, recognizing the child's limitations and knowing that they can not be changed right now, and seeking peace of mind, lifts the child up to see that "there is nothing up there." She doesn't feel beaten, because she recognizes the laws of child development. She might be tired of it, and as an authority figure will usually add: "Didn't I tell you? When Mommy says there's nothing there, there's nothing here. Remember that for next time honey."

Hanna was going through a similar process, although the last part of the scenario was, of course, quite different. On the street in front of that bank, I shared with her an intimate moment in which she expressed some of her true feelings towards her situation as an ultraorthodox wife.

That the orthodox Jewish wife is inferior to her husband is a commonly held view, and one that is confirmed in the academic literature (Koltun 1976; Heschel 1983; Schneider-Weidman 1984). While this is generally true, a glimpse into the orthodox woman's emotions and inner world provides a mixed picture of this inferiority. One comes to see the social and psychological means by which women live with this unbalanced situation. The technique described above is ancient. Every traditional Jewish mother bestows it on her daughter as part of her marriage dowry. "Men are like children," and satisfying them buys women their relative freedom. The possibility to experience inferiority in this "emic" manner, vis-à-vis the feminist "etic" way, was extremely valid.

Hanna never complained openly about her husband. That would have been unacceptable for a woman of her status. She did, however, lead me gently and subtly to her painful zones—the peripheral areas where she kept her anger, sadness, worries, and hopes. I knew from our conversations that she hardly ever opened the doors to those zones for others to come through. She had few girlfriends, and one sister she liked. All of them were orthodox, and not one was suitable as a confidant, at least as she saw them.

After ticking off most of the day's tasks, we went to the home of one of Hanna's girlfriends. We all needed a rest, and Hanna wanted to breast feed her baby. The building was on a main street, and while only about 30 years old, it was quite dilapidated. We climbed a dark dirty staircase to the apartment of Rachel, who was glad to see us.

Hanna introduced me as a friend. Rachel had her wig off and wore a scarf as women tend to do when at home. She kept pushing it forward on her head as orthodox women do. Rachel was 26 years old, 4 years younger than Hanna and me. She had 4 children, the eldest 6 and the youngest 3 months old. The flat was dark, the night smells still prevailed, and it seemed that Rachel had not yet declared it daytime although it was already noon. We sat in the living room on an old sofa, and she brought us cold water. Rachel's husband went to the same *yeshiva* Hanna attended, which had brought them close for the last two years. Her eldest daughter went to school with Hanna's third child. It was a small school and fairly new. The language of instruction was Yiddish, unlike most of the other orthodox girls schools in the town, where Hebrew was spoken; this characterized it as a more religious school than the others since today Yiddish is considered more sacred than Hebrew. The school enrolled girls from all orthodox streams, and promised the parents that all groups would be respected. Hanna and Rachel discussed a violation of that promise.

> Rivke came home crying. I couldn't get it out of her. I hoped it wasn't something to do with her learning because we'd already been through that at the beginning of the year. At that time the teacher said Rivke didn't concentrate, and dreamt and played with the things on her desk while she was telling the girls the Torah portion, anyway, this time Rivke finally told me that the teacher won't let her pray in her way. Well this was too much. Picking on her for not listening when she's only in the first grade is one thing, but telling her how to pray is an altogether different story.
>
> Well, the other Friday, when my husband came home, he went to talk to the headmaster. He was so mad. First of all he says that Rivke is a good girl. She helps me a lot at home, takes care of the little ones and has good *midot* [the moral and ethical traits considered important for girls]. Isn't it what a girl should strive for? He claims that schools nowadays push the girls too much towards learning. When he went there I was a bit worried, I didn't want him to have an outburst or to embarrass Rivke. He can forget himself every now and then when dealing with important matters. Before leaving the house I reminded him to try and remain calm, so he started to heat up right here.

Rachel had a shy little smile on her lips. She bent her face down and pushed the scarf forward again. She spoke quickly, as if this was the only way she could get the story out. Hanna turned red. She knew that Rachel was sharing an intimate feeling with us. Rachel talked about her daughter's problems, and revealed a clash with her husband. She also revealed short temper, which is generally an intimate subject, and is not viewed positively among the orthodox.

Hanna kept quiet for a while, smiled, and said:

> Well, same here. When Rabbi Liberman came to talk us into sending our children to the new school, he too said that the girls would be free to pray their own way. For you it's all new because Rivke is there for the first year, but our eldest had this conflict last year. She too was deeply hurt when the teacher told her she should change. Well, you know her, she wouldn't say anything, until one Saturday my husband hears her singing differently. He couldn't wait for the following Friday, called Rabbi Liberman during the week, and then went there. You know him when he gets angry.

Hanna became very red, and a large embarrassed smile covered her little face. She felt more mature and experienced than Rachel, both in child rearing and in marriage, yet she wanted to be open with her and give her the feeling that she was not the only one to have these kinds of problems. Rachel had opened the intimate stage, and Hanna didn't want to leave her there all by herself. Hanna too could use a short performance on that stage.

In that stuffy flat, on an old sofa, Hanna and Rachel shared some emotions, opinions, and stress which in my surroundings would never be considered particularly intimate. For those two young women, married to ultraorthodox men who spend the week away from home furthering their careers as scholars, this was pure intimacy. Listening to their voices, looking at their cheeks, watching their eye movements, one could discern the boundaries of intimacy.

Hassidic women are not supposed to criticize their husbands' behavior, and they avoid comments about their personality traits, whether positive or negative. The women evade direct references to conflicts with their husbands. In a casual conversation one might catch a glimpse of conflict through double entendres, deliberately unclear comments, laughter, blushes and the like. An intimate conversation might go a bit further. In such an exchange one might hear a fuller portrayal of a couples' disagreements, an admission of the difficulties encountered in the orthodox way of life, an awareness of one's status within the community which is accepted but as an underestimation of oneself as an adult.

These topics and feelings are suppressed most of the time, but sometimes, with certain people, they emerge and reveal the depth of the oppressing mechanism. Being "normal" means not talking about intimate issues, as if they do not exist at all. Avoiding intimacy indicates a recognition of the community's social and mental boundaries, which is, in a sense, sanity. The women I knew had to be very careful any time they exposed their hidden worlds. Doing it at the wrong time, in front of inappropriate people, or in an unsuitable place, might present them as fragile, bewildered, or even crazy.

The information conveyed in the scene described above and the context in which it was exposed indicate the delicate skin overlaying intimacy, separating the overt and the covert, the normal and the abnormal, and maintaining the dichotomy drawn by the orthodox between a "weak woman" and "strong woman." In the first category the orthodox community puts women who find it hard to manage their large families, women who are not involved in any activity outside the house such as classes, charity, and volunteer work, and women who act "weird" with regard to the above-described limits. At the other end of the continuum, in the respected category, are the strong women. They are recognized for managing the never-ending housework and limited assistance with ease, speed and acumen. They are the ones with extra time for activities like volunteering, but never boast about it.

Strong women help weak women, thereby strengthening the dichotomy between them. Hanna was known for her strength. She had five children, a husband on weekends only, a meager income, and a tiny flat. Yet she stood as a paradigm of steadfastness. She wore a scarf while the other wore elegant wigs, giving up beauty for modesty. She sent her children to schools that were more orthodox than others of her sect. She never spent time chatting outside with her neighbors, and she kept her flat empty of unnecessary objects like kitchen accessories, pictures, house plants, superfluous furniture and extra toys. Hanna was isolated in her milieu as a strong woman, and had few opportunities to express her stress, fatigue, uncertainties and complaints. The few incidents witnessed and described here all centered around the themes of marital relationships, familiarities and the status of women. The rarity of these incidents in which Hanna shared her despair, worries, anger, and hurts gave them great significance.

ADJUSTING THE LIMITS OF INTIMACY

Being so close to someone who strives to be perfect, who does what she says she is going to do or should do, who sets an example for her peers, was very complicated for me. I could learn from being around her what all ethnographers have learned from their marginal informants. Hanna was my age, she lived five minutes away from my house, spoke Hebrew, and was Jewish like me. We shared a similar sense of humor, similar opinions on certain topics, and similar ways of dealing with children's problems. But, the enormous distance between us on the topic of religion could never be bridged. Added to this was the prohibition against talking about "everything," in deference to her boundaries of intimacy.

Thus, I always suffered from the feeling that I didn't really know Hanna. I wanted to see her naked, free of the obligations one is able to put aside in my society. I wanted to see her in the flesh and blood, human, not an example.

Being so close to her for two years, and yet always somehow apart, I drew her into my world. I did it through dreams I had during the fieldwork. In those dreams, Hanna and her husband were sinners, liars, inconsistent and uncertain. Giving up the expectations of intimacy I had at first, the dreams served as compensation. In them I saw Hanna in a short skirt with no wig covering her long dark hair. Her husband wore jeans and both of them watched television— strictly forbidden in their community. One time I dreamt he was having an affair with a young man.

Certain expectations I had about our relationship were not being met. Being "there" and at home at the same time drove me to share my frustrations with friends. Such a remote alternative way of Jewish life was a kind of threat to them. They filtered this cultural alternative through their attitudes towards "the black ones [reference to the black coats worn by Hassidic men]," with no interest in altering those prejudices. One of the most popular teases revolved around Hanna's husband's absence from home, and the comments ran something like this: "That's what he tells her, I bet you he's fooling around." "Tiberias? I'm sure he's somewhere around Tel Aviv having a good time." "Those blacks in their *yeshivot,* all they do is talk about girls. I know this guy who was once orthodox and he told me all about it." I met these provocations with smiles, sometimes playing along and only rarely becoming angry. The perception of orthodoxy as a forgery, religious life as a sham, and deep resentment towards religious people is part of the socialist-Zionist education of which I was also a product. Subconsciously I too wanted to strip them of their perfection, but on the professional level I went on accepting their borders while probing their inner world. The dreams reflect this ambivalence.

Patience, delicacy and sensitivity were required to carry this burden without letting it come between me and Hanna, and towards the end of my two years of research they enabled Hanna to come back to the topics we discussed during our first conversation, but on another level.

It was after a particularly stimulating lesson about the writings of the Jewish scholar, Maimonides. The lesson had been given by a bright rabbi who was broadly educated and treated the material in an academic manner. Hanna saw that I was intellectually stimulated, and a few minutes after I arrived home the telephone rang: "I can't let it wait until our next visit. I have to talk to you. When are you planning to come next?" Throughout the research I was in constant fear of being excluded from the community, and any unusual phone call made me nervous. "Well, if necessary I'll come tomorrow."

She had no intention of telling me not to come anymore. She was standing in her living room, rolling up some of her husband's religious paraphernalia he had left for her to put away. I told her how my husband had escaped many attempts by orthodox men in the bus station and airport to persuade him to don them and pray. She was shocked to hear that he never had, and that he had not celebrated his *Bar mitzvah,* the ceremony conferring adulthood on a 13-year-old Jewish male. "But," she said, "I wanted to talk to you about something else. Yesterday you were so alert and excited. How come you get like that only when it's on a theoretical level. Why don't you try to do a simple thing and see if it moves you too."

I could feel the thin ice, on which I was walking for the last two years, cracking. Hanna had never asked me to follow any of the commandments she and her family observed. She never asked me to bless food, or wash my hands in the special way they do before eating. She never inquired about my habits at home concerning keeping kosher, or observing the Sabbath and holidays. She respected my efforts to be frank with her, and avoided subjects that would embarrass me and force me to be untruthful. Just as I learned to avoid subjects that evoked canned answers from her, she avoided subjects that I could handle only by politeness or deception.

This mutual recognition of impersonal spheres granted us the special but restricted intimacy we had shared for two years. The tiniest fracture in this delicate balance would have exposed the deeper feelings on both sides, and Hanna was about to create such a fracture. The crack she opened up would uncover hidden untouchable layers, and create a hole that in time we would both fall into, finishing our relationship as ethnographer and informant.

> I have here two booklets which tell you how to maintain family purity. Why don't you read them and tell me whether you can practice any of it. This is the most important thing to start with, even if you don't do anything else. Read it and talk about it with your husband, don't say anything now, just think about it.

When I left Hanna's I knew that the end was near, but at the same time I saw the opportunity for a frank dialogue about purity, and remembering the one we had at the beginning of our relationship, I couldn't let this chance slip by. I wasn't afraid, as most of my family and friends were that I would become one of "them."

I wasn't afraid to try to obey some laws. My only concern was the loss of honesty. My conviction that this experience was mostly for the purpose of the research equalled my conviction that it signalled the end of the research.

ONE STEP TOO FAR:
THE DEMISE OF A FIELD WORK

And so, a few days later I returned to Hanna's home. It was Friday and the stairwell smelled clean. Behind the doors one could detect the Sabbath cooking. Friday is a short day and many things have to be done before the Sabbath brings everything to a stop. Hanna was in the kitchen washing the dishes. She boiled some water for that favorite of Israeli drinks, instant coffee, and cut me a piece of cake. I asked her if one is supposed to make a blessing before eating such a small portion of food. She said "Yes, and since you ask, why don't you repeat after me." After two years I found myself blessing the food she offered, mainly out of politeness but with no feeling of dishonesty.

> Nu? have you read the booklets? What do you say, is it going to be hard? What does your husband say?
> It doesn't seem so difficult, and my husband and I are very open with each other. He won't be the trouble. It's me. I have to see if I can do it. Don't you ever run into technical problems?

Hanna blushed and smiled. Being married for ten years—half of it pregnant and almost half of it breast feeding—left her very little time for menstrual periods. Still, she had unshared memories about her bathing in the *mikva,* confusion and distress because she couldn't tell for sure whether she was pure and allowed to have sex. That Friday morning, while the fish were waiting to be stuffed, she let some of these feelings out.

> It's been six months since I stopped breast-feeding Tzirale, and I haven't gotten pregnant yet, so now after a rather long time all those rules are relevant for me. There were times when I was pregnant, fed the baby for a year, stopped feeding, and got pregnant again without even having my period once. With God's help I hope it won't take much longer now. The most annoying thing is blood during your seven clean days, when you already started to count the clean days [the time between the last day of the woman's menstrual cycle and the day she goes to the *mikva* to purify herself; following these 7 days she is allowed to have sex with her husband], and suddenly—blood! This has to be carefully checked because you can't be forbidden more than necessary. I remember one time when I found blood on my underwear and it was way into the fourth day. Oi, I was so nervous.

I knew it couldn't be. Finally I spotted a little sore on my back that was bleeding. The other time it was a bleeding finger. Anyway, there is no one to talk to or show your body to—it took me forever to spot this sore on my back. The daily check is very important during those days. [Hanna dashes off to the bathroom and comes back with a small package in which she keeps square pieces of white cloth.]

See, you put one leg up on the bathtub or on a chair. You wrap the cloth around your finger, stick it you know where, and twist the finger around. It has to come out with no blood stains. Some women when they first hear it think it's disgusting—do you?

She looks at me and she is blushing again. I try to keep the subject on a practical level and equate the finger with an ordinary tampon. Hanna takes my silence to mean that I have no qualms about either the esthetic or religious aspects, and adds:

Well, according to your calculations you should be bathing this Sunday and so should I. Why don't we go together?

Sure, why not.

Driving home, the scarf lies on the seat next to me, my fingers work rapidly through my matted curls, and loud rock and roll music is playing on the radio. In my world this last step, to which I had agreed, looks like a risk. It doesn't feel like hypocrisy because I'm ready to do it, to bathe in the *mikva*. It just seems like this ethnographic work which I've tried to respect for 24 months as work has turned into an adventure.

Saturday night Hanna called and I told her my calculations show Monday. I didn't want to skip the matter entirely since I had promised I would try, but neither did I want to do it with her. Monday evening, when it turned dark, I took a towel and shampoo, evaded the hostile, worried looks of my husband, and went out. The *mikva* is very close to my home, near the community center and the family care clinic where my babies are checked and treated. A ring of the doorbell brought out a short lady: "Yes dear, please come in honey." I recognize her, she lives in the Gur community. She doesn't know who I am, but she gathers I am new. "Here honey, call me when you are ready."

The little stall I am in has a bathtub, some clothes hangers, and a chair. The bathing regulations are posted on the wall. I fill the clean tub with warm water, settle in, and hear voices through the wall. How strange to know that there is another woman who will be allowed to have sex from today. The bath feels so nice. I can see Hanna sitting here quietly, enjoying herself. No one knocks on the door, no one cries for her attention, and the place is physically nicer than hers. How nice, "a bath of her own."

When I call the lady she comes right in, checks my body to see no loose hairs are clinging to it, no open sores, and tells me I can keep my towel on if I am shy. "Well, some are you know. Where are you from. Oh, from here, I see. Ah, Hanna sent you, Oi our Hannele, such a saint. How many times did she say you have to dip? She didn't? Okay, then seven."

We leave the bathing room and enter the *mikva* room. I descend the steps into the middle of a small pool. She makes sure I submerge completely, and each time I come out she signifies the dip as *kosher.* "Mazel tov," she says, and looks at me with pleasant green eyes, and after I say the blessing she happily repeats "mazel tov." I look at the short old lady, and she is really happy, delighted to have purified another woman.

"Wasn't that horrible," I think to myself while dressing. "Disgusting," says my husband when I tell him about it at home.

Tuesday Hanna calls:

> It's not that I'm keeping checking up on you or anything, but I wondered whether you had gone to the *mikva,* You did? Oh, thank goodness, bless the Lord. I cannot tell you how happy I am. Each dip purifies this filthy world. I am really pleased. May the Lord bless your home and family, and may you enjoy purity and good luck.

Forget about this time, I say to myself, sharing her happiness, what about the next time?

There was no next time. I was trapped. It was clear that if I go on seeing Hanna, I would have to go to the *mikva* every month, because I promised her I would try. If I can't go to the *mikva,* I won't go to her.

What is the natural ending for a field work? My teachers used to say that one has to work for at least a year, to experience a full round of seasons, holidays, cycles of agriculture, and so forth. Some talk about an inner feeling signalling the right time to withdraw. Others have financial restrictions, like a limit on grant funds. Some say that, in a sense, most ethnographers never really leave their field.

It seemed like it took two years for a relationship to be built between two incongruous people: 24 months to realize that we would, never be able to be more than informant and ethnographer as long as we remained within the confines of those roles.

One can not afford the luxury of treating an ethnographic work as an adventure when studying modern societies, and probably any group of humans. The post-modern ethnographer must take into account that he or she is working in an open culture-market which gives meaning to the works and that the subjects are a vital part of that market. They read, discuss, and challenge the products of ethnography and by doing so give it new value. Thus ethnographic research demands solid working relations which can offer only a limited amount of intimacy. Breaking the rules and redefining the terms of the working relationship intensifies the intimacy, and might even lead to the revelation of how they actually make love. I'm glad I never found out.

Intimate relationships between researcher and informants, blur the subject-object connection they actually maintain. Being able to communicate on equal levels of everyday life, sharing feelings and thoughts, revealing anxieties, dreams or desires obscure the working bond they've agreed to preserve. Intimacy thus offers a cozy environment for the ethnographic journey, but at the same time an illusive one. The ethnographer wants information, this information happens to be someone else's real life. The informant's willingness to cooperate with the ethnographer might arise from different motivations, but it usually ends when the informant feels that he/she has become an object for someone else's interests. So it seems that intimacy and working relationships (if not under force or fallacy) go in opposite directions. Wishing to preserve the sociological endeavor through ethnographic methods, not via force or fallacy, puts a heavy burden on the depth and endurance of intimate and reciprocal relations.

"Do you still see Hanna a lot?" people ask me. "Do you keep in touch?" they wonder. "We only talk on the phone, I visited her when she had her new baby, we talked a lot during the Gulf war," I answer. We can't be friends because she was my object and we both know it.

NOTE

1. Conversations in this work are either direct quotes or reconstructions of dialogues from different times telescoped for the sake of brevity.

REFERENCES

Bar-Yosef, J. (1985). *A heretic despite himself.* Jerusalem: Keter Publishing House.
Berger, P., and Luckmann, T. (1966). *The social construction of reality.* London: Penguin Press.
Berger-Sofer, R. (1979). *Pious women.* University Microfilms Int.

Berger-Sofer, R. (1981). *Ideological separation and structural interaction.* Unpublished.

Clifford, J. and Marcus, G. E. (eds) (1986). *Writing culture.* Berkeley: University of California Press.

Friedman, M. (1982). The changing role of community rabbinate. *Jerusalem Quarterly,* 25, Fall.

Friedman, M. (1986). Haredim confront the modern city. In P. Medding (ed.), *Studies in contemporary jewry.* University of Indiana Press.

Friedman, M. (1986). Life tradition and book tradition in the development of ultraorthodox Judaism. In H. E. Goldberg (ed.), *Judaism viewed from within and from without.* New York: SUNY Press.

Geertz, C. (1988). *Works and lives.* Stanford University Press.

Harris, L. (1985). *Holydays.* New York: Macmillan.

Heschel, S. (ed.) (1983). *On being a jewish feminist.* New York: Schocken Books.

Jayanti, V. (1982). *Women in M'ea Shearim.* M. A. Thesis, The Hebrew University, Jerusalem.

Koltun, E. (ed.) (1976). *The Jewish woman.* New York: Schocken Books.

Levy, A. (1988). *The ultra-orthodox.* Jerusalem: Keter Publishing House.

Marcus, E. G., and Fischer, M. J. (1986). *Anthropology as cultural critique.* Chicago: University of Chicago Press.

Sangren, P. S. (1988). Rhetoric and authority in ethnography. *Current Anthropology* 29(13): 405-435.

Schneider-Weidman, S. (ed.) (1984). *Jewish and female.* New York: Simon and Schuster.

Shaffir, W. (1974). *Life in a religious community: The Lubavitcher Chassidim in Montreal.* Canada: Holt, Rinehart and Winston.

Shokeid, M. (1988). Anthropologists and their informants: Marginality reconsidered. *Archives* 21(1): 31-47.

PART II | Voice

9

The Myth of
Silent Authorship

Self, Substance, and Style
in Ethnographic Writing

Kathy Charmaz
Richard G. Mitchell, Jr.

[handwritten annotations: "thought's in head", "My Position innarrating story", "authority as authorship"]

Voice is the *animus* of storytelling, the manifestation of author's will, intent, and feeling.[1] Animus is not the content of stories but the ways authors present themselves within them. Scholarly writers have long been admonished to work silently on the sidelines, to keep their voices out of the reports they produce, to emulate Victorian children: be seen (in the credits) but not heard (in the text).

There are practical reasons for muting voice, for individuals and disciplines alike. Often enough in studies of human lived experience, people confound our expectations, even after long and diligent research. They say one thing and do another, conceal what seems obvious, find the ineffable in trivia, dramatize the routine, and otherwise act in ways that to us appear mysterious, courageous, mean-spirited, beatific, or silly. Candid reports of these experiences might give voice to an author's confusion, astonishment, ambivalence, revulsion, or awe.

AUTHORS' NOTE: Reprinted from *Symbolic Interaction,* vol. 19(4), (1996). Used with permission from JAI Press Inc. An abbreviated version of this chapter was presented in the session on symbolic interaction at the annual meetings of the American Sociological Association in New York, August 16-20, 1996. We thank David Altheide, David R. Maines, and Robert Prus for their comments on an earlier draft and Rosanna Hertz and Laurel Richardson for encouraging us to explore this area.

But reports of personal or collective confusion and phenomenal bewilderment without an organizing storyline make poor capital for disciplines seeking respectability in the intellectual marketplace or for intellectuals seeking recognition within those disciplines. Thus, modern social sciences regulate and restrain their authors' voices.

Silent authorship comes to mark mature scholarship. The proper voice is no voice at all. Disciplines cast out the image of scientist as icon, as responsible source of definitive knowledge, in favor of scientist as oracle, as the transparent mechanism through which empirical "facts," as in the case of uncritical positivism, or eschatological truths, as in the case of Marxism, express themselves. Voiceless reportage, modernist and otherwise, transcends the messy melange of fragmented meaning, elliptical referents, and shifting contexts that researchers may encounter in the phenomenal world. The "facts" speak for themselves, metaphorically, in mathematical models and formulas; the "natives" speak for themselves, narratively, in postmodern ethnography (see McCloskey 1990). Tales of research that collapse into narcissism and reflections upon the cultural cosmos that fly off into social science fantasy have their accorded places and permit authors a full range of voice, but these reports are only weakly linked to the intersubjective. For the most part, social science researchers are not expected to speak, and if they do, we need not listen. While positivism and postmodernism claim to offer open forums, both are suspicious of authors' voices outside prescribed forms. Extremists in both camps find corruption in speech. It lacks objectivity and value neutrality in the positivist idiom; it expresses racist, Eurocentric, phallocentric oppression in the postmodern view.

Our point is this: There is merit in humility and deference to subjects' views, and there is merit in systematic and reasoned discourse. But there is also merit in audible authorship. We speak of the writer's voice from the standpoint of ethnographers committed to the vocation of using all we can of our imperfect human capacities to experience and communicate something of others' lives. We go and see and sometimes join; we ask and listen, wonder and write, and tell our stories, not necessarily in that order. We believe that these simple acts of outward inquiry and inward reflection together with effort and creativity will give us something to say worthy of sharing. We do not pretend that our stories report autonomous truths, but neither do we share the cynic's nihilism that ethnography is a biased irrelevancy. We hold a modest faith in middle ground.

As ethnographers, our stock in trade is language, writing—words. These comprise some of the behavior we study and nearly all of the products we produce. The limitations of words, particularly descriptive language, concern us, but often these limitations are overstated on both sides of the modernist fence. Positivists have represented descriptive language as a vague, insipid veil for metaphysics, filled with meaningless references to private, incommensurable sensation, not to the solid realm of public physical events.[2] Postmodernists have reified descriptive language into a hidden power that commands and controls the intersubjective, while veiling sovereign dictates of a metonymic tyranny.[3]

From our perspective, words are both limited and useful; they are neither magic nor nonsense. Symbolic interactionists can tell a reasoned tale without retreat into scientific autism, and an interesting one without regress to arty irrationalism.

Evocative forms of writing are not merely desirable; they are essential. The interactionist charge is to involve readers' imaginative participation with subjects and authors in the described experience. It has been said of late that this project goes poorly, that ethnography and other practiced forms of interactionist research are outmoded and devitalized. No doubt stale and uninspired tales can be found in ethnography as in other forms of writing. But merely changing the presentation rules—writing reports as a haiku series or three-act plays or in unaccustomed meter or rhyme, exchanging prose for verse and verse for video— does not guarantee evocation. Indeed, unfamiliar forms in unaccustomed hands may produce products that are more self-conscious than evocative. Poetic writing is not necessarily profound or artistic any more than logical arguments are necessarily lucid or reasonable (see also Schwalbe 1995).

In our view, new forms of reportage should correspond to new phenomenal encounters.[4] Voice is not a technical feature of writing, like style, to be refined with practice or changed in form until the writer achieves "correct" effects. Nor is voice a bellwether of fieldwork maturation, a quality that "improves" as research progresses in time along some imagined continuum from first impressions to final analysis. Voice can be improved, but only as writers become more sensitive to communicating the fullness of fieldwork phenomena, green or ripened.

In the following pages, we offer two examples of the writer's voice that differ in many ways. First, Richard Mitchell recounts an early foray into the thickets of survivalism, the practice of paramilitary role-playing in preparation for the apocalypse. Second, Kathy Charmaz (1991) reflects upon chronic illness and the longtime sufferers who struggle to find meaning through "good" and "bad" days. Each of us writes in a distinct genre from different vantage points using disparate forms of knowledge for divergent purposes. Our writers' voices emerge from and reflect these differences, but they both derive from a common, uncompromising origin: fieldwork.

OPERATION AURORA BORALIS

After the interview with Kennedy, I went looking for more survivalists. I continued to read the papers and each new issue of *Survive,* where, a few months later, I found a small ad for Live Free, Inc., an Illinois-based organization claiming to have branches nationwide. I became a mail order member and soon received a letter from Live Free's local contact. We exchanged correspondence and phone calls. Then this note arrived:

> Wapaloosie Mtn. National
> Survival Association
> Group Icefield Operations HQ.
> [Address]
>
> Dear survivalists and patriots:
>
> Oct. 1-2 the American Pistol and Rifle Association in coordination with Live Free, Inc. will be holding a defense operations seminar on its permit in the Bakerville National Forest. Bring firearms. If you don't have anything more than a .22 bring it. This is a school, it is important you come, the instructors are good. Classes will cover map and compass problems, code, patrolling, ambush and counter ambush, recon and scout, night perimeter ops.
>
> Equipment: OD green clothing or cammies, canteen, small pack, rifle or shotgun.
>
> Rules:
> a. All participants will respect the flag and the US Constitution.
> b. There will be no profane language during the program.
> c. There will be no illegal weapons. . . .

Six more rules followed, then a hand-drawn map, an invitation to "bring your friends," and sketches of two fire-belching rifle barrels labeled "RAT TAT!!" and "LIVE FREE!!" It was signed, "Jim Hawkins." My colleague Eleen Baumann and I talked about it. At least the rules seemed reasonable. We called for final permission and directions. With trepidation, new camouflage clothing, and a borrowed shotgun, we went. It took 13 hours of driving across two states to reach the dirt-road junction designated as our rendezvous.

Saturday, 7:45 a.m., worn from sleeplessness and active nerves, we did as we had been told: We pulled to the roadside in plain view, shut off the engine, and remained in the vehicle. "Someone will come for you," Jim had promised. Who or how he had not told us. We watched the mirrors and road ahead and bolstered our courage by ridiculing our unseen subjects.

The media exaggerated things, we were sure. Survivalists were probably nothing more than play-acting weekend warriors, just wanna-be characters out of dime-novel westerns. With mock seriousness, Eleen called them "free rovin' anarchs, beholdin' to no men." We made nervous fun of the countryside nearby, too. "Yesterdayland," we called it, a forgotten Disney attraction. In appearance, the area through which we had driven since dawn did seem like a piece of America out of time if not place. Tiny towns were connected by dirt roads; pine and fir forest bluffs and hills were separated by clear streams. Road signs, gate posts, and the few people we saw suggested a sparse population of cattle ranchers, ever hopeful miners, out-of-work loggers, and ostracized Indians. Even names on the map fit the Old West theme. Bear Mountain, Cougar Mountain, Quartz Mountain, and Iron Mountain lay in the cardinal directions around us. The road ahead went down Refrigerator Canyon, along Rabbit Creek, and around Gold Hill, just south of the all-American town of Republic. At the general store and gas station a few miles back, we got orange juice and directions from a proprietor who, it seemed to us, wore his holstered revolver as casually as his cowboy boots. "Good fight at Rosie's [bar] last night," he confided, nodding toward the two bruised and disheveled coffee drinkers on the front porch.

At 8:15, amid dust and loose engine noises, a car pulled in behind us. I met my second survivalist. Like the displaced gentry of industrializing England, Jim Hawkins was a man of many titles but few possessions. In his correspondence he called himself the "Wapaloosie Mountain National Survival Association, Group Icefield Operations Director," "Sergeant-Major Jim Hawkins, Member, Survival Base Board of Directors," the "Regional Director of Live Free, Inc." (LFI), the "Director of Affiliation" of the "American Pistol and Rifle Association" (APRA), and occasionally "Group Leader Icefield Unit APRA." Today, he was just "Jim." Jim's 18-year-old Chevrolet leaked fluids and fumes as we watched, and it was corrugated on three corners. "That's my Mexican APC," he joked. "APC" is military shorthand for Armored Personnel Carrier. The back seat was filled with plastic buckets, tools, blankets, camping gear, odds and ends of army surplus, and his "battle rifle," a World War I bolt-action British Enfield .303. Jim was in his early 30s, trim, about 5′ 10″ and wore a "uniform" of assorted Vietnam-era surplus garments. After some mutual identity checking, he told us the exercise was about to begin a short distance away. "You'll meet Henry there," Jim told us. "He runs the LFI group in your area." Henry, LFI, and APRA turned out to be real enough, but for much of the weekend we were not sure about Jim. He headed back toward his car. Then, to our surprise, he stopped, turned toward us, came to military attention, and started to salute. The gesture was interrupted only when his hand was above his shoulder. "Follow me," he instructed out the open passenger window as he drove by, jouncing down the hill toward the assembly point three miles away. We followed and in a few minutes found ourselves in the middle of an isolated clearing in heavily timbered forest. We were surrounded by survivalists. None of them were like Jim.

The clearing was ringed with primer-spotted domestic pickups and four-door sedans with blackwall recaps and six-digit mileage. Men with guns—large and small caliber assault rifles, side arms, grenade launchers, submachine guns—stood about chatting, smoking, loading ammunition magazines, and examining each other's weapons. They wore well-used military camouflage over modest denim and polyester ready-wear. Their billed caps and the buckles of their necessarily ample belts proclaimed allegiance to brands of trucks and farm machinery. Two men performed the survivalists' toilette—sharing a truck side mirror as they painted their faces, ears, and neck with dappled green and brown makeup. These two, and others, looked martial; the man squatted before us across the smoldering campfire looked primeval. This apparition was wearing a gillie suit—the ultimate in portable concealment, a handmade hood and cloak of dark fish net through which uneven earthtone rag strips had been woven and tied. Twigs and leaves were added for accent. Imagine a Big Bird pelt, darkened, tattered, and soiled. As we watched, he carefully poured a half cup of water from his canteen into a pile of ash at the fire pit's edge. Then, with both hands, he began kneading this slurry into a loose paste. Small amounts of dirt and spittle were added; the paste stiffened. He looked up from his work and gave us a steady glance. Then, to our amazement, he lowered his face into these handfuls of mud and began smearing the mixture carefully into creases and hollows and over all the exposed skin on his head. For several moments, just the rustling gillie suit was visible; then he again looked up. Only the eyes reminded me of humanity. The rest was transformed into a kind of filth-covered, primitive man-thing. I stared at it. It stared back. The thing fastidiously wiped its hands on a patch of grass, rose from its haunches, stepped around the fire and stood square in front of me. It extended one hand and, almost to my surprise, spoke. "Hello," it said, "I'm Henry."

We had tried to prepare for this moment. We followed directions, were on time, and brought what we could of the required gear. We wanted to be unobtrusive, to "blend in." Henry's direct stare now joined the others we had received since our arrival. We had not been overlooked. Into this circle of camouflaged men riding in battered Detroit iron and armed to the teeth, we had come, nearly empty handed, driving a late model diesel-powered Peugeot station wagon, "disguised" for the occasion in freshly pressed discount-store duck hunting outfits over preppy L. L. Bean pants, Patagonia jackets, and Nike trainers. In a few minutes, the training, ambush maneuvers, and gunplay began.

What happened that day and the next would be discussed by the participants for many months and analyzed by others for even longer. In those 36 hours, we learned how to whisper and creep, how to handle the weapons, how to shoot at people, and one certain thing. Our attempts at "disguise" were a paradox: successful failures. Instead of hiding us, they made us the center of positive attention. After all, who else but naive enthusiasts would wear such ludicrous costumes? We were accepted, treated with gentle respect, and even praised. But we never went unnoticed.

GAINING ENTRY, MAKING SENSE

This sample of Richard's tale begins and ends in puzzlement and ambiguity. It is an early fragment from a much longer description of first impressions. Survivalism reveals itself to the author as an assortment of surprises and seeming contradictions from which meaning must be wrested as events unfold. The writer's voice is that of the eyewitness, the narrator in the trenches with an identifiable persona and a stake in the action. The scene comes alive in its stark strangeness and in its characters' foreign ways. Readers become allies with whom Richard talks in a conversational style (Card 1992). By writing the scene, he writes himself—not only as a surprised novice but also as a skilled craftsman. Richard paints an image of the surroundings and of his feelings that set the stage for the action to follow.

This tale is as much a "character story" as it is a "milieu story" and "event story" (Card 1992). A protagonist enters an alien environ to join in uncertain events. Richard tells his story in a series of images by which we come to "see" the goings on (Stephens 1986). Richard's voice reveals tensions between nearness and distance. He penetrates the scene, describing as he goes, and then loses the upper hand. The scene enfolds him, imposing its own demands. He pushes back this encroachment with jokes and surprises. Resistance works—but only for a time.

> We made nervous fun of the countryside nearby, too.
> "Yesterdayland," we called it, a forgotten Disney attraction. In appearance, the area through which we had driven since dawn did seem like a piece of America out of time if not place. Tiny towns were connected by dirt roads; pine and fir forest bluffs and hills were separated by clear streams. Road signs, gate posts, and the few people we saw suggested a sparse population of cattle ranchers, ever hopeful miners, out-of-work loggers, and ostracized Indians.

Details underscore the immediacy, the "seeing" of the experience (Denzin 1991; Wolcott 1990).

> The clearing was ringed with primer-spotted domestic pickups and four-door sedans with blackwall recaps and six-digit mileage. Men with guns—large and small caliber assault rifles, side arms, grenade launchers, submachine guns—stood about chatting, smoking, loading ammunition magazines, and examining each other's weapons. They wore well-used military camouflage over modest denim and polyester ready-wear. Their billed caps and the buckles of their necessarily ample belts proclaimed allegiance to brands of trucks and farm machinery. Two men performed the survivalists' toilette—sharing a truck side mirror as they painted their faces, ears, and neck with dappled green and brown makeup.

Such detailing brings us as strangers into a strange land, distinguishes survivalists' actions from our own, and creates a drama. The resultant voice is immediate, furtive, questioning. Richard is the reporter here, the "observer-as-participant," to use Gold's (1958) terms, but there is no univocality. He builds tension into his narrative, potentiates dramaturgic moments (Stephens 1986:5), and cues the reader to his feelings throughout the tale:

With trepidation . . .

We . . . bolstered our courage by ridiculing our unseen subjects . . .

. . . to our surprise, he stopped, turned toward us . . .

. . . almost to my surprise, spoke . . .

We had tried to prepare for this moment . . .

Richard's voice is neither neutral nor muted. He expresses events as he faced and felt them. Early in the story, Richard reveals his vague hope that survivalists will be not more than "play-acting weekend warriors," just "wanna-be characters," but the fieldwork soon thickens. Jim Watkins is discovered to be "a man of many titles but few possessions," and Henry's appearance pushes the limits of imagination.

Images are built on what is unsaid as well as what is said. We sense, at times, a pause, a hesitant silence carrying part of the tale's rhythm. We enter the scene knowing little of the players or the play. What will happen? What is intended? Prior experience is a poor guide. Yet the researchers, too, pose puzzlements of their own. What is a "sociologist"? Jim and Henry and the others must decide. And they have no more to go on than Richard and Eleen's immediate appearances and behavior. In the end, the judgment is positive. The researchers are affirmed; they are odd but acceptable. "After all, who else but naive enthusiasts would wear such ludicrous costumes? We were accepted, treated with gentle respect, and even praised. But we never went unnoticed."

The story builds on subtle ironies:

Ric explained the first and frequent order of the day: Wait . . .

Like much of survivalism, the exercise was rich in plans and complex in design. On paper, and there was plenty of paper, survivalism looked serious and substantial. . . .

What guides the action? The invitation to the "Defense Operations Seminar" provided ground rules. But over and again, through these samples and the 50+ pages that follow, the author and reader are overtaken by surprise and contradiction. Ordinary conceptions are discredited; new meanings come suddenly upon the scene. Received sociological theory has not paved a way through this alien world. In the weekend of gun-filled woods action, there is not yet time for patient analysis.

BETWEEN GOOD DAYS AND BAD

What's a good day now? There is no good day. . . . Well, a good day now is sort of a neutral day. That's you know, there are never days when I have . . . almost never when I have lots of energy and run around! . . . I really don't pay that much attention [to my body], and never have. I do pay more attention now because I am limited [by severe emphysema]. . . . I don't know if you could say I monitor; I observe [laughs]. Yeah, I'm forced to observe it.

It's [his emphysema] accelerated. . . . I mean there has been a decline in the last couple of years from Point A to Point B but I haven't noticed all that much. . . . I'm doing less than I did before . . . all of a sudden [I] see myself as an invalid [laughing], you know, an old invalid.

EDITOR'S NOTE: Material in this section is excerpted from Kathy Charmaz's *Good Days, Bad Days: The Self in Chronic Illness and Time,* copyright © 1991 by Kathleen C. Charmaz.

all that much. . . . I'm doing less than I did before . . . all of a sudden [I]
see myself as an invalid [laughing], you know, an old invalid.
    I asked, "How is that for you?" He said:
    It's no picnic [laughing]. Yeah, I guess you come more to grips with
    your mortality. . . . I see my dying as much more of a possibility than I
    did a few years ago.

Slow in pace. Low in energy. Short of breath. John Garston's former
daily round receded into the past as his emphysema progressed. His
apparent ease in moving around his tiny cabin belied how hard he found
it to walk around his favorite flea market, or to climb a staircase, or even
to manage the short distance to his mailbox. . . . At forty-six, John
Garston's aging rapidly accelerated and death drew closer. John
Garston's illness had become intrusive. He could not ignore it. It cut into
his life and circumscribed his choices. Nonetheless, he tried to live with it.
    What is it like to live with unremitting symptoms? What are "good"
days and "bad" days? How do people accommodate and adapt to
intrusive illnesses? What stances do people take toward them? How
does having an intrusive illness affect relationships? How do ill people
try to keep their illnesses contained?
    An intrusive illness means that the effects of illness continue; they
do not simply disrupt ill people's lives temporarily. From ill people's
views, an intrusive illness forces them to accommodate, or to suffer the
consequences, which can be both immediate and devastating. How they
accommodate to their illnesses shapes whether or not they can live as
they choose.

"Good" Days and "Bad" Days

Dividing life into "good" days and "bad" days provides one measure
of experiencing an intrusive illness and a part of the taken-for-granted
lexicon through which illness becomes understandable and explainable.
Differentiating good and bad days in illness reflects a more intensified,
focused version of evaluating days more generally, such as in work,
child care, and love. "Good" days and "bad" days also implicitly
concede the limits of self and reveal images of self. Telling identifications emerge. What assumptions lie embedded in good days and bad
days? What kind of experience do the terms denote? How does a "good"
day contrast with a "bad" one?

Most fundamentally, ill people define good and bad days according to their evaluations of the amount of intrusiveness of illness. The relative presence or absence of symptoms figures here. Ill people weigh their symptoms as they learn which ones they can dismiss or ignore. Certain symptoms may remain more or less present but vary in severity and intrusiveness. Hence, the amount of suffering and infirmity that ill people experience differentiates good and bad days.

Subsequently, suffering and infirmity create other important criteria for evaluating the day such as the amount of time taken for illness and regimen. In addition, the kinds of activities possible, amount of productivity, degree of choice, and amount of control all figure heavily in evaluating the day. These criteria flow from the initial assessment of amount of intrusiveness. When intrusiveness is low, most people have more choices and can exert greater control over them and over themselves. Conversely, when intrusiveness is high, choices narrow, and ill people have less control over them and over themselves.

Intrusive illness may lead to loss of control. The relative visibility, embarrassment, or stigma produced by illness or the subsequent loss of control can significantly define a day. Feelings of control, therefore of personal competence, shape whatever definition one makes.

Definitions of good and bad days result from juxtaposing and comparing one day with another. Decided disjunctures between the types of days lead to developing precise, explicit definitions of good and bad days. An elderly woman with cancer remarked, "Today's a good day, but yesterday was hell."

Evaluations of days are fundamentally intertwined with evaluations of self. Ill people measure the quality of the day against the self they recognize, acknowledge, and wish to be. Thus, they judge whether the day is consistent with the self they wish to affirm and present to others.

A "Good" Day

A good day means minimal intrusiveness of illness, maximal control over mind, body, and actions, and greater choice of activities. Ill people concentrate minimally, if at all, on symptoms and regimen during a good day, or they handle them smoothly and efficiently. Illness remains in the background of their lives. Spatial and temporal horizons expand and may even become expansive during a good day. When illness abates, people have much better days. Like ex-convicts just released from jail, they may wish to make up for lost time all at once.

A single mother's temporal horizons had consisted of physically getting through the day and financially keeping her children fed through the month. Her spatial horizons had been limited to the distance between her bed, the bathroom, kitchen, and living room in her tiny apartment. When she began to have good days, her temporal horizons lengthened to ideas about how she wanted her family to live in the next few years and what kind of a future she desired for herself. She exclaimed in wonder, "Before, I dragged through the day, wondering if I could get through it. Now I have a whole life in front of me." During her past bad days, she had felt locked into an uncontrollable present. As the possibility of a long future stretched out before her, she began to see a chance of exerting control over it. In short, expanding time horizons characterize a good day.

Good days are, of course, relative to an ill person's criteria and experience of chronic illness. For some people, a good day means functioning as they had before chronic illness became intrusive. Quiescent or controlled symptoms contribute to feeling relatively "normal" between exacerbations. Definitions of a good day shift and change according to ill people's experience of the progression of their illnesses. For Patricia Kennedy who had had debilitating flare-ups of multiple sclerosis, "A good day means to be able to get up and get out of bed by myself, to eat breakfast, to shower, now it means to go off to school, to participate in class, to rest and then go on [with household and family tasks]."

Definitions of a good day derive from a sense of being in character, being the self one recognizes and acknowledges. On a good day, ill people have more opportunity to be the selves they wish to be. In addition, on a good day, the earlier jarring questions about present self, the doubts, the eroded confidence, the nagging fear about the future all recede into the past, or may be completely forgotten.

A "Bad" Day

A bad day means intensified intrusiveness of illness, less control over mind, body, and actions, and limited choices about activities. Illness and regimen take center stage. On a bad day, people cannot ignore or easily minimize illness. Further, their intensified symptoms may then elicit uncontrolled feelings. Charlene Danforth, the receptionist with lupus erythematosus and Sjögren's Syndrome, described a bad day:

> I find that I'm really a lot more tired than, you know, if I just have a regular day. I have a lot more memory loss, ah, frustration and then I get depressed and angry . . . I just blew [up] that day.

Frustration marks a bad day and leads to fury, often at self. Lora Cobart recalled her bad days:

> My speech would slur a little bit, I get really pissed off or I'd go to pick something up [and drop it] . . . I mean I got really annoyed when I dropped things and that was counter-productive only it didn't do me any good to get annoyed. George [her partner] would point out that getting angry at myself didn't do anybody much good. It's hard to accept things like that and you don't want to accept them on one level or on the other, there's no point at being angry. So, I guess I felt angry at myself, at my body.

Spatial and temporal horizons shrink on a bad day. When people take for granted that their activities will be curtailed, they voluntarily limit their spatial and temporal boundaries. When they struggle to remain active, they test and measure exactly what their spatial and temporal boundaries are. Patricia Kennedy stated, "On a bad day I can't get up, I have to stay home—I have no choice. I have symptoms—yes, strength, lack of balance. It's hard for me to go out—I only go to safe places. Thrifty's [store] too crowded—too many visual stimuli, too confusing. Somebody may knock me over . . . On a bad day either I need to go with someone or take a cane. I know I should stay home and rest. On a real bad day, I can't do anything."

Like many other ill people, Patricia Kennedy graded bad days. Her definition of bad days changed when her illness flared. She commented, "I deal with time differently and time has a different *meaning* to me." Patricia Kennedy said, "being sick is a waste of time," which profoundly reduced time for tasks or for personal goals. Bad days elicit anger and frustration because they negate being one's preferred self. Bad days reflect a frustrating and frightening self for this self limits the present and might foretell the future.

How do people handle bad days? They revise expectations downward of self and of the day. For example, some ill people try to use the day for undemanding tasks. By revising the day downward, they try to prevent bad days from becoming "lost" days.

Spatial and temporal boundaries can shrink so radically during a bad day that ill people seem to sink into self. In turn, their boundaries for interacting and functioning steadily contract. As people sink into self, they experience a kind of self-involvement that probably feels alien or distasteful. Under these conditions, people feel out of self. That is, the self presently experienced bears little resemblance to someone's "real" or "ideal" self. Hence, ill people often say, "I'm not myself today."

A REALIST RENDERING

In Kathy Charmaz's (1991) analysis of time, illness, and self, she constructs conceptual categories to illuminate her respondents' experiences and concerns, thereby telling a "collective story" (Richardson 1988). Rather than aiming for ethnographic detail, this style of writing emphasizes analytic incisiveness. Criteria for this style rest upon "getting it right," but that means more than mere accuracy. It means portraying something significant of human experience (Richardson 1990, 1994). How the writer's voice emerges and develops contributes to the success or failure of this endeavor. This writer does not fashion a narrative of the self, but she does create a textured, interpretive voice.

Kathy's writing consists of an analysis of meaning. Her analysis is a realist tract (Van Maanen 1988) that describes, explicates, and synthesizes multiple statements and observations. Would any other observer have echoed her voice by writing in a similar way? Probably not, unless another observer held an equivalent relationship to the observed, asked parallel questions, and had done similar things with the collected observations. Ways of viewing the experience shape what is viewed as well as the voice of the viewer. Kathy's multiple, extensive, and intimate involvements with the phenomena made her familiar with the scene. She brought analytic questions to this experience from the start and built upon a partially developed framework from earlier pursuits. Voice becomes interactive and emergent. Yes, it reflects what the author brings to, aims for, and does with the material, but voice is always mediated through self and others, those within the field and beyond.

This kind of writing is more than bland reporting. Although analytic, it also has evocative elements. Kathy invokes the language of everyday life and asks us to look deeply into it rather than simply through it. Everyone "knows" what "good" days and "bad" days are, but what do they mean?

Kathy leads us into the topic, sets the candid tone, and shows us how good days dwindle as health fails. John Garston's frank statements match the incisiveness of Kathy's analysis and provide a counterpoint to the rhythm of her voice. She, in turn, picks up and repeats the rhythm of John's day within her writing. The short sentences recreate John's slowness and lack of energy. She reveals his experience in her narrative. Her wording collapses the past and forecasts the future:

> Slow in pace. Low in energy. Short of breath. John Garston's former daily round receded into the past as his emphysema progressed.

Through her analytic rendering, Kathy presents respondents' seldom spoken views, explicates hidden assumptions, and offers pithy definitions. Like others, neither John Garston nor Patricia Kennedy had articulated the measure of their days with such precision before their respective relationships evolved with Kathy. As she sifts and sorts her respondents' words and feelings and synthesizes their unstated, but implied, collective concerns, Kathy slips into the phenomena and into respondents' hidden assumptions. "Definitions of a good day derive from a sense of being in character, being the self one recognizes and acknowledges. On a good day, ill people have more opportunity to be the selves they wish to be." Similarly, Kathy relates definitions in a reporter's voice, but it resounds with respondents' experiences. "From ill people's views, an intrusive illness forces them to accommodate, or to suffer the consequences, which can be both immediate and devastating."

Although Kathy seldom writes in the first person, her voice pervades the passage and persuades the reader. She renders the described experience as her own through word choice, tone, and rhythm.[5] In the following paragraph, we feel space and time disappearing, slipping away, and sense that the person is also slipping away, descending into declining health and sagging spirits:

> Spatial and temporal boundaries can shrink so radically during a bad day that ill people seem to sink into self. In turn, their boundaries for interacting and functioning steadily contract. As people sink into self, they experience a kind of self-involvement that probably feels alien or distasteful.

A sympathetic tone comes through these stark statements. Through matter-of-factly reciting details, Kathy digs into the experience and excavates meaning. As the details pile upon each other, she helps the reader understand what good and bad days mean to chronically ill people *as they live them*. Behavior that the reader might otherwise attribute to an ill person's irksome personality becomes understandable, even predictable. "Bad days elicit anger and frustration because they negate being one's preferred self. Bad days reflect a frustrating and frightening self for this self limits the present and might foretell the future."

Throughout the passage, Kathy's voice resonates with respondents' experience, as evident in her use of metaphors and similes. Illness comes and goes and comes again, holds center stage, then fades into the wings, only to reappear in the next act, the next bad day. Fears nag; confidence erodes. Ill people find themselves in or out of self, as if it is an elusive object that they can lose. Kathy deepens the analysis and lightens the tone when she likens people with chronic illness to dissimilar others: "Like ex-convicts just released from jail, they may wish to make up for lost time all at once."

CONSTRUCTING VOICES

Herbert Blumer (1969) argued that people construct conduct in response to and from within situations that possess obdurate properties. Our job as symbolic interactionists is to study and report those situations as encountered and lived by others and ourselves. Description tells the reader what happened: the who, what, where, and when of things. Voice clarifies the researcher's place in, and experience of, that action. David Maines locates voice squarely in this Blumerian tradition: When free of artifice, "our writing becomes a kind of data itself, reflecting the phenomena we've studied, such that when the reader reads our accounts, a kind of deeper sense of the situation under scrutiny is conveyed" (personal communication, April 11, 1996). Voice forms another dimension of the ethnographic report; voice is one more source of insight from which readers can construct images of the goings-on.

Maines's point, and ours, is the inexorable link of voice to empirical experience, to our relationships with the denizens and domains of our inquiry (see also Maines 1989, 1993). Thus, there is no one "correct" voice, dictated in advance by disciplinary expectations, any more than "facts" of human nature or "truths" of history subordinate our discoveries in the field. The intentional construction of a "sensitive, empathic, othering" voice remains as duplicitous as the figment of a "distanced and objective" research discourse. Candid voice resonates with empirical experience; it does not improve it.

Sometimes, we find an illustrative (not imperative) regularity in voice, and we can readily envision examples of such situations beyond the excerpts above. For instance, when situations are instrumental, rule governed, or referential and our experiences of them are congruent (staid, explicit, understood, or well defined), our voice may be formal, routinized, as in a yearly university budget report or an external reviewer's report on an academic department. However, our experiences may deviate from situational appearances. If a review of the university's accounting books reveals hidden surprises and suggests intrigues, routine work may hold unexpected drama. Then, voice grows more animated, vivid, sensate. Other combinations can be imagined.

When fieldwork is committed and consequential, the writer's voice both shows and tells. It describes the action found and the experiences in finding it. Voice serves as a passive, willfully manipulated instrument only for those writers whose research is largely disengaged from the empirical. Literary critics or rate-data analysts who write with autonomous voices teach us as much about the limits of their intersubjective knowledge as the power of their pens.

Voice varies along these main dimensions: (1) the freshness of the inquiry, (2) the relationships that researchers craft with their informants, and (3) the place of the studied phenomenon in larger systems of meaning and practice. Thus, voice depends on the answer to three questions: Where does the tale begin? How are subjects involved in the telling? What are we studying?

Where Does the Tale Begin?

All research beyond the banal begins in uncertainty, where action is unantici-pated and anticipations are unrequited. We enter slippery, uncertain ground. Paths grow faint, the footing unsound. In real beginnings, we nearly always stumble, are misunderstood, and lose our confidence or our way some of the time. This awkwardness seems unsightly and unprofessional, so we rarely tell beginning tales. Beginnings are reconstructed at the end, in appendices and footnotes. In retrospect, what we did becomes what we should have done. Our temperate voices tell measured tales of just means and ordered findings. No false starts are in these stories—no confusion, trepidation, quandary, infatuation, or terror. Only when fieldwork can make sense in personal and professional terms does the tale get told. Unfortunately, this Procrustean treatment leaves out much that might be of value to the reader and diminishes our potential understanding of the phenomenon in question.

How Are Subjects Involved in the Telling?

What we make of studied life depends in part on what it makes of us. The notion of writer's voice as an autonomous and self-directed creation is mislead-ing. Ethnographers do not "choose" or "construct" or "impose" their voices onto writing with the vigor or certitude these active verbs suggest. We have made this point elsewhere (Mitchell 1993; Mitchell and Charmaz 1996). We may seek to present ourselves as "friend" or "disinterested bystander" or "novice," but subjects can and usually do reinterpret, transform, or reject these presentations in favor of their own. Our voices, if candid, reflect this reassignment of role.

Informants may play a special part in moderating relationships between researchers and members but with diverse intentions and consequences. Informants provide access, smooth the way, and answer questions. They *may* bring the researcher into their worlds of meaning. In the Chicago ethnographic tradition, such researchers as William F. Whyte (1943) and Robert Prus (1996; Prus and Irini 1980; Prus and Sharper 1977) have demonstrated immense skill in cultivating and using informants to enhance their research. Whyte, Prus, and others in this tradition have formed strong alliances with informants, leading to expanded research relationships based on mutual acceptance. But not all researchers possess the skill and fortunes of Whyte and Prus. Acceptance is not certain.

Sometimes, informants may not share the researcher's objectives. They may see researchers as what Wax (1980) called prey—fair game, suckers, marks. If so, then researchers' quest for data make them easy targets for informants to exploit for personal gifts and favors or to manipulate impressions on behalf of their group or class. Even when informants and researchers do share bonafide trust, other problems of communication can persist. Genuine intimacy carries with it implicit expectations constraining the scope and forms of inquiry. Friends know "we just don't talk about" some things. Researchers who establish deep and abiding relationships with their informants may feel obligated to disattend to proscribed but significant phenomena, or they may omit relevant data from their reports in deference to their perceptions of members' expectations.

If we view our relationships with subjects as affectively strong and of common purpose, our voices will no doubt reflect this view. Informants may bolster our confidence. Our reports may brim with enthusiasm and conviction, all of which may be accurate or entirely mistaken. With (or without) the help of informants, there will be times when we think we know, and we don't. Voice reports the researcher's involvement with phenomena. It is not phenomena themselves.

What Are We Studying?

The examples of voice in the preceding excerpts reveal substantial but not surprising variance. When social life comes upon us full force, we may have something to say, but the words and forms of our speech are not just writing options. To repeat, all ethnographic voices have their origin in empirical experience. And, to state the obvious, survivalism is not chronic illness.

Later, Richard would learn more about survivalists. In spite of survivalism's initial appearances of calculation and utility, he would discover that it is primarily a celebration of irrationality—an encompassing, compelling game of make-believe. This is not to suggest that it is a trivial experience. Survivalists' end games are times of enchantment when worlds that never were, nor could have been, nor ever will be, are crafted and momentarily admired. But these enchantments are temporary and must stand on their own.

Survivalism lacks empirical confirmation, and survivalists know it. No apocalypse has occurred. America has not fallen into economic ruin or the clutches of alien invaders. Participants are not joined in some folie à deux. Their game has limits—on time, place, rules of engagement, and decorum. Richard's experience was with the ingenious daydreams and make-believe of a marginal few. They surprise him and themselves. Their play transforms a corner of the world into a stage of action, a place of unambiguous meaning, high drama, obvious objectives, and fair means. With will and wit and help from a few friends, survivalists can occasionally turn an ordinary day into a "bad" one, a day filled with fast and furious and fateful action, at least in imagination.

Survivalism remains cut off from core affirmations of self in daily life. Survival action takes place in the interludes and on the side. It is sporadic, infrequent, peripheral—a weekend a month, an evening a week, a letter in the post office box, a trip to the gun shop or hardware store. These are the epiphanies of survivalism, events easily diluted in the swirl of more potent and compelling life currents—family, work, and friendships. Richard gives voice to action on the fringes of his subjects' lives. Kathy's voice arises from the center. She speaks for us all, sooner or later.

Chronic illness is as old as humankind and as common as death. We all decline, debilitate with the passing of years and the coming of disease, with injury and accident and the obsolescence of our parts. Kathy gives voice to an experience at the very heart of the human condition. Whereas survivalism is optional, infrequent, and barely believable, chronic illness is unrelenting, unavoidable, and all-encompassing. Survivalists choose their action; sufferers bear what comes to them. Survivalists construct consequentiality; sufferers seek to minimize it, to make today as good and ordinary and unremarkable as before—a "good day" when illness slides into the background.

Kathy's task, finding the collective in the subjective, is not easy. Unlike Thomas Mann's (1927) characters, chronically ill people seldom launch into a soliloquy on the seeds of time. Kathy sought shared meaning in individual suffering sensible, to make it ordinary and unquestioned. Through over 100 interviews and a decade of time, in casual encounters and on formal occasions, both coincidental and directed, Kathy stayed in touch with suffering—others' and her own. Her voice does not transcend experience but re-envisions it. Kathy's voice brings fragments of fieldwork time, context, and mood together in a colloquy of her several selves—reflecting, witnessing, wondering, accepting—at once.

CONCLUSION

The myth of silent authorship is false but reassuring. In nervous times, when faced with personal doubt or phenomenal puzzlement, we strike a noble pose or familiar chord. We act as if we can cover up confusion, as if ignorance does not show. We change our voices or try to. When the appearance of understanding must be created in the face of confusion or ignorance, we often tighten the text around familiar themes or distract our readers with unexpected forms. "New" processes are discovered to be only variants of the old; old ideas are wrapped in new packaging. Method bequeaths meaning. Disciplines encourage this camouflage of the author's uncertain voice and sometimes require it. If subjects act in unexpected ways and authors insist on sharing their befuddlements in language that affronts positivist sensibilities with excessive subjectivity or offends postmodernists with political impropriety, peer review and rebuttal provide ample opportunities to bring errant authors back on course. The author's voice is modulated and muffled until indistinguishable from the metanarrative chorus of the discipline. The flight from ambiguity is joined.

The speech of sociologists is worth hearing, but it is not magical. There is little to fear from candor. Accusations concerning the abuse of our authority exaggerate its occurrence. Our pronouncements are rarely definitive or consequential. The forces loosed in naming remain as modest as the speaker's knowledge of real things. Words mediate; they do not create. We need all our words to tell the whole story. And, in the end, we can only stand upon our stories.

We do ourselves and our disciplines no service by only telling half-tales, by only reporting finished analyses in temperate voice, by suppressing wonder or perplexity or dread. Alternatively, writing tricks and data transformations may distract us, but they do not guarantee a clearer tale or a greater truth. Turning Henry and Ric into iotas of a path model or changing John and Patricia into stanzas of a song will not make their lives more vivid or true than candid description. Henry and Ric and John and Patricia have every right to expect us to represent their lives as something more than scientific artifacts or art objects.

In ethnography, the emergent self is acculturated; it learns the limits of its own power. Fieldwork leavens immodesty but does it imperfectly. And that is good. Authors should have something to say that we can't anticipate from the title page and the publisher. There is work to be done that can only be done "down and dirty," face-to-face confrontations with the lives and works and worlds of those about whom we would write. Good writers of all kinds know this. Sometimes, the great ones tell us so: "I don't much care for analysis or examining literary currents," Pablo Neruda ([1970] 1990) said in an interview shortly before his death. He had little use for books about books and the dry arguments of academic critics. Neruda ([1954] 1970), the greatest of Latin American poets, the voice of revolutionary consciousness for half a century, described the origin of his voice, in the way he knew best, in a poem:

> *Ode to the Book**
>
> I don't come out
> of collected works,
> my poems
> have not eaten poems—
> they devour
> exciting happenings,
> feed on rough weather,
> and dig their food
> out of earth and men.
> I'm on my way
> with dust in my shoes
> free of mythology;
> send books back to their shelves,
> I'm going down into the streets.

Symbolic interactionists who have something to say and a voice to say it with would do well to follow.

NOTES

1. See Gaskin (1995) on Epicurius and his varied understandings of *animus* (p. xxxv).
2. Otto Neurath (1959) describes the positivist's agenda as taking the "imprecise, unanalyzed terms" of natural language and "purifying" it until every word is replaced "by terms taken from the language of advanced science" (p. 200). For Carnap (1959), his article "The Elimination of Metaphysics through Logical Analysis of Language" meant the ruthless expungement of "pseudo-

---

*This poem was reprinted with permission from Random House UK Ltd. © 1970.

concepts" from scientific reporting, including words that were ill defined, were used asyntacti-
cally, or were out of place. When put to the test, these systems produced little unequivocal
knowledge. Carnap's publication of the grandly titled *International Encyclopedia of United
Science* in the late 1920s consisted of only a small collection of short brochures (Ayer 1959:7).

3. Postmodernists are inclined toward a faith in the metonymic power of words. Metonymic
("other name") magic reduces things to objects, specifically words, before the spell works.
Knowing the name of a thing and uttering it in proper ritual form (like the voodoo priest and her
doll) gives power over that object to the speaker (or writer). Donald McCloskey (1990) reminds
us that this is a long-standing notion in literary criticism.

4. Voice has been treated as a professional problem for at least half a century. In his 1929
presidential address to the American Sociological Association, William F. Ogburn (cited in
Bannister 1987:161) insisted that scientific sociology could only progress if its practitioners
adopted a "wholly colorless literary style." The American Psychological Association's (1994)
"style" requirements impose a general frame for presentation, yet its positivist presumptions
remain implicit. The postmodernist rejection of descriptive writing is analogous; it represents an
attempt to modulate content by regulating form. In our view, all presumptions about voice are
inappropriate in advance, or independent, of fieldwork.

5. In this kind of writing, the writer remains in the background and becomes embedded in the
narrative rather than acting in the scene. The reader hears the writer's words, envisions the scenes,
and attends to the story, not the storyteller (see Provost 1980).

REFERENCES

American Psychological Association. 1994. *Publication Manual of the American Psychological
    Association* 4th ed. Washington, DC: Author.
Ayer, A. J. 1959. *Logical Positivism.* New York: Free Press.
Bannister, Robert C. 1987. *Sociology and Scientism: The American Quest for Objectivity,
    1880-1940.* Chapel Hill: University of North Carolina Press.
Blumer, Herbert. 1969. *Symbolic Interactionism.* Englewood Cliffs, NJ: Prentice Hall.
Card, Orson Scott. 1992. "What Kind of Story Are You Telling? Pp. 45-55 in *The Writer's Digest
    Handbook of Novel Writing,* edited by Tom Clark, William Brohaugh, Bruce Woods, and
    Bill Strickland. Cincinnati, OH: Writer's Digest Books.
Carnap, Rudolph. 1959. "The Elimination of Metaphysics through Logical Analysis of Language."
    Pp. 60-81 in *Logical Positivism,* edited by A. J. Ayer. New York: Free Press.
Charmaz, Kathy. 1991. *Good Days, Bad Days: The Self in Chronic Illness and Time.* New
    Brunswick, NJ: Rutgers University Press.
Denzin, Norman K. 1991. "Representing Lived Experiences in Ethnographic Texts." Pp. 59-70 in
    Studies in Symbolic Interaction (vol. 12), edited by Norman K. Denzin. Greenwich, CT:
    JAI.
Gaskin, John, ed. 1995. *The Epicurean Philosophers.* London: Everyman.
Gold, Raymond L. 1958. "Roles in Sociological Field Observations." *Social Forces* 36:217-23.
Maines, David R. 1993. "Narrative's Moment and Sociology's Phenomena: Toward a Narrative
    Sociology." *Sociological Quarterly* 34:17-38.
Maines, David R. 1989. "Herbert Blumer on the Possibility of Science in the Practice of Sociology:
    Further Thoughts." *Journal of Contemporary Ethnography* 18:160-77.
Mann, Thomas. 1927. *The Magic Mountain.* New York: Knopf.
McCloskey, Donald. 1990. *If You're So Smart: The Narrative of Economic Expertise.* Chicago:
    University of Chicago Press.

Mitchell, Richard G., Jr. 1993. *Secrecy and Fieldwork.* Newbury Park, CA: Sage.

Mitchell, Richard G., Jr. and Kathy Charmaz. 1996. "Telling Tales, Writing Stories: Postmodernist Visions and Realist Images in Ethnographic Writing." *Journal of Contemporary Ethnography* 25:144-66.

Neurath, Otto. 1959. "Protocol Sentences." Pp. 199-208 in *Logical Positivism,* edited by A. J. Ayer. New York: Free Press.

Neruda, Pablo. [1954] 1970. "Ode to a Book." Pp. 284-89 in *Neruda: Selected Poems,* edited by Nathaniel Tarn. Boston: Houghton Mifflin.

———. [1970] 1990. "Introduction" to *Neruda: Selected Poems,* edited by Nathaniel Tarn. Boston: Houghton Mifflin.

Provost, Gary. 1980. *Make Every Word Count.* Cincinnati, OH: Writer's Digest Books.

Prus, Robert. 1996. *Symbolic Interaction and Ethnographic Research: Intersubjectivity and the Study of Human Lived Experience.* Albany: State University of New York Press.

Prus, Robert and C. R. D. Sharper. 1977. *Road Hustler: The Career Contingencies of Professional Card and Dice Hustlers.* Lexington, MA: Lexington Books.

Prus, Robert and Styllianoss Irini. 1980. *Hookers, Rounders, and Desk Clerks: The Social Organization of the Hotel Community.* Salem, WI: Sheffield.

Richardson, Laurel. 1988. "The Collective Story: Postmodernism and the Writing of Sociology." *Sociological Focus* 21:199-208.

———. 1990. *Writing Strategies: Reaching Diverse Audiences.* Newbury Park, CA: Sage.

———. 1994. "Writing: A Method of Inquiry," Pp. 516-29 in *Handbook of Qualitative Research,* edited by Norman K. Denzin and Yvonna S. Lincoln. Thousand Oaks, CA: Sage.

Schwalbe, Michael. 1995. "The Responsibilities of Sociological Poets." *Qualitative Sociology* 18:393-414.

Stephens, Michael. 1986. *The Dramaturgy of Style: Voice in Short Fiction.* Carbondale: Southern Illinois University Press.

Van Maanen, John. 1988. *Tales of the Field.* Chicago: University of Chicago Press.

Wax, Murray L. 1980. "Paradoxes of Consent to the Practice of Fieldwork." *Social Problems* 27:272-83.

Whyte, William Foote, 1943. *Street Corner Society.* Chicago: University of Chicago Press.

Wolcott, Harry F. 1990. "Making a Study 'More Ethnographic.' " *Journal of Contemporary Ethnography* 19:44-72.

10

Personal Writing in Social Research

Issues of Production and Interpretation

Marjorie L. DeVault

In the past few years, I have been drawn into two writing projects that called for an explicitly autobiographical approach. When my friend and colleague Tracy Paget learned that she was dying from a rare cancer she began work on a series of essays about her situation: She was an analyst of medical error who had become an example of her topic. She asked me to edit the book (Paget 1993); in an attempt to resolve and express my complex feelings about this work, I decided to add to her text an epilogue that told the story of my involvement with Tracy during her illness. More recently, I was asked to contribute to a collection of autobiographical essays written by feminist sociologists. We were to tell the stories of our lives and work, with the idea that the collection would illuminate the development and institutionalization of feminism in our discipline. This collection took shape alongside several others published recently and constituting a small wave of autobiographical writing in our discipline, undertaken especially although not exclusively by feminists, e.g., *Authors of Their Own Lives* (Berger 1990), *Gender and the Academic Experience* (Orlans and Wallace 1994), and *Individual Voices, Collective Visions* (Goetting and Fenstermaker 1995). Also of note, the February 1993 special issue of the British journal *Sociology* (vol. 27, no. 1) was devoted to "Biography and Autobiography in

Sociology." The topic there is broader than mine, for those articles consider not only sociologists' own autobiographical writing but also their use of others' life writing as data.

I was quite ambivalent about both of my autobiographical projects. While writing, I experienced more than the usual highs and lows, vacillating between euphoria and despair. I was exceedingly dubious at the beginning about my ability to do this kind of writing, but by the time I finished I felt that I was reasonably good at it. Both projects represented work that I thought of as "not quite sociology," but I have also felt, at times, a desire to present and defend them as sociology because they express many of the same analytic themes as my more conventional scholarly work. I know that I would not have embarked on either project if not for my grounding in feminist scholarship and my interest in experimental genres for social science writing—these relatively new lines of thought gave me the confidence to proceed. But my forays into autobiographical writing left me somewhat unsettled about the place of this kind of writing in sociological work. My purpose in this chapter is to identify and discuss some of the questions raised by incorporating personal writing into empirical studies.

We sociologists tend not to be very self-conscious about our own writing: indeed, Howard Becker (1986) suggests that "literary types" can make jokes just by saying "sociology"—the way comedians use words like "Peoria" (p. 1). The scientific underpinnings of our discipline lend credence to the idea that we work with a transparent medium, simply "writing up" our "findings." Social scientists recognize that some of us write "well," and others don't, but we rarely talk very explicitly about what that means; our disciplinary culture does not make writing a focal concern. In fields that take writing more seriously—among writers and critics, for example—practitioners share more fully developed vocabularies and attitudes toward writing. I mention this difference at the outset to suggest that some of the bafflement and criticism directed at new forms arise from sociologists' relatively impoverished understandings of writing. My aim is not to convert sociologists to a more literary culture or simply insert literary understandings into the writing culture of our discipline but to suggest that social scientists might be more conscious of our own assumptions and practices—of how we talk about writing issues and handle them in our texts. Rather than simply criticize or defend personal writing (the most common sociological responses to date), I propose that we consider in a more thoughtful way what is involved in the production and interpretation of research texts that include personal accounts. My discussion is located within a qualitative fieldwork tradition, not because personal writing is irrelevant to other modes of sociological analysis, but because my own training and experience are in the qualitative tradition and because that is where sociological experiments with personal writing have been most evident.

WHAT'S NEW? TRADITIONS OF PERSONAL WRITING IN FIELDWORK ACCOUNTS

I use the term "personal writing" here to refer to sections of text that present autobiographical or introspective material in the service of a sociological analysis. Although such material has often been included, in some way, in fieldwork accounts, personal material has typically been used to frame the substance of an analysis. More recently, in the wave of rhetorical innovation that has developed in the social sciences, some researchers have begun to construct analyses that make personal writing an integral part of the analytic work of the research text. This strategy has been developed most fully by anthropologists; well-known and successful examples are works by Myerhoff (1978), Shostak (1981), Rosaldo (1989), Kondo (1990), and Behar (1993). Similar moves can be seen in other fields, most notably among legal theorists, where the work of Patricia Williams (1991) is exemplary. In sociology, two relatively early examples are Reinharz (1979) and Zola (1982). More recent work in this vein includes Orr (1990), Stacey (1990), Krieger (1991), Ronai (1992), Linden (1993), Paget (1993), and Ellis (1993).

This new personal-reflexive writing arises in part from postmodernist thought, and any attempt to locate it in relation to a fieldwork tradition runs up against the uneasy relationship between qualitative sociology and postmodernism. The postmodern critique of positivism, with its emphasis on multiple and shifting perspectives, seems compatible with long-standing tendencies within the interactionist fieldwork tradition, which emphasizes close attention to meanings that arise in particular settings. It is instructive to identify these parallels; however, I want to resist the interactionists' comfortable but misleading claim that "we've been doing that all along!"

In one sense, almost any fieldwork report can be considered a personal narrative of sorts. The discussion of method required in a scientific report is a story of the project and field-workers are central actors in their projects. Stories of gaining access, and the vicissitudes of entry to the field, are conventional parts of an ethnographic report and, to varying degrees, reveal the field-worker as a vivid individual character in the research narrative. But traditionally, fieldwork texts have been built upon a separation between this kind of storytelling and the portions of the text that present a substantive analysis. Stories in which the researcher appears as a character are typically contained in introductory chapters. Often, they are elaborated in a methodological appendix, a placement that defines them as inessential to the analysis, interesting only as an aside to specialist readers. (But how many of us turn to these appendixes first? And what does that tell us about the insights and pleasures they provide?)

The kinds of stories that researchers tell about their fieldwork are a curious mix of disclosure and discretion. Placed in a section on "method," the story of a research project serves a legitimizing function: The story that is told provides a warrant for the analysis to follow (Clifford 1983). It should reveal a researcher who is intelligent, responsible, thorough, and objective (at least as much so as is humanly possible). Here, the purpose of personal storytelling is to establish the researcher's authority: The story is meant to say, "Believe me, because I did it right." These purposes are highlighted, I think, by the existence of a popular mini-genre in the field of qualitative research, the account—published quite separately from the research results—of "what really happened in the research" (e.g., Johnson 1988; Stacey 1991; Thorne 1988; Van Maanen 1988). Often, these kinds of accounts are written some time after the fieldwork has ended and the research report has been published. Perhaps the best-known example is William Foote Whyte's (1993) appendix to *Street Corner Society,* added 12 years after the first edition's publication. It is strikingly autobiographical, beginning with Whyte's background and youthful aspirations, and provides a quite detailed account of his personal experience of his years conducting the research. Some authors of these accounts seem to imply that the distance of elapsed time facilitates useful reflection on the research story. Whatever the merits of this claim, the separation of analysis and reflection gives the impression that "personal" elements of the research story are inessential to its core.

While explicitly personal writing in published texts has traditionally been limited and contained in these ways, field-workers also produce snippets of "autobiographical" writing routinely in the notes we keep as part of any research project. Standard ethnographic practice involves keeping a fieldwork log or chronicle of some sort; developing a "quarry" of thinking about a project in analytic memos; or including "self-examination" writing in our notes, more or less consciously (perhaps formalized in "observer comments"). And of course the core of ethnographic work involves the production of field notes, a specialized form of "reportage" (Emerson, Fretz, and Shaw 1995). These different kinds of personal writing parallel the types identified by journal writer Ira Progoff (1975), who helps his workshop students develop their journals by calling attention to these admittedly artificial categories and asking them to experiment with each mode. My point here is that sociologists write themselves into their projects in various ways, sometimes without much noticing that we are doing so. We learn and then teach—either consciously or not—ways of working with personal experience and placing it within our texts. In these ways, standard ethnographic practice both relies on and obscures personal experience.

It is becoming commonplace to recognize that fieldwork is all about text and that we produce, interpret, and present data only through writing. My point here is more specific: that personal narrative is woven into the production of fieldwork at the most fundamental level. Conventionally, however, we have been most tolerant of personal elements in the writing that only the researcher reads. The classic realist ethnography is produced for presentation to a wider public by removing most of the explicitly personal material—or at least moving it to a subordinate place in the text. What is new, then, is a greater tolerance (or demand) for the personal to appear differently in our writing—to be expressed and placed more prominently and to be read as having greater significance for our findings and interpretation.

The impetus for this development is surely grounded in recent criticism of the notion of scientific "objectivity" and perhaps also in questions that ethnographers have asked about the researcher's responsibilities to informants. Social scientists are being pressed to acknowledge that all writing is located and tells at best a partial truth. Including the researcher more explicitly in the text offers the reader additional information which may be used in evaluating the account. From a traditionally positivist point of view, introducing a personal dimension may seem to bias our analyses and weaken our claims to "truth." But some philosophers of social science suggest that acknowledging our partiality can move us toward a stronger form of objectivity (Harding 1986, 1991). And Patricia Hill Collins's (1990) outline for an Afrocentric feminist epistemology (pp. 217-19) suggests that recognizing the producer of any knowledge claim allows a fuller and more robust evaluation of its merits (see also Stanley 1993).

GENRE: THE TRUTH, THE WHOLE TRUTH,
AND NOTHING LIKE THE TRUTH AT ALL

Genre is the literary term that refers to texts of a particular type or form that work in the distinctive ways of that form. Sociologists, I would argue, tend to take genre for granted. The research report is a rigid, controlling genre and one that we learn so early in our science training and use so routinely that it seems a "natural" and efficient way to convey the results of our investigations. (Even when it may not seem so appropriate, its conventions are enforced very effectively through peer reviewing and the editorial practice of professional journals and publishing houses.) Perhaps because there is a single dominant and controlling genre in the social sciences, sociologists seem to read other kinds of work without much awareness of how they work as forms. Thus, my intention in this section is to call attention to "generic" features of personal writing—that is, the conventions of telling that are characteristic of personal accounts.

Personal writing can be more or less self-conscious, but it is most often designed to appear immediate and confessional. It speaks to readers with an individual voice, and that voice often claims something like "Here is my truth, complete and unvarnished." A personal account works well when it reads easily and gives the impression of direct access to an individual reality. The author disarms (and thus wins the reader) by telling it "like it is." But, of course, these are impressions created by the skillful writer in this genre (just as the skillful statistical analyst convinces readers that numbers on a page "explain" the variance in some piece of the social world). In fact, any story of one's life is a truth that is highly selective and crafted for particular purposes, both conscious and not.

Sitting down to write my autobiographical essay brought this feature of the genre clearly into view. When I was asked to participate in the autobiography project, my first reaction was that I simply couldn't do it because there were some things I was unwilling to tell for public consumption. It took a few days worrying to realize that I could tell what I wanted and keep my secrets. But that first insight led to a more complex and continuing meditation on what story to tell, how, and to what end. I began to realize that my story would have a plot and that I would need to consider where it should lead. Did I want to tell a "success story," for example? If I highlighted "troubles," would I be read as "whining"? As the daughter of a professor, I wanted to give some sense of the way that my class background had eased my entry to professional life, but I wanted to do that in a way that would include my ambivalence about the meaning of "ease" and "comfort" in a relatively privileged segment of a stratified society. I needed to make these kinds of purposes explicit—at least to myself, and sometimes to readers—in order to decide what to tell and how.

Kathryn Addelson (1991) uses an interesting and effective technique to address this kind of issue when discussing her working-class background in the autobiographical material she wove into her collection of philosophical essays, *Impure Thoughts*. She begins by quoting a brief autobiography written some years earlier to introduce a collection of working-class life histories produced by a community-organizing group. "This little autobiography," she explains, was written to make a point, and, of course, it leaves out many important things" (p. 4). Then she proceeds to tell another, expanded story of her life, and in the chapters that follow, more stories from that life. This technique encourages her readers to recognize the constructed character of her personal writing and to read it more carefully for its analytic significance and connections to the substance of her essays. Berger (1990) also takes note of the crafted and selective character of autobiographical writing in the introduction to the collection he edited, by reference to Pierre Bourdieu's characterization of autobiographers as "ideologists of their own lives" (p. xvii). But he seems not to have taken the full significance of the phrase, since he transmutes "ideologist" into "author" in the title he chose for the book.

Sociologists are not taught to do autobiographical writing, and most of us who attempt it proceed, I presume, somewhat intuitively, learning by imitation. In fact, the study of examples—whether conscious or not—is probably the way most practitioners learn any form of writing. One key to producing useful personal writing seems to be an ability to reflect on experience so that the account does more than simply report the facts. One must consider not only what to write about but also why and how. It is also important to consider what is appropriate and useful—what kinds of everyday accounts move readers beyond the mundane, for example, and what kinds of important material one might be censoring out of shame or fear. Sometimes, self-censorship is prudent: When one includes personal-reflective material in a research text, it may be read as evidence of problems and "weaknesses" that more abstract texts conceal. But revelation has the virtue of challenging the fictions of "hygienic research" (Stanley and Wise [1983] 1993:114-15) that sustain such readings.

Social scientists are trained to think analytically, but we are perhaps less prepared to apply our analytic skills to our own experience. We are certainly not taught to write about whatever self-analysis we can achieve; rather, we are encouraged to edit these insights out of our texts. What I mean to suggest here is that we need to become more sophisticated and reflective readers and writers in order to consider where our personal stories lead and what they convey.

QUESTIONS

New forms incorporating personal writing raise many questions. The brief discussion that follows identifies a few of these and provides some preliminary thoughts. I offer them not as answers but as invitations to further discussion.

• *How should we write personally about others?*

Recent formulations of fieldwork ethics include increasingly stringent review of research by human subjects boards as well as new questions about the possibilities of obtaining "informed consent" (e.g., Goduka 1990) and the virtues of confidentiality for informants (see Linden 1993; Myerhoff 1978). When we write from personal experience, we must consider how these formulations speak to our responsibilities to other people who appear in the texts. If I write about my parents or teachers, for example, do I need their consent? What about friends and acquaintances? Do I have an obligation to identify characters in my story, or the right to do so if I wish, even against their will? What if they remember things differently?

Ruth Behar (1993) includes in her innovative ethnography, *Translated Woman*, an autobiographical chapter that sketches some of the parallels and intersections between her life and that of her informant, a Mexican peddler. More recently, she has written about her father's painful response to the way she portrayed them there and how his wounded anger mixed with pride in her accomplishment (Behar 1995). She also describes participating in a writers' conference, where she wondered about hurting those we write about, and the teacher—a prominent memoirist—provided what may be one of the standard literary answers: "People aren't emotional hemophiliacs. . . . They can take it better than you think" (Behar 1995:69).

Whether one approves or disapproves of this relatively cavalier response for the journalist or fiction writer (and it seems likely that researchers' evaluations would diverge sharply; see Punch 1994), it seems important to consider why social scientists might be held to a different standard. To the extent that social scientists claim to produce authorized knowledge of society, we seize a power to define realities of and for others. Legitimacy in this enterprise rests on adherence to systematic methods of investigation and seems also to carry an implicit assumption that we study general, replicable processes in which individuals are interchangeable. Personal writing may challenge this assumption, exposing some of the fictions of our tradition of systematic inquiry. It may require new ways of thinking about confidentiality and identification. An autobiographical account brings a more immediate kind of disclosure than the typical empirical study together with more intimate reasons for concern about others. It can also provide opportunities for more sustained collective work on narratives of social life, since those closest to us may be more easily recruited into close collaboration than other research participants (see Mykhalovskiy 1997 [this volume] on the collective production of autobiography).

- *How do we evaluate and critique personal writing?*

Sociologists are unaccustomed to evaluating personal writing; the standards for critique and discussion seem "slippery" to many in comparison with more familiar criteria associated with the scientific research report. Cotterill and Letherby (1993) point out that some readers "may feel unable to criticise the work without appearing to criticise the researcher personally" (p. 75). Indeed, Eric Mykhalovskiy's (1997 [this volume]) analysis of the common charge of "self-indulgence" suggests that this critique, apparently aimed at the author of an autobiographical text, functions as a regulatory practice and conceals a series of unstated assumptions about social analyses.

As personal writing becomes more common among social scientists, researchers will need to develop new avenues of criticism and praise for such work. One element in this new evaluative understanding might be a clearer sense of how to combine "scientific" with "literary" standards, without mystifying the latter. People in their social contexts learn to know in a tacit way—through listening and telling—what makes a good story. Groups of readers develop (more or less) common understandings of the bases for evaluation, partly explicit and partly arising from a tacit sort of judgment. As we gain experience reading and discussing, we become "better," "more sophisticated" readers who feel more certain about these judgments, make them more consciously, and have access to a fuller vocabulary with which to articulate them. Presumably, a "good story" in some contexts, for some purposes, may be not so good for others. Such criteria for evaluating personal writing as sociology have barely begun to develop.

Howard Becker (1982) discusses these kinds of evaluative processes in *Art Worlds,* as among jazz musicians and theater people, who express such tacit evaluation with phrases like "it swings" and "it works" (p. 199). These judgments are learned over time, although not always articulated in abstract form, and are based partly on assessments of how others will respond to a performance or text. Social scientists already use this kind of tacit evaluation without much awareness alongside the explicit "scientific" standards—this is the point of recent analyses of the rhetorical dimensions of classic works in the social sciences (see Clifford and Marcus 1986; Hunter 1990; McCloskey 1990). As we see this kind of evaluation more clearly and understand it better, we will perhaps become more comfortable with it and articulate these judgments more clearly. Developing a fuller sense of these standards will, I think, involve closer attention to readers and their likely responses to texts.

- *How much reflexivity is enough?*

I am generally enthusiastic about the reflexive turn in sociological writing, and I feel impatient with charges that personal writing is "self-indulgent" or "narcissistic." Still, I sometimes worry that the recent emphasis on the personal may signal a retreat from the attempt to interpret a wider social world. Many field-workers seem to have turned to personal writing in part as a response to concern about the difficulties of protecting informants' views and interests. Recent writing in our field has generated a profound skepticism about the bases for our interpretive authority and the value of writing about others at all (see, e.g., Patai 1991; Stacey 1991). In this context, writing that reveals personal sources for a research endeavor can be seen as an attempt—although a futile one—to balance the positions of researcher and subjects. It may also serve as a kind of "confession" that explains and perhaps goes some way toward excusing the researcher's activity.

My own research, for example, has focused recently on work in the predominantly female profession of dietetics and community nutrition. As I began to write about this field, I was painfully aware that many of my informants will not share my critical stance toward "professionalism" and its effects and may take my writing about their difficulties as yet another attack on their subordinated professional ranks. Increasingly, I saw that my questions about "profession" have arisen from my own ambivalence about my situation as a professional sociologist. As I considered this possibility, it seemed only fair—and perhaps a way to explain to informant readers why I see them as I do—to include some discussion of these personal sources for my work. Having worked with this insight for a couple of years now, I have mixed feelings about the strategy: Although it provides some insight, I see that it does not solve the fundamental problem, and I fear that it has sometimes provided an excuse for spending more time at my computer than in the field. In each particular case, then, it seems important to consider what a personal element does in an analysis and how it contributes to a larger project.

- *Who writes personally, and why?*

Finally, I want to consider how autobiographical strategies are likely to be related to inequalities of status and power. I am concerned here with the structured organization of silence and self-disclosure: Which of us will be motivated to tell truths about our lives? Which truths will we be willing to tell? On the face of it, we might assume that those who are most vulnerable will be least likely to reveal personal information. Yet such a view seems too simple, especially when one looks at the body of work in this area: The autobiographical impulse seems common among working-class academics, women, and those from other groups underrepresented in the professions. In part, it may be that these accounts make "good stories": The story of one who succeeds against the odds is likely to be "interesting," whereas an account of more "ordinary" success is perhaps not so easily conceptualized as a story at all. This observation about what "works" as a story may help illuminate the effectiveness of personal narrative in a more general sense. The personal account makes excluded voices "hearable" within a dominant discourse—it is compelling in part because it reveals in vivid detail those whose presence might not be noticed if they spoke abstractly.

This observation might be seen as either promising or worrisome. It suggests that personal writing is useful for exploring the unexpected and thus for bringing to light aspects of "ordinary" experience that are typically obscured. However, the observation that "outsiders" may be more likely than the powerful to tell compelling personal stories could also be cause for concern if this asymmetry marks personal writing as a technique for "others" and therefore a site that reproduces "otherness" (see Fine 1994).

Here, those writing personal texts may benefit from the experience of feminists working with the insight that "the personal is political." Despite the productivity of this original insight, two decades of feminist writing have brought a keen awareness of how the slogan can be misused. Subjecting "the personal" to sustained analysis can make its political grounding visible, but no adequate politics can be developed from a single individual's personal testimony—unless it is considered as one piece of a larger conversation. Personal writing in social research may ground our analyses more clearly in the particular situations that produce them. But it will be most productive if we proceed with attention to the social sources for personal stories and to what's missing as well as what we tell.

REFERENCES

Addelson, Kathryn Pyne. 1991. *Impure Thoughts: Essays on Philosophy, Feminism, and Ethics.* Philadelphia: Temple University Press.

Becker, Howard S. 1982. *Art Worlds.* Berkeley: University of California Press.

———. 1986. *Writing for Social Scientists: How to Start and Finish Your Thesis, Book, or Article.* Chicago: University of Chicago Press.

Behar, Ruth. 1993. *Translated Woman: Crossing the Border with Esperanza's Story.* Boston: Beacon.

———. 1995. "Writing in My Father's Name: A Diary of *Translated Woman*'s First Year." Pp. 65-82 in *Women Writing Culture,* edited by Ruth Behar and Deborah A. Gordon. Berkeley: University of California Press.

Berger, Bennett M., ed. 1990. *Authors of Their Own Lives: Intellectual Autobiographies by Twenty American Sociologists.* Berkeley: University of California Press.

Clifford, James. 1983. "On Ethnographic Authority." *Representations* 1:118-46.

Clifford, James and George E. Marcus, eds. 1986. *Writing Culture: The Poetics and Politics of Ethnography.* Berkeley: University of California Press.

Collins, Patricia Hill. 1990. *Black Feminist Thought: Knowledge, Consciousness, and the Politics of Empowerment.* Boston: Unwin Hyman.

Cotterill, Pamela and Gayle Letherby. 1993. "Weaving Stories: Personal Auto/Biographies in Feminist Research." *Sociology* 27:67-79.

Ellis, Carolyn. 1993. " 'There Are Survivors': Telling a Story of Sudden Death." *Sociological Quarterly* 34:711-30.

Emerson, Robert M., Rachel I. Fretz, and Linda L. Shaw. 1995. *Writing Ethnographic Fieldnotes.* Chicago: University of Chicago Press.

Fine, Michelle. 1994. "Working the Hyphens: Reinventing Self and Other in Qualitative Research." Pp. 70-82 in *Handbook of Qualitative Research,* edited by Norman K. Denzin and Yvonna S. Lincoln. Thousand Oaks, CA: Sage.

Goduka, Ivy. 1990. "Ethics and Politics of Field Research in South Africa." *Social Problems* 37:329-40.

Goetting, Ann and Sarah Fenstermaker. 1995. *Individual Voices, Collective Visions.* Philadelphia: Temple University Press.

Harding, Sandra. 1986. *The Science Question in Feminism.* Ithaca, NY: Cornell University Press.

———. 1991. *Whose Science? Whose Knowledge? Thinking From Women's Lives.* Ithaca, NY: Cornell University Press.

Hunter, Albert. 1990. *The Rhetoric of Social Research: Understood and Believed.* New Brunswick, NJ: Rutgers University Press.

Johnson, John M. 1988. "Trust and Personal Involvements in Fieldwork." Pp. 203-15 in *Contemporary Field Research: A Collection of Readings,* edited by Robert M. Emerson. Prospect Heights, IL: Waveland.

Kondo, Dorinne K. 1990. *Crafting Selves: Power, Gender, and Discourses of Identity in a Japanese Workplace.* Chicago: University of Chicago Press.

Krieger, Susan. 1991. *Social Science and the Self: Personal Essays on an Art Form.* New Brunswick, NJ: Rutgers University Press.

Linden, R. Ruth. 1993. *Making Stories, Making Selves: Feminist Reflections on the Holocaust.* Columbus: Ohio State University Press.

McCloskey, Donald N. 1990. *If You're So Smart: The Narrative of Economic Expertise.* Chicago: University of Chicago Press.

Myerhoff, Barbara. 1978. *Number Our Days.* New York: Dutton.

Mykhalovskiy, Eric. 1997. "Reconsidering Table Talk: Critical Thoughts on the Relationship between Sociology, Autobiography, and Self-Indulgence." Reprint. Pp. 229-251 in *Reflexivity and Voice,* edited by Rosanna Hertz. Thousand Oaks, CA: Sage.

Orlans, Kathryn P. Meadow and Ruth A. Wallace, eds. 1994. *Gender and the Academic Experience: Berkeley Women Sociologists.* Lincoln: University of Nebraska Press.

Orr, Jackie. 1990. "Theory on the Market: Panic, Incorporating." *Social Problems* 37:460-84.

Paget, Marianne A. 1993. *A Complex Sorrow: Reflections on Cancer and an Abbreviated Life.* Edited by Marjorie L. DeVault. Philadelphia: Temple University Press.

Patai, Daphne. 1991. "U.S. Academics and Third World Women: Is Ethical Research Possible?" Pp. 137-53 in *Women's Words: The Feminist Practice of Oral History,* edited by Sherna Berger Gluck and Daphne Patai. New York: Routledge.

Progoff, Ira. 1975. *At a Journal Workshop: The Basic Text and Guide for Using the Intensive Journal.* New York: Dialogue House Library.

Punch, Maurice. 1994. "Politics and Ethics in Qualitative Research." Pp. 83-97 in *Handbook of Qualitative Research,* edited by Norman K. Denzin and Yvonna S. Lincoln. Thousand Oaks, CA: Sage.

Reinharz, Shulamit. 1979. *On Becoming a Social Scientist.* San Francisco: Jossey-Bass.

Ronai, Carol Rambo. 1992. "The Reflexive Self Through Narrative: A Night in the Life of an Exotic Dancer/Researcher." Pp. 102-24 in *Investigating Subjectivity: Research on Lived Experience,* edited by Carolyn Ellis and Michael Flaherty. Newbury Park, CA: Sage.

Rosaldo, Renato. 1989. *Culture and Truth: Renewing the Anthropologist's Search for Meaning.* Boston: Beacon.

Shostak, Marjorie. 1981. *Nisa, the Life and Words of a !Kung Woman.* Cambridge, MA: Harvard University Press.

Stacey, Judith. 1990. *Brave New Families: Stories of Domestic Upheaval in Late Twentieth Century America.* New York: Basic Books.

———. 1991. "Can There Be a Feminist Ethnography?" Pp. 111-19 in *Women's Words: The Feminist Practice of Oral History,* edited by Sherna Berger Gluck and Daphne Patai. New York: Routledge.

Stanley, Liz. 1993. "On Auto/Biography in Sociology." *Sociology* 27:41-52.

Stanley, Liz and Sue Wise. [1983] 1993. *Breaking Out Again: Feminist Ontology and Epistemology.* 2d ed. London: Routledge.

Thorne, Barrie. 1988. "Political Activist as Participant Observer: Conflicts of Commitment in a Study of the Draft Resistance Movement of the 1960s." Pp. 216-34 in *Contemporary Field Research: A Collection of Readings,* Prospect Heights, IL: Waveland.

Van Maanen, John. 1988. "The Moral Fix: On the Ethics of Fieldwork." Pp. 269-87 in *Contemporary Field Research: A Collection of Readings,* edited by Robert M. Emerson. Prospect Heights, IL: Waveland.

Whyte, William Foote. 1993. *Street Corner Society: The Social Structure of an Italian Slum.* 4th ed. Chicago: University of Chicago Press.

Williams, Patricia. 1991. *The Alchemy of Race and Rights: Diary of a Law Professor.* Cambridge, MA: Harvard University Press.

Zola, Irving Kenneth. 1982. *Missing Pieces: A Chronicle of Living With a Disability.* Philadelphia: Temple University Press.

11

Reconsidering "Table Talk"

Critical Thoughts on the Relationship Between Sociology, Autobiography, and Self-Indulgence

Eric Mykhalovskiy

There is a lot at stake in this writing. I am confronting ghosts, evils and I do, so much, want to come through it. Although I would rather it be otherwise, I feel not being able to write this chapter would be devastating. A failure of self.

I want to write about self-indulgence. More specifically, I want to write about how self-indulgence and related namings such as narcissism and self-absorption are used as regulatory charges against certain forms of sociology. Recently, those who use autobiographical perspectives to do social science have expressed concern with the characterization of their work in these terms (DeVault 1994; Jackson 1990; Okely 1992; Kreiger 1991). This chapter builds on these expressions. It turns analytic attention to the charge of self-indulgence itself, scrutinizing the claims it makes about the use of autobiography in sociology.

EDITOR'S NOTE: This chapter originally appeared as an article in *Qualitative Sociology,* Vol. 19, No. 1, 1996. Reprinted by permission of Human Sciences Press, Inc.

The chapter takes as its point of departure the naming of my own work as self-indulgent in the context of an effort to enter the academy. Its basic strategy is to write through that experience in order to explore implications of the charge which transcend that particularity. Fundamental to its defense of autobiographical sociology, then, is its use of an autobiographical perspective to fashion that defence. Throughout the chapter I refer to "Table Talk" (Peters 1993),[1] the article I wrote which was described as self-indulgent. To allow for an engaged reading of the present chapter, I provide a brief account of this earlier written text.

"Table Talk" is an autobiographical essay which I wrote for an anthology of sociological papers exploring the construction of masculinities (Haddad 1993). Together with two other pieces of critical autobiography (Weatherbee 1993; McKenna 1993) it forms a section in the anthology which, as a whole, is prefaced by an introduction that explores our use of autobiography as a method of thinking and writing (McKenna et al. 1993).

"Table Talk" reads as an exercise in ethnographic autobiography which describes some of the ways my gendered subjectivity was produced through the detail of everyday living. It focuses on an experience familiar to many of us; that of family talk in which, as children, we are described as "like" our mother's or father's sides of the family. These moments of talk are presented in the article as forms of categorization through which gendered subjectivities are partly accomplished.

The textual form of "Table Talk" is somewhat unusual for an academic article. The essay is written as five dated journal entries. The first four entries describe how the categories are grounded in stories and experiences of my grandparents and tell what it was like to be categorized as a Mykhalovskiy or a Krewesky.[2] Through accounts such as the one provided in Appendix 1, the four entries narrate my contradictory relationship to hegemonic masculinity by describing how it was that I was categorized a Krewesky—a feminine family category, while my sister was named in relationship to the masculine Mykhalovskiy category.

The fifth journal entry takes the form of a commentary on the previous four. In general, it problematizes and complicates the representation of categorization offered in the earlier sections. For example, it notes that the gendered character of my categorization is more enigmatic than suggested by the sex-role model implied in my rendering of them. It unsettles this rendering by wondering how my description and valorization of the categories is structured by patriarchal family relations and how processes of gender formation are connected with those of ethnic identification. The final entry closes by raising questions about the analytic use of memory and notes how categorization produces and reproduces family through a form of embodied talk that links present and past subjectivities.

In using "Table Talk's" academic reception as a basis for teasing out the implications of designating autobiographical sociology narcissistic, self-indulgent, or self-involved, the present chapter also makes use of innovations in textual form. It reads as an interplay between a "personal" narrative written in italicized text and a narrative more recognizable as academic in style. The "personal" narrative describes four instances in which I was textually represented in relation to the charge of self-indulgence (in a letter of rejection from a university graduate programme, in a letter of appeal to that programme, in a conference paper and in this chapter). Through these instances I indicate how the production of proper academic subjectivities comes at a personal cost of self-regulation, guilt, pain, the denial of pleasure and the silencing of voice. In writing personal narrative in the second person voice I also hope, in part, to upset I/you, writer/reader, individual/social and other dichotomies upon which the charge of narcissism rests.

In the more "academic" text, I use the device of irony to explore the charge's assault on the sociological relevance of autobiography. My concern is to explore the insular character of the social relations of readership, content, and authorship that the charge of self-involvement invokes. In asking to whom autobiographical sociology speaks, for example, I begin with my own alienated experiences of academic reading and argue that the charge's assumption that autobiographical sociology speaks only to those who produce it rests in how the latter challenges disciplinary reading practices. By questioning what autobiographical sociology speaks of, I try to display how the claim of narcissism rests in an individual/social dualism that obfuscates how writing about the self involves, at the same time, writing about the "other" and how work on the "other" is also about the self of the writer. Lastly, I critique the notions of authorship implied by the charge of self-indulgence. I draw a parallel between the synecdoche of the solitary writer and the self-indulgent writer and argue that the latter obscures the collective process through which texts of autobiographical sociology are often written. Overall, by pointing to the self-involved practices of standard sociology and the reliance of the charge on the conventions of a masculine academic discourse, the analysis exposes the charge's contradictory and ironic character.

FIRST FEELINGS

It's late Spring 1993 and you are half way through a trip to Europe that you planned for over a year and saved for, even longer. During a phone call "home" you hear that your application for doctoral studies has been rejected. Your stomach drops. You are in shock, disbelief: When doing your M.A. you were talked about as a "top" student. Away from the academic world for four years now, you wonder how standards may have changed. Or was your M.A. just a big joke, a masquerade after all? In the end, you take the rejection as an indication of your merit. You feel stupid but also uneasy.

Later, you receive a fax giving an "official account" of your rejection. Your disapproval, it seems, was based on reviewers' reservations with the writing samples submitted as part of your application. One evaluator, in particular, considered your article "Table Talk" to be a "self-indulgent, informal biography . . . lacking in accountability to its subject matter." You feel a sense of self-betrayal. You suspected "Table Talk" might have had something to do with the rejection. It was an experimental piece, not like other sociological writing— YOU SHOULD HAVE KNOWN BETTER!

Slowly, self-indulgence as assessment slips over the text to name you. You begin to doubt your self—are you really self-indulgent? The committee's rejection of your autobiographical text soon feels, in a very painful way, a rejection of you. All the while you buy into the admission committee's implicit assessment of your work as not properly sociological.

REDISCOVERING
AUTOBIOGRAPHICAL SPEECH

In my initial approach to this chapter, I thought to write about autobiography, sociology and self-indulgence in relation to feminist critiques of social science knowledge production. (Westkott 1979; Smith 1987, 1990, 1990a; Harding 1986, 1987; Spelman 1988). I hoped to benefit from the challenge to dominant intellectual traditions made by these critiques and, in particular, from their debunking of a "universal," "neutral" social science by their indicating how its knowledges are gendered, as well as raced and classed. In thinking about self-indulgence, I was particularly drawn to feminist postmodernist critiques that called for a more self-reflexive social science (McKenna 1991; Krieger 1991; Richardson 1988, 1993; Walkerdine 1990). These analyses supported my view that the abstract, disembodied voice of traditional academic discourse was a fiction, accomplished through writing and other practices which remove evidence of a text's author, as part of concealing the conditions of its production. Susan Krieger (1991:47, 116) has written about the problems such practices pose for some social scientists:

Some of us have become increasingly dissatisfied with the tone of remote authority commonly used in the writing of social science and with the way the personality of an author gets lost in social science texts. . . . Social science is premised on minimizing the self, viewing it as a contaminant, transcending it, denying it, protecting its vulnerability, yet nonetheless mobilizing it as a tool for representing experience. . . . As social scientists . . . we paint pictures in which we hope not to exist; or, if we exist, our role is presented as subordinate, or as nearly invisible.

Krieger's work helped show me the intellectual heritage that grounded the naming of autobiographical sociology as self-indulgent. This heritage includes a commitment to rationality, objectivity and subject/object as well as other dualisms, all often subsumed in the notion of an autonomous masculine academic subject or voice (Seidler 1989). Clearly, it is from a place of commitment to a view of the self of the social scientist as contaminant that sociological work writing in an author's presence can be named self-indulgent.

At first, I wrote this chapter within a fairly standard academic discourse; with proper forms of linear argumentation and appropriate distance from its subject matter. I am surprised at the extent to which I invoked standard academic rhetorical strategies in this effort; of how they arose in me as the first order of things, even as I set out to critique them. It is only now, as I re/write, that I fully see the contradiction of defending sociological autobiography through its abandonment. I can feel now, in its negation, the falsity of using the masculine academic subject in defense of a project which stands against it.

Perhaps even more interesting than this contradiction, is the extreme difficulty I experience as I try to write about self-indulgence from a more distanced stance. For with each such effort, my writing freezes. Rather than seeing these as problematic episodes to be ignored or resisted, I want to follow Krieger's suggestion to view personal experience as a source of insight in analysis. In her article "Beyond Subjectivity: The Use of the Self in Social Science" Krieger (1985) writes about how feelings of distance and estrangement prevented her from following through with an analysis of a lesbian community she had researched. In an effort to move forward, she re-examined her experiences of interviewing and found that they were times when her "self" felt most threatened and in need of confirmation. She came to see the interviews as a microcosm of the social dynamics of the larger lesbian community and used this insight to explore processes of differentiation, rejection and confirmation through which it functioned as an identity community.

In a parallel way, my writing blocks can be an insight into the nature of the charge of self-involvement. For as a practice of academic gate-keeping, naming the work of a writer as work that indulges only that writer's self is peculiarly silencing. My blocks have been bound up with a desire to speak through the voices of others. They have been times of great panic and anxiety when I have read other sociologists' work, trying frantically to find a source of something important to say. This is, of course, the charge of self-indulgence at work. My writing blocks are microcosms of the type of self-regulation that the charge of self-involvement puts in place. They are symptomatic of practices through which the proper academic subject is reproduced; one who in writing, above all else, writes about the other. I want to struggle against these practices through writing that is autobiographical.

FIRST WRITINGS

It's summer 1993 and you are back in Toronto, your trip cut short to organize an appeal of your application's rejection. You are angry. In part, you are enraged by the cost and lost opportunity brought upon by your rejection. But beyond this, you are angered by the shame and denigration you have felt in response to the criticism of your work.

You feel yourself at variance with how "Table Talk" has been named because you have never understood yourself to be self-indulgent. You were not raised to treat yourself as important. In fact, your childhood was mostly about putting other people's needs ahead of your own. In recent years, you have struggled hard to produce and recognize wants. Writing "Table Talk" was part of that process. You find it curious that just as you begin writing in ways that you want, the effort is named narcissistic. The religious, almost Protestant underpinning of the idea of self-indulgence becomes clearer to you. You come to see that an important part of the charge of self-indulgence is the denial of self-pleasure.

Minding your previous textual mistake, you work hard to represent yourself as a proper sociologist in your letter of appeal to the university. You flatly reject the association of "Table Talk" with narcissism and suggest that its naming as such is an ad hominem criticism without scholarly merit. Perhaps, you suggest, your evaluator is unfamiliar with the wealth of work by women of colour and other feminists which adopts autobiographical forms to explore issues of sociological relevance (Ellis 1993; hooks 1989, 1994; Pratt 1984; Steedman 1988).

More than ever, you adopt a stance of defense against the charge and argue for a strong relationship between autobiography and sociology. While you do not see it as such at the time, there is a way that your complete rejection of the charge only partially challenges it. You do not stand in relation to the charge in such a way that permits you to invert its moral claim. You are unable to examine how autobiography does indulge the self of the writer by treating the writer's experience as worthy of inquiry. At this point, you do not see that that may not be a bad thing after all.

TO WHOM DOES THE
AUTOBIOGRAPHICAL SELF SPEAK?

Naming an autobiographical text like "Table Talk" as self-indulgent is, in large part, to comment on an experience of reading. It is to suggest that in reading the text, very little is offered up that is of value, as the reader experiences the text as one that speaks only the indulgence of its author. Here, the charge of self-indulgence is a contradictory reading, which as a specific or particular response invokes a universal reader who shuts out the possibility of the text speaking to others.

I think there is an important irony in suggesting that autobiographical sociology speaks only to those who produce it. I came to the writing of "Table Talk" with a profound sense of mistrust about more standard forms of academic knowledge-making. During my M.A. I was struck by the extent to which academics spoke only to themselves. Contrary to what I had expected, the university and the work of its intellectuals seemed very insular and isolated, as if cut off from the lives and experiences of people outside the academy. When thinking about the social organization of scholarly work I would imagine, among its other aspects, academics writing abstract, esoteric articles about other people that were read by a handful of other academics.

Much of the sociology I was reading at the time left me with similar feelings of insularity. In particular, I remember reading social science work on masculinity (Pleck and Sawyers 1974; Pleck 1981; Farrel 1974) and being struck by how the texture and variety of men's experiences had been written out by its authors. It seemed also the case that in always speaking about "other men," and in extremely voyeuristic terms at that (see Connell 1990; 1991), much of this work reproduced masculinist assumptions in its research and writing practices. Most of all, I found it difficult to locate my own experiences in this work or to use it to better understand my self and life.

Writing sociology autobiographically, it seemed to me, offered the possibility of reading experiences not mired in this kind of self-alienation. More so than with other forms of academic writing in which I had been engaged, doing autobiographical sociology challenged me to think about my relationship to readers. As I set out to write "Table Talk" I became concerned with accessibility to lay audiences (Richardson 1988) and so, I tried to write sentences that would not be boring and would not rely on sociologese. Like Richardson (1993) I, too, wanted to write a "sociology that move[d] people emotionally and intellectually," and so, I wrote in my feelings and the contradictions of my experiences and tried not to present myself through a seamless, rational narrative.

My reading of the literature on masculinity had suggested to me the kind of writing practices which excoriate the character of human lives from a text. I wanted to correct this problem in my own work, in large part, by speaking to readers through detail. My hope was that rich description of categorizing talk—including its physical setting and the emotions in me it provoked—coupled with detailed stories of my grandparents and my relationship to them would bring enough of the "stuff of living" to the text to which people could react. I did not expect a facile response of identification with my categorizing experiences on the part of readers but, instead, one of resonance and engagement.

Poststructuralist work that critiques notions of authorship by examining how texts are produced in their reading are a good source of description of the type of active reading response I was looking for. While I do not fully agree with the "death of the author" perspective of some poststructuralist approaches to authorship (Foucault 1979; Clifford and Marcus 1986), I do find value in the work of feminist poststructuralists such as Nancy K. Miller and Eve Sedgwick, who write insightfully about new ways of understanding readership.

> In the notes to "A Poem Is Being Written," an autobiographical essay. . . . Eve Kosofsky Sedgwick writes: "Part of the motivation behind my work [on the essay] has been a fantasy that readers or hearers would be variously—in anger, identification, pleasure, envy, 'permission,' exclusion—stimulated to write accounts 'like' this one (whatever that means) of their own, and share those." What Sedgwick records here as the author of a personal spectacle is the desire for a response—beyond the specular. This might take the form, for instance, of more personal criticism . . . but also of gestures not predetermined, that would bring out other voices from their own shadows. (Miller 1991:24)

My hope was that in its reading, "Table Talk" would not speak a knowledge that was given—that was there for incorporation. My own experiences of academic reading had shown me that the possibility for reading practices that go beyond spectatorship is, in part, a question of the kind of text one confronts.

What I want to suggest here is that the charge of self-indulgence, the notion that autobiographical sociology speaks only to its authors, arises out of how academic writing conventions are transgressed when trying to write for the possibility of new reading practices.

The dismissal of autobiographical sociology as self-indulgent is realized through processes not unlike those Trinh T. Minh-ha (1989) describes in her account of Western anthropological responses to "Third World" storytelling. When viewed through a structural universalism typical of the Western mind (i.e., all good stories have a beginning, a succession of events, a turning point and a closing) non-Western stories which often "have no development, no climax that forms the story's point, or no end that leaves the mind at rest," "fall straight into the category of 'bad' stories" (Trinh 1989:142). In a similar fashion, when read through the standard criteria that make for a good sociological telling, autobiographical work will always disappoint.

I have come to think of the criteria of sociological orthodoxy as expressed by a masculine academic discourse or voice, itself propped up by forms of thinking, writing, doing research and so on. As sociologists, this is a voice with which many of us are familiar; which we listen to and often reproduce as part of our apprenticeship. Authoritative, at times arrogant, it is a voice that speaks unitarily and with confidence. At its worst, it floats depersonalized, above actual speech, booming loudly with knowledge of the other, inviting its listeners/readers to be persuaded through its reason and reasonableness.

Autobiographical sociology gives offense to this voice. As sociology, it comes to "not" speak in that it does not rely on standard ways of being sociologically meaningful to readers. Autobiographical sociology does not, for example, deploy a calculative reasoning through which the social is understood as the interplay of variables. It does not present the results of research on others. It does not reach for the heights of theoretical abstraction, nor present evidence in test of a theory. To the extent that the experiences of its authors are its subject, those experiences are not presented as data; are not worked up as a case or instance of something else.

"Table Talk," more specifically, violates any number of criteria that might make it a good sociological "story." It is not told as rational discourse that moves from a concise statement of problematic through to its considered exposition and concluding resolution. It is not told by a single narrator, but instead, engages multiple voices. Written in part through the recounting of memories, the text blurs the distinction between past and present, fact and fiction. The article ends with a new beginning which raises questions about the account of categorization given in the text and wonders how it might be made otherwise.

The intent of these textual moves is to create an open text whose voices welcome reading practices different than those entered into when reading a knowledge organized for transmission. In doing autobiographical sociology, I hoped for a text that in recognizing the possibility of many readings, left spaces for others to speak. I wished for a text that welcomed, rather than concealed, contradiction and tension (Richardson 1993) and that would allow readers to include feeling and participatory experience as part of knowing and reading (Ellis 1993). I hoped to write a text that would make possible a reading stance that moved away from incorporation or abstract theoretical rumination; one that in its reading, would encourage the writing of other lives, the telling of new stories. In light of this invitation, to name me as the sole reader of "Table Talk" and to see in it only self-absorption is, like Trinh's anthropologists, to miss an opportunity to hear a new way of telling. It is a response that is not only ironic, but deeply unimaginative.

FIRST SPEAKINGS

It's November 1993 and you are at a men's studies conference at the University of Toronto. You are somewhat apprehensive about being there. You don't support the institutionalization of men's studies and you've never liked any of the "men of men's studies" that you've met. You've been invited to speak on autobiography and masculinity, but what you really want to talk about is self-indulgence. Months have passed since your university application was rejected and you feel less threatened by the charge of self-involvement. Your appeal was successful and, eager in their support, your colleagues reject the association of your work with narcissism. Others are less dismissive and urge you to more fully consider what the charge can possibly mean. Your stance toward self-indulgence begins to shift; you begin to view it as an opportunity for exploration.

Still you are uncertain. Although the conference is only "quasi-academic" you wonder how your credibility will be affected by telling about your rejection. In the end, you speak about the process of writing "Table Talk" and leave self-indulgence to a few closing remarks. You ask what it can mean to indulge the self, to give up to, or yield to the self in one's writing. You propose that the characterization of your work as self-indulgent interprets the content of auto-biographical sociology as excessively focused on the self of the writer. You argue against this interpretation, suggesting that "Table Talk" and similar work (McKenna 1993; Weatherbee 1993) is about more than the writer's self.

OF WHAT DOES THE
AUTOBIOGRAPHICAL SELF SPEAK?

To characterize autobiographical sociology as self-indulgent is also to make claims about the nature of its content. Just as the charge collapses the text's author and reader into one, so too it posits the writer's self as the text's object. This is a reductive practice which asserts that autobiographical sociology is about the self of the writer and no one or nothing else. It is also a contradictory practice; for in positing a pristine asocial self, it is the charge of self-involvement more so than autobiographical sociology, that yields to or indulges "the self."

There is, however, a truth in the use of self-involvement as a metaphor for describing the object relations of autobiographical sociology. To name my self as the content of autobiography is one way to describe its specificity; its distinction from work in which the self of the writer is not deemed worthy of inquiry. Left as a singular description, however, this account becomes problematic. The charge of self-indulgence privileges one named aspect of autobiographical content—the socially suspended "me of the writer." By relying on a strict individual/social dichotomy, it obscures how work about the writer's self is at the same time about the "other" and how work on the "other" is also about the self of the writer.

Those concerned with the sociological implications of autobiography have spoken similarly about standard responses to their work. In his book *Unmasking Masculinity,* David Jackson (1990:11) argues that critiques which view autobiographical sociology as self-indulgent or excessively introspective, rest in a dualistic way of thinking that "wrenches apart the interlocking between self and society that is at the heart of" the project. Stanley (1993), although not concerned with responses, argues in a similar way about the intent of "auto/biography" in sociology. She suggests that recent work challenges the conventional genre distinction between biography and autobiography. " 'A life,' whether of one's self or another is never composed of one decorticated person alone" (1993:51). For Stanley, "auto/biography in sociology calls attention to how the writer's life is lived and understood in relation to social networks of people."

In writing "Table Talk" part of what I hoped to accomplish was to show that to write individual experience is, at the same time, to write social experience. While I am the central character of the story the article tells, I do not stand alone in the text as Stanley's decorticated self, but instead am written in relation to others, specifically my grandparents. Even so, "Table Talk" is about more than a series of biographies refracted through one another. Like other works of autobiographical sociology, it takes as its object, the social processes through which subjectivities are formed. More specifically, it draws attention to how our experiences of our selves are mediated by language as a practice of categorization. Family talk about how I had my grandfather's nose or was otherwise "like my mother's parents" was a way of producing me in relation to a family and to particular others who were my family. Its interpellative success rested in the weight of family history, the authority of an interpretive voice, and the social malleability of the body. An object fundamental to the article, then, is how categorization, organized as a form of naming in a patriarchal family context, accomplishes subjectivity.

Making connections between individual experience and social processes in this way, is a practice to which autobiographical sociology is particularly well-suited. In my own work, this capacity derives from an understanding of social organization developed by, and in response to the work of, Dorothy Smith (1987, 1990, 1990a). Smith proffers a form of sociological analysis that begins with the particularities of local events, including their language, but that explicates the operation of the social beyond that particularity. Intrinsic to this work is an exploration of the socially organized nature of human existence without reliance on a notion of a pristine "individual" and a reified "social structure" that stand in opposition to one another. Instead, the concept of social relation is used methodologically to consider how a particular someone's daily experience is organized by concerted human activity not experienced in its immediacy by that particular someone.

This approach points to the fallacy of self/other, individual/social dichotomies by demonstrating that "a whole social organization is needed to create each unique experience" (Bannerji 1991:85). In writing "Table Talk," I was very much intrigued by such notions of simultaneity: by how particular experiences both constitute and are constituted by social relations which transcend a given particularity. The article takes one such particularity—family talk that took place around the kitchen table—and explores its relationship to the social. These moments of talk were not epiphanies (Denzin 1989:33) but, instead, typical almost trivial occurrences that often lasted no longer than a minute or two. Their power to define and construct, then, came out of my desire for family identification and out of all that happened before and outside the moments themselves. Experiences of immigration, Ukrainian ethnicity in Canada, patriarchal family relations, family violence and anti-Semitism, all narrated in the article through descriptions of my grandparents, gave the categorizing moments their power.

At the same time, these moments of categorization are constitutive of the social. They invoke a past to produce a future; one that is tied to me as an individual, but also social, as I exist and struggle in contradictory ways in relations of gender, ethnicity and anti-Semitism.

21 and 22 December 1991

She [my grandmother Anne] will be eighty-six in January. Silver-haired with small eyes. Her skin is olive-coloured and she is short. When she hugs me, the top of her head reaches just below my chin. . . . The skin on her hands is loose. It moves freely, glides across the bone when pushed from side to side. When I was young, we used to compare each other's hands; mine, white and taut and always smaller, but with the promise of bigness. "You grow up be big man, OK." Her will, her massive will and resourcefulness speaking during these moments, as if to rub off somehow, instilling gleeful hope and competence . . .

My grandmother Anne is an abundant racist and a fervent Ukrainian nationalist, part of the second wave of Ukrainian emigration to Canada—the conservative one. Residues of her anti-Semitism have taken root in my body. At first, it happened with [her] jokes about *zhydy* [Jews]; jokes that I did not understand. Later on it was more blatant. "You know, the *zhydy* are *paskoodni*." I look up *paskoodni* in my Ukrainian-English dictionary, searching for the exact meaning of this word that I know is bad. *Paskoodniy*—abominable, wicked, filthy, foul, vile, loathsome. My father tries to explain her behavior, tries to explain away her behaviour, saying she was probably molested or abused by the Jewish tailor from whom she learned how to sew. I suspect my father learned to be an anti-Semite from her too. He, complete with conspiracy theories about the Jews using the holocaust to monopolize world-wide sympathy. An abominable, wicked, filthy, foul, vile and loathsome legacy. I fight to make it go away. I want to puke it out of me once and for good. . . . (Peters 1993)

A text exploring the social production of subjectivity, there is at least one other way in which "Table Talk" is about more than the self of its author. In my work and thinking, I am committed to an actual world. A world of social relations and experience, of human practices and activities, of embodied joys, pleasures and pains. In this world, texts are but a part of life, often for some people more than others. At the same time, I recognize that the textual rendering of life, of experiences, lives, social organization and the like is a necessarily interpretive, representational and theoretical practice. In the case of "Table Talk," I am present in the text not only as a central character of the story it tells, but as its narrator. This reflexive character of the work shows how writing about our lives also "produces" our subjectivities.

The reflexive challenge to strict self/other distinctions raises interesting questions about the charge of self-involvement. For the latter's suggestion that only autobiographical work is about the writer's self, presumes that there is work that is not autobiographical; that sociological work about "others" is not at the same time about the self of the writer. This assumption is challenged by work in both postmodern ethnography (Clifford and Marcus 1986) and feminist methodology, (Gluck and Patai 1991; Stacey 1991). By exposing the power relations inherent in description, analyses of the textual production of ethnographic authority have shown how "Western" ethnographies of "other" cultures are themselves cultural constructions or "inventions" (Clifford 1986) which tell as much about the West as they do about other cultures. In like fashion, feminist oral historians such as Gluck and Patai (1991) have noted that there can be no transparent representation of women's experiences. Texts, as outcomes of feminist oral history, involve acts of framing and interpretation which transform women's spoken words or narratives into written form. Points of emphasis, forms of description, and omissions, such as the importance of race and class in women's lives tell much about the selves of those who write women's oral history.

Recent work on autobiographical sociology (Haug 1992; Denzin 1989; Stanley 1993) has similarly emphasized that writing one's own history is not a practice of unproblematic representation. For the autobiographer, the self of the writer exists as other, known only partially, remembered and understood in different ways in different contexts. My experience, your experience, do not stand before us unmediated. To re/consider, re/present or write about experience is to engage in an act of the present, or at least of the time of its execution. In this way, experience is always both of a past and a present. Feelings, desires, discourses and all else present in a moment of re/consideration are all constitutive of the past experience that is evoked.

Autobiographical sociology speaks to these concerns by considering the ways in which subjectivity is produced in acts of memory and writing. Part of what "Table Talk" is about, then, is my textual rendering; that is, the rhetorical practice of autobiography. In questioning my self-production in "Table Talk," I do not embrace textuality in such a way that writes out the very possibility of my existence outside the text. Rather, I try to consider the social organization of my consciousness and writing.

I consider, for example, how the then current "opening up" of Eastern Europe may have mobilized my desire to tell the story in ways that conjoined my ethnicity with the process of becoming gendered. I write about how a shift in discourse from sex-roles to social organization altered my rendering of the gendered character of the categorizing process. I also write about the omissions and forgettings which made possible a particular version of what happened. Writing in these shifts and considerations intends a destabilization of textual authority and emphasizes how autobiographical sociology stands as a partial interpretation of remembered and reconstructed experience. In writing a text that questioned my rhetorical self-production, my intent was not to simply write about myself. Nor was it to posit representation as all-embracing or to defer to the nihilism of deconstructionism. Rather, I hoped to emphasize the truth in re-experiencing experience through consideration of its inscription.

WHO SPEAKS
AUTOBIOGRAPHICAL SOCIOLOGY?

As with questions of readership and subject matter, I experience the relations of authorship evoked by the charge of self-involvement with extreme tension. As I reconsider the charge in this writing, I want to give expression to how naming me as author of "Table Talk" both conveys and misconstrues my experience of its writing. In the context of self-indulgence, locating authorship in me is suggestive of writing as a highly individualized, unique and solitary effort. While naming myself as author of "Table Talk" redresses a certain academic predilection to write ourselves out of our texts and view our authorship as unimportant, I also want to recognize the ways I am not alone in my work and writing.

In my view, there is an easy fit between the notion of the self-indulgent autobiographer and the image of "the solitary writer" (Brodkey 1987).

Even when not specifically named self-indulgent, autobiography can call to mind highly individualized writing practices. One easily thinks, for example, of the autobiographer alone at his desk, turning inward in search of experiences that can represent the truth of his life. Critical work that challenges the ideology and practice of "masculinist autobiography" (Jackson 1990:21) can also support highly individualized conceptualizations of writing.

For example, Krieger's (1991) call for a fuller recognition of individual perspectivity in social science often relies on almost romantic notions of an inner self. Krieger writes persuasively against a social science tradition which requires that the presence of its writers be excised from the texts they produce. In pushing us to more fully consider how we impact our work, however, she draws on problematic notions of individuality and personal uniqueness. This is most apparent in her discussion of the relationship between art and social science. Here, Krieger selects the socially isolated life of Georgia O'Keefe as an exemplar of creativity and of speaking an inner truth against which public response to one's work is largely ignored or seen to miss the point. I find little inspiration in such a creativity or in the social relations of work of the isolated artist who seeks truth in his or her inner self. There can be a danger in this kind of insularity, in claiming to speak only from within, in not caring about what others think or feel, in seeing in others not an opportunity for engagement, but only a prescriptive conformity that must be resisted.

Overall, Krieger writes about the self in a language of internality. Her text is permeated with references to "individual senses of things," "private inner worlds," and "speaking only of one's experience." This discourse of the self promotes an individualization of knowledge and offers up knowing as a process that is not social, but that somehow obtains from within; that proceeds from a deep unknowable inner life. This outcome of Krieger's critique of dominant social science traditions leaves me somewhat unsatisfied, for it leaves in place the self/other dichotomy upon which such traditions are partly based. In response to the curious existence of a social science that shows no evidence of its production by actual individuals, Krieger posits a social science that is not socially produced, but reflects only the unique personal selves of its writers.

The metaphors of isolation and insularity with which Krieger constructs authorship and writing are challenged by Linda Brodkey (1987) in her book *Academic Writing as Social Practice.* In this book, Brodkey describes how images of the solitary writer are pervasive in Western culture:

> Writing is a social act. People write to and for other people. Yet when we picture writing we see a solitary writer. We may see the writer alone in a cold garret, working into the small hours of the morning by thin candlelight. The shutters are closed. Or perhaps we see the writer alone in a well-appointed study, seated at a desk, fingers poised over the keys of a typewriter. . . . Whether the scene of writing is poetic or prosaic, the writer above the madding crowd in a garret, only temporarily free from family and friends in a study, or removed from the world in a library, it is the same picture—the writer writes alone. (1987:54)

In Brodkey's view, the writer who writes alone is a dominant image, a prevailing synecdoche which tells as a complete story only a partial aspect of writing. Brodkey does not claim that solitude is not necessary for writing. Rather, her concern is to demonstrate how the image of the solitary writer limits our understanding of writing by obscuring its collective and social character.

The charge of narcissism works in a parallel way to Brodkey's "reigning trope" of writing. When conjoined with the charge's insular description of autobiographical subject matter and reading relations, naming me as author of "Table Talk" specifies a circumscribed authorship, accomplished through a feat of self-absorption. This description prevents an understanding of how "Table

Talk" was a collective writing project which, in part, depended on the work of others who have woven self-narrative with critical argument (hooks 1994; Walkerdine 1990; Ellis 1993).

I wrote "Table Talk" in a writing group with my friends Doug Weatherbee and Kate McKenna. Over a four month period, we met every other week in each other's homes to read our journal entries and share our responses to one another's work. Working together was at once profoundly moving, angering, joyous and challenging. Writing sociology collaboratively breathed a transformative excitement into the more isolated ways of writing I had learned as part of my academic training. I have been left craving similar experiences, in large part because of how good it felt to listen, talk, think, feel, write and rewrite in a context of support and caring.

In our sessions together, we did not orient to one another's work from a standard academic stance, whether one of seeking out and obliterating contradiction, reciting the ideas of great thinkers, or distantly ruminating about theory in some other form. The process in which we did engage involved practices unlike those I typically use in the academy. In part, we used our knowledge of one another to consider how we spoke of ourselves in our writing, without making excessive claims to understand from a particular speaker's perspective. At the same time, we tried to do "positioned listenings" in which we concentrated on how our own experiences were evoked by another person's writing. These often offered useful insights into how, as writers, we were represented in our stories.

We did not adopt a countering or oppositional stance toward one another's work. Rather, our critiques focused on a desire for elaboration. In listening to one another's writing, we tried to hear what was taken for granted. We tried to problematize the gaps, the silences, the places where the detail was missing, with an understanding that such omissions often signalled what was in greatest need of explication. We drew parallels between this way of working and feminist strategies for doing interviews and analysis. Marjorie DeVault (1990) and Marianne Paget (1983), in particular, emphasize how the knowledge produced in an interview does not emanate from a single individual, but is shaped out of the interaction of two communicating people. They also underscore the importance for researchers to listen to participants' silences and "you know" expressions in interviews, for these often indicate experiences for which language fails, but which are worthy of description and analysis (McKenna et al. 1993).

Writing "Table Talk," then, was fundamentally grounded in a process of social reflexivity, as Doug and Kate responded to the parts of my journal entries which needed to be elaborated, pried apart or reconsidered. In one such instance, they questioned how my recollections of categorization were remembered not in English, but in Ukrainian. This led to a discussion of how I had taken for granted the relationships between extended family ethnicity and gender, in how I had thought about "Table Talk" as simply an account of the production of gendered subjectivity.

Through this discussion, I came to recognize that I was writing about a social process in which becoming gendered was, at the same time, a process of becoming Ukrainian-identified. This shifted my analysis and subsequent writing in ways that more fully examined how relations of ethnicity and gender are lived in simultaneity. In writing this shift into the article, I tried also to locate its point of origin in Doug and Kate's responses to my earlier writing. In doing so I recorded collaboration into the text. I wanted to show how the article's production was not my singular achievement but rather, involved a dialogic and collaborative process (Becker et al. 1991). Without Doug and Kate's particular and sustained engagement with the article, "Table Talk" would not have been written as it was. The charge of self-involvement cannot capture this quality of authorship. When used as a basis for describing "Table Talk," the charge once again produces irony, in this case through its support of a solitary, authorial voice who writes a text disembodied from the individuals involved in its production.

RECONSIDERATIONS

It's spring 1994 and you are in Toronto writing a paper about self-indulgence. Its a hard thing for you to do. For one thing, you have written through illness, fatigue and feelings of vulnerability. You wonder at how these states arose just as you went to write about an experience that left you feeling tired and vulnerable. Any earlier feelings of strength in challenging the charge escape you now. You thought writing this chapter would free you from the charge, make it go away; but this hasn't happened. You don't feel strong, you feel spent.

When you started writing this chapter you were overwhelmed by the complexity of your experience of self-involvement. It was as though there were too many layers to unpack too many stones to tell at once. As you went to write, you found that standard academic forms of expression limited how you could speak about self-indulgence so you tried to write another way. You wanted to take what you had learned about textual form and subjectivity seriously. You wanted your writing to represent how you differently experienced, felt, interpreted and understood the charge of self-involvement over time and in different social contexts.

As you read the text you have written now, something is wrong. There is something in it that is too careful, too clean. Especially as you read the larger pieces of text, you have difficulty hearing the sound of your voice. Where did the violence of your experience of the charge go? You also wonder about your use of "you." Why did you use the second person voice to describe your experience? Why did it turn out that way?

You have any number of "academic" responses to the question. For example, you might argue that in using the second person voice you hoped to disturb rigid self/other relations by emphasizing how writing about one's self involves problematic access to the past and so, implies an "invented" other. Or you might argue that in using the second person voice you wanted to unsettle the dichotomy between author and reader The "you" of the text's second person discourse refers to the author's experience, but also invites the reader to replace him or her self as author.

Neither of these explanations is quite right. In attributing a self-aware analytic intent to your use of "you," neither gets at how this voice arose in you spontaneously as you went about writing "personal" narrative. Reading over these sections now, you see that the second person voice holds or records the social organization of an academic regulatory practice. While you have found it difficult to write about self-indulgence from a distance, the pain and anguish brought by the charge has made writing from a place of closeness also a problem. Reading over your 'personal' narrative, you wonder how it could have been written otherwise. You wonder about how you needed the "you" discourse; about how its specifically othering practices offered as close a stance as you could assume to your experience of self-indulgence in this writing. You come to think of your "I" as a casualty of the charge and the use of the second person voice as a way of representing the charge's impact in how you write. You decide to leave the "you" discourse for now. It seems to write the charge quite well.

ACKNOWLEDGMENTS

I owe a special debt to Himani Bannerji and especially Karen Anderson whose support of autobiographical sociology made possible the writing of this chapter. I thank Carol-Anne O'Brien, Rita Kanarek and Richard Willis for their support in the experience of rejection the chapter describes. Blye Frank, Penni Stewart, Kate McKenna, Mary Louise Adams and Carol-Anne O'Brien gave extremely helpful comments on earlier drafts of the chapter. I am most grateful to Marjorie DeVault for her generous feedback and encouragement to see the chapter through to publication. I would also like to thank Rosanna Hertz, editor of *Qualitative Sociology* and four reviewers including Carolyn Ellis, Norman Denzin, and Laurel Richardson for their constructive comments and suggestions in revising the original chapter. An earlier version of this chapter was presented at the Annual Meetings of the Canadian Sociology and Anthropology Association, Learned Societies Conference, University of Calgary, Calgary, June 1994. I would like to acknowledge the financial assistance of the Social Sciences and Humanities Research Council of Canada.

NOTES

1. The article was written under a pseudonym.
2. For the present chapter I have replaced the fictitious names Petrovsky and Kaminetz used in "Table Talk" with my actual family names Mykhalovskiy and Krewesky.

REFERENCES

Bannerji, H. (1993). But Who Speaks for Us? Experience and Agency in Conventional Feminist Paradigms. In H. Bannerji, L. Carty, K. Delhi, S. Heald & K. McKenna, *Unsettling Relations: The University as a Site of Feminist Struggles* (pp. 67-107). Toronto: Women's Press.

Becker, H., McCall, M. M. & Morris, L. V. (1991). Theatres and Communities: Three Scenes. *Social Problems,* 36: 93-116.

Brodkey, L. (1987). *Academic Writing as Social Practice.* Philadelphia: Temple University Press.

Clifford, J. (1986). Introduction: Partial Truths. In J. Clifford & G. E. Marcus (Eds.), *Writing Culture. The Poetics and Politics of Ethnography* (pp. 1-26). Berkeley: University of California Press.

Clifford, J. & G. E. Marcus. (1986). *Writing Culture: The Poetics and Politics of Ethnography.* Berkeley: University of California Press.

Connell, R. W. (1990). An Iron Man: The Body and Some Contradictions of Hegemonic Masculinity. In M. Messner & D. F. Sabo (Eds.), *Sport, Men and the Gender Order* (pp. 83-95). Champaign Ill: Human Kinetics Books.

Connell, R. W. (1991). Live Fast and Die Young: The Construction of Masculinity among Young Working-Class Men on the Margin of the Labour Market. *Australian and New Zealand Journal of Sociology,* 27(2): 141-171.

Denzin, N. (1989). *Interpretive Biography.* Newbury Park, CA: Sage.

DeVault, M. (1994). Personal Writing In *Social Research.* Paper presented at the Qualitative Research Conference, University of Waterloo, Ontario, Canada.

DeVault, M. (1990). Talking and Listening from Women's Standpoint: Feminist Strategies for Interviewing and Analysis. *Social Problems,* 17(1): 96-116.

Ellis, C. (1993). " 'There are Survivors': Telling a Story of Sudden Death." *The Sociological Quarterly,* 34(4): 711-730.

Farrell, W. (1974). *The Liberated Man.* New York: Random House.

Foucault, M. (1979). What Is an Author? In J. Harari (Ed.), *Textual Strategies: Perspectives in Poststructuralist Criticism* (pp. 141-160). Ithaca: Cornell University Press.

Gluck, S. & Patai, D. (Eds.) (1991). *Women's Words: The Feminist Practice of Oral History*. New York: Routledge.

Harding, S. (1986). *The Science Question in Feminism*. Ithaca: Cornell University Press.

Harding, S. (1987). Is there a Feminist Method? In S. Harding (Ed.) *Feminism and Methodology: Social Science Issues* (pp. 1-14). Bloomington: Indiana University Press and Open University Press.

Haug, F. (1992). *Beyond Female Masochism: Memory-work and Politics*. London: Verso.

hooks, b. (1989). *Talking Back: Thinking Feminist Thinking Black*. Boston: Southend Press.

hooks, b. (1994). *Teaching to Transgress: Education as the Practice of Freedom*. New York: Routledge.

Jackson, D. (1990). *Unmasking Masculinity. A Critical Autobiography*. London: Unwin Hyman.

Krieger, S. (1985). Beyond 'Subjectivity.' The Use of the Self in Social Science. *Qualitative Sociology,* 8(4): 309-324.

Krieger, S. (1991). *Social Science and the Self: Personal Essays on an Art Form*. New Brunswick: Rutgers University Press.

McKenna, K. (1991). Com(e) (a)part (m)entalizations. Forming Academic Subject(ivitie)s. Unpublished Master's Thesis. OISE, University of Toronto.

McKenna, K. (1993). (Dis)Honouring Father(s). In T. Haddad (Ed.), *Men and Masculinities: A Critical Anthology* (pp. 59-75). Toronto: Canadian Scholars' Press.

McKenna, K., Peters, E. & Weatherbee, D. (1993). Reconstructing Masculinities through Autobiography. In T. Haddad (Ed.), *Men and Masculinities: A Critical Anthology* (pp. 59-75). Toronto: Canadian Scholars' Press.

Miller, N. K. (1991). *Getting Personal. Feminist Occasions and Other Autobiographical Acts*. New York: Routledge.

Okely, J. (1992). Anthropology and Autobiography: Participatory Experience and Embodied Knowledge. In Okely & H. Callaway (Eds.), *Anthropology and Autobiography* (pp. 1-28). New York: Routledge.

Paget, M. (1983). Experience and Knowledge. *Human Studies,* 6:67-90.

Peters, Eric. (1993). Table Talk. In T. Haddad (Ed.) *Men and Masculinities: A Critical Anthropology* (pp. 77-90). Toronto: Canadian Scholars' Press.

Pleck, J. H. (1981). *The Myth of Masculinity*. Cambridge: MIT Press.

Pleck, J. H. & Sawyers, J. (1974). *Me and Masculinity*. Englewood Cliffs: Prentice Hall.

Pratt, M. B. (1984). Identity: Skin Blood Heart. In E. Bulkin, M. B. Pratt & B. Smith, *Yours in Struggle: Three Feminist Perspectives on Anti-Semitism and Racism* (pp. 11-63). Brooklyn: Long Haul Press.

Richardson, L. (1988). The Collective Story: Postmodernism and the Writing of Sociology. *Sociological Focus,* 21(3): 199-208.

Richardson, L. (1993). Poetics, Dramatics, and Transgressive Validity: The Case of the Skipped Line. *The Sociological Quarterly,* 34(4): 695-710.

Seidler, V. J. (1989). *Rediscovering Masculinity: Reason, Language and Sexuality*. London: Routledge.

Smith, D. E. (1987). *The Everyday World as Problematic: A Feminist Sociology*. Toronto: University of Toronto Press.

Smith, D. E. (1990). *The Conceptual Practices of Power: A Feminist Sociology of Knowledge*. Toronto: University of Toronto Press.

Smith, D. E. (1990a). *Texts, Facts, and Femininity: Exploring the Relations of Ruling*. London: Routledge.

Spelman, E. V. (1988). *Inessential Woman: Problems of Exclusion in Feminist Thought*. Boston: Beacon Press.

Stacey, J. (1991). Can There Be a Feminist Ethnography? In S. Berger Gluck & D. Patai (Eds.)
    Women's Words: The Feminist Practice of Oral History (pp. 111-119). New York: Routledge.
Stanley, L. (1993). On Auto/Biography in Sociology. *Sociology,* 7(1):41-52.
Trinh, Minh-ha T. (1989). *Woman Native Other.* Bloomington: Indiana University Press.
Walkerdine, V. (1990). *Schoolgirl Fictions.* London: Verso.
Weatherbee, D. (1993). "You Gotta Learn to Take Care of Yourself." In T. Haddad (Ed.) *Men and
    Masculinities: A Critical Anthology* (pp. 91-103). Toronto: Canadian Scholars' Press.
Westkott, M. (1979). Feminist Criticism of the Social Sciences. *Harvard Education Review,* 49(4):
    422-430.

APPENDIX I

19 November 1991 and 5 January 1992

To be a Mykhalovskiy means to be like my father's father Izidor. Izidor
with the accent on the second syllable. . . . To be a Mykhalovskiy means
to be a raw vibrant energy, a live wire sparking dangerously in the dark.
The part of him that endures as the Mykhalovskiy character is his
passion for having a good time. [My father and grandmother Anna]
reach for this quality of his when they tell stories about him. . . .

   But I know this is not all that my paternal grandfather was. Because
at other moments, my father chose to reveal a different truth. My father
. . . who was abused by Izidor, permitted himself to name my grandfather's horror in a way that Anna, his wife, never would. He told us about
the relentless physical beatings, about how Izidor beat his wife too,
about his drinking . . . about how she sewed dresses all night in their
home until she collapsed, about how she kept them alive. . . . Yet these
parts of the story were somehow set aside, covered up, passed over,
semi-forgotten. All that was raised during the moment of categorization
that I am choosing to remember now was the positive valuing of his
ability to have a good time. . . . And I wonder why it is that they would
resurrect and re-package him in this way. Why did they choose to
transfer any part of him to Helen at all?

   A few nights ago at my [sister Helen's] birthday party I was reminded
that she is good at being a Mykhalovskiy. She was full of energy,
excitement and vitality with loud, heavy laughter from the gut. At ease
with other people; often centre stage and entertaining. . . . She sat on
Izidor's knee. He was dead before I was born. We are both glad that he
died before he could do any direct damage to us. And yet his blows at
my father transmute, and endure in my father's words, loud and angry,

a discourse of disappointment and hatred at me. They persevere, I fear, in the blows that lurk in my mind, waiting to be discovered and unleashed. It's funny that while they chose to name his impact on Helen as a transfer of fun-loving carefreeness, his real legacy, to us both, was one of fear, violence and anger (Peters 1993:79-80).

12 | Communication Problems in the Intensive Care Unit

Albert B. Robillard

MONITORS AND COMMUNICATION

I was initially interested in writing about Jean Baudrillard's television screens as a displacing hyperreality of today (Baudrillard 1983, 1990). I proposed to use the idea of screens and the displacement of the person and experience in the context of the monitors in the intensive care unit (ICU). The monitor screens, in my experience as a hospital patient, seemed to constitute multiple shifting loci of the self, consonant with Fredric Jameson's description of the postmodern self and identity (Jameson 1984). I sometimes thought I had become like William Gibson's (1984) characterization of a human with cyborg parts. I had to look at the monitor screens to find out if I was alive, how close to death I was, and if I were making any progress to recovery. The monitors were my constant focus when I was alone. They were, as well, the focus of those taking care of me. My heart rate was monitored, as well as my blood pressure, respiration, oxygen saturation level of my blood, the other blood gases, my temperature, urinary output, the infusion rate of my medications, and my prostrate body was moni-

EDITOR'S NOTE: This chapter originally appeared as an article in *Qualitative Sociology,* Vol. 17, No. 4, 1994. Reprinted by permission of Human Sciences Press, Inc.

tored by a television in the ceiling. I lived in and by the collective scanning of the monitors by me and by my caretakers.

Let me illustrate this point about living in the monitors. When an ICU nurse would come into my room she or he could flick a remote switch on their belt and the monitor readouts of other patients would be projected on my monitor screen. That way she or he could keep track of other patients while working in my room. I was at first unaware that my nurse routinely switched on my neighboring patient's readout on my monitor. I would look at and listen to my monitor and become alarmed at the falling blood pressure, the irregular cardiac rhythm, the low oxygen saturation level, and the bells and buzzers that would go off to signal the other patient was in need of immediate life saving assistance. Thinking it was my readout, my blood pressure would jump to near 200, my respiration rate would increase to 40 per minute, my oxygen saturation level would sink to 80s, and my own monitor alarm bells and buzzers would go off.

It was this confusion of living in monitor screens, whether your own or mistakenly other's, that caught my analytic attention. I proposed to write about the displacement of the self by the screens, with the added dimension that the monitor screens were not only located in my room but also at the nursing station, about 100 feet away. The displacement was not only characterological, in terms of finding the truth about who you are in the screens, but spatial, as well. Most of the monitor reading, so at least you thought and hoped, took place at the nursing station. The placement of careful and continuous reading of the monitors at the nursing station may have been a panoptic dream, but it effectively removed critical reading of factors concerning life and death, as well as televised bodily behavior, to a remote unseen location. Additionally, the actions derived from this information were formulated in an invisible place, a site beyond personal influence.

However, when I started writing the chapter on the monitor screens, I piled page after page on my communication problems with the nursing staff, physicians, and other workers on the hospital floor. I am afflicted with a neuromuscular disease and I cannot talk or communicate in anything approaching the social consensus of "real time." I came to feel as if I had deserted my initial project of describing my uncomfortable journey in the cyberspace of the monitors. I faced a dilemma of putting aside the description of my communication problems and proceeding with the theme of the monitor screens. The more I worked on the chapter, the larger my failure at consensus "real time" communication appeared to be the source of my discomfort in the ICU, even with the monitors. The direction of the chapter seemed clearer, and I eventually came to see the dislocating, self-distancing (Zola 1982) trouble with the monitors was not all that different from most nurses falling to use my alphabet board, to talk with me. The sense of loss of personal control with the monitors was roughly approximated in the refusal of most nurses to use my alphabet board. When I could not communicate I had no participation in my care or the way I was regarded and the way I came to view myself.

THE ILLNESS

This chapter is based on three and a half months of hospitalization, most of it in the ICU.[1] This fieldwork is not recommended. I have had a neuromuscular disease since 1985 and an acute episode of pneumonia in 1991 suddenly brought me to the hospital in an ambulance. My lungs had filled up with fluid; I was having extreme difficulty breathing. The emergency medical service crew of the ambulance stuck a tube in my nose and down to my lungs and pumped air in with a bag. I was air bagged for the twenty minute ride to the hospital. Attached to the bag was a cylinder of oxygen. When I arrived at the emergency room, I was rushed inside to a room where seven people began to work on me. I was reintubated, a new tube stuck in my nose, down my throat, and into my lungs. The fluid was suctioned out of my lungs. The suctioning of my lungs would become a permanent feature of life.

I cannot talk. I can communicate by forming individual letters with my lips. I could emit some vocal sounds before the hospitalization but I did not have enough muscle strength and control to articulate words. I spoke by spelling out words by moving my lips. This is a slow process and does not match the real time order of natural conversation. Moreover, the number of people who can read my lip movements is highly limited. My lip movements are restricted, due to weak lip muscles, and it takes intensive training and exposure to be able to read my lips. The students who work for me as research assistants can read my lips, as can my wife, daughters, and my mother-in-law. Otherwise, I have to communicate by using an alphabet board, an even slower process than lip reading. Most of the time when I was in the hospital I had to use the alphabet board, with nurses, nurses' aides, and respiratory therapists. Occasionally, a student research assistant would work with me on a book, and for that time I could communicate more rapidly by lip movements. My wife spent most nights with me in the room and she could read my lips and tell the staff what I was saying.

I found not having a real time voice was the equivalent to not having any defense to what was done to my body, and once my body was touched I had no control over the intensity or the painful effects of the procedure. I came to visualize having a voice as having a defense of making assertions about myself, making threats, and counter threats, and otherwise carrying out and maintaining an interfactional space for myself. Not only could I not control what was happening to my body, I found I could not control the interactions which largely made up my person. I could not even communicate simple information about my condition to my doctors and most of my nurses. It was very difficult to gain people's attention and maintain that attention through a course of conversation. The physicians, operating under tremendous subjective time pressures, would limit their visits to my room to fifteen minutes, time enough for only a few, if any, of my laboriously formulated sentences. The physicians would suggest that I formulate what I had to say before they came. This suggestion left out the possibility to respond to any emergent conversation while they were in the room. It also assumed that I would remember what I wanted to say in conversational contexts long after the conversation had passed. Some physicians made decisions in the room about treatment, including surgery, and I could not respond, besides giving a simple yes or no with head movements. If I wanted to enter a qualified answer, it was impossible and many times the physician would leave the room while I was trying to spell out a reply. Often the physician would not see himself being addressed by my reply, the time lag was too great and his attention had switched to a new task, and the person interpreting what I was trying to say was so concerned about reading my lips or using my alphabet board that she or he forgot to signal the physician that I was saying something to him.

Not being able to conversationally influence most aspects of my experience in the hospital generated frustrations, resentments, and attributions about my intelligence, my motivations, and, equally from my perspective, about the intelligence, motivations, sensitivity, and the irrationality of the entire health care delivery system.

FLYING NURSES

The communication problem with most nurses was the same as with physicians. Most of the nurses in the ICU were visiting nurses from the U.S. mainland. In my experience the visiting nurses were uniformly Caucasian or *haoles,* as they are known in Hawaiian. These nurses call themselves "flying nurses." Flying nurses sign short term contracts to work three months to a year. Most of them worked on three to six month contracts. Most worked three twelve hour shifts a week and would have four days off to enjoy Hawaii. The hospital paid roundtrip airfare to Hawaii and subsidized the apartment rent of flying nurses. The flying nurses lived in the same large apartment building (appropriately named the Marco Polo) and mainly socialized with each other. It is not too strong to say the visiting nurses lived an Anglo-like colonial compound existence. Many of these nurses had worked in major medical center ICUs on the U.S. mainland. The national need for ICU nurses was so severe that some were able to spend years making the circuit of resort areas in the United States.

It was my feeling the flying nurses were almost impossible to communicate with. I had a much easier time talking with local nurses. Unfortunately the number of local nurses in the ICU was small. By local nurses I mean nurses who lived in Hawaii, whether they were immigrants to Hawaii or were born and raised in Hawaii. The flying nurses knew little of the social structure, culture, and history of Hawaii. They knew the Hawaiian pidgin English word for urine (*shi shi*) and the Hawaiian word for finished (*pau*), but little else.

It was not by intention, but the flying nurses could not locate me in their conversations. The "me" they could locate was a generic person, but not the "me" that lived in Hawaii, had friends, worked, had a history in Hawaii and the Pacific Islands. The flying nurses could talk about where they were from, where they had gone to nursing school, where they had worked, and where I had lived and worked on the U.S. mainland. When the Dean of the School of Nursing at the University of Hawaii would visit me the flying nurses did not recognize her. When clinical instructors in the School of Nursing would visit me they would be unrecognized. The local nurses would quiz me about my relationship to nursing faculty. When my research assistants would come to work with me they had to fight being hurried out of the room. I was treated as a standard sick person, someone too sick to be working and in command of his circumstances. It appeared to me that the flying nurses could not conversationally formulate me except as a sick person. I had no local personality. I felt as if I were one more sick person, equivalent to countless others in their experience. It was not that the visiting nurses wanted to treat me in crass, generalized ways but hardly one of them inhabited the particulars that illuminated my social circumstances in Hawaii.

The relevance of describing the context of interaction with flying nurses is that the commonplace, generalized methods of treating me appeared to not include a personal status whereby I could get them to use the alphabet board. None of the flying nurses would use the alphabet board. A few would try but they would become frustrated and stop the effort. The most common problem is that the nurses could not remember the letters of the words as I selected them from the alphabet board. They would not write the letters and words down. They would reverse letters, forget the last letter of the sequence, and would quickly lose all sense of progression through words, sentences, and paragraphs. Frequently when we would move from the first word to the second and third, the first word would be forgotten.

I discovered that when most nurses correctly spelled out the words without writing them down, they could not recognize the word, even after repeatedly saying each letter in the word. I learned that spelling out words is not equivalent to word recognition, especially among native speakers of English. This would happen for short words such as "what," "is," "the," or for longer words like "responsible," "routine," "medication," "procedure." A nurse would stand before me and spell "W-H-A-T" over and over again without recognizing the word.

I had a hard time separating words, many would run the words together as in "Iwanttocallmywife." This was completely unintelligible. I got as lost as the nurses when they would spell out run together words. I would have to start over again from the first word. Separating words became a paramount problem. I would try to stop after spelling out a word to indicate a separate word had been completed. But, as I came to learn, most people could not recognize a word even after they had spelled it correctly and had repeated it several times. I would try jerking my head to the right to indicate a word had been completed but this was too easily mixed up with saying no by shaking my head from side to side. Indicating the stops between words was and is a continuing problem, even for those who write down the letters as I sequentially spell them.

These communication troubles were encountered or anticipated by most flying nurses. Many would say, "I am not even going to try the board." Others would say, "It is no sense in trying to communicate. I know what needs to be done and I am going to do it." Some few would say, "I have a job to do, so don't give me any trouble by trying to talk." The most memorable nurse told me the first time I met her, "I am the nurse from hell and do not try any of that communication shit with me." Working with a patient in my condition, it was thought, could be accomplished without any communication with the patient. I was made aware that "most" patients in the ICU could not communicate by any means and I was using up critical time from the care of other patients by using an inefficient communication process. There was a flutter of talk about outfitting me with a speech prosthesis, as if such an instrument would cure my communication problems. There was a naive belief that a speech prosthesis would operate in real time of normal conversation.[2] My insistence in talking and being heard, expecting what I said to influence behavior, lead to a spiral of mutual antagonism between myself and the flying nurses. Communication with flying nurses was a lost cause. I quickly came to think of them as nearly anonymous parts, universally interchangeable, mirroring what I thought they thought of patients.

LOCAL NURSES

I had more success with the few local nurses serving in the ICU. But this success was not general to all local nurses. Some local nurses are military dependents, working here for three or four years and then moving on to the site of the new assignment. Another but small portion of local nurses are the newly arrived. They are usually Caucasian, dependents of business people or professionals who have just moved to Hawaii. A few of the newly arrived are nurses that have been recruited from the mainland. The military dependents and the newly arrived cannot be seriously considered authentic local nurses.

What I mean to indicate by the term local nurse is either locally trained nurses or long time residents of Hawaii. Local nurses need not have been born and raised in Hawaii. Many authentic local nurses are from the Pacific Islands and the Philippines or are Caucasians from the U.S. mainland who went to college in Hawaii. But most local nurses were born, raised, and educated in Hawaii.

Authentic local nurses could by glances, gaze, facial expression, vocabulary, syntax, cadence, dialect, body language, and topical reference conversationally locate themselves and the patients as members of and constrained by the same local culture and social structure. We could exchange information about neighborhoods, schools, places of employment, local and national cultures, food, life histories in the context of Hawaii, or, in short, the conversational formulation that we belonged to this place, something which pervades and appears as essential in social interaction among "local" residents. I had a personality with local nurses, to the extent that I could use my knowledge about Hawaii and the Pacific to locate them specifically. There was a reciprocity of highly detailed knowledge which located me and them. I felt that they knew me as a unique situated individual. I felt I knew them as situated individuals. We did not deal with each other in generic, universal categories.

Not all local nurses could communicate with me. No male nurses even attempted to use my communication board. This experience is consistent with my extra-hospital experience. Males, in general, appear not to have the patience or the multiple communication rhythms to be able to use alternative means of communication. There were three nurses and one respiratory therapist who would consistently use my communication board. One nurse was a local Chinese, whose first language was Cantonese. Although she spoke English without any accent, she only spoke Cantonese till she entered elementary school. The other nurse was a Chamorro from Guam. Her first language was Chamorro. The third nurse was a Hawaiian from Hilo. She did not speak Hawaiian or any other language except English. All three nurses were trained at the University of Hawaii. The respiratory therapist was a Caucasian from Indiana. She had lived in Hawaii for fifteen years.

Interaction with local nurses began much the same as it did with flying nurses but it progressed much faster in getting into biographical particulars. Both kinds of nurses would enter the room the first time and introduce themselves and say "I hear you are a professor at UH." I would nod my head. The next question would be what department was I in. This was the first hurdle. The flying nurses would guess and would almost never be right. The flying nurses would not usually use my alphabet board, even though it was lying next to my bed and they had been shown how to use it. The local nurses would begin to use my board, perhaps because they had the knowledge and motivational culture to conversationally formulate themselves as members of the same social space. Hawaii has a strong culture of differentiating those who belong and those who are visitors or just passing through. Once my department was identified the local nurses would know where my department was located, "You are in Porteus Hall." Then there would be statements like, "I took a sociology class from Ikeda or Sakumoto." I could then ask "Who did you have for medical-surgical-nursing?" We could progress quickly to a conversational exchange of personalities, "What did you think of X?, How did you like the class?, Where did you go to high school and where did you grow up?" I could tell the local nurses I lived in Kailua and they would immediately ask me what neighborhood. They would know a lot about me from the neighborhood.

The local nurses had the conversational moves which both indicated the detailed knowledge of place and the motivation to use this corpus as the basis of formulating co-membership in the social topography with me. This shared body of knowledge was identical with who, with substantial variation, we were. We, me and the local nurses, could be called out and motivated by these deep attachments.

OTHER INTERACTIONAL PROBLEMS

There are a number of routine interactional problems I encountered with flying and local nurses and with other direct care providers. I call the first two problems "Not Now," and "Out of Context." "Not now" would occur when I either indicated I wanted to say something or when I was in the middle of formulating a sentence. I would be told "not now" as a way of breaking the interactional focus, rearranging the interaction to permit something else to happen. I would be interrupted from speaking when the portable x-ray machine crew would appear in my doorway, when my physicians or residents would enter the room, when any new machine would be set up, when my medications would be administered and when I would be fed. Even when I was speaking about the procedure underway or about to begin, I would be cut off. Frequently I was trying to tell personnel how to handle my body in the procedure. I had gained a lot of experience about what worked in these procedures in the positioning of my body. Certain positions would cause coughing spasms and delay or abort the procedure. "Not now" would happen every morning at seven when the x-ray crew would reposition me for a chest film and I was interrupted from telling them how to position me. Ignoring what I was trying to say, the crew would begin to move me and I would invariably go into a muscle and coughing spasm, ruining the x-ray. I found little collective memory among x-ray crews, or among hospital staff about what worked and what did not work, belying the fiction of nursing notes and staff conferences. I felt it necessary to direct each staff away from problem areas in the handling of my body but because I could not overlay my speech with on-going action, and the attention to my speech required such a focus, I was usually unsuccessful in using my speech to guide the interaction.

"Not now" is directly related to "Out of Context." "Not now" can take three avenues. The first is simply saying "Not now" when I am trying to speak. The second is when the party I am speaking to cuts me off by attending to another task, usually walking away in mid-sentence. The third possibility is when another interrupts my conversation, taking over the interactional focus. "Not now" does not occur only when I am about to start a treatment or a procedure. It can happen anytime when I am trying to speak.

"Out of Context" happens when I am able to resume speaking to the topic that I was addressing when I was interrupted with a "Not now." Usually the interaction has moved along so far that when I address an old topic my conversants have a hard time seeing the relevance of what I am saying. It takes so much effort to spell out what I am saying I could not easily recycle the topic by saying "You know what we were speaking about a little while ago, the X topic." I could only, because of time and energy, speak directly to a former topic. This speaking out of context would generate many complaints and confusion. It would often break off further communication. Speaking out of context would be like an ethnomethodological experiment, producing comments like "Are you crazy?", "What the hell are you talking about?", and so on. The local nurses came to learn that this was a standing problem with my speech and would try to remember the course of our conversation. But it was often problematic whether they could remember and it was an opportunity for closing the conversation, much to my frustration.

I found I could not do the constant reparative work that goes on in normal conversations. I did not have the temporal dimension to say, "You know what we were talking about before," as a method of reintroducing a topic I was talking about. I could not layer my speech with the body gestures and differentiations in pitch, volume, tone, stress, or pace of voice to keep my present turn at talk, keep from being cut off, and keep from having my sentences completed by others. Some people would anticipate the spelling of words as I was progressing through spelling them, unintentionally giving me words I had not thought of. The more common problem was and still is that people finish my sentences, usually making me say what I had not intended. This has caused many sharp disagreements. Because I could not talk while my translator was reading what I said, I frequently experienced gross editing of what I said. Sometimes the translator would refuse to say my thoughts. More frequently the translator would not be assertive and translate my thoughts at the proper spot in the conversation, choosing to wait, delaying my participation and leading to further out of context remarks.

Another trouble I had was that it was difficult to tell when my turn at talk was coming to an end and without the paralanguage of intonation it was difficult to know when I had actually ended a turn. This was so disassembling to the conversation that my conversant could not remember what I had just said and we had to start all over again spelling out the sentence.

The last example of trouble in this brief sample of interactional difficulties in the hospital was the absence of redundancy. Normal conversations are filled with countless restatements and qualifications of topic and its predicates as the conversants continuously negotiate and respecify meaning. My spelling out sentences was too labor intensive and focused to be context sensitive to the need to rephrase and reinterpret what I meant. Tied down to looking at the spelling as it was written, I was usually unaware of behavioral signs of the need to respecify and was at a loss in formulating a proper interpretational context. Sometimes it seemed as if my statement came out of the blue, obscuring the interactional fit and meaning of what I said.

CONCLUSION

This chapter started out with the intention of describing the ontological insecurity experienced in personal absorption into a complex of monitor screens in the ICU. I had been interested in the fragmentation of the postmodern personality, described by Jameson, and Baudrillard's hyperreality of TV monitor screens as a site of the shifting postmodern personality. I thought my experience in the ICU was a good example of fragmentation and ontological insecurity in the context of remote monitoring and my own viewing of the monitor screens.

When I started writing I entered the qualification that I cannot talk. I thought this colored my experience, making a difficult time even harder. However, when I began to think of how my body and my person was fragmented by the monitors, I could not get beyond the thought that there was a learning process of me looking at the nurses looking at the monitors and talking about what they saw. I was directed to look and read the monitors from their attention to them. It became a coordinated looking and reading. Because I was alone much of the time and could not talk to ask questions about the monitors and what they meant, I tended to spend a lot of time looking at the screens and trying to figure out what they meant. When I tried to communicate with the nurses I was unsuccessful most of the time. Ninety percent of my nurses were flying nurses. I could not tag them with my face, gaze, or my identity, pulling them into conversations.

As much as I was attracted to the notion of monitor screens, I came to doubt the source of my trouble was in the monitors. Further, I came to see that postmodern social theory, at least as represented by Jameson and Baudrillard, has no sense of social interaction (Tucker 1993). If the social is dead, as Baudrillard would have it, this common culture truth is an interactional achievement of talk, writing, film, TV, broadcasting, drama, teaching, and other forms of discourse. The source of my difficulties in the ICU was in the daily social interaction with nurses, physicians, and technological people and in the meaning this interaction generated for the social and physical environment, including machines in the room. The absorption into monitor screens was produced, in large part, by the comparative isolation and inability to get information about the monitors and their read out values.

I have described some of the communication problems I experienced in the ICU. I have come to see interaction, from its earliest phases of glancing and starting to talk, as the site of personal integration or fragmentation, security, power and powerlessness, anger, patience, memory and context relevance in my attempts to talk in the hospital. The institutionalized, naturalized, socially consensual order of conversation has a time order, a rhythm, that assumes an intersubjective coordination of physical human bodies. Having a body which could not inhabit this time order was a breach of the normalized conversational environment every time I tried to talk. Yet, as I learned from the local nurses, there are a few people who demonstrated the normal time order is but one among many time orders and structures for communication.

ACKNOWLEDGMENTS

The Social Science Research Institute at the University of Hawaii supported the time and provided the facilities to write this chapter. I am indebted to the research assistance of Anthony Bichel, Yi Ding Chen, Zhuo Miao, and Jennifer Spector. I received criticism and encouragement from Jack Bilmes, Ken Liberman, Peter Manning, John O'Neill, Divina Robillard, Kay Toombs, Don Topping, and Eldon Wegner.

NOTES

1. This chapter explicitly uses the self as the primary source of data. I have long ignored this experience in doing sociology. I feel like Irving Zola (1982) when he wrote in the first paragraph of his book, *Missing Pieces,* "Yet for over two decades I have succeeded hiding a piece of myself from my own view." While I have suffered this illness since 1985 and have been in a wheelchair since 1988, I have felt constrained from consulting this experience until this chapter, written in 1993. I implicitly regarded personal experience as a "forbidden pool" of knowledge, used but never acknowledged (Fine 1992). This diffidence toward describing my experience of disability is also shared by the late disabled anthropologist Robert Murphy (1987), in his book *The Body Silent.*

This reluctance is, in retrospect, strange for someone trained as an ethnomethodologist. The "unique adequacy requirement" (Garfinkel 1984; Schutz 1967) for beginning a study of a social setting states that the analyst must be a recognized member of the practices he or she is describing. However, most ethnomethodological studies after assuring the reader they are a proficient practitioner of the setting described, quickly turn into third person accounts. The use of the "I" as the subject of analysis is an embarrassment for many. It remained for Dorothy Smith (1987) to explicitly theorize the self as the source of both analytical knowledge and the subject of official research.

I was encouraged to use the experience of my disability as a broad sociological by Irving Zola. He gave a colloquium in Honolulu in the spring of 1993. In his talk and in personal conversation after, he used his disability to open up broad issues of social order, for both the able and disabled.

2. I know of no computer assisted speech device that speaks in real time. I have made a thorough investigation of the synthesized speech market.

REFERENCES

Baudrillard, Jean. 1983. *In the Shadow of the Silent Majorities . . . or, the End of the Social.* New York: Semiotexte.
Baudrillard, Jean. 1990. "Xeros and Infinity." In Jean Baudrillard, *The Transparency of Evil: Essays on Extreme Phenomena.* London: Verso.

Fine, Michelle. 1992. *Disruptive Voices: The Possibilities of Feminist Research.* Ann Arbor: The University of Michigan Press.

Garfinkel, Harold. 1984. *Studies in Ethnomethodology.* Cambridge: Polity Press.

Gibson, William. 1984. *Neuromancer.* New York: Ace Books.

Jameson, Fredric. 1984. The Politics of Theory: Ideological Positions in the Postmodernism Debate. *New German Critique.* No. 33, Fall.

Murphy, Robert. 1987. *The Body Silent.* New York: Henry Holt.

Schutz, Alfred. 1967. *Collected Papers: The Problem of Social Reality.* The Hague: Martinus Nijhoff.

Smith, Dorothy. 1987. *The Everyday World as Problematic: A Feminist Sociology.* Boston: Northeastern University Press.

Tucker, Jr. Kenneth H. 1993. "Aesthetics, Play, and Cultural Memory: Giddens and Habermas on the Postmodern Challenge." *Sociological Theory.* Vol. 11, No. 2, pp. 194-211.

Zola, Irving. 1982. *Missing Pieces: A Chronicle of Living with a Disability.* Philadelphia: Temple University Press.

13 Breaking Silence

Some Fieldwork Strategies in Cloistered and Non-Cloistered Communities

Mary Anne Wichroski

This chapter deals with some methodological problems encountered during fieldwork I conducted among communities of Roman Catholic nuns. To investigate the decline of female religious orders in the United States, including the ways in which the nuns remaining in these communities have adapted to life in the 1990s, I selected two types of orders from one diocese in the Eastern region of the United States. One group was an "apostolic" or "active" order—that is, sisters affiliated with a particular community, but actively working in the world as teachers, nurses, and social workers. The other order was a "contemplative" or "monastic" community of nuns, living by the rule of "enclosure"—a traditional cloistered existence, whereby members do not generally leave the grounds of the monastery nor permit the entry of outsiders.

The study of each type of order would present specific methodological problems with regard to language and communication. While all fieldwork,

EDITOR'S NOTE: This chapter originally appeared as an article in *Qualitative Sociology,* Vol. 19, No. 1, 1996. Reprinted by permission of Human Sciences Press, Inc.

regardless of the degree to which one is an observer or participant, requires awareness and the ability to intuit what is hidden, to grasp implicit meanings, etc., the degree to which this is possible is also influenced by the type of social milieu within which we are operating and the extent to which we can establish common cultural ground therein.

As a social scientist, I entered the field equipped with certain skills and enculturated with the norms of the academic, sociological community; but I was also a person—American, Catholic, and female—living in the 1990s. As I moved towards less familiar territory (from the more open to the less open type of community), my prior training and knowledge became less useful and my cultural assumptions more glaring. More specifically, linguistic difficulties arose because of: (1) a closed culture of "we-ness;" (2) articulation problems (lack of language); (3) meaning inversions; and (4) silence as a mode of communication. These four problems might be seen as a continuum—a progression from least to most problematical in terms of linguistic barriers representing different degrees of connection between researcher and researched. While the reticence of some of the sisters to express themselves and lack of language were features of my interviews with the active sisters, meaning inversions and silence were encountered later in the cloistered community, pointing out that as a fieldworker, I was moving through a set of methodological problems that became increasingly difficult to overcome through conventional verbal exchange.

After several stages of resistance and disappointment, I began to adapt, to question the scientific ways of seeing and knowing, and to finally accept with gratitude those very difficulties which helped me to see better some aspects of the lives of the nuns which I could not possibly have understood without them. It was often *through* these linguistic challenges and the subsequent emotional reactions to these "breaches" in understanding, that important data emerged. In this chapter, I argue that by adopting a research stance appropriate to the groups being studied—that is, by moving from observer to participant and back, stretching our capacities, using our emotions, working actively with those barriers that confront us—we may learn more *from* those very obstacles than if they had never presented themselves.

BACKGROUND OF THE STUDY

My data on religious orders of women came from a variety of sources, including in-depth interviews with sisters, historical records, Church documents, and participant observation over an 18 month period of fieldwork. I interviewed 23 members of the active community, visiting several convents, residences, and workplaces, as well their Motherhouse, where I spent time in the archives and was allowed to interview, as well as have informal conversations with, several of the sisters in residence. Although a prepared interview guide was used, open-ended questions often allowed extended discussion and emergent themes to develop. Questions addressed included their reasons for choosing the religious life, descriptions of the training period, how they interpreted and coped with the changes leading up to and following Vatican II, how their work lives changed, living arrangements, relations with their communities, their beliefs on current theological, as well as secular political questions, and their thoughts on the future of religious orders of women.

Because of restrictions on the interactions with contemplative nuns, my fieldwork on this group consisted of four lengthy interviews with the Mother Superior and four additional day-long visits as a guest of the community, during which I was assigned a room, was allowed to observe and to participate in some of their daily activities, and to have some, although limited, interactions with several of the sisters. Ongoing written correspondence and telephone conversations with the Mother Superior were invaluable in supplementing information on the order.

Additional sources of data included official Church records, the documents of Vatican II, histories of the orders, often published by and provided by the sisters themselves, and other archival materials, such as letters, journals, and membership records provided by the orders. The major source of data, however, was the sisters themselves, who shared many hours with me in conversations, both formal and informal, and provided me with documents and references several times during the course of this fieldwork.

Despite the cooperation of the sisters, this project forced me to confront several problems, not the least of which was researcher bias. As noted by other qualitative researchers, in many ways the fieldworker *is* the research instrument; that is, the observer is part of what is observed (Khleif 1974:396), the biography of the observer crucial to analysis (Agar 1986; Loftland and Loftland 1984; Johnson 1978; Khleif 1974; Reinharz 1979), and "we must consider who we are and what we believe when we do fieldwork" (Kleinman and Copp 1993:13). Although my background as a Catholic allowed me easier access to respondents and provided a working knowledge of religious language, tradition, theology, and scripture, my personal knowledge of nuns was limited to retrospective material. I knew virtually nothing about female monastic communities, other than what I had learned from historical studies, but I did have much exposure to active nuns; my contact with them extended over the course of my childhood and we did at one time share a common culture.

While my training as a sociologist helped me to see things from a different perspective, I would be remiss if I did not admit a struggle with preconceived notions regarding religious orders of women. The nuns I knew were strong authority figures, not perceived as victims of a traditional, patriarchal institution. I did not think of them as "persons," nor did I see them in terms of their gender. We did not interact with them on a personal level; yet there was something appealing and liberating about being in contact with them. As an adult, I was intrigued by what seemed to me to be their pro-feminist characteristics and had difficulty reconciling this with other notions about their secondary status within the Catholic Church. There were negative memories associated with them as well, such as the harsh discipline and dogmatic nature of their convictions which we were asked to accept without question. I had mixed feelings towards these women who had helped shape my childhood, a combination of respect and abhorrence, awe and fear.

It was only later, after studying the social psychology of community living and reading about some of the cultural conflicts taking place in convents in the 1960s (see for example, Curran 1989 and Neal 1965; 1984; 1990 on the value conflicts for American teaching sisters trying to motivate students to be competitive and responsible individuals while they themselves were living under different rules) that I felt in a better position to analyze the phenomenon of religious orders of women in a sociological context. However, trying to think in terms of organizational types—that is, concentrating on systems and patterns rather than people or spiritual matters—was often difficult. Cultural misunderstandings continued to surface and had to be addressed throughout the entire fieldwork experience.

In summary, I was entering the field as a female, American, Catholic sociologist with some degree of knowledge about the subject at hand but hardly prepared for some of the methodological dilemmas that would arise with regard to language. As mentioned previously, these problems also parallel the movement from more to less familiar cultural territory. Each of these issues will be addressed below along with illustrations of the kinds of data that emerged as a result.

A CULTURE OF WE-NESS

I began this fieldwork by interviewing the active sisters. My Catholic background gave me easier access to them, as well as the advantage of some familiarity with religious language. I did not consider the initial reluctance of some of the sisters to engage in full disclosure as unusual at first. Many of the nuns expressed concern about why I was interested in researching them and several asked for reassurances along the way, showing apprehension about how their comments might be interpreted or whether their statements might reflect poorly on their order. Several of the nuns also expressed concern that they were giving me the type of information I really wanted. While this is not an unusual aspect of fieldwork, a recurrent feature of these interviews alerted me to an interesting dynamic—that is, the reluctance of the sisters to speak in terms of the self without reference to the community.

Most of the sisters spoke in terms of "we," rather than "I." When asked for self-descriptions, phrases such as "our life," "our community," and "our future" were often used. For example:

> . . . there isn't the depth of our life that we had when we were a community . . . we are so diverse . . . different jobs with different hours (Field Notes 4:56, 10/19/92) We are independent, intelligent women capable of making decisions (Field Notes 3:38, 9/30/92). Everything that reflects on me reflects on others (Field Notes 20:245, 12/29/93).

Even when speaking of independence and the more democratic structures within convents at present, these notions were stated in terms of the group. Reticence about self revelation was evident in the comment of one nun who stated, "I hope you don't mind if I give my personal views," (Field Notes 1:2, 9/15/92), as though I might think this inappropriate for a nun to do. The traditional personal interview, during which I expected to hear individual thoughts and opinions, was grounded in my own American cultural assumptions regarding individuals in interaction and my negative reaction to this statement was an indication of my personal distaste for self-denigration in women. My impatience might also have been a result of my own nervousness about asking inappropriate questions, since my previous experience with nuns had not been characterized by self-disclosure of a personal nature. (Having been taught self-effacement by them, I may have expected them to exhibit this, while still resenting the kinds of emotional barriers that this represents.) What I later came to understand was that this aversion on the part of some of the sisters to self-revelation was less an indication of self-effacement or even a sense of exclusion towards outsiders, but more of a manifestation of their communal lifestyle, which had become second nature to them. This barrier was in many ways a function of my own emotional reactions to them and was easier to cross than I first anticipated in that many of them spoke at great length of their personal experiences, once encouraged to do so. In this same regard, I was also struck by the uniformity of speech among the nuns; after the first few interviews, I came to realize that they all used similar phrases and word choices, even though some of their responses to individual questions were very diverse.

While most of the sisters showed an air of deference and humility at times (perhaps a result of their earlier socialization, which they described as a type of deindividuation process, characterized by exercises in humility and self-effacement), this was always balanced by a sense of pride and specialness and a respect for their community. These points of congruence between the interviews with the active sisters helped to reinforce to me the extent to which they were a community, despite the fact that many of them are not living communally on a daily basis.

LACK OF LANGUAGE

While as a group, the active nuns appeared forthright and articulate, on some occasions, self-deprecating remarks were noted which seemed to signal something other than a common culture of humility and modesty; that is, at times I detected an inability, rather than a conscious reluctance, to describe aspects of their experience. Commenting on the linguistic aspects of interviewing, Marjorie DeVault (1990) affirms that "language is often incongruent with the realities of women's experience" (DeVault 1990:96). She systematically noted hesitancies in speech during explanations women gave of their household tasks and developed strategies for "recovering" those aspects of experience that are left out when women "translate" their accounts, eliminating what they feel is unimportant or difficult to explain. Women translate by using words that are as close as possible to what they mean but often miss the mark, for example, using "housework" to refer to all their work tasks in the home (DeVault 1990:102). Difficulties in expression may stem from feelings of unimportance of the work, as Daniels (1988:57-63) noted in her analysis of the self-deprecating remarks of female volunteer civic leaders which she saw as an indication of low self-confidence and anxiety about their own achievements. This self-doubt helps to sustain a "linguistic void" in that women have not adequately developed a comfortable way of discussing their own work, even with each other. Dorothy Smith (1987) refers to this problem as a gap in social knowledge or a "line of fault" in women's experience in that they are forced to view their activities through male eyes, rather than on the basis of their own interpretations. Aspects of family work are difficult to label and therefore are not a part of shared

language. The work of caring and service, which relies on an emotive component, has also been identified as "invisible work" in that the worth of women's
work hinges upon its value on the labor market (Daniels 1987; Wichroski 1994).
It is difficult to conceptualize the caring and nurturant aspects inherent in social
relations as "work," because of the "folk understanding" of work as paid labor
(Daniels 1987:403).

Similarly, the work of nuns is not necessarily conceptualized in their own
minds as "paid labor," perhaps reinforced by their earlier training. (One nun
recalled being reprimanded for referring to the baking of altar bread as a "job"
and was reminded that this task was a "privilege.") While women in general
perform the tasks of nurturing and caring in the home and are also overrepresented in service jobs requiring similar skills (Hochschild 1983; Wichroski
1994), these nuns too are now more actively engaged in social work and health
care fields.

As with other women, these aspects of labor are often difficult to articulate;
for example, one sister had difficulty describing her work as head of food
services in a novitiate (a training school) and this required extensive probing.
When asked about how she felt about her job, she said, "What I did was me"
(Field Notes 4:85, 10/19/92). From here we engaged in a long discussion about
the creative ways she had devised to make the food more appealing. My
interpretation of her original statement, as she explained it to me, was that she
felt "invested" in the work because it was a reflection of her satisfaction in doing
something more than merely serving food; that is, being creative in her work
and showing her concern for the young postulants. In her own words, "Although
this may sound silly, I could make a hotdog look good!" (Field Notes 4:86,
10/19/92). Prefacing her statement in such a way indicated that she thought I
might feel this type of work to be insignificant or degrading and it was difficult
for her to articulate specific aspects of it for this reason. It should be noted here
that while gender probably facilitated my entry into the convent for interviews,
her statement indicating that she "did not feel comfortable with intelligent
women," signalled that her perception of me "as professional researcher"
superseded any connection we were making by virtue of gender. She indicated
that she was often reluctant to speak of her jobs with the other sisters who were
better educated and had professional and administrative jobs, indicating a type
of occupational differentiation within the convent. Troubled by the reference to
domestic work as "dirty work," Sister referred to a Biblical passage in Luke
(10:38-42), the story of Mary and Martha. The common interpretation was that
Christ was partial to Mary, who sat and listened to Him, while Martha was busy
in the kitchen. Sister refused to accept this interpretation of Christ's preference

for those who worship over those who do necessary tasks in the service of others. Overall, this exchange showed the difficulties of describing aspects of work experience, in particular the nurturant element of it, and in reconciling her perception of her work within the established parameters of the institution—that is, the Catholic Church.

What I also came to realize was that these nuns, who had once lived a semi-cloistered existence, now had much more contact with priests and laypersons with whom they worked and in some cases, reported to. The new division of labor within the Church requires that nuns often work for parish priests and bishops, resulting in the loss of some of their former autonomy in managing their own institutions, such as hospitals and schools. Several of the sisters reported on what they felt to be sexual discrimination within the Church. It may be that their conceptions of work now more closely parallel those of the outside world, as there was evidence of a certain occupational differentiation within the community which may not have existed before Vatican II. (The responses of several of the nuns indicated that they may now be viewing themselves more in occupationally-based terms, and their new exposure to the outside world has brought them closer to secular women in tasks and concerns.)

On several other occasions passages from scripture and quotations from their foundress were used by the nuns to help explain their reference points, legitimations for their actions, and sometimes discrepancies between the interpretations of male clerical authority and their own experience. The actions and teachings of Christ and other historical role models associated with their order seemed to serve as guidelines for their current decisions, rather than formal decrees from the Vatican.

Allowing the nuns to digress from the standard interview format and to explain their own frames of reference helped in the articulation process and afforded me opportunities to better understand their lives and work and the ways in which they interpreted and legitimated them. The problem of lack of language indicates the need for the researcher to become an active listener, employing a "third ear" so to speak, to capture the essence of experience in the absence of vocabulary. Often facial expressions, body language, and particularly paralanguage, such as pauses, silence, hesitancies, tone and pitch, are signals that indicate a need for assistance and further attention. Just as phrases such as "you know" came to seem like a request for understanding (DeVault 1990:103), there are a variety of signals that may indicate that people need encouragement to explain experience and statements that appear incongruous at first, or even trivial, may be a source of important information.

In summary, unearthing clues to lifestyle patterns and values in their responses helped me not only to facilitate dialogue with the active sisters, hut to extract valuable information. As a product of Catholic schools where the nuns I knew had been trained during the same period as those in my sample (the median age was 62 years), I found I could often relate to some of their experiences. As a woman, I could understand some of their problems of articulation and reticence, and finally, these nuns were now working in the outside world. They were aware of current social problems, were highly educated, and many had been exposed to feminist ideas. A new division of labor had entered convents, perhaps changing their conceptions of themselves as professional women.

While conversations with the active sisters were very open, and often humorous exchanges, where I was able to ask questions continually, to encourage them to respond as individuals, and to try to "get around" difficulties of articulation, new methodological problems would characterize my fieldwork in the cloistered community, where verbal exchange would not always be sufficient to overcome them.

MEANING INVERSIONS

I indeed expected to encounter a more fully contained communal society when I visited the cloistered order, but I also expected that my religious orientation, as well as my new knowledge about religious orders would serve me well. What I found here was a new problem in that my interviews with the Mother Superior were characterized by a series of misinterpretations which could be attributed not only to unshared cultural assumptions, but to the actual use of common words themselves. Several times the latter helped to illustrate the former; that is, my interpretations of their words (both written and spoken) were culturally biased.

In many ways the cloister represents a reversal of the cultural underpinnings or assumptions found in the outside world. Individualism, freedom, and physical comfort are not valued as they are in contemporary society; for example, reference by the Mother Superior to "strength" as important in the cloister was misinterpreted by me to mean emotional stability. She later clarified what she meant; that is, physical stamina is required of the fully cloistered nun, while weaker individuals were often assigned physical tasks which might require outside labor or contact with outsiders. This did not make sense to me, as she had previously described the social organization within the monastery as comprised of three levels: the "choir sisters," who were the most educated and could hold office, "lay sisters," who perform domestic duties within the monastery; and "extern sisters," who performed more physical types of labor on the grounds and ran errands, such as food shopping. Asked how sisters were put into these categories, the Mother Superior explained that physical health was taken into consideration because the fully cloistered nun was required to recite the "divine office" seven times daily, including midnight prayers, and that the tensions and lack of distractions inside were physically demanding. Sister's explanations made clearer to me what I saw as the "heroic" aspects of their rigorous religious practices which were both physically and emotionally challenging, contradicting my earlier images of a passive life of meditation.

I also came to realize that their vows of poverty, chastity, and obedience are not self-explanatory terms; that is, poverty means "having just enough" and chastity may not be so much a separate vow but another form of poverty, what Williams (1981:120) referred to as a "poverty of the heart" that is, separation from friends, family, and social relations on the outside create an inner void to make room for spiritual fulfillment. Similarly, the vow of obedience conjures up visions of blind adherence to formal rules. Yet their definitions of hierarchy and authority were not consistent with this: for the cloistered nuns, hierarchy means in order of closeness to God, what comes first—not deference to the power of a punitive authority; nor did it mean that those who were more highly educated and could hold office were held in higher esteem than those performing physical or domestic labor. All forms of labor were considered done in service to God.

Finally, perhaps one of the most striking things about this community was their conception of gender, which I had expected to be characterized by passive acceptance of a secondary role within the Church. By virtue of their sexually-segregated lifestyle, the nuns have limited interactions with males. While their internal structure might be characterized as familial, rather than patriarchal, I assumed that they were ultimately subject to male, clerical authority. This is in some sense true; however, it appeared that for these nuns, gender was a source of institutionalized protection and legitimation, rather than a symbol of secondary status. While they have rejected the sexual and biological functions of womanhood for themselves, they appeared to have a sanctified view of these functions as being important in a spiritual sense. The celebration of womanhood is evident in their writings, art work, metaphors, and prayers, which reflect a special spirituality dependent upon gender. In addition, the nuns seemed to show a certain assertiveness in the kinds of work they will perform (despite reported pressure from the local Bishop), pride in their community and way of life, and a firm protectiveness of their members. It seemed that there were many aspects of the life of the contemplative nun that appeared gender affirming, relegating the issue of female inequality to a feature of the outside world and not of concern to them. The autonomy of the community, facilitated in some ways by gender, became another important theme in my final analysis.

In summary, these "breaches" in understanding, while confusing at times, served to clarify for me some of the faulty preconceptions that I carried by virtue of culture—that is, cultural conditioning—and the importance of shared meaning systems (including specific words) in sustaining communication.

Thus far I have dealt primarily with aspects of verbal communication and the ways in which meaning can be extracted by paying attention to those very difficulties that tend to inhibit it. Moving further into the closed community of the cloister, however, my role as observer (that is, active researcher) became more one of participant in the sense that there were many occasions when I was forced to abandon reliance on verbal exchange altogether; I refer here to the rule of silence.

THE RULE OF SILENCE

One of the first things I noticed on arrival at the monastery of the contemplative order was a sign that read, "Silence is a beautiful hymn we sing to God." It did not take me long to realize that this is a value that the cloistered nuns take seriously and truly uphold, yet is not as straightforward as it at first appeared. Thus, along with verbal misunderstandings in general, there is the problem of how to interpret the dynamic of self-imposed silence. This would require cutting through cultural misunderstandings, as well as abandoning what might be considered a more scientific sociological approach—that of recording and relying upon the spoken word.

My assumption had been that the rule of silence is a form of penance; that is, that the nuns impose this rule upon themselves to create an inner sense of mortification, curbing individualism and free expression in order to promote inner spirituality. In fact, the Rule of St. Benedict, the model for most monastic communities, makes this clear:

> Indeed so important is silence that permission to speak should seldom be granted even to mature disciples, no matter how good or holy or constructive their talk,

because it is written: "In a flood of words you will not avoid sin" (Prov 10:19); and elsewhere, "The tongue holds the key to life and death" (Prov 18:21). Speaking and teaching are the master's task; the disciple is to be silent and listen. Therefore, any requests to a superior should be made with all humility and respectful submission. We absolutely condemn in all places any vulgarity and gossip and talk leading to laughter, and we do not permit a disciple to engage in words of that kind (St. Benedict s Rule, in Fry (ed), 1982:31).

While silence may serve to curb gossip and hurtful words and signifies an overall respect for authority, which seems consistent with their ideology, the rule of silence does not mean that the nuns are mute; rather, they are polite and welcoming but do not engage in what they consider to be "unnecessary talk." Silence is greatly honored, while talk is seen as useless and tiring. The cloistered nuns observe this rule all day, except as dialogue becomes necessary in the course of their work. Silence is observed at meals (at the discretion of the Mother Superior), but one hour of recreation time is taken in the evenings, during which the nuns are permitted to converse, play games, play musical instruments, sing, or do handwork. The Mother Superior described this as "individuals expressing themselves according to their own need, but not necessarily in conversation" (Field Notes 10:167, 5/5/93). The sisters do not discuss their respective families nor personal histories with one another. Trivial conversation is discouraged: for example, one sister explained that she would express concern for another by making a statement, such as "I hope you had a restful night," rather than "How are you today?" which might invite discussion or complaints from the other (Field Notes 15: 201, 10/18/93).

This way of communicating reflects a worldview that is diametrically opposed to that of mainstream American culture. Most contemporary Americans take it for granted that people want to talk. We are encouraged by our ethos of individualism and a self-focused psychology which promotes competitiveness, to seek and maintain attention in interaction-a type of "conversational narcissism" (Derber 1983:5-6), which we also expect others to engage in. Modern American cultural norms include self-expression and venting our feelings as a means to self-fulfillment. While open verbal exchange may be taken as a sign of sincerity, openness, and honesty, we seem to abhor silence and are trained to avoid it, both socially and professionally, making it difficult for us to interpret as something other than rudeness, weakness, or apathy.

In terms of a research problem, if the observer cannot speak directly with respondents, observation of them in spoken interaction is useful, but how do we interpret interaction when there is no spoken language? Without clearcut frames of reference for what was going on, I was at first confused and disoriented by this confrontation with silence. Yet the time I spent in the cloister afforded me an opportunity to better understand what nonverbal communication can mean in a community of this type. Upon "checking in" to the monastery, there is a feeling of isolation for the outsider. I was greeted by a nun who I could not see but whose voice came through a screen. A key, a daily schedule, and a piece of paper with my room number on it were deposited in a revolving hatch and extended towards me. After hearing the automatic locks on the inside doors open, I entered and was left to my own devices. I remember feeling that I would have to devise ways of making contact with the nuns so that I could speak with them, if only fleetingly.

Two incidents highlight my desperate attempts to make verbal contact. On one occasion, a young nun delivered a tray of food to my room and asked me if I had a "vocation." She was probably curious about what I was doing there. I took this as an invitation to talk, but when I told her that I was simply a temporary guest of the community, she quickly retreated. Another more embarrassing situation occurred one morning when I inadvertently took the wrong door on my way to the Chapel and found (to my horror) that it automatically locked behind me. I found myself on the outside grounds, forced to walk the full length of the building to re-enter through the formal foyer and explain my predicament to the nun greeting visitors. Another nun was quickly dispatched to "rescue" me and guide me back upstairs; as embarrassing as this was, it gave me the opportunity to speak with this woman who was very pleasant and began to talk of her family and the business her brother owned in the city. As we reached the top of the stairs, I asked her if she had grown up in this area; immediately, she seemed to show visible signs that she had overstepped protocol; that is, she remained silent and when we reached my room, she retreated quietly.

While these experiences were somewhat frustrating, my emotional responses to these rebuffs—often ones of disappointment and guilt—served to reinforce for me the "realness" of the barriers between the nun and the outside world. In addition, they illuminated for me my own somewhat stubborn expectations regarding the value of verbal communication. What I failed to see at first was that, despite the lack of open invitation for discussion and sometimes strained responses to my questions in conversation, the nuns were communicating with me in other ways. Through direct eye contact and facial expressions, such as a warm smile, they welcomed me into their community. On several occasions, after having left my room, I would return to find gifts left for me—a calendar, cookies, a note or card—attempts to make me feel welcome. The nuns spoke with me only on their terms; for example, many said that they were praying for me and what they called "my project." Their daily prayers and singing, which they kindly allowed me to witness and take part in, seemed to be a special type of group communication, a tacit understanding to one another that they share the same symbolic world.

Similarly, Japanese culture is noted for the mistrust of words and its emphasis on non-verbal communication (Lebra 1976:252-253). The word "haragei" connotes a kind of visceral communication" (Rheingold 1988:53-54) where words are not trusted. This may be more common in homogeneous societies whereby unspoken values are commonly shared. Zen Buddhism also denies to verbal language the role of communication of information and of logical reasoning; hence, the suppression of verbalism and an emphasis on indirection and intuiting what is hidden (Befu 1983:176). Goffman (1959) also noted the importance of non-verbal communication in maintaining the definition of the situation.

For the contemplative nuns, it may be that their mode of silence is merely another way of communicating in that this rule is accepted and carried out by all; it contributes to a common definition of the situation, and is more easily upheld in a homogeneous community where meanings are shared. Their community may, in fact, sustain itself in this way, using a form of interaction not dependent upon individual disclosures through talk and intimacy. The "shared silence" of the community may fulfill the human needs for self-expression and a sense of belonging, which is not contingent upon social relations as we know them—that is, verbal affirmations. This is consistent with an overall ideology which de-emphasizes overt expressions of individuality or self-centeredness, as well as "small talk," which in contemporary society is considered polite and/or supportive of others and is generally welcomed and expected.

Social relations in the cloister are grounded in a specific cosmology, a worldview which in many ways is an "inversion" of life on the outside. Denial is pleasurable, material possessions irrelevant, individualism submerged and replaced with interdependence within the group. I also came away with a feeling of specialness, of pride in womanhood, a sense of spirituality that was dependent upon gender. Stripped of the encumbrances of the outside world—the pleasures, excesses, and demands we live with—the weight of these things being lifted, provides space for another level of experience. Silence is not interpreted as a void, but as shared experience which in and of itself helps to sustain this particular type of community. By giving myself up to the silence of the community, I was better able to grasp the sense of security and even a kind of freedom that this way of life affords the individual.

DISCUSSION

The tensions between my scientific sociological training and my socialization as a traditional Catholic were similar to those identified by Joseph (1988), who returned to her homeland in Lebanon as an anthropologist. She described her role as passive observer as much more comfortable but less "intellectually legitimate" from a methodological point of view (Joseph 1988:40). On the other hand, as field workers, when we lack an experience of "immersion" in the social setting, we may also feel inauthentic (Kleinman and Copp 1993:10). These conflicting feelings represent the tension between participation and observation in fieldwork. As Levi-Strauss had said, the "observer" gets to understand structure and also culture, the elements of stability; the "participant" sees process, the equilibrium of things, the ingredients of change, the dynamism beneath the surface. Yet this is not always an "either-or" proposition, nor a conscious choice for the researcher, who is often required to move back and forth between these two poles, depending upon the social context.

When actively seeking numerical data, reading archival material, and interviewing, I was taking an active stance; in essence, controlling what was being researched by asking questions and seeking information, having already decided what was important. In contrast, as a silent observer, I became a "participant" by blending into the background, letting the data come to me, a more passive and less traditional means of gathering data. While in the active mode, I needed to stand out to assert myself as the researcher, the objectifier, the "observer;" when in the passive mode, I needed to blend in so as not to disturb the ongoing social milieu; I was a "participant," and as such, I had returned to a world closer to the traditional, 1950s Catholic one that I remembered, muting at times the role of the fully conscious and focused fieldworker. Yet this connection, by virtue of past experience, served to facilitate my understanding at times, similar to what is argued by others who have returned to familiar fields after having been trained as anthropologists (cf., for example, Shami 1988:115-116 and Morsey 1988:70).

It was my sociological training which allowed me to view religious orders of women in a new way as normative organizations experiencing relative rates of decline. My interviews required verbal aggressiveness and probing, yet many times I was forced to hold back, to revert to a silent observer, learning to rely upon and trust my own emotional reactions as sources of potential data. As Copp (1993) points out, "feelings can suggest hypotheses" (31). My role as participant, while assumed reluctantly at times, required a more passive stance while interacting in the field, but a far more rigorous and aggressive one in the interpretive and analytic phases of the fieldwork, which were often simultaneous and on-going. In retrospect, the passive mode was sometimes preferable; for example, the clash between secular values and the unique atmosphere of "other-worldly" concerns, as well as the shared silence of the cloister, could probably only be understood by living out firsthand what the nuns call a "day in the desert." In many ways this phase of the fieldwork reinforced and/or clarified some of my earlier findings, such as the difference in perceptions of gender between the two communities. Using both active and passive research modes, I adapted my stance in order to accommodate and account for the types of social entities I was studying.

CONCLUSION

This chapter has dealt with some of the methodological problems encountered during fieldwork conducted among two types of Roman Catholic religious orders of women. Each would require some adaptability on my part. I have addressed the linguistic problems of reticence on the part of respondents, lack of language, meaning inversions, and the interpretation of silence. From the confrontation with each of these problems important data emerged, which might be summarized as follows:

1. Paying attention to the nuances of the nuns' responses helped to clarify and reinforce the communal culture of active sisters, their previous socialization, and the extent to which community can sustain itself in the absence of the formal structures present in the past.
2. Cutting through the lack of language for certain aspects of their experience revealed new perceptions of the active nuns about their work; i.e., the difficulties they seemed to have in reconciling a work identity with a religious one, and their new experiences with sexual discrimination.
3. Seeking clarification of words, phrases, and metaphors, rather than presuming common definitions, helped me to better understand the culture of the cloistered nuns, including the way their vows are interpreted and the importance of gender as a source of spirituality, autonomy, and legitimation.
4. Experiencing firsthand a culture of silence helped to clarify the structure and patterns of the closed community. Confronting my own feelings (i.e., being forced to see myself as a symbol of the barrier between inside and out) helped me to identify cultural assumptions and to reinforce the clash between the contemplative culture and mainstream society.

I hope that these strategies will prove useful to other qualitative researchers who choose to study non-mainstream groups. To abandon that which cannot be measured easily is to overlook a portion of reality simply because it is not easily accessible or cannot be converted into conventional raw data. Confronting one's own emotions in the field can help in extracting valuable data and can be just as rigorous a research technique as the use and interpretation of quantitative measures. While different interaction styles and discrepant meaning systems can be overcome, lack of language and interpretations of silence create special difficulties in the final analysis. Yet the problem of translating knowledge gained in this way into sociological discourse is not an insurmountable one. With regard to articulation, DeVault points out, "By noticing silences and absences, we begin to talk and write beyond them" (DeVault, 1991:227). Although it is valid to proceed with analysis despite the available labels for things, it is equally valid to attempt to name things that EXIST. By doing so we are contributing to a growing body of knowledge on women's experience and generating new research questions to explore. With respect to silence as a preferred means of communication, we can investigate what is being communicated and its significance as a type of interaction distinct from commonly-accepted, American cultural rules regarding it. In the first case, we wish to break the silence, and in the second, to understand it better. In both cases we can train ourselves to recognize the silences we are confronted with, discuss what they mean, and even use them as important clues to understanding.

REFERENCES

Agar, M. (1986). *Speaking of ethnography.* Newbury Park, CA: Sage.

Befu, H. (1983). *Japan: An anthropological introduction.* San Francisco, CA: Chandler.

Curran, P. (1989). *Grace before meals: Food ritual and body discipline in convent culture.* Urbana: University of Illinois Press.

Daniels, A. K. (1987). Invisible work. *Social Problems* 34:403-415.

————. (1988). *Invisible careers: Women civic leaders from the volunteer world.* Chicago: University of Chicago Press.

Derber, C. (1983). *The pursuit of attention: Power and individualism in everyday life.* New York: Oxford University Press.

DeVault, M. L. (1990). Talking and listening from women's standpoint: Feminist strategies for interviewing and analysis. *Social Problems* 37(1): 96-116.

————. (1991). *Feeding the family.* Chicago: University of Chicago Press.

Fry, T., O.S.B. (Ed.) (1982). *The rule of St. Benedict in English.* Collegeville, MN: Liturgical Press.

Goffman, E. (1959). *The presentation of self in everyday life.* Garden City, NY: Doubleday Anchor Books.

Hochschild, A. R. (1983). *The managed heart: Commercialization of human feeling.* Berkeley, CA: University of California Press.

Johnson, J. M. (1978). *Doing field research.* New York: Free Press, MacMillan.

Joseph, S. (1988). Feminization, familism, self, and politics: Research as a Mughtaribi. In S. Altorki & C. F. El-Solh (Eds.), *Arab women in the field: Studying your own society* (pp. 25-47). Syracuse, NY: Syracuse University Press.

Kleif, B. B. (1974). Issues in anthropological field work in the schools. In G. D. Spindler, (Ed.), *Education and cultural process: Towards an anthropology of education* (pp. 389-398). New York: Holt, Rinehart & Winston.

Kleinman, S. and Copp, M. A. (1993). *Emotions and Fieldwork,* Newbury Park, CA: Sage.

Lebra, T. S. (1976). *Japanese patterns of behavior.* Honolulu, Hawaii: University of Hawaii Press.

Loftland, J. and Loftland, L. H. (1984). *Analyzing social settings* (2nd edition) Belmont, CA: Wadsworth.

Morsy, S. (1988). Fieldwork in my Egyptian homeland. In S. Altorki & C. F. El Solh (Eds.) *Arab women in the field: Studying your own society* (pp 69-90). Syracuse, NY: Syracuse University Press.

Neal, M. A. (1965). *Values and interests in social change.* Englewood Cliffs, NJ: Prentice Hall, Inc.

————. (1984). *Catholic sisters in transition: From the 1960s to the 1980s.* Wilmington, DE: Michael Glazier.

————. (1990). *From nuns to sisters: An expanding vocation.* Mystic, CT: Twenty-Third Publications.

Reinharz, S. R. (1979). *On becoming a social scientist.* San Francisco: Jossey-Bass.

Rheingold, H. (1988). *They have a word for it: A lighthearted lexicon on untranslatable words and phrases.* Los Angeles, CA: Jeremy P. Tarcher.

Shami, S. (1988). Studying your own: The complexities of a shared culture. In S. Altorki & C. F. El Solh (Eds.), *Arab women in the field: Studying your own society* (pp. 115-138). Syracuse, NY: Syracuse University Press.

Smith, D. (1987). *The everyday world as problematic: A feminist sociology.* Boston, MA: Northeastern University Press.

Wichroski, M. A. (1994). The secretary: Invisible labor in the workworld of women. *Human Organization* 53(1):33-41.

Williams, D. (1981). The brides of Christ. In S. Ardener (Ed.), *Perceiving women.* London: Dent & Sons, Ltd.

14 | The Case of Mistaken Identity

Problems in Representing Women on the Right

Faye Ginsburg

> *Dialogue represents not just a literary technique, or a way of connecting the isolated person to the outside world, but a reinterpretation of the nature of the self . . . the self cannot be understood or expressed except in relation to an audience whose real or imagined responses continually shape the way in which we define ourselves.*

(Kelly 1992:44)

The question of how anthropologists achieve some sense of participation and empathy with *some* "other" despite difference has been central to the ethnographic enterprise in its conventional cross-cultural form. However divided the field of sociocultural anthropology has become, Malinowski's axiom—that the ethnographer's task is to represent the native's point of view—is still widely accepted. The assumption is that the ethnographer should take a sympathetic position vis-à-vis his/her subjects. While this stance of identification informs much of the discussion on field methods and ethnographic writing, it is rare that audiences read into even the most seamless of ethnographic accounts a confu-

EDITOR'S NOTE: This chapter is reprinted from *When They Read What We Write: The Politics of Ethnography,* edited by Caroline Brettell, 1993, Westport, CT: Greenwood. Reprinted with permission of Greenwood Publishing Group, Inc.

sion between the identities of the anthropologist and the native. Malinowski's talent for grasping the native's point of view, for example, has not been mistaken for his becoming a Trobriand Islander (whatever other questions have been raised about his work). What happens, however, when the anthropological gaze is turned toward those with whom the investigator—and most of his or her anthropological colleagues—disagrees in some significant way?

In his pioneering study, *Tuhami* (1980), Vincent Crapanzano discusses the recognition of other ways of constituting reality in anthropological research as a sort of "epistemological vertigo." The threat of such an encounter and its possible transformative effects is striking when the subject is at some cultural or historical remove. When the "other" represents some very close opposition within one's own society, taking on the "native's point of view" is problematic in different ways, not only in the research but in the response of professional colleagues, especially when the work is focused on a social and political conflict that engages the hearts and minds of other anthropologists. This chapter explores a particular instance of this general case through discussion of work with American right-to-life activists.[1] In particular, I want to focus on the dilemmas of developing effective ethnographic representation for potentially hostile audiences; discuss textual strategies for encompassing the tensions between compassion and disagreement; and suggest how such ethnographic mediation can illuminate important social issues in our own society.

Most of the anthropological writing on methodological problems addresses the research process. Much ink has been spilled over questions of rapport, objectivity, reflexivity, selection of informants, and the ethics and politics of the field situation. For those working in their own societies, the question of gaining distance and *de*familiarizing oneself takes on prominence. Recently, there has been a surge of interest in ethnographic writing itself and how the relationships made in ethnographic fieldwork are reconstituted textually (Geertz 1988). Such work raises questions about the representation of the anthropologist's voice in relation to that of the (often less powerful) natives (Clifford 1988). A number of writers have suggested less authoritative and more experimental rhetorical strategies, the better to represent the experience of cultural anthropology in a postmodern world (Marcus and Fischer 1986; Clifford and Marcus 1986).

With all this self-reflection, relatively little attention has been paid to problems of *reception* of ethnographic texts. The tropes and strategies used to familiarize so called exotic cultures assumed a fairly predictable response to such material on the part of most readers. Whether or not that assumption was correct, it cannot be applied so easily to audiences for ethnographies written about people from the same society as the reader's. Texts must be written with an awareness that they will be read by those studied; *other* natives—even anthropologists—inevitably find it difficult to suspend judgment, particularly when they disagree politically with those represented. In my own anthropological research with right-to-life grassroots activities in the United States, I found that when I began to present my work and explain the way the world looked from the point of view of these "natives," I was frequently asked if I had, indeed, become one of "them." For the sake of discussion, I will call this problem "the case of mistaken identity." The challenge for the ethnographer is to find methods that anticipate and effectively counter such reader reactions.

This chapter addresses this challenge through a discussion of the strategies I chose to enable audiences momentarily to set aside preconceptions. Unlike the Nuer, Australian Aborigines, or a variety of American subcultures, the people I studied are considered by most of my colleagues to be their enemies. When I offered representations that rendered the right-to-life position sensible or even as powerful as it is to those who adhere to it (as any good ethnographer must), often my "objectivity" or results were called into question, framed by queries as to whether I had "gone native." In this case, my colleagues (most of whom are in favor of abortion rights, i.e., pro-choice, as am I) meant that I had come to understand the right-to-life position, implying as well that this would undercut my credibility to make a valid ethnographic analysis.

In response, I shifted from a strategy of mediation, which sets up the anthropologist as defender and spokesperson for "the native." Instead, I used devices that (1) helped me to recreate for readers the counter-intuitive encounter that I experienced, (2) drew attention to the interpretations offered by informants, and (3) resituated the ethnographic case in the context of historical material, thus drawing attention away from the immediacy of politics and toward broader cultural patterns that are often "too close" to see in one's own society. The more general concern is how the interpretation of research is shaped when home audiences are often directly engaged in the issues being studied. This is the central point to which I will return. but first I want to provide some background and case material.

BACKGROUND

The example used here is a study of grassroots activists on both sides of the abortion conflict in the United States. I worked with pro-life and pro-choice women engaged in a struggle over the opening of the first abortion clinic in Fargo, North Dakota, which I followed closely from 1981 to 1984 (including two periods of fieldwork totaling twelve months). Though I was concerned with activists on *both* sides of the abortion issue, the work focused on the pro-life position because of the prominent role this movement has played recently in American politics and culture.

I began to explore the idea for this research on female grassroots abortion activists in 1980, the year Ronald Reagan was elected President of the United States, an event that has come to be associated with what is called the rise of the New Right.[2] My interest was in investigating the role played by women in this rightward swing in the United States from the point of view of those engaged in conservative social movements at the local level.

The activism of women on the right was, by 1981, a topic of concern among feminist scholars in particular, although few had had direct contact with any of these right-wing women working at the grassroots. These grassroots activists offered an important challenge to the burgeoning work in feminist scholarship in the United States that began in the 1970s and has proliferated since then.[3] The first premise of such research was an acknowledgment of women as active agents rather than passive victims, as well as a respect for how women cross-culturally shaped their identities and interests from their experiences as *female* social actors. What were feminist scholars to do with this right-wing social movement claimed by and for women? The right-to-life movement put forward an agenda that seemed contrary to American feminist desires, and yet had thousands of "average" white, middle-class American women (the same socio-logical profile of most feminists) across the country as its supporters. On more political grounds, I wanted to understand why feminism was losing its persua-sive grip, and was interested to see if indeed there was any broader common ground between women opposed on single issues such as abortion.

The development of the right-to-life movement was part of the emergence of the American New Right in the 1970s, the rather peculiar coalition of economi-cally and socially conservative politicians, fundamentalist Christians, and peo-ple enraged in single-issue social movements intended to reverse liberal gains of the 1960s such as abortion, affirmative action, and gun control (Himmelstein 1990). While most of these groups did not share ideologies with each other, their different interests in having a conservative president brought them together to gain a minority for the election of Ronald Reagan in 1980 and 1984 and then George Bush in 1988. With some exceptions (Fitzgerald 1986; Harding 1987; Klatch 1987; Luker 1984; Paige 1984), most authors who were writing on the New Right in the 1980s focused on the political organization and leadership of a few well-known groups and leaders who were central to these organizations. Few had gone out and talked to the different people these movement leaders claimed as their supporters, to find out who they are, how they live, and what motivates them. In particular, I wanted to understand what motivated women to become so active in political causes that, in my view as a feminist, were against their own interests.

THE RIGHT-TO-LIFE WORLDVIEW

In the 1980s, pro-life activity was most engaged and effective at the local level, and for that reason offered a setting particularly appropriate for anthropological research. In general, right-to-life groups draw their strength from local social life. Their activity, unlike the direct mass-mail organizing of many of the New Right groups, is embedded in the kind of ongoing face-to-face interaction that is the stock-in-trade of the anthropological enterprise.

Contrary to stereotype, the pro-life movement, like many other single-issue groups, encompasses a broad range of ideological positions, from radical pacifism— Pro-Lifers for Survival, an antinuclear group, for example—to progressive Catholics and Protestants, to fundamentalist Christians. While right-to-lifers are frequently considered to be unswervingly hostile to feminism, much of their rhetoric seeks to claim the same territory charted by the women's movement. In the book *A Private Choice* by John Noonan, one of the key philosophers of the movement, abortion is cast as anti-woman, the agenda of upper-class men. Noonan writes:

> When strong and comprehensive anti-abortion statutes were enacted in 19th century America, the militant feminists had been outspoken in their condemnation of abortion. . . . Who wanted abortion in 1970? Only a minority of any section of the population favored it, but the stablest and strongest supporters of the liberty were white upper-class males. (1979:48-49)

Noonan goes on to quote from Eugene O'Neill's play *Abortion,* written in 1914. In it, the protagonist Jack Townsend, a rich young college student, impregnates a local girl for whom he arranges an abortion, which proves fatal to her and the fetus. Noonan musters this, along with statistics and legal arguments, as evidence for his case that abortion casts women as the victims of male lust and the uncaring penetration of upper-class privilege into the ranks of the less fortunate.

Noonan provides an example of how right-to-life activists' concerns go beyond the goal of recriminalizing abortion; they see abortion as symptomatic of other social problems. In particular they are concerned that materialism and narcissism are displacing nurturant ties of kin and community. Much of their agenda could be interpreted as a desire to reform the more dehumanizing aspects of contemporary capitalist culture. In this respect, although their solutions differ, many right-to-life concerns more closely resemble those of some of their pro-choice opponents than those of their supposed allies on the New Right who favor a more libertarian conservative social philosophy (Klatch 1987).

This complexity of position is not confined to leadership but was apparent among grassroots activists as well. "Roberta" provides a case in point. I first met her at a pro-life banquet and fundraiser. Born in 1953, Roberta is now married to an auto mechanic. Before giving birth to her first child, she worked as a college teacher and a graphic designer. In 1984 she was a full-time homemaker, raising two children, expecting a third, and active in the pro-life movement as well as Democratic politics.

> They paint the job world as so glamorous, as if women are all in executive positions. But really, what is the average woman doing? Mostly office work, secretarial stuff. Even teaching gets routine after awhile. When you watch TV, there aren't women pictured working at grocery store checkouts. I just don't see homemaking as any worse than eight to five. I really like homemaking. It's something I've chosen. I bake, I garden, I sew, I see it as an art. I don't say everyone should do it that way. And my husband likes to do it too. People should be able to do what they like to do. That's the part of the women's movement I've really been in favor of.

In Roberta's construction, this is not simply a defense of homemaking as a choice of vocation. Her description of her own life is embedded in a critique of what she considers to be the dominant culture. What she *does* defend is the social and economic consequences of having made a decision that she senses is unpopular.

> There are a lot of pro-life people who choose to stay at home with their children like me. A secondary income is not that important to us. My income would be pretty darn good if I took off for the work force again. My husband alone can support us but we have to pinch and budget and so we don't go to the fundraisers. And now that my husband and I have become evangelicals, we don't really believe in drinking for the sake of drinking. So we're severely criticized for that. Anyway, to completely exclude us for that one reason, being pro-life, just blows my mind.

In choosing to leave the work force, Roberta knew she would be greatly reducing the disposable income of her household. The economic consequences of her ideological choice, then, have restricted the activities in which she and her husband can participate. (Interestingly, pro-choice women only ten years senior to Roberta felt that their decision to do the opposite, leave homemaking for the work force, was similarly controversial. This indicates how rapidly the definition of "normal female behavior" has changed.) Roberta sees in the lack of recognition for domestic work an extension of a more pervasive condition: the increasing commercialization of human relations, especially those involving dependents.

> You know, the picture painted these days is how much kids cost. These are the reasons given for most abortions. How much work kids are, how much they can change your lifestyle, how they interpret the timing of your goals. What is ten years out of a seventy-year life span? You know, I've done a lot of volunteer work in nursing homes and it's just a lonely world to see women who don't have families. If you don't have your family, if you don't have your values, then what's money, you know?

In her narrative, abortion is threatening because it suggests the public acceptance of sexuality disengaged from family formation and the values associated with the latter. Metaphorically, Roberta represents this as the triumph of material interests over the care of human beings, a loss of a locus of unconditional nurturance in the social order.

In general, pro-life activists stress the negative consequences for women of the dismantling of a system that links male sexuality to childbearing and marriage. Sally, a friend and pro-life colleague of Roberta, for example, uses her experiences as a social worker as evidence that abortion undercuts women's ability to gain the support of a man.

> In my work, I saw a lot of people who were part of the middle class and then because of a divorce or having a child out of wedlock, they became part of the welfare system. I saw how really necessary, how many reasons there were to really maintain that relationship. There's a very real world out there. I feel sorry for men that they can't have the same feelings I do about pregnancy. But in the situation of a woman, where all of a sudden after twenty years of a marriage she has nothing, and he at least has a business or a job or whatever. . . . Women just have a different kind of investment in the marriage situation.

Ironically, the same sorts of cases are used by pro-choice activists who attribute the viewpoints of their opponents to ignorance of the difficulties many women face. Almost all of the Fargo pro-life activists were aware of these stereotypes and addressed them in a dialectical fashion, using them to confirm their own position. Roberta, for example, expressed it in the following way:

If you take the pro-life stand, you're labelled as being against anything else that women stand for. And ironically, it's mostly women in our movement. The pro-choice people say about us, "Well, they must have feelings but they're so put down they can't make up their own minds, you know." And they think we're just saying what we do because that's what men have taught us. Well, if the men have taught us, why aren't the men helping us?

To write off the views of a Sally or a Roberta as naive is as much a misreading as are their claims that pro-choice women are unconcerned with raising families. They, along with other right-to-life activists, are well aware of the fragility of traditional marriage arrangements and recognize the lack of other social forms that might ensure the emotional and material support of women with children or other dependents. As Roberta made clear,

> The women I have been talking to are strong and independent, hardly weak women, homemakers by choice because they value that. They support equal pay for equal work. I know about that because I sued the company I worked for and won. . . . No we aren't quiet. You know, we couldn't have a movement if we were all the way we're stereotyped.

For the most recent wave of right-to-life activists in particular, the pro-life movement speaks to their concerns. Through it, their own dilemmas are framed as part of a larger struggle to reform the culture in the interests of women. For Roberta, the right-to-life cause legitimates choices she has made—as a woman, mother, and political activist. As she explained to me while I cleared my tape recorder from her kitchen table to make room for freshly baked bread:

> The image that's presented of us as having a lot of kids hanging around and that's all you do at home and you don't get anything else done, that's really untrue. In fact, when we do mailings here, my little one stands between my legs and I use her tongue as a sponge. She loves it and that's the heart of grassroots involvement. That's the bottom. That's the stuff and the substance that makes it all worth it. Kids are what it boils down to. My husband and I really prize them; they are our future and that is what we feel is the root of the whole pro-life thing.

The collective portrait that emerges from such stories is much more complex than stereotypes that portray pro-life women as reactionary housewives and mothers passed by in the sweep of social change. They are astute, alert to social and political developments, and on many issues are not antifeminist. They approve of and endorse women seeking political power and economic equity. Roberta, for example, brought a comparable worth suit against a former employer. Most held or had held jobs, and some had careers. In the marriage relationships I observed, husbands helped regularly with domestic duties and were pragmatically and emotionally supportive of their wives' political work.

What is striking in the pro-life narratives is how most of these women had assimilated some version of feminist thought and woven it into their life choices. The plot of almost every story hinges on how the narrator either repudiated or reorganized these ideas into a right-to-life framework. Sally's narrative of how her ideas have changed since she joined the pro-life movement is illustrative.

> You're looking at somebody who used to think the opposite. I used to think that sex outside of marriage was fine. Now I see I don't believe that anymore. I believe when you practice sex outside of marriage you are taking all kinds of chances, including walking out on each other and not having to accept the responsibility of children or whatever. And to me, once you engage in the act of sex, it's a big emotional commitment. If my boyfriend walked out on me I would be devastated. I think the world preaches you can have it all . . . doing lots of things without getting caught and I guess over the last few years, I've really changed my mind about a lot of things. And when I see the abortion clinic, there's proof positive to me that my values are right and an innocent human being is paying the price for all this.

This sort of negotiation of feminism into their life story distinguishes younger right-to-life women in particular, although it is present in more muted form with older activists. Rather than simply defining themselves in opposition to what they understand feminist ideology and practice to be, many, like Sally, claim to have held that position and to have transcended it. Sally, for example, describes her former "liberated" ideas about sexuality and heterosexual relationships as a repression of her true self.

> I think there was part of me that never fully agreed. It wasn't a complete turnaround. It was kind of like inside you know it's not right but you make yourself think it's okay. When I was in college, I loved to read *Cosmopolitan* magazine, all kinds of magazines and I thought, "This is the kind of life I was meant to lead. . . . " You know, I think part of it is rebellion.

The same kind of appropriation of feminism is incorporated into political rhetoric; for example, a pro-life lecture popular in 1984 Fargo was entitled "I Was a Pro-Choice Feminist, but Now I'm Pro-Life." While such a claim provokes discussion of how the ideas of feminism are distorted, my concern here is to analyze what such assertions mean for those who make them. The lecture title is only one of many examples of right-to-life narratives in which activists assert a prior alliance to feminism, usually framed as a period of separation from the narrator's mother. The "conversion" to the pro-life position often follows a first birth or pregnancy. Thus, they narratively subsume their opponent's ideology into their own and thus claim authority over it.

In much the same way that pro-choice women embrace feminism, pro-life women find in their movement a particular symbolic frame that integrates their experience of work, reproduction, and marriage with shifting ideas of gender and politics that they encounter around them. It is not that they discovered an ideology that "fit" what they had always been. Their sense of identification evolves in the very process of voicing their views against abortion. In the regular performance of their activism, they are transforming themselves and their community, while projecting their vision of the culture into the future, both pragmatically and symbolically.

What underlies these narratives is a partially shared world of reference, the sociohistorical context of American women's lives and the social and cultural understandings of procreation and sexuality in particular. One can hear in the different emphases of activists' stories the dramatic shape of contradictions experienced by American women over the female life cycle in particular, the opposition between motherhood and wage work.

Proposed solutions to this dilemma are being argued in the abortion debate, a social arena marked as a contested domain. To succeed, each side must see and present its understanding of the cultural and personal meaning of reproduction as "natural" and correct. In order to legitimate their own position, proponents must make a persuasive case so that the formulations of the opposition appear unnatural, immoral, or false. On an individual and organizational level, then, each side constitutes itself in dialogue with the "enemy," real and imagined. The opposition is both incorporated and repudiated, understood and denied. This process is what gives the abortion debate its dialectical qualities. The "other" becomes a critical counterpoint on which one's own stance depends. While activists' actions are cast against each other, both sides provide ways for managing the structural opposition in America between wage work and parenthood that still shapes the lives of most women in this culture, and differentiates them from those of men.

Such data suggest to me that the we/they dichotomy marking the public side of the debate masks the points on which activists converge: issues such as comparable worth, women embracing political power, women reshaping the economy to meet their needs and responsibilities, and opposition to "male culture" insofar as it is identified with materialism and achievement and detrimental to women's needs as mothers. In addition, these activists' lives are embedded in social worlds with significant empirical and ideological overlap. Neighborhood and state politics, school boards, churches, PTA, pot lucks, canoe trips, backyard picnics are the arena of "local knowledge" occupied by activists on both sides.

The pro-life and pro-choice stances, like all genuine dialectical oppositions, have a number of elements in common, and both draw on an overarching understanding of gender prevalent in American society. Both sides voice a critique of a culture that increasingly stresses materialism and self-enhancement while denying the cultural value of dependents and those who care for them; in each case, they tie this perspective to women, claiming that it is women who represent nurturance, whether in the family or in the society at large. While their solutions differ, each group desires, in its own way, to ameliorate the unequal conditions faced by women in American culture.

THE RETURN OF THE NATIVE

Despite their obvious differences, the shared concerns of women activists on both sides, such as those that I have presented above, continued to come up, and so I wove the thread of their common discourse into my writing. After I returned from the field and began to present these ideas in public, the reactions of colleagues raised new problems for me. It is one thing, I learned quickly, for an anthropologist to offer her analysis of the native's point of view when the subjects are hidden in the highlands of New Guinea and have little impact on the lives of the assembled audience. Relativism has its limits, I discovered, especially when the subject is a controversial group from one's own society.

At first, I used a conventional anthropological strategy of attempting to mediate social distance by stressing what I saw as shared concerns in terms that the "natives" (pro-life activists in this case) would not use but which would be familiar and evocative to mostly liberal anthropological audiences. For example, I would speak of the critique of materialism and conspicuous consumption in American life that fuels much right-to-life sentiment as "critical of capitalism's dehumanizing effects," a phrase I think appropriate but one most pro-life people would be unlikely to use, because it suggests ties to secular, left-wing ideologies which they eschew but which most anthropologists hold dear.

Initially, I was more successful at engaging my audiences when I began framing my material in this way; this rhetorical strategy succeeded in disarming those armed with preconceptions. However, in the end the overall effect was to create further hostility and doubt on the part of certain audiences who took offense at any possible identification between themselves (many of whom also were critical of materialism in capitalist life) and these "others" to whom they were politically opposed, I found myself fielding hostile responses from colleagues; one skeptic actually suggested that my data—transcripts of life story interviews—simply were not true!

As a way out of the dilemma, I decided to put less effort into mediation and to create a more direct sense of confrontation between the right-to-life activists and the audiences I was addressing. Because my work took place in the context of a social drama—a contest around an abortion clinic—the multiple points of view of activists and their dialectical intertwining could be presented and compared. My hope was that the response could no longer be deflected onto me as if I had become an advocate rather than an analyst of these people.

While the social drama of clinic protests allowed the complexities of perspectives to be presented, it became apparent to me that abortion activism also needed to be contextualized as an ongoing social form rather than an isolated phenomenon. The metaphors and issues of gender articulated in the abortion debate are not new in American history, as many scholars have pointed out. I began to read extensively the feminist research on women's social history in America (Cott and Pleck 1979; Degler 1981; Gordon 1977).[4] This perspective gave me a powerful historical framework for examining the cultural and historical roots of contemporary debates over gender as they are played out in the abortion debate. Such a framing drew attention to the structural determinants that have shaped American women's lives for over two centuries, allowing me to resituate both the specific ethnographic case and the broader abortion controversy as part of a legacy of women's activism in the United States. This drew attention away from the immediacy of politics and toward broader cultural patterns regarding gender that are often too close to see in one's own society. The danger of such a long view, however, is that one loses a sense of the social actors themselves, the complexity of their motivations, and the cultural possibilities of their actions.

DISTINGUISHING IDENTITIES/
POLYPHONIC STRATEGIES

In trying to understand the meaningful location of abortion in the lives of contemporary women, I elicited "life stories" (Bertaux and Kohli 1984) from women from both sides, as part of an interest in activists' subjectivity. My initial intention in using this method was to grasp the significance that activism assumed in people's lives, to clarify the connections they saw between their sense of personal identity and abortion activism, and to see how engagement in these social movements was itself transformative. Life stories allowed me to present to readers long sections of narratives in which subjects interpreted their own actions, deflecting attention away from me as ethnographer and forcing a vicarious encounter between the reader and the subjects.

My method was simple. How, I asked activists, did they see their own lives in relation to their current work on the abortion issue? During my fieldwork, I carried out thirty-five such interviews, twenty-one from pro-life activists, and fourteen from pro-choice activists. The result was a set of narratively shaped fragments of more comprehensive life histories in which women used their activism to frame and interpret their historical and biographical experiences, in ways that distinguish the memberships of each group. I call them "procreation stories" because in them, activists on either side constituted provisional, narrative resolutions of their dissonant experience of what they regard as a coherent cultural model for the place of reproduction, motherhood, and work in the female life course in contemporary America.[5]

When I began to carry out these interviews, I discovered that most of the activists shared my interest in these questions. We were, in a sense, interested in figuring out the same problems. People seemed to enjoy the process, and when I would see them after the interviews, they would often recall things they had forgotten to tell me. This desire to continue telling me a life story indicated to me that the interview was part of an active reconstruction of experience, providing continuity between the past and current action and belief. These women also are engaged in convincing others of the rightness of their position; in a sense, I had positioned myself as a potential convert. Certainly the life stories were shaped in part by what these women imagined would persuade me to agree with them. This response was not entirely unexpected; what had not occurred to me was that the material generated by this method would help me to mediate their worldview to incredulous audiences to whom right-to-life activists otherwise had no access; finally, it became apparent to me that my informants saw me as a vehicle for doing so.

To capture the tension that framed the life story interviews, I realized I needed to generate a more direct sense of confrontation between the right-to-life activists and the audiences I was addressing to avoid the trap of mistaken identity, as if I had become an advocate rather than an analyst of these people. I turned to the emerging feminist scholarship on women's personal narratives which has developed more dialogical approaches to the representation of textual material—drawing on the use of extensive direct quotes, presented as a counterpoint to the author's words.

I used personal narratives as a central element in the text, which helped me to recreate for readers what I experienced and drew attention to the contrast between my interpretations and those offered by the women themselves. To clarify and elaborate this distinction is part of a larger trend in work with women's personal narratives, as noted by the editors of a recently published collection on that topic:

> In positing the centrality of the interpretive act, we recognize the possibility that the truths the narrator claims may be at odds with the most cherished notions of the interpreter. Personal narratives cannot be simply expropriated in the service of some good cause, but must be respected in their integrity. . . .
>
> The interpretation of women's personal narratives often entails a cautious juxtaposition of alternative truths and feeds into the feminist project of revising not merely the content of our knowledge of human society, but the very criteria that guide our search for truths. (Personal Narratives Group 1989:264)

By juxtaposing sections of life stories with my analyses of them and of other women activists in American history, I hoped to create a richer sense of the positions held by activists and how their identities emerge from lived experience as well as the historical construction of gender in the United States.

CONCLUSION

Working in as contested a situation as the one I had chosen, I could not rely on prior styles of ethnographic representation in which the cultural object is presented as homogeneous and stable, nor could I let my voice stand for my subjects. I also had to consider a complex readership, which included other anthropologists and feminist scholars, as well as my informants and other activists on both sides of the abortion debate. This was not simply a problem of popularizing, which was not my goal, but of developing a representational strategy that would challenge preconceptions of received political wisdom.

My struggle for an approach that more accurately reflected my experience coincided with the emergence of a greater "experimentalism" in the writing of ethnography that challenged its underlying political and poetic conventions (Marcus and Fischer 1986). Texts in which the voices of the anthropologists and subjects are made distinct and placed in dialogue with each other and with historical material can help to render sensible challenging cases such as that of women right-to-lifers, and ensure that they are not mistakenly identified with the anthropologist. Such polyphonically structured strategies reflect recent feminist anthropological work, which has insisted on a complex interrogation of the ways in which a text emerges out of relationships between the ethnographer and the subject, and which has drawn attention to the often forgotten historical dimensions that illuminate the lives and often contested social action of contemporary women.

A number of people interested in innovation in ethnographic writing have been influenced by the work of the late Russian social and literary theorist Mikhail Bakhtin. In particular, they took up Bakhtin's idea of "polyphony" as a rhetorical strategy in which "no single voice is the bearer of definitive truth," especially characteristic of complex heterogeneous societies such as the United States (Kelly 1992:44). For example, in his introduction to the book *Writing Culture,* historian of anthropology James Clifford invokes Bakhtin's ideas of dialogue and polyphony in both language and literature as guides to ethnographic textual production:

> [Dialogism] locates cultural interpretations in many sorts of reciprocal contexts, and it obliges writers to find diverse ways of rendering negotiated realities as multisubjective, power-laden, and incongruent. In this view, "culture" is always relational, an inscription of communicative processes that exist, historically, *between* subjects in relations of power. (1986:15)

In creating a text that convincingly represented opposing political positions to anthropologists and activists alike, I would invoke Bakhtin even more radically than Clifford does. While Clifford argues in favor of the decentered, complex text, Bakhtin himself refused to draw the line between text and context. In his ideas of historical poetics, no cultural production exists outside of language; the context is already textualized by what he calls "prior speakings" and the "already said" (Stam 1990). When an anthropologist's informants are close but controversial neighbors, one is made acutely aware of the power of prior speakings in one's own community of academia, as these become particularly loud and difficult to subvert.

By shifting from a strategy of analytic mediation, which inevitably sets up the anthroplogist as spokesperson for "the native," to one of a dialogue in which the voice of the "other" is audible, the author is able to recreate for her audience the counterintuitive encounter that she herself experienced across a boundary of difference in her own society. In this way, the audiences for such work must encounter this other set of voices more directly. Such polyphonically structured encounters are, of course, still mediated by the author. However, when the voices of the anthropologist and the informants are presented, distinguished, and placed in dialogue with each other, our efforts to render sensible the lives of controversial subjects in our own society are less likely be misapprehended as cases of mistaken identity.

NOTES

I would like to thank Caroline Brettell, Fred Myers, and Susan Carol Rogers for their insights in editing this chapter. Research was funded by the Charlotte Newcombe Fellowship in Ethics and Values, an American Association of University Women Fellowship, a Sigma Xi Research Award, and a David Spitz Award in the Social Sciences, CUNY Graduate Center.

1. "Right-to-life" (or "pro-life") is the name used by American social activists who are against abortion and euthanasia. Following standard anthropological practice, I will call members of the group by the name they prefer.

2. More recently, conservative analyst and New Right architect Kevin Phillips has argued that the Reagan administration was the economically destructive finale of a coalition built by Goldwater, Nixon, and Wallace in the 1960s rather than the debut of a new conservativism (Dionne 1987).

3. For example, see M. Rosaldo and Lamphere 1974; Reiter 1975; and MacCormack and Strathern 1980.

4. A more obvious context that I also addressed was the long history of changes not only in the interpretation of abortion, but in its practice as well (Luker 1984; Mohr 1978).

5. For a full discussion of my analysis, see Ginsburg 1987.

REFERENCES

Abu-Lughod, Lila. 1991. "Writing Against Culture." In Richard G. Fox, ed., *Recapturing Anthropology: Working in the Present.* Santa Fe, N.M.: School of American Research, pp. 137-162.

Adams, Jad. 1989. *AIDS: The HIV Myth.* New York: St. Martin's Press.

Adams, Timothy Dow. 1990. *Telling Lies in Modern American Autobiography.* Chapel Hill: University of North Carolina Press.

Agar, Michael. 1980. *The Professional Stranger: An Informal Introduction to Ethnography.* New York: Academic Press.

———. 1986. *Speaking of Ethnography.* Beverly Hills, Calif.: Sage Publications.

Allport, Gordon. 1942. *The Use of Personal Documents in Psychological Science.* Social Science Research Council, Bulletin 49. New York: Social Science Research Council.

Alverson, H., and S. Rosenberg. 1990. "Discourse Analysis of Schizophrenic Speech: A Critique and Proposal." *Applied Psycholinguistics* 11:167-184.

American Anthropological Association. 1989. "Report of the Administrative Advisory Committee," *Anthropology Newsletter* 30 (8):22-23.

———. 1990. "Revised Principles of Professional Responsibility." Ballot to Members, March 15, 1990. Washington, D.C.

Appadurai, Arjun. 1981. "The Past as a Scarce Resource." *Man* 16:201-219.

————. 1988. "Introduction: Place and Voice in Anthropological Theory." *Cultural Anthropology* 3 (1):16-20.

Arensberg, Conrad M., and Solon T. Kimball. 1940. *Family and Community in Ireland.* Cambridge, Mass.: Harvard University Press.

Asad, Talal, ed. 1973. *Anthropology and the Colonial Encounter.* New York: Humanities Press.

Bertaux, Daniel and Martin Kohli. 1984. "The Life Story Approach: A Continental View." *Annual Review of Sociology* 10: 215-237.

Clifford, James. 1986. "Introduction: Partial Truths." In James Clifford and George Marcus, eds., *Writing Culture: The Poetics and Politics of Ethnography.* Berkeley: University of California Press, pp. 1-26.

Clifford, James and George Marcus, eds. 1986. *Writing Culture: The Poetics and Politics of Ethnography.* Berkeley: University of California Press.

Cott, Nancy and Elizabeth Pleck. 1979. "Introduction." In Nancy Cott and Elizabeth Pleck, eds., *A Heritage of Her Own,* New York: Simon and Schuster, pp. 9-24.

Crapanzano, Vincent. 1980. *Tuhami: Portrait of A Moroccan.* Chicago: University of Chicago Press.

Degler, Carl. 1981. *At Odds: Woman and the Family in America from the Revolution to the Present.* New York: Oxford University Press.

Dionne, E. J., Jr. 1987. "High Tide for Conservatives, But Some Fear What Follows." *New York Times.* October 13, A 13.

Fitzgerald, Frances. 1986. *Cities on a Hill.* New York: Simon and Schuster.

Geertz, Clifford. 1988. *Works and Lives: The Anthropologist as Author.* Stanford: Stanford University Press.

Ginsburg, Faye. 1987. "Procreation Stories: Nurturance, Reproduction, and Procreation in Abortion Activists' Life Stories." *American Ethnologist* 14(4): 623-636.

Ginsburg, Faye. 1989. *Contested Lives: The Abortion Debate in an American Community.* Berkeley: University of California Press.

Gordon, Linda. 1977. *Woman's Body, Woman's Right: A Social History of Birth Control in America.* New York: Penguin Press.

Harding, Susan. 1987. "Convicted by the Holy Spirit: The Rhetoric of Fundamental Baptist Conversion." *American Ethnologist* 14(1): 167-181.

Himmelstein, Jerome. 1990. *To the Right: The Transformation of American Conservatism.* Berkeley: University of California Press.

Kelly, Aileen. 1992. "Revealing Bakhtin." The New York Review of Books 39(15): 44-48.

Klatch, Rebecca. 1987. *Women and the New Right.* Philadelphia: Temple University Press.

Luker, Kristen. 1984. *Abortion and the Politics of Motherhood.* Berkeley: University of California Press.

MacCormack, Carol and Marilyn Strathern, eds. 1980. *Nature, Culture, and Gender.* New York: Cambridge University Press.

Marcus, George and Michael M. J. Fischer. 1986. *Anthropology as Cultural Critique: An Experimental Moment in the Human Sciences.* Chicago: University of Chicago Press.

Mohr, James. 1978. *Abortion in America: The Origins and Evolution of National Policy.* NY: Oxford University Press.

Noonan, John. 1979. *A Private Choice: Abortion in America in the Seventies.* New York: The Free Press.

Paige, Connie. 1984. *The Right-to-Lifers.* New York: Summit Books.

Personal Narratives Group. 1989. *Interpreting Women's Lives.* Bloomington: Indiana University Press.

Reiter, Rayna Rapp. 1975. *Toward an Anthropology of Women.* New York: Monthly Review Press.

Rosaldo, Michelle and Louise Lamphere, eds. 1974. *Women, Culture, and Society.* Stanford: Stanford University Press.

Stam, Robert. 1990. "Mikhail Bakhtin and Left Cultural Critique." In A. Kaplan, ed., *Postmodernism and Its Discontents.* Bristol, U.K.: Verso, pp. 116-145.

15 | Gender and Voice, Signature and Audience in North Indian Lyric Traditions

Geeta Patel

Poetry is one of the predominant modes through which cultural subjectivity in South Asia is articulated (Abu-Lughod 1986, 1993). Poetry can be thought of as "high" cultural practice, read by afficionados and studied by scholars. But it is also oral, transmitted and remembered through recitation, and therefore available for a different kind of use. As the opening sequences of this chapter show, children learn poetry as practice, learn singing and recitation at home, and pick up on film songs that are memorized.[1] Literacy in poetry does not require that one read, just that one be cognizant of different kinds of verse. It is transmitted locally. Poetry is a way of expressing how one feels and who one is. Poetry can animate everyday street encounters and give symbolic substance to ordinary conversations. As a major style of speaking, as an important, even essential kind of voice that women and men resort to frequently, poetry can be a fruitful site for discussions on gender and voice that allows such discussions to be carried beyond merely academic ruminations.

READING POETRY, READING VOICE

People speak in the voice of an "other," often in the form of poetry, to articulate sentiments that they would not in their own (Parker and Willhardt 1996). This kind of cross-voicing can traverse the bounds of gender, and men can speak as women, women as men. However, when that kind of voicing is collected and read in retrospect, the crossing over has sometimes been eliminated. Those voices are then read as direct mimetic representations or records of a gendered position.

In this chapter I explore two instances of voice cross-over—in Bhakti poetry and in Sanskrit lyric. Both kinds of poetry are widely known, circulated, and spoken. I am versed in both and have chosen them because both together form the basis for my understanding of my own subjectivity. I learned Bhakti and Sanskrit poetry in two different sites—as a child in India and as an graduate student in the United States. Sanskrit lyric is the literary ancestor of Bhakti poetry. My study of Sanskrit as an adult gave me the early symbology through which I could translate my own childhood acquisition of Bhakti. Through it I began to unravel the tangled language of authorship and voice in which I had learned to speak myself.

Beginning this chapter with a set of anecdotes that place me as a participant in the production and reading of Bhakti poetry, I go on to articulate a series of questions about voice, gender and signature, performance, audience, and crossing over. The next section lays out the history of collecting Sanskrit texts, followed by analyses of some poems from one Sanskrit collection in which I look at different combinations of crossing—men writing as men, men writing in women's voices, women speaking as women, and women appearing under other aegis. I conclude by bringing the kinds of issues I raise around gender and signature in Bhakti poetry to the Sanskrit texts. In the process, I hope to open a space for an expanded investigation of voice, subjectivity, gender, and reading.

STORIES FROM "THE FIELD":
LEARNING POETRY, PERFORMANCE, VOICE

I stood on a flat patch of mud holding my four-year-old cousin's hand. I was six at the time and on one of the monthly pilgrimages my family made in the 1960s from the city to my father's village in Gujarat. Laughing, my cousin and I were making wet circles with hennaed heels in thick pools collected after the last blinding monsoon shower. In preparation for the women's dance to welcome the rains (closed to men), my aunts had dressed us in vivid pink and green taffeta skirts topped with *cholis* and long *duppatas* rimmed in braided silver thread that we were tossing up in the air and trying to snatch as they floated down. We'd galloped out of the two-room, streaked adobe house my father's parents in Danilimda owned to fill in a circle of women forming in random snatches in the space outside that was used as a courtyard for the village. The woman who drummed for dances was standing in the center tap-tapping the dholak she held tight against her hip. Suddenly, the circle closed, expanded, the noise of quick talking and calls to different houses muted/dulled, and the drummer tapping eight-time began to sing in her high thin voice, "Sister, I had a dream I wed . . . "

Later, squatting on my heels before the coal stove with my mother, the room sharp with the tart spiciness of marigolds strung on doorways, I asked with the sudden rash of curiosity that can overtake kids, "Ma, where'd that song come from?" "Mira," my mother said concentrating on flattening chapptis between her palms. "It's Mira's." "Who is Miras?" My mother's look twitched in amusement: "M-I-R-A, honey, Mira's a woman, was . . . a queen who lived a long time ago. . . . She left home because she loved Krishna, you know, the god. She made songs that we sing on festivals sometimes, like today." She paused and said slowly, You've heard that song before . . . but not in Gujarati, we sang it in Hindi at home last year, in Bombay after Divali, but it was a little different. . . . Remember, you and Mridula tried making up new lines and singing them and we joked that you were both little Miras reborn.

Years later, at Columbia in the 1980s, learning to read Mira's poetry in a class on Bhakti (medieval, mystical, devotional) religion, I recited the "same" song, drumming the meter against my knee with a pencil. The class opened up with questions about whether "Mira" actually existed, how the "corpus" grew over time, whether it expanded or contracted in different areas of the subcontinent where songs attributed to Mira were commonly sung, and who (women or men) composed some of the songs now commonly associated with her and for whom all of this mattered. The discussion brought home to me in an American classroom my artless questions to my mother from the 1960s: "Where did that song come from?" and "Who is Miras?"

FIELDING QUESTIONS ABOUT VOICE
AND GENDER, AUDIENCE AND SIGNATURE,
CONTENT AND CROSS-DRESSING

The kind of discussion we shared in our class on Bhakti was comparatively new to the study of Indian poetry. Scholars of religion had recently moved away from scrutinizing texts to understanding how texts were produced in the context of local practices and beliefs (Hawley 1988a, 1988b; Kishwar 1989).[2] In the 1970s and 1980s, influenced by feminist critics and literary theorists who advocated context-based readings of texts, scholars of India turned to the field to gather ethnographic material for a different kind of investigation of texts. As field researchers began doing ethnographic work on Mira's poetry, they quickly realized that singers (like me as a child) often composed "new" songs that then became part of the oeuvre of poetry attributed to the poet "Mira." When scholars asked singers what it was about these songs that made them Mira's, the singers would point to the imbrication of content and context—words, themes, and scenes, with attending explanations of where a song might fit into others that were also considered Mira's songs and when songs were likely to be sung.

This process of collection opened up several very fruitful avenues in discussions of voice and gender. One of the avenues I discuss here is the different ways that audiences read—from audiences who participate in the performance of the songs and are also potential composers of the songs (local audiences) to audiences who read or listen to the songs but do not participate directly in the performance (academic audiences like collectors, theorists of religion, and critical commentators).[3] Because I traverse the divide between participant and researcher, my role as an audience member in the three stories above is obviously quite complicated and changes with the circumstances under which I interact with Mira's poetry. In the first story, I am a participant in a village ritual, a member of a collective of women who gather together to sing songs by Mira. In the second story, I am a young child (a local) who is taught by her mother about the "legend of Mira." While inculcating me into local lore, my mother reminds me that I and my cousin were also composers of songs that then probably became songs we called "Mira's." In the third story, I am part of an academic audience studying Mira's poetry. In the process, I bring to my understanding of a "tradition" of poetry in women's voices my memories of being a participant/composer of those same "traditions." So I am a researcher/participant, someone who looks retrospectively and critically at texts, and a person who, if she were in the field, might have been studied by such a researcher.

Another related avenue is the question of signature and how different kinds of audiences understood it. Clearly, not all the songs that are supposedly by Mira (that is, signed by the author Mira) were produced by a historical person called Mira. In discussions of poetry that rely on textual information, critics make assumptions about who the poem is actually written/composed by. They assume that the poem is by the person whose name is appended to the poem as the "author." This presumption relies on a notion of property. The person who signs the poem is the "owner" of the poem and therefore *is* the person who composed the poem (Foucault 1977). However, performance-based poetry often has a different relationship to signature than text-based poetry. Performance allows someone (either man or woman) to compose as Mira or use Mira's signature and add that composition to Mira's corpus. A reader of Mira's poetry who does not understand the exigencies of performance and the way signature works as a pen name is clearly a different kind of audience member than one who shares the space of performance and composition and participates in the use of a poet's signature.

The third avenue is the relationship of voice to content in tandem with multiple audiences and consequences for perceiving cross-over, cross-dressed voices. When researchers in the field asked performers how poems by Mira might be identified, they were pointed to content and context. Certain themes that occurred in Mira's poetry were considered themes that "defined" it. The poetry was also characterized by the situations when it was likely to be sung. In these cases, the poet's signature did not tell a potential reader about the "real" person Mira. Instead, signature was an indication of or a shorthand for the inflections (themes, images, language, scenes) of *a particular kind* of voice—Mira's voice—sung under very specific circumstances. That voice may have been composed by either a man or a woman. If the audience understood that it was composed by a man, the male composer could be thought of as cross-dressed in Mira's voice and signature. When the audience did not or could not comprehend the possibility of voice cross-over, then the composer can be said to have passed as the woman "Mira."

POETRY AND VOICE

Articulating the problem of voice this way opens up a gendered space between singer/reciter, composer, attributed author, and/or the person whose signature is on the poem, so that the "one" who speaks sits in an uneasy relationship to all these locations. So too does the "one" who reads, if reading can either close or open that space between singer, composer, and signature. Focusing on desire (*sringar, kama*) in poetry from the exemplary anthology of Sanskrit love lyrics, *Vidyakara's Treasury* (see Ingalls 1975), I will historicize these concerns to complicate the ways in which voices have been produced in current research on voice, subjectivity, and gender.[4] I have chosen the love lyric because it is the predominant lyric tradition and also because women's voices represent the sine qua non of love lyrics.

COLLECTING DATA, THINKING GENDER

In its most conventionalized form, the topography of love (*sringar, madhuriya, kama*) is commonly believed to have reached its apogee in Sanskrit anthologies from the 7th through 12th centuries. Poems from the anthologies are archetypal love lyrics. This Hindu lyric tradition supposedly came into its own as part of a production of so-called classical (authentic) Indian literature in the 18th and 19th centuries by Orientalist Indologists like William Jones (1726-1794) and Max Muller (1823-1900), when texts like the anthologies ostensibly embodied *the* period (7th-12th centuries) of cultural and political eflorescence in "Indian" history (Niranjana 1992).

The "classical" Sanskrit "tradition," assembled in the 18th and 19th centuries as a textual one, was one that did not have to bear the burden of gender. Orientalists like Jones (who were scholar-administrators) constructed a history for South Asia that justified colonial power and expansion in the subcontinent (Nirajana 1992; Sarkar 1989). All such histories were marked by the teleological twists peculiar to Orientalist representations. They were written in reverse—beginning by positing contemporary South Asia as degenerate and debauched (Hegel 1899; Mill 1975). Jones then excavated for "natives," whom he thought of as too incompetent to speak for themselves, past moments when Indians had a glorious civilization. Jones's project consisted of hiring pandits to transcribe works as well as advise him on their translations, turning, in the process, often fluid, multiversion works into fixed textual *Critical Editions* (Niranjana 1992:16). Having mined pandits' knowledge, Jones dismissed them with the arrogance of a colonial administrator and took upon himself the job of gifting natives with their own authoritative texts.

For both British Orientalists and Indian proto-Nationalists in this colonial period, one of many ideological failings of contemporary "Indian" culture was its horrendous treatment of women (Grewal 1996; Kumar 1993; Mani 1989). There is ample documentation of the immediate effects of this posited shortcoming, including salvage attempts by both groups to find evidence of times, for example the Vedic period, when women had power and prestige (Chatterjee 1989; Kumar 1993; Mani 1989). But since the "classical" period (7th-12th centuries A.D.) escaped that kind of scrounging, it was probably excessively masculinized, a domain of male poetry afficionados, arbiters, and authors. Works attributed to women were relegated to and later reconstituted from its interstices.

SANSKRIT LYRICS:
INTRODUCTION TO VIDYAKARA

One of the best known Sanskrit anthologies, *Vidyakara's Treasury (Subhasitaratnakosa)*, was ostensibly compiled by a Buddhist monk, Vidyakara, the abbot of a monastary in Jagaddala around 1100 A.D.(dates are rarely completely acertainable). Such anthologies were court based, either written by courtiers and poets who were attached to courts, or collected under the patronage of a ruler. Organized by subject, with desire predominating, *Vidyakara's Treasury,* like most other anthologies consists of *muktaka,* single-stanza poems released or liberated presumably from longer pieces and attributed to different writers who were mainly male, although some lyrics were assigned to women and others were anonymous.

POETIC CONVENTIONS IN SANSKRIT LYRICS:
WHAT EVERY COURTIER SHOULD KNOW

Readers of Sanskrit rely on what an afficionado of poetry who lived in the period when it was composed would be likely to know. To understand a poem one must be fluent in its coded language. The typical afficionado is a courtier, a member of an urban elite versed in a literary grammar (seasons, landscapes, and types of protagonists) that forms the basis for all such poetry. Each object in a poem must be decoded to read delicately delineated shifts in mood and desire.

In this world of "classical" poetics, love came alive in season; the flora, fauna, air and texture of spring and the monsoons turned into erotically charged symbols and heron and peacock, *kadamba,* heavy wind, sudden thick downpours, and stark, vivid lightning became signifiers of latent or expressed desire. Poetry dramatizing a dance of nuanced gestures between two extremes, love in union and love in separation, drew on an iconography of emotions—from the cold desolation of abandonment and the vivid fire of anguish or anger to the lush throes of consummated passion and the loose langor of its aftermath.

The cast of characters that played on the straight lyric stage included a *nayaka* (male lover), his *sakha, sahachara* (male confidantes), a *nayika* (female lover), her *sakhi, sahachari* (circle of friends), and a *duti* (go-between) who relayed messages among the protagonists.[5] The female lover, portrayed *nakh-shikh* (literally from head to foot) in graphic detail, often had almond eyes that stretched to her ears, a plump bee-stung lower lip, breasts like full jars of water, a waist with three folds and thighs like the trunk of a banana tree. Female types, put together from the conventions of head-to-foot descriptions, were also characterized relationally, strung out between a range of relationships with men. For example, *svakiya* (of one's own, of one's own family) women were the man's own, and *parakiya* was a woman who belonged to another. The category "*parakiya* women" incorporated other men's wives, unmarried women, or courtesans (*ganita*). These women were considered sexually transgressive, that is, their desire disrupting the boundaries of kinship.

Vidyakara's anthology organizes the love lyric into four categories based on types of desire—latent, unfulfilled, fulfilled, and transgressive. Rather than follow his schema, I reorganize the poems to elaborate the connections between signature, gender, and voice. The first set of poems is by "men" who write as men, the second by men writing in women's voices, the third by women who speak as women, and the fourth by women appearing under other aegis.

MEN WRITING AS MEN

All the poems in this category are assigned to male poets. Many of these are miniatures (*svabhavokti*) in which men gaze at objects of latent desire, mainly adolescents and young women. Their masculine voyeur's gaze roams women's bodies, embodying them in exquisite detail. In some poems, the descriptions appear to be neuter. That is, the poem gives a reader no information about the gender of the person looking but merely offers up the person being looked at. The commentaries on such poems assign gender to the implicit voice in the poem—its gender is male.

Another type of poem in this category depicts scenarios in male and ungendered voices that describe lonely (*sunya*) places where women came ripe for sexual picking (sometimes to be caught unguarded) or barren moments as women longed for lovers on the road. These verses, marked by crookedness, duplicity, and double meaning (*vakrokti*), are emblematic of women's learned seductiveness, sending deliberately double, contradictory messages of denial and hunger to ensnare men:

> Those who chance to catch a woman in a lonely place
> and find her overcome with love
> ever more charming for her feigned refusal
> which yet leads on to secret kisses, as her eyes
> dart here and there in fear;
> they are the men who know the taste of bliss.
>
> (No. 813, Ingalls 1975)

Written in a male voice and ascribed to a male poet, this is an extreme version of a prototypical poem from this section. The very emptiness (*sunyata*) of "a lonely place" as signifier that opens the space up for incursions of male desire carries the erotic charge in this poem. The play (*vakrokti*) between feigning and refusal read straight, that is, read from the position of a male reader who echoes the expectations of the male voice in the poem, speaks to a woman's duplicity; she really wants it even as she pretends she doesn't. The erotic charge, then, is further incited by the possibility of violence/violation promised in the woman's (feigned) refusal. Read against the grain (*vakrokti*), so that the seeming duplicity is turned on its head and the "feigned" is inflected with fear (*bhaya*), the poem speaks of violence; it becomes the foreshortened story of a woman unwittingly caught alone trapped by a man who refuses to take "no" straightforwardly.

MEN WRITING IN WOMEN'S VOICES

The category of poems in women's voices is the most interesting in that it contains all the poems attributed to female authors in this collection. The women whose voices are represented here are picked out from the usual roster of characters in the game of love—lover, friend of the lover, and the person who carries messages back and forth between lover and beloved. Such poems carry a charge of an emotional semantics of mutual duplicity (*vakrokti, vyajokti*—partially concealed fact) and deceit between the women. Women friends mislead one another in order to acquire a male lover. Friend metamorphoses into a rival. The go-between lies to both parties so that she can thwart their desire for each other. All the women circulate around men who are portrayed as so irresistible that women would forgo and betray each other for them. The commentarial literature uses this kind of voice to explain the "nature" of women. Since women speak ostensibly for themselves while conversing crookedly with women and men, *vakrokti* (deceit, duplicity, double meaning) is supposedly intrinsic to female behavior.

WOMEN SPEAKING AS WOMEN

Not unexpectedly, the few poems attributed to women are in the *asati* (untrue, false, against one's being—*sat*) or "wanton woman" section. Most of these verses are by Vidya (knowledge, wisdom) or Vijjika, a woman whose name appears consistently in many collections as well as in commentaries on aesthetics and poetry; some, though, are by Shilabhattarika. Many poems in this section on women's voices echo themes from the others. But all the poems by Vidya are laments by *parakiya* women, who slip away from socially acceptable relationships with men, to meet clandestinely with lovers.

WOMEN APPEARING UNDER OTHER AEGIS

Although very few lyrics attributed to women can be found in other anthologies or in the commentarial literature,[6] there is evidence in texts like the *Kavya Mimamsa* of Rajashekara (dated approximately A.D. 900) of a long history of royal women such as princesses, daughters of prime ministers, actresses and courtesans, including his wife Avantisundari, who were poets and scholar-critics. Certainly, collections under the name of a single male poet like Amaru (*Amarushataka*), known for its particularly adept representations of love in women's voices, which were probably not composed by one person, let alone in one period, raise the possibility that women's signatures may have been subsumed under other names.

GENDERING VOICE, READING
SIGNATURE IN SANSKRIT LYRICS

Women's voices in the available Sanskrit anthologies are vocalized by both male and female poets. If one reads these poems against the grain, perusing them as a feminist reader/audience member who refuses to take the self-evident for granted, their attributes come into focus differently. Poems recorded under men's and women's signatures share presumptions about gender embodied in common semantic and poetic conventions. If the poet's name were excised from the poem, and the poem was left to float nameless, unauthored, it would be very hard to distinguish "men's" from "women's" writings.

Within the geography of the poetry, relationships between men and women were unbalanced. Men controlled visual codes; they stood behind a camera photographing female bodies, but the lens was never angled their way. They were never pinned in a portrait as the specularized objects of female desire. Both men and women in the poetry spoke in emotional color, but unlike women who were unfailingly *vakrokti* (crooked), men were animated by more complex motivations. The unevenness of gendered positions within the poetry carries over to the relationship between the gender of voices within and the gender of the signature that frames a poem.

Even a quick perusal of the genre shows that "women" who were anthologized *always* spoke in women's voices, whereas "male" poets conversed with a great deal of facility as both men and women.[7] If a poem ostensibly signed by a woman were in an anthology, then she could speak *only* in the voice of a woman who lived in that poetic universe (as *nayaka, sakhi,* or *duti*), and the untowardness of her speaking at all meant that she was likely to be allocated to the *asati* (not quite right) space given to transgressive women.[8] So the confluence of gender and naming became, among other things, a way of foreshortening possibilities for (voiced) gendered mobility within the space of a poem.

However, we now know that there were many women composers whose lyric is no longer extant. It is possible that other uses of gender and naming, as well as poems that realized various geneologies of desire, disappeared during a period of collection (by colonializers and proto-Nationalists) in the 1800s when such poems did not satisfy the ideological requirements for what came to be called "classical" and "traditional."

TURNING BACK TO MIRA

Sanskrit critics have tended to take for granted both the texts they study and the signatures appended to them. Like an earlier generation of scholars of Indian religion, they have preferred to hold texts steady and use signatures as literalized information about the gender/sex of the writer. But, if audiences could be construed as multiple—those that share performance, those that read in retrospect, and those that, like me, want to push the boundaries between participant/reader—then the exigencies of gender, signature, and voice can become more transgressive.

Signature could be used as a signifier in Sanskrit lyrics, as in Mira's poetry, to mark certain traits embodied in poems. Name, then, and the gender of the name could cross gender and be worn by somebody of a different sex if maleness was about a latitude allocated to poetic personae and femaleness about its constriction. However, to provide the space to read these possibilities into poetic voices, one needs to be open to differently inclined reading habits. When one is not so inclined, gender is read as passing. Men who write under women's names and women who are transferred without their names to "male authored" anthologies pass into the domain of another gender.

NOTES

1. Film songs constitute a "popular" poetic genre that have continuities with "high" literary traditions. They are often exquisitely composed pieces of poetry that audiences discuss, parse and analyze, and recite under appropriate circumstances.

2. Before the move to local uses of text, historians of religion had concentrated almost exclusively on critical editions of poems attributed to particular literary figures. This kind of analysis relied on internal investigations of texts. Texts were treated as though they were closed entities, with all the material for investigating them contained within the text itself. Although scholars did use data external to texts (like the commentary literature) to understand their content, the kind of close readings they performed attended exclusively to information gleaned from grammar (syntax, semantics) and vocabulary.

3. Other elaborations on audience and reading practices include those by Fish (1980), who looks at the ways in which audiences actually produce the texts they read, and those by feminists like Flynn and Schweickart (1986) and Bobo (1995), who delineate the practices of women readers turning texts available to them to suit their needs.

4. I use "North India" advisedly, partially as a short (although historically troubled) designator for the northern part of South Asia. The geographical region I talk about predates the idea of India as a nation (although Sanskritists like Sheldon Pollock are trying to prove otherwise) and includes regions of Pakistan and Afghanistan. But the lyric traditions I talk about have now come to be associated with India, as a geographical site as well as a nation, so I have stayed with that term when I talk about poetry.

5. Heterosexualized desire is not a given in the entire Indic lyric tradition, because poetry that comes out of an Islamic (Persian, Urdu, Hindi) lineage includes poems written in men's voices to beautiful boys. So if one included such poetry, one would have to expand the cast to boy lovers (*saqi*) and the socially correct, sanctimonious nag (*nasikh*).

6. For example, in Anandavardana, Manamatta.

7. Commentators reading poems by "Amaru" eulogized "his" ability to speak as and for women. For many, "Amaru's facility with women's voices was proof that lyrics collected under "Amaru's name were in fact composed by women.

8. Another way of making this "chicken before the egg" statement is that her untowardness was indicated by where she was included. *Asati* (not-*sati*) is a curious descriptor (it can be an adjective as well as nominal descriptive term) because it plays off *sati* (virtuous woman) as well as *Sati* (a woman who gives herself up to her husband's pyre and goddess who dismembers and scatters herself in response to a slight faced by her husband).

REFERENCES

Abu-Lughod, Lila. 1986. *Veiled Sentiments.* Berkeley: University of California Press.

————. 1993. *Writing Women's Worlds.* Berkeley: University of California Press.

Bobo, Jacqueline. 1995. *Black Women as Cultural Readers.* New York: Columbia University Press.

Chatterjee, Partha. 1989. "The Nationalist Resolution of the Women's Question." Pp. 233-53 in *Recasting Women,* edited by Kukum Sangari and Sudesh Vaid. New Delhi: Kali for Women.

Fish, Stanley. 1980. *Is There a Text in This Class?* Cambridge, MA: Harvard University Press.

Foucault, Michel. 1977. "What Is an Author?" Pp. 113-38 in *Language, Counter-Memory, Practice.* Ithaca, NY: Cornell University Press.

Flynn, E. A. and P. Schweickart, eds. 1986. *Gender and Reading.* Baltimore, MD: Johns Hopkins University Press.

Grewal, Inderpal. 1996. *Home and Harem.* Durham, NC: Duke University Press.

Hawley, J. S., ed. 1988a. *Songs of the Saints of India.* New York: Oxford University Press.

————. 1988b. "Author and Authority in the Bhakti Poetry of North India." *Journal of Asian Studies* 47(2):269-90.

Hegel, J. W. F. 1899. *The Philosophy of History.* Translated by J. Sibree. New York: Colonial Press.

Ingall, D. H. H. 1975. *The Subhasitaratnakosa: Vidyakara's Treasury.* Cambridge, MA: Harvard University Press.

Kishwar, Madhu. 1989. "Introduction." *Manushi* 50-52 (January-June):3-9.

Kumar, Radha. 1993. *The History of Doing.* London: Verso.

Mani, Lata. 1989. "Contentious Traditions: The Debate on Sati in Colonial India," Pp. 88-126 in *Recasting Women,* edited by Kumkum Sangari and Sudesh Vaid. New Delhi: Kali for Women.

Mill, J. S. 1975. *The History of British India.* Chicago: University of Chicago Press.

Niranjana, Tejaswini. 1992. *Siting Translation.* Berkeley: University of California Press.

Parker, A. M. and M. Willhardt, eds. 1996. *The Routledge Anthology of Cross-Gendered Verse.* London: Routledge.

Sarkar, Sumit. 1989. *Modern India: 1885-1947.* New York: St. Martin's.

About the Contributors

Patricia A. Adler and Peter Adler received their Ph.D.s in sociology from the University of California, San Diego. He is Professor of Sociology at the University of Denver, where he chaired from 1987 to 1993. She is Associate Professor of Sociology at the University of Colorado, Boulder. They have written and worked together for over 25 years. Their interests include qualitative methods, deviant behavior, sociology of sport, sociology of children, and work and leisure. They have published numerous articles and books, including *Momentum* (Sage, 1981), *Wheeling and Dealing* (1985), *Membership Roles in Field Research* (Sage, 1987), *Backboards and Blackboards* (1991), and *Peer Power* (forthcoming). The Adlers have served as editors of *Journal of Contemporary Ethnography* (1986-1994) and as the founding editors of *Sociological Studies of Child Development* (1985-1992).

Hale C. Bolak received her doctorate in psychology with a specialization in gender from the University of California, Santa Cruz. She was on the faculty of Psychology and Women's Studies at Santa Cruz before taking her current position as the director of the Feminist and Cross-Cultural Graduate Psychology Program at New College of California in San Francisco. She is a native of Turkey where she carried out several research projects, including a study of children's perceptions of the social division of labor that was part of a cross-cultural project sponsored by the Social Science Research Council of England. Her doctoral research was on working-class households in Istanbul. Her publications from this research include a chapter in an edited book by Sirin Tekeli titled *Women in Turkish Society* (1995). She continues to teach and do research in the area of feminist studies from an interdisciplinary and cross-cultural perspective.

Kathy Charmaz is Professor of Sociology at Sonoma State University. She was the recipient of the 1992 Charles Horton Cooley Award from the Society for the Study of Symbolic Interaction and the 1992 Distinguished Scholarship Award from the Pacific Sociological Association for her book *Good Days, Bad Days: The Self in Chronic Illness and Time.* For nine years, she was enrolled in the Alternative English Major at Sonoma State University and for six years taught courses on writing in the School of Humanities. Her current projects include an empirical study of bodily experience in health and illness and didactic works on conducting and writing qualitative research.

Marjorie L. DeVault is Associate Professor of Sociology and a member of the Women's Studies Program at Syracuse University. She has written on household work (in *Feeding the Family: The Social Construction of Caring as Gendered Work*) and feminist research strategies. Her current research interests include constructionist approaches to family studies and gender dynamics of professional work in nutrition and dietetics, and constructionist approaches to Family Studies.

Carolyn Ellis is Professor of Communication and Sociology at the University of South Florida. She is author of *Final Negotiations: A Story of Love, Loss, and Chronic Illness* and coeditor of *Investigating Subjectivity: Research on Lived Experience* (Sage) and *Composing Ethnography: Alternative Forms of Qualitative Writing* (AltaMira Press). Her current work focuses on narrative, autoethnography, qualitative methods, and subjectivity.

Tamar El-Or is Lecturer of Sociology and Anthropology at the Hebren University, Jerusalem. Her book *Educated and Ignorant: Ultraorthodox Jewish Women and their World* (1994) focuses on a matrix of literacy, gender, and religion. She currently studies the constitution of gender, national, and Jewish identity among religious Zionist young women.

Faye Ginsburg teaches in the Department of Anthropology at New York University, where she directs the Program in Culture and Media. Her research on social movements and cultural activism has focused on the abortion debate and more recently on indigenous media makers. Her books include *Contested Lives: The Abortion Debate in an American Community* (1989); *Uncertain Terms: Negotiating Gender in American Culture* (edited with Anna Tsing, 1991); and *Conceiving the New World Order: The Global Politics of Reproduction* (edited with Rayna Rapp, 1995).

Rosanna Hertz is Professor of Women's Studies and Sociology at Wellesley College. She received her Ph.D. in sociology from Northwestern University. In past years she has also held visiting scholar or postdoctoral appointments at Harvard Medical School, the Center for Research on Women at Wellesley College, and the Florence Heller Graduate School for Advanced Studies in Social Welfare at Brandeis University. She is author of *More Equal Than Others: Women and Men in Dual-Career Marriages* and *Heartstrings and Purse Strings* (forthcoming). Recently she coeditored *Studying Elites Using Qualitative Methods* (Sage) and since 1991 has been the editor of *Qualitative Sociology*. She is presently working on a study of single mothers and their children.

Christine E. Kiesinger recently received her Ph.D. in Communication from the University of South Florida where she teaches courses in communication and close relationships. Her scholarship is centered in the area of female identity, with a specific focus on the lives and experiences of anorexic and bulimic women. Mostly autobiographical in nature, Christine's research aims to capture the texture and details of emotional experience in descriptive ways. Her work is often cast in narrative and poetic form and is written to evoke connection and understanding, and ultimately, to heal.

Raymond J. Michalowski is Professor and Chair of Criminal Justice and Adjunct Professor of Sociology at Northern Arizona University. His published works span a variety of topics including criminological theory, comparative ethnography of law and justice, political economy of crime and punishment, sociological analyses of lawmaking, justice policy, and corporate and upper-world deviance. This seemingly eclectic array of topics are actually part of a larger project to comprehend (or perhaps represent) the relationship between political-economic systems and the cultural and organizational processes that determine the social understanding of harm and the selection of harm-reducing strategies. Off on yet another tangent, he is currently engaged in an ethnographic study of codes of resistance within biker cultures.

Richard G. Mitchell, Jr. is Associate Professor of Sociology at Oregon State University. He is an ethnographer with interests in avocational risk adventure, professional ethics, and separatist, segregationist, and millennial social movements.

Eric Mykhalovskiy lives in Toronto, Canada where he is completing his doctorate in sociology at York University. His dissertation explores how health services research functions as a contemporary organization of power. Further research interests include the sociology of health and illness, the social organization of knowledge, the use of autobiography in sociology, and activist sociology. He is a contributor to *Medical Alert: New Work Organizations in Health Care* and coauthor of *Hooking Up: A Report on the Barriers People Living with HIV/AIDS Face Accessing Social Services.* He is a member of the board of directors of the Community AIDS Treatment Information Exchange and has been involved in AIDS activism for the past eight years.

Nancy A. Naples is Assistant Professor of Sociology and Women's Studies at the University of California, Irvine. Her work focuses on understanding how low-income community residents interpret as well as politically respond to economic and social change. As a feminist ethnographer, she is interested in developing self-reflective and interactive methodological strategies that remain sensitive to the shifting dilemmas of field-based research. Her work has appeared in *Social Problems, Gender & Society,* and *Rural Sociology.* She is currently working on a book titled *Grassroots Warriors: Activist Mothering and Community Work and the War on Poverty* and an edited collection *Community Activism and Feminist Politics: Organizing Across Race, Class and Gender.*

Geeta Patel is Assistant Professor of Women's Studies at Wellesley College. She received her Ph.D. in Urdu and Sanskrit from Columbia University. Her work on gender and sexuality focuses on poetry composed in Urdu, Hindi, and Sanskrit. She is presently completing a book titled *Poetry in Movement: Gender and Colonialism.*

Shulamit Reinharz is Professor of Sociology and Director of the Women's Studies Program at Brandeis University, she also taught at University of Michigan. She is author of numerous article and books, including *On Becoming a Social Scientist, Qualitative Gerontology, Feminist Methods in Social Research* and *Psychology and Community Change.* From 1982 to 1987, she served as coeditor with Peter Conrad of *Qualitative Sociology* and since then has served on its editorial advisory board. She also serves on the editorial boards of the *Journal of Aging Studies, Gender & Society, American Journal of Community Psychology, Israel Studies,* and *Qualitative Inquiry.* She recently created the International Research Institute on Jewish Women, sponsored by Hadassah and situated at Brandeis University. This interdisciplinary institute is the only one in the world devoted to research on this topic. She is also the 1997-1998 Robin Williams Lecturer of the Eastern Sociological Society.

Albert B. Robillard teaches Sociology at the University of Hawaii at Manoa. His research interests include disability, face-to-face interaction, medical services in Hawaii, Micronesia, and the Philippines, Filipino and Chinese cultural identity, social change in the Pacific islands, mental health in Micronesia, and tourism. He is director of the Health and Social Science Project in the Social Science Research Institute and has served as a research Fulbright Professor at Ateneo de Manila University. He has held appointments in the Department of Pediatrics at Michigan State University and in the Department of Psychiatry at the University of Hawaii. He was the National Institute of Mental Health grant director for training mental health counselors in the Marshall and Caroline Islands. His new book is *Meaning of a Disability: The Lived Experience of Paralysis.*

Lisa M. Tillmann-Healy moved to Tampa, Florida in 1993 to join the Ph.D. program in communication at the University of South Florida, where she developed interests in relationship, interpretive, and narrative studies. She is currently writing an ethnographic dissertation on the experiences and relationships of gay men participating in a community softball league.

Rahel R. Wasserfall was born in France and moved to Israel in her late teens. After completing her Ph.D. in Anthropology at Hebrew University of Jerusalem, she was a Fulbright Post-Doctoral Fellow and Visiting Scholar at the Institute for Sociology at Eotuos Lorand University in Budapest. She is currently a Research Associate and Lecturer in Women's Studies and Sociology at the University of Boulder, Colorado. She has published numerous articles on the intersection of ethnic and gender identities in Israel and on the anthropology of gender. She is currently editing a book titled *Thou Shall Immerse Thyself: Gender and Ritual of Purification in Judaism.*

Mary Anne Wichroski received her Ph.D. in sociology from the University of New Hampshire where she currently teaches Social Psychology, Research Methods, and a capstone course in Sociology for majors at the University of New Hampshire, as well as Research Methods for the Social Work Department. In the past, she has taught courses on aging and the family at other colleges in the Northeast. Her publications are in the areas of women and work, women and religion, and qualitative research methods. She is presently working on a book on religious orders of women in the United States. In the future, her research will focus on women and aging.